What people are saying about M. William Phelps:

"M. William Phelps is the rising star of the true crime genre, and his true tales of murderers and mayhem are scary-as-hell thrill rides into the dark heart of the inhuman condition." —Douglas Clegg, Bram Stoker Award-Winning author of *Afterlife, The Abandoned, The Halloween Man, The Hour Before Dark,* and *Nightmare House*

Praise for *Perfect Poison:*

"Captivating, exciting, a jolt-a-minute. With this tour de force M. William Phelps earns a deserved place among the best true-crime writers. Plain and simple, *Perfect Poison* is one of the best true crime books I've ever read!" —Harvey Rachlin, author of *The Making of a Detective* and *The Making of a Cop*

"*Perfect Poison* is [the] horrific tale of a nurse Kristin Gilbert's insatiable desire to kill the most helpless of victims—her own patients. A stunner from beginning to end, the story expertly rendered by Phelps with flawless research and an explosive narrative. Phelps is the best nonfiction crime writer to come along in years . . . the future of the genre." —Gregg Olsen, *New York Times* bestselling author of *Abandoned Prayers*

"M. William Phelps isn't content with a retelling of what people think they already know. . . . He is reporting and writing at a level that has become rare in today's true crime genre. The result is the kind of compelling account of terror that only comes when the author dedicates himself to unmasking the psychopath with facts, insight and the other proven methods of journalistic leg work." —Lowell Cauffiel, *New York Times* bestselling author of *Forever and Five Days* and *Eye of the Beholder*

"Phelps is a first-rate investigator." —Dr. Michael Baden, host of HBO's *Autopsy,* author of several books

Praise for *Lethal Guardian:*

"An intense roller-coaster of a crime story. Phelps's book *Lethal Guardian* is at once complex, with a plethora of twists and turns worthy of any great detective mystery, and yet so well-laid out, so crisply written with such detail to character and place that it reads more like a novel than your standard nonfiction crime book." —Steve Jackson, *New York Times* bestselling author of *Monster*

Also by M. William Phelps

Perfect Poison

Lethal Guardian

EVERY MOVE YOU MAKE

M. WILLIAM PHELPS

PINNACLE BOOKS
Kensington Publishing Corp.
http://www.kensingtonbooks.com

Some names have been changed to protect the privacy of individuals connected to this story.

PINNACLE BOOKS are published by

Kensington Publishing Corp.
850 Third Avenue
New York, NY 10022

All Kensington Titles, Imprints and Distributed Lines are available at special quantity discounts for bulk purchases for sales promotions, premiums, fund-raising, and educational or institutional use. Special book excerpts or customized printing can also be created to fit specific needs. For details, write or phone the office of the Kensington special sales manager: Kensington Publishing Corp., 850 Third Avenue, New York, NY 10022, attn: Special Sales Department, Phone: 1-800-221-2647.

Pinnacle and the P logo Reg. U.S. Pat. & TM Off.

First Printing: June 2005

10 9 8 7 6 5 4 3 2 1

Printed in the United States of America

In memory of my brother,
Mark Anthony Phelps, Sr. (1957–2004),
and all the good times.

And to his children,
Mark Anthony Phelps, Jr., Tyler Phelps
and Meranda VanDeventer—
he loved you.

FOREWORD

This incredible true story, which, in my opinion, includes the most shocking and surprising ending in the history of true crime, begins and ends at a section of the Hudson River near downtown Troy, New York. Because the Hudson, called "the River of Steep Hills" when adventurer and explorer Henry Hudson discovered it in 1609, plays such a figurative role in this story—as if it, too, is a character—I feel obligated to give you, the reader, a brief description of the river, the towns and cities along its banks where the book takes place, and the surge of crime that has infected the region throughout the years.

Considering the role the river plays in this story, in a twist of irony only nature could invoke, the Hudson—315 miles of stunning waterway that empties into the Atlantic Ocean at the southern tip of Manhattan—is fed by Lake Tear of the Clouds, a body of water about the size of a football field, shaped like a teardrop, in the Adirondack Mountains. As one travels north from Manhattan along the Hudson's banks and into upstate New York, there are areas littered with debris: pieces of old Styrofoam cups that take decades, if not centuries, to decompose; beer bottles without labels floating aimlessly; used condoms; bits of newspapers and magazines;

driftwood; and just about anything else the river decides to consume, or people discard inconsiderately. Along certain sections of the river, large, boulderlike rocks, sharp and jagged to the touch, are grouped together like swarms of gnats, the water crashing off them as high and low tides rise and fall against the ebb and flow of the moon. The sand along the shore is like clay: gritty, the color of coffee. The water, in some areas, is as clear as cellophane straight down to the bottom, the pebbles and rocks on the river floor staring up at you; while in others, it is as murky as melted milk chocolate. In recent years, polychlorinated biphenyls (PCBs) have been the hot topic of debate when communities along the river get together and talk about dredging the bottom to clean it up. Some say it will only stir up tons of poisons collected throughout the years, while others argue it is essential to the ecology and survival of the river's two hundred different species of fish.

Located 138 miles north of New York City and 144 miles west of Boston, Massachusetts, the city of Albany is not only the capital of New York, but the crossroads of the Northeast. Described as the "humblest city in the state," always taking a backseat to its more popular sibling, New York City, this industrial town of about 130,000 residents sits thirty feet above sea level, with the hum, serenity and mirrorlike reflection of the sky bouncing off the Hudson on its doorstep.

Shortly after World War II, Albany, the unassuming hub of New York's government, enjoyed its most populated era with about 140,000 residents. That number has declined some over the years as people have moved outward into the suburbs of the "Capital District"—Rensselaer County, Saratoga County, Schenectady County—which is about eight hundred thousand people strong today.

Metropolitan areas around the Capital Region include four central cities—Albany, Schenectady, Troy and Saratoga Springs—and are surrounded by dozens of suburban and rural communities. Interestingly, Chester A. Arthur, the twenty-first president of the United States, is buried in Albany. Up the road from Arthur's grave is the burial site of Erastus Corning, who sat in the Albany mayor's chair for an unprecedented forty-one years. William Kennedy, the acclaimed novelist, whose most esteemed books include Ironweed, Billy Phelan's Greatest Game *and* Legs*—"the Albany trio"—writes of a fictional Albany, dark and unfashionable, during the hardscrabble Depression-era times of the late '30s when the city was brimming with thieves, mobsters, union busters and murderers. In the popular film* Ironweed, *actor Jack Nicholson plays Francis Phelan, perhaps Kennedy's most famous creation. Phelan is a drunkard, an ex–baseball player turned gravedigger who bounces around Albany with his drinking partner, Helen, trying to figure out where he fits into society.*

Like a majority of its surrounding counties, Albany County has its lion's share of crime to contend with, and has, historically, been marred by the highest crime rates in the north country. Between 1996 and 2000, for example, the county reported some fifty murders, which is rather low considering the population boom in the county during that same period. Rape is a crime that is hard to track because the numbers fluctuate so much from year to year—sixty-four rapes were reported in 1996, while, just a year later, the numbers doubled. By far, however, the most popular crimes in Albany County have always been burglary, robbery and aggravated assault. During that same five-year period—1996–2000—there were nearly 2,500 robberies and 4,000 reports of aggravated assault—staggering numbers by any count.

Under New York State penal code, robbery is the "forcible taking" of someone's possessions and/or cash—a convenience store or bank holdup, for instance. Also under the robbery code is "taking from a person forcibly"—walking up to someone on the street, perhaps, and demanding their money or possessions.

Burglary falls under three different degrees. Third degree is "unlawfully entering a building and committing a crime therein." Second degree is entering a "dwelling." First degree involves breaking and entering someone's residence and forcibly taking a "person or thing."

This story is about one of the Northeast's most prolific burglars—whom authorities later found was also a serial murderer—and the cop who pursued (and befriended) him for thirteen years. Nothing in this book has been made up; every bit of dialogue, every circumstance and thought, and every single fact in this book is real. I conducted over 150 hours' worth of interviews, studied thousands of pages of public records and had access to nearly one hundred letters written by Gary Charles Evans. That research, plus the scores of other documents, court records and interviews I used, have convinced me that this true-crime story is the most incredible you will likely ever read. There are events in this book that may be hard to believe; but trust me, everything in this book actually happened.

—M. William Phelps
March 2005

PART 1

LADY IN RED

CHAPTER 1

What I must do is all that concerns me, not what the people think. . . . You will always find those who think they know what is your duty better than you know it. It is easy in the world to live after the world's opinion; it is easy in solitude to live after our own; but the great man is he who in the midst of the crowd keeps with perfect sweetness the independence of solitude.

—Ralph Waldo Emerson, *Self-Reliance* (1841)

Friday, October 3, 1997, had been a hectic day for *Caroline Parker**, an unassuming, moderately attractive thirty-seven-year-old wife and mother of three. The following afternoon, at four o'clock, Caroline's sister was getting married. In what had been planned as a rather large family event through months of preparation, Caroline had a list of errands for her husband of almost four years, Tim Rysedorph, to run after he got off work.

For starters, Tim needed a haircut. Then he was supposed to get the family car washed, stop to buy a new suit and drop by Sam's Club to pick up a few last-minute items for the reception.

*Italics on first use represents pseudonym

Tim had left work at noon; by 3:30 P.M. Caroline was seething with anxiety because she hadn't heard from him yet.

When it came down to it, Caroline really didn't have any reason to fuss. Whenever she needed help, she turned to Tim, who had turned thirty-nine back on June 2, and whatever it was she needed, Tim was usually right on top of it. Anyone who knew him, in fact, later recalled how he would go out of his way for Caroline whenever she snapped her fingers.

Tim met Caroline on June 21, 1983. A mutual friend, Michael Falco, who lived in the same Troy, New York, neighborhood where they had all grown up, introduced them. Caroline was in the process of going through a divorce. Tim, who had been living in a New Jersey hotel shortly before he'd moved back to Troy, shared an apartment in town with his boyhood friend Falco and another old friend of theirs, Gary Charles Evans, a well-known burglar.

Caroline grew up in the Lansingburg section of town, and had flirted with the prospect of singing in a band. Tim, whom family members and friends later described as a "gifted" drummer, was in a fairly successful bar band called the Realm. Because of "their mutual love for music," Caroline later told police, they hit it off immediately when she showed up one night to audition for a vacant singer's position in Tim's band. Although she never got the gig, they started dating about a week later.

Tim stood about five feet eight inches, 160 pounds. He had a noticeable receding hairline, the crown of his forehead big and round, with strands of dirt brown hair, like frayed rope, protruding down his shoulders. Friends said he was a casual, easygoing guy who liked to please people. Tim's band played regularly at bars and nightclubs in and around Albany, New York. Usually, on Friday and Saturday nights, he was off with the band making extra money while Caroline stayed home with their nine-year-old boy, *Sean*. Known as a "comical joker" by his coworkers, during the day Tim held down a job driving a recycling truck for BFI Waste Systems.

Life had been fair to Caroline and Tim. They seemed to be making a go of it. Yet, some would later question the strength of their marriage, saying Tim could "never do enough" for Caroline, who, for the most part, hadn't worked a steady job throughout 1997.

Before Tim took off for work on Friday morning, October 3, he read a note Caroline had left him the previous night on the kitchen counter. Mainly, it was a list of the errands he had to run before the big day on Saturday. Because of the shift Tim worked at BFI, Caroline later told police, they often communicated through notes.

During the first ten years they were together, Tim and Caroline lived in Mechanicville, New York, just outside Albany. After getting into some rather enormous financial problems in 1995, they rented a small, two-bedroom apartment in Saratoga Springs and had lived there ever since. About fifteen miles north of Albany, Saratoga Springs is, historically, known for what locals call its "healing waters." Part of the Hudson River Valley, the town boasts one of the oldest thoroughbred racetracks in America, Saratoga Raceway. Victorian houses and ancient apartment complexes line the streets, while Starbucks and Borders cater to the middle class.

Tim had worked at BFI since the fall of 1995. His shift was not what most Americans would jump at when looking for work. He was expected at the office at 5:00 A.M. on Mondays, Wednesdays and Fridays, and would get out at about 12:00 or 1:00 P.M. On Tuesdays and Thursdays, he worked from 6:00 A.M. to 2:00 P.M. If he ran behind because of traffic or inclement weather, he would have to stay for maybe an hour longer. Either way, he was generally home by no later than 4:00 P.M. on any given day.

Tim enjoyed the job and hours. Getting out early freed him up for rehearsal with the band Monkey Business he had been in for several years. On the days when he didn't have rehearsal, he would make time for family. When work was done, a coworker later said, Tim often headed home. He didn't run out like some of the other guys and "grab a beer or two and watch the game." He did his time at work and, while pursuing his dream of making it in the music business, rushed home to be with his family. On top of that, Sean was an avid soccer player and Tim rarely missed one of his games.

On Friday, before Tim left for work, after reading the note Caroline had left, he sat down at the kitchen table and dashed off a note to Sean. He told him to have a "great day in school." He wished him "luck" in his soccer game later that day, ending the brief note: *Love, Dad.*

Tim didn't mention why, but he wasn't going to make Sean's soccer game on Friday night. With the wedding one day away, perhaps he felt he had too many things to do after work. After all, what was one game? Caroline and Sean could count on one hand the number of games Tim had missed over the years.

CHAPTER 2

Throughout the day on Friday, October 3, Caroline Parker, perhaps overjoyed and anxiety-ridden over her sister's wedding the following day, left Tim numerous messages on his pager. Finally, at about 3:30 P.M., after not talking to her all day, Tim called home.

"I'm still running errands," he said. "I'll be home soon."

Caroline had spent the day sewing a comforter for her bed. It was a way, one would imagine, to burn off all that wedding stress. Tim had promised to bring home dinner.

At around 7:00 P.M., Caroline, wondering what she, Sean and Tim were going to have for dinner, paged Tim again and left another digital message.

What's for dinner? We're still waiting.

After thirty minutes went by, getting no response, Caroline ordered takeout from a deli up the road. She was getting upset because Tim wasn't home. The wedding was fewer than twenty-four hours away. She wondered if he had finished all the errands.

When Caroline and Sean finished dinner at 7:30, she paged him again.

Where are you? Call me . . . [Caroline].

"Where are you?" was the first thing out of her mouth

when Tim called a few minutes later. Her aggravation had now turned to anger.

"Listen—" Tim said before Caroline cut him off.

"Forget dinner. We already ate."

"I have a few more errands to run," he said. "I'll be home soon."

Before Caroline put Sean to bed at 9:30, she sent Tim another message.

I need to talk to you right now! Call me.

When Tim failed to call back, she dozed off while lying on the couch watching the nightly eleven o'clock news to see what kind of weather to expect for the wedding.

By 11:30, she woke up and, rubbing the sleep from her eyes, walked downstairs into the bedroom to see if Tim had come home yet.

Near midnight, she paged him.

Call me right away. . . .

Tim called back immediately.

In what Caroline later described to police as a "broken call," she said she thought Tim had said he was "surrounded by the police," but the line had gone dead midway through the call. Later, when police asked her to describe the call a second time, she said she wasn't sure if she had been dreaming, watching something on television, or if it was, indeed, Tim.

After he told his wife he was surrounded by the police, Caroline recalled later, she said, "Now you won't be able to get a suit for the wedding." Then she said they argued about Tim's having to wear an old suit.

"That's the least of my worries," she thought Tim said before the line went dead again.

An hour later, at about 1:03 A.M. the following morning, as Caroline tossed and turned on the couch worrying not only about her sister's wedding but where in the hell her husband was, the phone rang.

"It's me, Caroline," Tim said.

"Where are you?"

"I'm in Latham. I'll be home in forty minutes."

* * *

A few hours after the sun broke over Tim Rysedorph and Caroline Parker's Regent Street apartment on October 4, 1997, Caroline woke up and immediately realized that Tim hadn't come home. After paging him—*Where are you? Call me right now!*—she walked up the stairs to the kitchen, made a pot of coffee, threw some laundry in the washing machine and tried to sort out what was going on.

With no response to her first page, she sent another.

Tim, please call me now. . . . I need to speak to you now. . . .

Fifteen minutes later: *Tim, Sean has a soccer game soon, he can't miss this one, too.*

Sitting on the sofa, contemplating what to do next, the telephone startled her.

Tim!

When she answered, all she could hear were "Touch-Tone noises," as if, she said later, "the call was being made from the outside. But I don't know why I thought this. I assumed it was Tim, and he sounded like he was out of breath . . . that he was scared, or running."

That's when she said, "Tim? Tim? Is that you?"

Sean, who had been sleeping on the couch, got up when he heard his mother screaming and crying into the phone: "Tim? Tim? Speak to me?"

"Yes . . . ," the caller said quietly.

"Are you all right?"

". . . call . . . not working . . . doesn't work" was all Caroline remembered hearing before the line went dead.

When that happened, she sent him another digital page. *Tim, I couldn't make out anything you were saying. . . . Please call me.*

For the next hour, Caroline paced in the living room . . . waiting, wondering. In her heart, she felt something was wrong—terribly wrong. Tim was not in the business of running off without telling her. They'd had problems in the past and Tim had slept at a friend's apartment or his brother's house for the night, but this was different. They hadn't been fighting. Tim had promised to take care of several errands before the wedding.

Where the hell is he?

At some point before the wedding, after not hearing from Tim all morning, Caroline called her mother.

"Tim did not come home last night. He's missing. I can't find him."

"What? Caroline, are you—"

"Don't tell anyone in the family, Mom. I don't want to ruin the day."

"Okay."

While Caroline was putting the finishing touches on her makeup after talking to her mother, the phone rang. Nearly jumping out of her dress to reach for it, she said in desperation, "Hello . . . hello?"

"Is Tim there?" a man's voice asked.

"Who is this?"

"Lou."

"Are you a good friend of Tim's?" Caroline couldn't recall anyone by the name of Lou that Tim had ever known.

"Yeah. I'm a friend. I work with Tim."

"Have you seen him lately . . . Have you seen him"—Caroline was jumpy, frenzied, barely able to get the words out fast enough—"he's missing."

"I'm just returning his call; he left me a message."

Caroline couldn't handle it; she started to cry. "I'm sorry. I . . . I . . . We need to find him."

"Don't cry," Lou said. "Everything is going to be all right. I'll make some phone calls around town and see what I can find out."

"You will? Yes. Do that. Please."

"Maybe he's in a place where he can't call you?"

"What . . . where? What do you mean by that?"

"Maybe he got into trouble and got picked up and is in jail."

"I would have heard something."

"Not necessarily."

Confused, Caroline asked, "What do you mean?"

"Listen, don't worry. I will try to find out what's going on and call you back later."

"Thanks."

Before Lou hung up, he had one last bit of advice.

"Maybe you should call the police."

CHAPTER 3

Minutes before Caroline left her apartment to make her sister's wedding on time, she phoned the Saratoga Springs Police Department (SSPD). Hysterical, she asked the officer who picked up if he could find out if Tim had been involved in an auto accident, or if he had been arrested.

"No, ma'am, I don't see anything," the cop said a few moments later.

At 1:42 P.M., Caroline sent Tim a message.

It's almost time to leave for the wedding, call now.

Two hours later, about twenty minutes before the wedding, she sent Tim one last message: *Emergency with wife, call home right away.*

Tim never called.

The wedding obviously turned out to be an uncomfortable affair for Caroline, but she had to attend, nonetheless. Her sister counted on her.

Minutes after the wedding, she called the state police, the sheriff's department and the Colonie Police Department, a nearby town Tim occasionally frequented. She asked the same set of questions she had posed to the SSPD earlier.

At the urging of the Colonie Police Department, the SSPD sent a uniformed officer to interview Caroline and write up an official missing person report. The SSPD's initial thought was that the case would not amount to anything. So far, all they had was a husband missing fewer than twenty-four hours who had not shown up for his sister-in-law's wedding.

It was hardly enough to panic.

Ed Moore had been a detective with the SSPD for the past twenty years. Promoted to chief later in his career, Moore knew his business as a cop perhaps better than a lot of his colleagues, and relied, like most cops, on his instincts.

When Caroline got home from her sister's wedding early in the evening on October 4 and telephoned the SSPD, demanding it do something about what she insisted was her "missing husband," Moore heard what he later said was genuine pain and anguish in her voice.

Moore spoke to Caroline briefly, trying to reassure her that he was going to do everything he could to find her husband.

After hanging up, weighing what she had told him, taking the sincerity she had displayed into account, Moore told himself something wasn't right.

Tim Rysedorph had a good job, apparently loved his wife and son, had made specific plans to go to his sister-in-law's wedding and rarely ever failed to come home from work—at least that's what Caroline had claimed. To top it off, he had missed the wedding.

Something wasn't adding up.

By Sunday morning, October 5, Caroline had called several of Tim's friends to see if any of them had heard from him. She even had a friend page Tim and leave his phone number as a callback—just in case Tim had been screening his calls and, for whatever reason, didn't want to talk to her.

Nothing.

At about noon, Lou called back. After hitting the streets

and asking a few people about Tim's whereabouts, he said he couldn't offer much.

But Caroline, as worried as she appeared, began to float her own theory.

"Tim's still not back, Lou," she said in a rush. "I'm getting really scared . . . and, well, he's probably dead because I haven't heard from him yet." Caroline was, she later told police, rambling on and on, just blurting out words as they passed through her mind, not thinking too much about what she was saying.

"What are you talking about?" Lou asked.

"They're probably going to find him dead," Caroline said, "in the trunk of my car at the bottom of the Hudson River."

"Don't say that," Lou said. "That's not going to happen. Or else, he'll never be found—just like what happened to his friend Mike."

Lou was referring to Michael Falco, who had been missing for about twelve years. Shortly after Falco introduced Caroline and Tim, he went out one night and never returned. It had been rumored that Tim and Michael Falco's old friend Gary Evans, who had lived with them at the time, was responsible for Falco's disappearance. Evans, who had been partners with Falco on a number of profitable jewelry heists, denied the stories, telling people Falco had gone "west."

Caroline didn't know what to say after Lou compared Tim's situation to Falco's.

"Like I said, maybe he's in a place where he can't call," Lou told her.

"I called the police like you suggested and reported Tim missing."

"Maybe you should call the police back and tell them you've heard from him?"

Caroline screamed, "No! I can't do that! They will stop looking for him."

"Calm down. Keep your chin up. Everything will be okay." But Caroline could do nothing more than cry. "I'll call you back at dinnertime," Lou added, and hung up.

After that, Caroline began phoning the SSPD almost hourly, wondering what it was doing to find her missing husband. Tim had been gone for three days now.

Something's wrong!

Although the SSPD is a full-service police department, fully capable of any type of investigation, Detective Ed Moore decided to call the New York State Police (NYSP)—if only to quell Caroline's constant phone calls and inquiries. She was becoming quite the pain in the ass.

Established in 1917, the NYSP is one of the ten largest law enforcement agencies in the country, and the only police department in New York with statewide jurisdiction. The breakdown of troops within the structure of the department is rather extensive simply because New York encompasses some fifty thousand square miles of land. The division headquarters of the NYSP is located in Albany, with eleven separate troop barracks spread throughout the state. Since Tim Rysedorph lived in Saratoga Springs, Troop G, in Loudonville, had authority over the missing person report Caroline had filed.

NYSP troops, like in most states, provide "primary police and investigative services across the state." Any cases requiring "extensive investigation or involving felonies" are referred to the NYSP's principal investigative arm—the Bureau of Criminal Investigation (BCI). In house, investigators call it "the Bureau." The Major Crimes Unit (MCU), a separate division of the Bureau, is used for homicides and high-profile cases.

As far as Tim Rysedorph's disappearance, the Bureau from Troop G in Loudonville, despite its reluctance of getting involved in a case of a married adult missing only three days, was brought in to assist the SSPD. Following up on a missing person report wasn't what Bureau investigators liked to spend their time doing. But most investigators agreed it was part of the job. People went missing, for any number of reasons, all the time. Generally, the Bureau could come into a case and—with its manpower and carefree access to the latest, top-notch technology—solve it quickly.

Although missing person cases came in on a regular basis, the Bureau dealt mostly with narcotics cases, violent and serial crimes, child abuse and sexual exploitation matters, computer and technology-related offenses, bias-related crimes, auto theft, consumer product tampering and organized crime. Murder cases, Bureau investigators have said, are one of its foremost priorities, taking precedence over just about any other cases that don't involve missing or exploited children.

Little did anyone involved in Tim Rysedorph's disappearance know then that within twenty-four hours of Ed Moore's call to the Bureau, every available Major Crimes Unit investigator from Troop G in Loudonville would be working on the case.

CHAPTER 4

SSPD detective Ed Moore contacted Senior Investigator Jim Horton from the Troop G Bureau on Monday, October 6, regarding Tim's disappearance. Known as "Big Jim" to his Bureau brethren, Horton stood about six feet, 180 pounds. He had been on the job since February 20, 1978—almost nineteen years now—and had been promoted to senior investigator back in 1990, a job, colleagues later said, he took more seriously than life itself. The oldest of four siblings, Horton kept what little hair he had left parted to one side, blade-of-grass straight, always well-manicured. He wore a scraggly mustache that he had been contemplating shaving lately.

More of an athlete than a student, growing up in the Capital District area, Horton didn't have aspirations of becoming a cop, but instead wanted to be a physical education teacher. It wasn't until a friend from high school had mentioned one day he was taking the state trooper exam that the seed was planted in Horton. But when he came home that afternoon and told his mother about becoming a cop, she blasted him.

"No son of mine is going to be a pig!" she said. Horton's father, standing next to him in utter shock at the prospect, just shook his head and walked away.

In 1975, two years out of high school, Horton decided to take the state police entrance examination and, surprising everyone in his family, did extremely well on the test and was accepted into the academy right away.

"Up until then," Horton noted later, "I worked construction. I had grown up in a blue-collar family. My brother became a professor. My sister Pam has a master's degree in education, two kids, and was very influential in helping and looking out for our baby sister, Kathy, who is deaf. My father was a mechanic and my mom grew up with a silver spoon, rebelling against her mother by marrying my motorcycle-/stock car-driving dad. To me, they were hippies. My mom marched on Washington, DC, did the Woodstock thing, and smoked pot."

The State Police Academy was, when Horton entered it in 1978, run like a paramilitary camp. Cadets marched like soldiers and were mandated to salute higher-ranking officers. After graduating, disappointedly, just below the top 10 percent in his class, Horton excelled as a trooper. By 1981, he was being asked to go back to the academy to train recruits, but refused, vowing never to "treat people the way [he] had been treated in the academy." An admitted type A personality, he had bigger plans, which didn't include spending his days on the interstate chasing drunk drivers and speeders. He wanted that coveted gold shield, to become an investigator. Wayne Bennett, Horton's supervisor at the time, encouraged him to apply to the Bureau when he had three years on the job. To be accepted, a trooper needed four years. But Bennett, who would later become the superintendent of the state police (the top cop, if you will), told Horton to apply anyway.

As senior investigator of the Bureau, investigating and solving nearly two hundred homicides throughout his career, Horton thought he had seen it all by the time Tim Rysedorph's name crossed his desk on October 6, 1997. In the latter stages of what amounted to a stellar career that included solving some of New York's most famous murder cases, Horton was a celebrity of sorts in the Capital District. There were countless stories written about him in the newspapers, and he seemed to enjoy the notoriety it brought him. Two of his cases had even been featured on renowned forensic pathologist Dr. Michael Baden's popular cable television show, *Autopsy,* and Horton gladly appeared on the show to discuss both cases.

Throughout his career, certain cases haunted Horton. One in particular involved the death of several children in upstate New York. Horton, who had married his high school sweetheart, Mary Pat, and quickly had two children, a boy, Jim, and a girl, Alison, had little tolerance, like most cops, for criminals who targeted women and children.

"The cases I remember most," Horton recalled later, "are the ones where children were murdered . . . truly innocent victims, as opposed to people who put themselves in a position of danger by flirting with drugs and hard-core drug dealers."

Horton wasn't a fan of spending his time on the job tracking down husbands who had been missing for what amounted to, in Tim Rysedorph's case, seventy-two hours. But he decided to take along one of seven investigators he supervised, a cop he had been working with a lot lately, Chuck "Sully" Sullivan, and head over to Caroline Parker's apartment to ask her a few questions.

"With these types of cases," Horton said later, "you generally have a husband who has run off with his girlfriend. We knew Tim Rysedorph had been in a band. It wasn't a stretch to think that he had met another woman and had just up and taken off somewhere."

Caroline Parker called one of Tim's ex-brothers-in-law, Nick DiPierro, who had also worked with Tim at BFI, on Monday. The first question out of her mouth was "Do you know someone named Lou who works with Tim?"

"No," DiPierro said.

"Are you sure? This is really important."

"Well, there's this guy named Louis, but I don't know his phone number."

Caroline looked in Tim's personal address book for anyone named Lou and found "Louis." Instead of making the call herself, she called Nick back and gave him the phone number.

"You call Louis," she said, "and call me right back. Ask him if he called the house this past weekend."

Within ten minutes, Nick called back. "Louis said he never called the house."

A few minutes later, Louis called Caroline and repeated what he had told Nick.

"I could tell that it wasn't the Louis who called me those few times," Caroline recalled later, "because of his voice. Louis stuttered. He spoke very differently."

Horton had found out from several of Tim Rysedorph's eight siblings that Tim and Caroline, at times, hadn't gotten along as well as Caroline had said. There were several instances, family members told Bureau investigators, when Tim had taken off for periods of time to get away from Caroline.

While the Bureau continued questioning Tim's family members, SSPD detective Ed Moore took a ride to Caroline's apartment to see if there was anything else she could add. Maybe she had overlooked something important.

Caroline told Moore she and Tim had a loving relationship and Tim would not "do this to us," adding, "I don't know of any reason Tim would leave without first telling me, or at least calling me to let me know he's okay."

"What else can you tell me?" Moore asked. "I feel like we're missing something here."

"I think something bad has happened to Tim," Caroline said. "Someone is making him do something he does not want to do. Either that, or somebody is after him."

"What makes you say that?"

"I think he witnessed a crime, or knew something about someone. Maybe they're after him for it and he's running from them."

This was an interesting development. It appeared Caroline knew more, but was obviously holding back.

Caroline then explained Tim's relationship with Michael Falco. She said Falco had been missing for many years. "Tim and Michael were good friends."

Was there a connection?

After leaving Caroline's with a sour taste in his mouth, Moore suggested the Bureau begin interviewing Caroline to see what else she knew. If there was one cop who could get her to open up, Moore knew it was Jim Horton. He was considered one of the top interrogators the NYSP employed. If Caroline knew more than she was offering, Horton was the man to get it out of her.

CHAPTER 5

When it came to police work, Jim Horton was a pragmatist. He knew more about homicide investigations, larcenies and missing person cases than most cops with the same time on the job put together—and there weren't many who would argue that fact. Working in Major Crimes for the past decade or so, however, had hardened Horton. He knew firsthand what human beings were capable of doing to one another. On some nights, he would arrive at home docile and withdrawn, beaten down by the violence he had witnessed that day, wrestling with the disgust he felt for certain criminals and the crimes they committed.

At the tail end of his career in the Bureau, Horton had been thinking about retirement lately. It wasn't the job, he said later, but the baggage that came with it. He loved the job. The thrill of the chase. Putting "bad guys" in jail. It was everything he had thought it would be, and perhaps more. He wasn't a perfect cop, by any means, and was the first to admit it. But he took the job seriously and had a record of arrests, convictions and awards far surpassing most other cops. Moreover, despite how some felt about his relationship with a career criminal, Gary Evans, all those years, he knew it was something he had to do for the sake of the job.

But the stakes had changed over the past year where Gary Evans was concerned. For the first time, Horton and other Bureau investigators believed Evans—who was known to use several aliases—had been involved in much more than just burglaries and a few arsons to cover up those thefts. Bureau investigators now had good reason to believe Evans had murdered at least two men, maybe more. What they needed, however, were bodies and evidence.

Thus far, they had neither.

By late 1997, forty-three-year-old Gary Evans, with his piercing blue eyes, was on the run, far away from the Capital District. Horton knew Evans would never stop stealing, no matter where he went. It was in his blood. Like an addict, he couldn't help himself. Whether he was scaling the roof of an antique-store barn, or tunneling his way underneath a jewelry store, Evans could—Horton had always said—"find his way through a straw if he needed to." By far, he was the most prolific serial burglar the Bureau had ever encountered—not to mention the fact that he was good at it.

There was one time when the NYSP had been called to the scene of a tripped alarm. It was in the early '80s, shortly before Horton had met Evans. When two troopers arrived on the scene, they shone their lights into the jewelry store, only to watch Evans, as if he were Batman, drop himself from the ceiling by means of a knotted rope. As the troopers approached the front door to go into the building, they watched Evans pull himself back up the rope. Yet, after surrounding the building with several more troopers who had since arrived on the scene, there was no sign of him. Just like that, he was gone.

At just under five feet six inches, 185 pounds, Evans had built his body throughout the years into a machine, lifting weights, carving it like a Greek statue. He never drank alcohol or used tobacco or drugs, and hated anyone who did. He lived on a simple, yet disciplined, diet of cereals, breads, pasta, rice and sweets. He despised meat of any kind. Even in prison, he would trade meat for bread. As a criminal, he took pride in his work and tried to outdo himself with each crime. He spent every hour of each day planning and thinking about his next job, and how he was going to avoid being caught. He had never worked a full-time job and had told Horton numerous times he never would. Horton had even pulled some strings and found him jobs. But he'd always quit after a few days.

Horton's last encounter with Evans was the final blow to their relationship. In 1995, Horton needed Evans to testify in a rape-murder case involving a known rapist and alleged serial murderer. Evans had befriended the guy, under the direction of Horton, after being put in a jail cell next to him, and eventually got him to incriminate himself in an unsolved murder. All Horton asked Evans to do was stay out of trouble until the trial was over.

Months before the trial, Evans stole a rare book worth nearly $100,000 and ended up with the FBI on his trail. Horton was livid. After the trial, Horton ended the relationship.

They hadn't spoken since.

CHAPTER 6

As Horton and Charles "Sully" Sullivan made their way over to Caroline Parker's apartment on Monday evening, October 6, to begin trying to find out where Tim Rysedorph had been for the past three days, they had no reason to believe it was anything more than a cheating husband running off on his family, regardless of the wild accusations and theories Caroline had whipped up while talking to Detective Ed Moore.

"Why are we even getting involved in this?" Horton lamented as they trekked up the pathway toward Caroline's apartment.

"Don't know, Jim. It's our job, maybe?"

Before they got to Caroline's front door, Horton told Sully to take care of the introductions. Sully would act as the quiet cop who took notes, while Horton would be the abrasive cop, asking the tough questions, trying to empathize with Caroline and, at the same time, pulling information out of her without her even knowing. They wanted to wrap up the case as quick as they could and move on to what they presumed were more important cases: homicides, missing children, rapes.

Horton, who had worked for years as a polygraphist, was

a first-rate interviewer, well-versed in these types of interviews. They hadn't called Caroline to warn her they were coming. The element of surprise worked best. A cop could learn many things by just studying body language and listening to the way a person spoke when he or she was confronted with certain questions.

When Caroline came to the door, Horton and Sully could tell it had been a long three days for her. She looked distraught. Crying. Shaking. Her face vacant, withdrawn.

Earlier that day, Horton had run Tim's name through the system to see if anything came up. Besides a child endangerment charge when Tim was in his early twenties—most likely buying alcohol for someone underage—and a petit larceny—a stolen car stereo or something—he was clean.

On the surface, Tim and Caroline appeared to be middle-class people living in a clean apartment in a good section of town. Nothing more, nothing less.

"The apartment was very neat and clean," Horton said later. "I remember what looked like a brand-new leather couch in the living room and several expensive-looking items—knickknacks, that sort of thing—all around the place. The couch was gorgeous. I recall saying to myself, 'How the hell does a guy like Tim Rysedorph afford a couch like this?'"

Horton and Sully already knew Tim was pulling down no more than $350 a week as a truck driver for a garbage company. So, as Horton walked into the apartment and began looking around, his instincts told him immediately that Tim was also making money somewhere else.

How can he afford to live like this?

Running his hand along the smooth leather of the couch, Horton, dressed in his customary dark blue suit, white shirt and tie, began by offering casual conversation. "Boy, what a nice couch. This thing is gorgeous. How much was it? How do you afford something like this?"

"Tim's in a band," Caroline said. "He probably makes more money with the band than he does driving a truck. He's a drummer."

Superficially it made sense. Horton shook his head. *Okay*.

Over the next ten minutes, Caroline explained how Tim was supposed to be home for her sister's wedding. There was no reason for him to be missing. At times, she would become a bit impatient, as if she felt Horton and Sully weren't taking her seriously.

"Can we look around the apartment?" Horton asked at one point.

"Okay."

The kitchen was nothing special, Horton remembered. But he noticed a few incredibly expensive appliances most families don't have the means to afford. There was also a chrome refrigerator that piqued his interest.

Must be a pretty damn successful band Tim is in.

"Why aren't you out there looking for him?" Caroline blurted out as they made their way around the apartment.

"Well," Horton said, "these questions may seem trivial to you, but we have to ask." Then he tried to lighten the mood a bit. "The questions may seem obvious, ma'am, but I'm not the smartest guy in the world. I need to keep asking the same things over and over."

Sensing Caroline's anger, Horton decided to hit her with a few hardball questions: Did she know of any girlfriend Tim might have had? How had the sex between them been recently?

Caroline seemed blindsided at first, yet kept her composure. It was clear she honestly believed Tim was a stand-up guy—that he didn't have a girlfriend, or a second life she didn't know about.

"Has he changed recently? . . . Has anything come up lately?"

"No," Caroline said.

Dead ends. They were getting nowhere.

Tim and Caroline's bedroom was in the basement of the apartment. Tim had a practice drum kit set up by the foot of the bed. The bed itself was made. The room neat. Horton checked the closets.

Everything looked pretty normal.

On and off, Caroline cried and whimpered. Horton and Sully, studying her the entire time, began to sense after some time, as perhaps Caroline did, too, that something was horribly wrong. Tim wasn't coming home.

"The major thing that bothered us as we walked around the apartment and talked to [Caroline] was that Tim had missed his sister-in-law's wedding," Horton said later. "He had told her he was going. He also left his son a note. That was a big deal to us. He had planned to make that wedding, but something kept him from doing it."

When they made it back up into the kitchen, Horton figured he'd ask one more question to see where it led.

"Has anything changed recently? Tim's attitude? His demeanor? Anything? How did you two get along?"

"Well, there's this guy that Tim grew up with in Troy who's been hanging around lately. . . . I don't like him. I don't trust him."

Horton looked at Sully. *Now we're getting somewhere.*

"Do you know his name?" Horton asked.

Caroline went quiet for a moment, trying to think of the name. Then, "I know he is suspected of killing another guy Tim knows, Michael Falco."

Falco? Horton hadn't heard the name in years. "Go on," he encouraged.

"Michael Falco is the guy this guy is suspected of killing. Michael and Tim were best friends. They grew up together. This guy also grew up with Tim and Mike."

Gary fucking Evans, Horton thought. Without knowing it, Caroline had been talking about Evans, who was the last person to see Michael Falco, a convicted thief and former partner and roommate of Evans's, alive. They had done several jobs together throughout the late '70s and early '80s. Falco had been missing, along with another former partner of Evans's, Damien Cuomo, since the mid-1980s. Both men hadn't been seen for years, and as far as the Bureau was concerned, Evans was the prime suspect in both disappearances.

"At that moment," Horton said later, "the hair on the back of my neck stood up. I couldn't wait to get out of that apartment so Sully and I could talk about what Caroline had just said."

Horton then asked Caroline if the name Gary Evans meant anything to her.

"Yes!" she said instantly. "That's the guy Tim has been hanging around with lately. I don't like him. . . ."

Tim Rysedorph is dead. Michael Falco is dead. Damien Cuomo is dead, Horton told himself as Caroline spoke of her hatred for Evans. If there had ever been a doubt that Cuomo and Falco were dead, it was wiped clear by the simple fact that Tim Rysedorph and Evans had been hanging around together recently and now Tim was missing, too.

Liabilities, Horton thought, *all three of them*.

In recent years, Horton had been accused—mostly by the press and a few local defense attorneys, but also a few cops—of carrying on a relationship with Gary Evans, Tim Rysedorph and Michael Falco's friend and burglary partner.

When it came down to it, Gary Charles Evans was a twisted sociopath who had burglarized dozens of antique shops in New York, Vermont, Massachusetts and Connecticut. Horton had been playing a game of cat and mouse with Evans for the past twelve years, using him as an informant, while at the same time arresting him for various crimes. Evans, a master escape and disguise artist, had even helped the state police on a number of unsolved crimes, but Horton had developed a personal relationship with Evans throughout the years, which had infuriated some people.

Horton thought he had rid himself of Evans two years to the day prior to Tim Rysedorph's disappearance. They'd had an argument. After arresting Evans for the theft of a rare and expensive book, Horton told Evans he never wanted to see him again. Their relationship was over. Too many things had happened throughout the years. And after testifying in a case Evans and Horton had worked on together, Evans did just that: he disappeared from Horton's life and they hadn't seen each other since.

So it would have been a safe bet to assume the last name Horton had ever expected to hear while investigating the disappearance of Tim Rysedorph on October 6, 1997, was Gary Evans.

For a number of years, Horton and other members of the Bureau had suspected that Evans had killed Damien Cuomo and Michael Falco, but they had no proof. Cuomo's and Falco's cases, which were considered missing person cases, had gone cold years ago. No law enforcement agency had worked on the cases in over a decade and no family members of either men, according to Horton, had put any pressure on law enforcement to revive the investigations. Like many missing person cases that are actually unsolved murder cases, Damien Cuomo and Michael Falco were mere numbers on files in the state police records room. Sadly, until a hungry investigator decided to reopen the cases, or a family member began complaining to the district attorney's office, they would remain in the records room collecting dust like hundreds of others.

As Horton began working his way out of Caroline Parker's apartment, Sully by his side, he told himself that Caroline was never going to see her husband alive again. *If he's been with Gary Evans, he's as good as dead.*

CHAPTER 7

Horton and Sully figured there was only one reason Tim had been hanging around with Evans: burglary. There was no other purpose. Evans was a loner. He lived by himself. Traveled alone. And unless he needed a partner in crime, he never socialized with people.

From their brief conversation with Caroline, Horton and Sully knew she was either playing stupid, or was scared of aligning herself with stolen property, or she was in denial about her husband's criminal activity.

When Horton explained to Caroline shortly before he and Sully left that there was a good chance Tim had been involved in some illegal activity with Evans, the relationship between him and Caroline "turned very sour," Horton said later.

"No way would my Timmy do this!" Caroline had lashed out. "He's a good father. He's not a thief. He works his ass off."

"Well," Horton had replied, "if Tim has been hanging around with Gary Evans, he's up to no good. Gary has never worked an honest job in his life. He's a career thief. I don't see Gary and 'Timmy' hanging out together, ma'am, if they're not doing something illegal."

* * *

As Horton and Sully approached Horton's cruiser outside Caroline's apartment, Horton, shaking his head in disgust, said, "Holy shit . . . here we go again with Gary."

"What do you think?" Sully asked, opening the passenger-side door.

"We've got big problems. Gary's gone, that's for sure. He's definitely left the area."

Horton opened his door, sat down in the car and began to think.

There was a warrant out for Michael Falco's arrest that had passed through several Bureau investigators' hands over the years. Whenever Horton felt Evans was in the mood to talk about his crimes, he would ask him about Falco especially, seeing that they had grown up together in South Troy and were well-known partners in crime. Evans, though, had always denied any knowledge of Falco's disappearance. In fact, he said, he was in prison when Falco disappeared. But a careful check of Evans's record of incarcerations proved different. He had been incarcerated at Sing Sing prison, serving a two- to four-year bid for third-degree burglary, back on July 3, 1985. Falco had been reported missing about five months earlier.

But whenever Horton had questioned Evans about Falco, Evans would simply say, "Come on, Guy. I'm a thief, not a murderer."

For years, Horton had no reason not to believe him, nor had he any evidence to prove otherwise.

"I can't believe this motherfucker is back in my life, Sully," Horton said as he started the car. "Tim Rysedorph is dead. Where the hell do we begin?"

"What makes you so sure he's dead? He could just be off with Evans doing jobs."

"Tim doesn't have a record to speak of. Remember, we did a rap sheet on him. Gary always told me about liabilities.

He doesn't like them. He also told me one of the last times I spoke to him that he wasn't going back to prison. Rysedorph—believe me when I say it, Sully—is dead."

It was no secret that Horton had used Evans as confidential informant (CI) and kept in contact with him for the better part of the past thirteen years. Evans had even written Horton several letters throughout the years and Horton had, at times, written back. In those early letters, which Horton began to think about now more seriously as he and Sully batted around the possibility that Evans had murdered Tim Rysedorph, Evans had always made one thing perfectly clear: he hated prison.

Being a person who adored the outdoors, often sleeping in the woods and traveling on bicycle, being confined was the worst possible environment Evans could be placed in. He couldn't take the discipline and conveyor-belt routineness of daily life behind bars. He needed to be out in the world, roaming, doing what he wanted.

Cops weren't the only people Evans had to worry about. There were scores of local drug dealers and thieves who had it out for him because they knew he was a CI.

So with crooks and cops chasing Evans, Horton knew that finding him was going to be the biggest challenge. When Evans wanted to disappear, he did it with the ease of a snake in a cornfield. If he had indeed murdered Tim, there was a good chance he had left the country, or at least the Northeast. Disguises and obtaining false identification were two of Evans's greatest skills while on the run. If Horton wanted to find him, he knew it was going to take some sort of mistake on Evans's part.

CHAPTER 8

Tim's car, a blue 1989 two-door Pontiac Sunbird, was found late in the day on Monday, October 6. By the sheer logic of basic police work—tracking down leads and following up on them—the Rensselaer Police Department (RPD) responded to a report of a car parked at the Rensselaer County Amtrak train depot about ten miles from Latham, New York, the last town in which Tim had been spotted. A car in the parking lot fit a description of Tim's. Unlocked, the car had its parking lights on and driver's-side window open when police arrived. The keys were under the driver's-side floor mat, which, Caroline explained later, was totally out of character for Tim. What turned out to be a lead that would ratchet the investigation up a notch—a knapsack loaded with tools and some of Tim's clothes—had been found in the trunk. When Horton got a chance to look through the knapsack, he concluded that Tim probably wasn't carrying around pliers and glasscutters and other burglar tools because he was planning on doing some handyman work. Instead, as he had suspected all along, Tim had been pulling off burglaries with Evans.

Working off a lead he received from the Bureau, SSPD

detective David Levanites was dispatched later that day to Nick DiPierro's house, Tim's ex-brother-in-law.

Although they had gotten along well throughout the years, Nick said his relationship with Tim had never been that close.

"What can you tell me about him?" Levanites asked.

"I know Tim is involved with criminal activity with someone else he hangs around with. He told me one time not too long ago that they—him and his partner—were committing burglaries in New Jersey, Connecticut and Massachusetts."

"Did he say anything else to make you believe this?"

"He asked me, well, I mean, he showed me some coins one day and asked me if I wanted to buy any of them. They were old, from the 1800s, I think."

"What else?"

"I refused. But a little while later, I saw him again and he told me that he sold them for a thousand dollars."

When Horton heard what Levanites had uncovered, it only solidified his theory that Evans was, most likely, the last person to see Tim alive.

"It was the coins; the merchandise had Gary's mark all over it," Horton recalled later. "One of Gary's favorite items to steal was rare coins. He had stolen tens of thousands of dollars' worth throughout the years."

During the next few days, the Bureau kicked into high gear regarding their search for Tim and, now, Gary Evans. They knew if they found Evans, they would find Tim or his body.

Horton briefed his team several times throughout the week, mapping out a plan. There were leads to follow up on from the SSPD. People to interview. Background checks. Evans had a propensity to live in motels and hotels throughout the Capital District and was known to retreat into the woods when he felt the pressure was on. Part of his MO was to keep an apartment and a motel room at the same time so he could bounce back and forth.

"Finding Gary Evans if he didn't want to be found," Horton said later, "wasn't easy. That much we knew. Yet, sooner or later, I knew Gary would make contact with whatever woman he was sleeping with at the time. The only problem I saw right away was locating his most recent girlfriend—I hadn't seen or heard from Gary in almost two years."

The last known contact Tim had with his wife was at 1:03 A.M. on Saturday, October 4. Horton assigned an investigator to go to the Dunkin' Donuts in Latham to talk to anyone there who could identify him. A "lead desk," an exclusive office inside the Bureau designed to generate leads, was immediately set up. Horton put all seven investigators he had available on the case.

While his investigators were off and running, tracking down people and finding out more about Tim, Horton put in a call to Ed Moore, the SSPD detective who had taken Caroline's initial call.

"We've got a problem, Ed," Horton told Moore. They had known each other for years, had worked cases together and respected each other immensely.

"What's going on, Jim?"

"Well, I think we've got a homicide here with that Tim Rysedorph missing person case."

Moore went quiet. Saratoga Springs, a twenty-five minute trip up Interstate 787 from Albany, was an artsy type of refuge that horse fans flocked to during racing season. It was spread out and rural, with thick wooded areas; homicides weren't something the SSPD had to think about all that much.

"You've *got* to be kidding me?"

Horton gave Moore a quick rundown of his history with Evans, including his hunch that Evans might be involved with the disappearances of Michael Falco and Damien Cuomo. Moore said he'd put as many detectives as he could on the case, assisting the Bureau in any manner it needed.

Horton finished speaking to Moore and sat down at his desk, staring at a mugshot photo of Evans he had pulled from a file, contemplating his next move. Evans, Horton realized, was playing a game. Horton could sense it. Evans had always liked to be one step ahead of him. If he was responsible for Tim's death, Horton knew he was gone; they were wasting their time looking in the Capital District.

As much as Horton didn't want to admit it, having Evans back in his life was "exciting," he later confessed.

"I had spent a lot of my time watching him watch me—and vice versa. Gary always made my job more interesting."

By the same token, considering what Horton now knew, he didn't view Evans as just another serial thief he had come to know throughout the years and developed a relationship with for the sake of the job.

"With Tim Rysedorph," Horton added, "I knew it was going to be the last time Gary and I tangled. I really felt he had crossed a line at this point and was a murderer. The stakes were much different when Tim turned up missing. It wasn't about a game of cat and mouse anymore; it was possible Evans was a serial murderer, which I took very seriously."

Everything Horton had done for Evans (buying him food, stopping by his apartment just to say hello, getting him jobs) was done—ironically—with sincerity and deception. Horton cared about Evans, but he also kept tabs on him for law enforcement purposes.

"It was part of the game, yes—but also my job."

Nevertheless, Horton knew Evans was a career criminal, and by nature would likely never change his ways. Ever since he suspected him of murdering Falco and Cuomo, Horton convinced himself that in order to get him to confess to everything—however horrific and brutal—he had to get into his head and gain his trust. There were even several unsolved murders in states Evans had visited that Horton had now suspected him of being involved in, but he had to play things out and allow Evans to admit to it all without being pressured.

"If I got him to like me, I knew one day he would confide in me and tell me everything. When Tim turned up missing and Gary's name became part of the investigation, I knew it was the beginning of the end for Gary. How did I know that?"

Evans, Horton insisted, had warned him.

Nathan "Bud" York, a Bureau investigator, found out on October 7, Tuesday, that the Wappingers Falls, New York, division of the Bureau had been involved in an investigation with the Massachusetts State Police (MSP) regarding a burglary. The theft had taken place at the Emporium, an antique shop in Great Barrington, Massachusetts, about an hour's drive over the New York state line. Nine thousand dollars' worth of jewelry, antique vases, ceramic plates, statues, paintings and other assorted items had been reported stolen back in March 1997.

When Bud York explained to Horton what he had found, Horton knew right away it was another one of Evans's jobs. Evans was so renowned and feared on the antique circuit, his photo had been published in several antique magazines throughout the Northeast. There wasn't an antique dealer in the tristate region—New York, Connecticut, Massachusetts—who hadn't heard of the notorious Gary Evans. Shops as far away as Maine, New Hampshire, Delaware and New Jersey even knew of Evans.

As new leads poured into the Bureau, it became pretty clear Evans had been on a serial robbery spree for about the past eighteen months. With that in mind, if there was one thing Horton was sure of, it was that Evans, over the years, liked to keep his stolen merchandise hidden in self-storage units.

Armed with that knowledge, he called two of his investigators into his office. "Track down all the storage units in the Capital District and find out if Gary rented a unit recently."

In the meantime, he sent a pair of investigators in search of a visitor's list for Evans's most recent stay in federal prison. It would take some time, but if they could find out who was on the list and track down any names Horton didn't recognize, they might get lucky.

In the federal system, inmates are allowed to compile a list of visitors. If someone isn't on the list, that person is not allowed in to visit an inmate.

What turned out to be a laugh riot around the office was when the list came back, Horton's name was at the top of Evans's list.

After everyone had a good laugh, Horton pointed to a name on the list right below his. The name looked familiar, but he couldn't place it: *Lisa Morris*, a woman who, ultimately, would end up breaking the Tim Rysedorph missing person case wide open.

CHAPTER 9

When Horton found Lisa Morris on October 15, 1997, she was living at Rolling Ridge Apartments in Latham, a mere stone's throw from the Spare Room II self-storage facility on Watervliet-Shaker Road, where Evans and Tim Rysedorph, the Bureau found out, had rented two self-storage units, eight feet by ten feet, to house their stolen property.

Getting Lisa to open up about Evans, Horton realized quickly, was not going to be easy.

Like Damien Cuomo, Michael Falco and Tim Rysedorph, Lisa grew up in Troy. A bit on the "rough" side, she'd had her share of problems with alcohol and drugs throughout the years, but had no real rap sheet to speak of. A plain-looking woman with easy brown eyes, large shoulders over a medium build, long brown hair and a quiet demeanor, Lisa's pale-white skin gave away her full-blooded Irish heritage. She had met Evans in 1988—to no one's surprise later on—a few months before Damien Cuomo, her common-law husband, turned up missing. As calculating and manipulative as Evans was, he had moved in with Lisa after Cuomo disappeared. Shortly before moving in, he was showing up at her apartment, telling her that Cuomo had "run off" after committing several burglaries with him.

"He's not coming back," Evans said one day. "He told me to tell you that."

In the beginning, the relationship between them wasn't sexual, Lisa said later. Evans would stop by her apartment just to talk, "like friends," and, at Cuomo's request, "keep her company."

As the months passed, he began giving her money, as if paying off a debt. When he stopped by her apartment with the cash, he would tell her that he'd heard from Damien, saying things like, "He's hiding out down south. Write him off. Forget about him. He's not coming back."

In 1996, after Evans finished a two-year bid for burglary in Sing Sing, he began a more concerted effort to win Lisa's affection.

"Gary and I became very close," Lisa said later, "when he got out of prison. He would often stay with me."

As she and Evans described it later, they began having what Lisa termed "marathon sex" around this same time—and Lisa, then a thirty-two-year-old single mother, said she couldn't get enough of it as she began to fall in love with Evans.

During the week of October 15, Sully and Ed Moore took one more stab at interviewing Caroline Parker. They needed Caroline to sit down and write out a formal statement. Tim's photo had been all over the television news lately and missing person posters had been hung around the Capital Region. His siblings were pleading for his return. Caroline and Sean, devastated, had given interviews to local reporters, hoping, naturally, it would help.

Ed Moore, Sully and other members of the Bureau felt different, though. They knew if Evans was involved with Tim, it wasn't going to be good news. Keep the faith and hope for the best, but understand it may not turn out so pleasant at the end of the day.

When Moore and Sully first arrived at Caroline's apartment, they explained how Tim had been involved in the trafficking of stolen property. They needed Caroline to fess up to what she knew about Tim's criminal behavior. It had been weeks now. No more bullshit. It was time to talk truth.

Caroline was taken aback by their candor. "I know of no criminal activity that Tim was involved in and do not believe he would do anything illegal like that," she said with stern assertion.

After a bit more prodding, however, she finally admitted that she and Tim's relationship hadn't been as trouble-free as she might have first let on. Tim had left in 1996 for a period of time, she explained. They fought. They had financial problems. But Tim, she insisted, was a family man all the way. "I believe our lifestyle does not reflect Tim having a lot of money from illegal activity. . . ."

Moore and Sully looked at each other: *You are so full of shit.*

About a week prior to his disappearance, Caroline recalled, Tim had taken a day off from work. Moore and Sully knew—but didn't share it with her—that on that particular day Tim was south of Albany with Evans selling stolen merchandise to an antique shop that the two of them had been doing business with for years. The owner of the shop had picked Tim and Evans out of a photo lineup. The Bureau had three checks in the neighborhood of $10,000 written out from the shop owner to Tim Rysedorph.

Caroline continued to talk about Tim's mood around the house during the last few weeks, relating how he was an incredibly private person, especially when it came to whom he was speaking to over the telephone.

"Do you recall any strange calls the past few weeks?" Sully asked.

"I cannot remember any unusual calls except for one. About two months ago, I answered a telephone call from a person I thought was my uncle Gary *Ashton*. 'Hello, is Tim there?' the caller asked when I answered. I said, 'Hi, Gar, what's the matter?' The caller replied, 'Just let me talk to Tim.' He sounded mad."

Caroline said she realized later it wasn't her uncle Gary, but it was Gary Evans. Everyone in their old Troy neighborhood, where Michael Falco, Evans, Damien Cuomo and Tim had all grown up, she said, believed Evans had murdered Falco.

The last time, Caroline said, she saw or heard from Evans had been when Sean was born. Evans brought over a card and gave them an air conditioner because he was concerned that the temperature in the apartment was too hot for Caroline and the newborn. As the years passed, Caroline said she would mention Evans's name around Tim, but he would always get upset.

"Don't *ever* mention that name again," Tim would snap angrily at Caroline at the mere mention of Evans. There was obviously some tension and resentment between the two men, but Caroline continued to maintain she had no idea why.

"Anything else you can recall about your husband and Gary Evans," Moore prodded, "would be of great help to us." He knew she had more information.

"Well, I remember Tim telling me that if anything ever happened to him, or if he ever became missing, 'like Mike Falco,' that I was *not* to say anything to the police about Gary Evans. . . . He is dangerous."

Moore and Sully wondered why she hadn't offered the information weeks ago.

Continuing, she said, "Tim said that if anything ever happened to him, I should change our last name and move away."

Considering what had happened the past few weeks, Caroline perhaps realized for the first time that Evans had likely had a hand in her husband's disappearance. She said she now believed it *was* Evans, using the alias "Lou," who had called her the weekend Tim disappeared. Tim was scared of Evans, she added, and had probably gone with him reluctantly because Evans had threatened Tim with Sean's safety.

It was one of the last conversations she'd had with Tim that really scared her, she admitted. The night before Tim disappeared, a Thursday, she said they had a fight and talked about getting a divorce. "'I love you . . . but if you want a divorce,'" she said Tim wrote in a note to her that night, "'I will give you money for the divorce.'"

Later in the note, after he apologized for being "moody" lately and even "mean" at times, as if he had a premonition of what was to come, Tim wrote of his concern for Caroline and Sean's safety, should he ever not return home. He speculated that Evans would harm her and Sean and was worried about not being around to protect them.

CHAPTER 10

Lisa Morris lived a life of solitude in a modest apartment that was, by sheer luck, only about two miles from Jim Horton's home in Latham. Stopping by Lisa's apartment and badgering her, Horton knew, was going to be the conduit to making contact with Evans.

The first few times Horton popped in, Lisa was passive, unfriendly, and perhaps a little scared. During a Bureau briefing one morning after Lisa's name had been discovered, Horton told his investigators he had recognized her name as someone Evans had mentioned to him from time to time.

"Gary told me more than once that, in his words, Lisa was simply 'someone he stopped by to fuck' every once in a while. I had no reason not to believe him. Gary had a lot of those women in his life."

The first thing Horton noticed when he knocked on Lisa's door on October 15 was how homely her apartment, from the outside, looked. It wasn't run-down, but, as Horton peered through the window, he could tell she hadn't kept it up perhaps the way she could have. A cop is always studying people and places: body language, vocal characteristics, clothes, how someone walks, eye movement, the appearance of a home, car. Lisa spoke with a smoker's raspy voice. She wore plain clothes and little makeup. She hadn't really held down a full-time job, but would work occasionally as a process server, delivering subpoenas to people in civil cases.

It was obvious to Horton by just looking at her that first time that she liked to drink—a lot. She had bags under both eyes and loose, pale skin. She appeared lethargic, as if it had taken all of her energy just to answer the door.

"Paperboy," Horton said as Lisa opened the door. He was holding a day-old newspaper he'd picked up on her front steps.

Without Horton saying anything more, the initial look Lisa held told him she knew exactly who he was and why he was there. Although Horton never openly wore a shield or flipped it out like television cops, he had a look about him that screamed law enforcement. It was something most cops couldn't hide. They looked the part. What was more, he kept his handcuffs hanging not from his waist, but from the emergency brake lever in his cruiser, and hardly ever carried his weapon.

"I never wore those stupid tie tags—like a miniature silver or gold set of handcuffs, announcing that I was a cop," Horton said later. "But it was written all over my face . . . and, of course, the blue suit. I certainly wasn't a vacuum cleaner salesman."

As Lisa invited Horton in and began to talk, he realized the connection she'd had with Evans ran deep and, most important, *recent*. There was no doubt she had seen Evans within the past few weeks.

"He's talked about you," Lisa said, adding, "I've heard your name before."

"I need to know some things, Lisa."

Within a few minutes, Horton learned that he and Lisa had more in common than just Gary Evans: their daughters attended the same school. Twelve-year-old *Christina Morris*, had gone to the same school as Horton's daughter, Alison. They weren't friends, but they knew each other.

Even more remarkable was who Christina's father was.

"Damien Cuomo," Lisa offered. Cuomo was one of Evans's "business partners." He had been missing since 1989. Horton had no idea Lisa even knew Cuomo.

Horton sat back for a moment, took a breath. It was all beginning to make sense.

"Let me get this straight: Damien Cuomo is your daughter's *father*?"

"Yes," Lisa said, surprised as to why Horton seemed so shocked.

More evidence to Horton that Cuomo, Falco and Tim Rysedorph were dead—and that Evans had killed them.

"It just all made sense to me at that moment," Horton recalled later. "What had been a hunch for years turned into a fact for me."

The apartment complex where Lisa lived was located on a patch of land in back of a strip mall on Route 155 in Latham. A second-story unit, her apartment had two bedrooms, a small living room, eat-in kitchen, and a sliding door that walked out to a small deck. It wasn't a penthouse, but the school district for Christina was considered one of the best in the state and the apartment was affordable.

Evans liked the location because he could park his truck in the parking lot of T.J. Maxx, a retail clothing store located in the strip mall adjacent to Lisa's door, when he wanted to pay her a visit. The apartment complex was directly to the northeast of the loading dock area of T.J. Maxx. Evans would park his vehicle in the front parking lot of the strip mall and blend it into the store's parking lot of vehicles. It was just one more way for Evans to keep his whereabouts secret.

Every aspect of his life had been thought out with meticulous consideration. Even a seemingly innocent stop at a girlfriend's house for "a piece of ass," as Evans would jokingly put it, had to be planned with concerted effort to the finest detail—and Evans was a master at alluding authorities and tricking people into thinking he was somewhere other than where he was supposed to be. Being a criminal was his job, twenty-four hours a day, seven days a week. Everything he did consisted of him snooping around, looking over his shoulder, covering his tracks. He had to, he later admitted to Horton, have a system in place for every part of his life, or he couldn't function. One of his biggest fears about visiting Lisa was being bottled up at her apartment if push ever came to shove. If his truck were out in front of her apartment, he would have felt caged in. On foot, he believed, he could get away from any situation.

Scattered around Lisa's apartment were ceramic elephants, statues, figurines and knickknacks of all types. In the ashtrays were butts from marijuana cigarettes. When Horton took it all in, he had no choice but to think that every antique in the apartment had been stolen by Evans and given to Lisa as a gift.

"I need to talk to Gary," Horton said as Lisa continued to speak of menial, everyday things.

"I'm not sure where he is."

"Listen, Lisa. I don't know what Gary's told you about me, but we go back a few years. I really need to find him."

Horton brought the list from the prison with him, hoping to prove to Lisa that he wasn't just making things up to further his agenda. He had no idea what kind of picture Evans had painted for Lisa of their relationship.

"You see," Horton said, pointing to the list where his name had been written by Evans, "he doesn't write that I'm a cop; he writes 'friend' next to my name, just like yours."

Lisa appeared to ease up a bit, as though she had become unwillingly convinced she could trust Horton.

"I used to date Damien Cuomo," Lisa said.

Horton explained how he knew the name and why it shocked him so much to hear that Lisa's daughter had been fathered by Cuomo.

"Do you think Gary had anything to do with his disappearance—no one has seen Damien for almost ten years now?"

"No! He's a piece of shit for leaving me high and dry with Christina. Fucking deadbeat dad is all he is."

"You know that Gary and Damien are —" Horton didn't even get a chance to finish what he was saying.

"Yes . . . I know they're thieves," Lisa said. "So what."

Even though Horton thought there was a good chance Damien Cuomo was dead, he felt he needed to ask Lisa where she thought he was.

"I know exactly where he is," Lisa said. She seemed mad, raising her voice and looking away. "He's down in the Carolinas living it up!" She was convinced of it.

Over the course of the next ten minutes, Lisa confessed that she had been dating Evans on and off for about the past eight years, but had never visited him while he was in jail. It wasn't something Evans wanted, she claimed. She talked about him as though he were some sort of Prince Charming who had saved her and Christina from the mess Damien Cuomo had left them in.

"I know Damien is on the run. He could have given himself up, done his time, and he could be sitting here right now with his daughter. But he left us instead! He never calls at Christmas, her birthday. Nothing. Thank God Gary came into our lives."

After a few simple questions, Horton understood Lisa's role in Evans's life. Gary Evans never considered Lisa to be anything more than a "quick lay." He felt nothing for her emotionally. He liked Christina, as he did most kids, and treated her with respect, but Lisa was a mere stepping-stone along his path of crime.

"Can you tell me when you saw Gary last?" Horton asked, ratcheting his voice up a level, letting Lisa know he was serious. It was time for answers. He didn't want to mention the stolen antiques in the house or the marijuana she was obviously smoking, but felt she wasn't being totally honest with him and would use it if he had to.

"Sunday . . . I saw him on Sunday," Lisa said, putting her palm under her chin, cradling her head, staring at the floor.

"This past week? Or last week?" Horton asked. He then pulled out a small calendar and pointed to the past two Sundays. "Which one?"

Lisa put her finger on October 5.

"What time?"

"About nine-thirty in the morning."

Evans had stopped by for about twenty minutes, she said. He was driving his green Toyota pickup.

"How was he?"

"Very scared . . . pale-looking."

There was more, of course, but Lisa paused, stood up and walked around the living room. She realized she was letting Evans down by saying things she shouldn't. Evans had warned her that Horton would be coming around.

"What did he say?" Horton asked.

"He told me that he had done something he was going to get caught for and didn't want to go to jail for twenty-five years." She sat back down.

"Is there anything else you can think of, Lisa? This is *extremely* important."

Neither Horton nor Lisa had mentioned Tim Rysedorph's name, which was the main purpose of Horton's visit.

Lisa then got up off the couch again and walked toward the door. As she opened it, suggesting it was time for Horton to leave, she said, "Gary told me he would contact me."

"When?" Horton asked as he walked over the threshold.

Lisa smiled as she closed the door. "In a few years."

CHAPTER 11

The fact that Lisa Morris knew Evans and Damien Cuomo were thieves told Horton that she knew a hell of a lot more than she was admitting. With certain sources, especially "key" sources, experience told Horton patience was his most productive asset. Lisa would come around. It would take time, but she would crack. All he had to do was continue pestering her: stopping by on his way home from work, and on his way to work, calling her and just keeping the pressure on. Establish a rapport, maybe even a personal relationship. He had to break that bond between Lisa and Evans and somehow make her trust him. Since Lisa was the last known person Evans had contacted before leaving the area, and had made a point of telling her he was going to get in touch with her, Horton felt she could ultimately be his "lady in red."

Horton recalled later, "In thinking about how to handle Lisa Morris, I figured I had to become her Columbo. It wasn't my style . . . bothering people like that until they just got sick of me. But Lisa knew something. She had been sleeping with Gary Evans."

A day later, Horton popped in unexpectedly. "Can I do anything for you?" he asked.

"Come in," Lisa said, opening the door.

She looked like she hadn't slept. It was either that, Horton guessed, or she had been drinking most of the night.

"What's up?"

"I wasn't all that truthful with you yesterday," she admitted.

Here we go . . . ,Horton thought as Lisa fired up a cigarette, took a deep pull from it and, while exhaling, ran her hands through her hair.

"Go ahead. I'm all ears, here, Lisa."

"Gary showed up that Saturday morning, not Sunday. I don't know, maybe nine or ten o'clock. He came to the door"—her hands were shaking—"and wanted to come in."

"So you let him in?"

"Not at first. He was dirty . . . covered with mud. I told him to go hose off downstairs in the laundry room and come back up."

"Relax, Lisa," Horton said, trying to calm her. She was getting antsy, getting up and walking around the apartment, thinking about things before she spoke.

"He was sweaty and really scared," she continued. "He kept some of his things here, so he had a change of clothes. 'I have to leave town,' he told me. He was nervous."

"Did he leave right away?"

"I guess. He was jumpy, looking out the window while getting dressed. He didn't want to hang around too long. He sensed you guys were on his trail."

"He didn't say anything else: where he was going, who he had been with, what happened?"

"No," Lisa said. "He gave me a few hundred dollars and told me he'd be in touch with me in a few years."

"Listen, I appreciate what you've told me here. If Gary happens to call you or make contact with you in any way, just promise you'll contact me."

Horton gave Lisa his business card, flipped it over and wrote his cell phone and home number on the back. "If you need anything, Lisa, just call."

Holding the card, Lisa stared at it for a moment. "I will, Jim. Thank you."

A clearer picture of Caroline Parker's relationship with Tim and his family began to emerge as Bureau investigators began talking to Tim's siblings.

Molly Parish, Tim Rysedorph's sister, said she hadn't seen Tim for almost a year, and no one in her family cared much for Caroline. "If Timmy left," Parish said, "it was because of [Caroline] and his not being able to provide for her needs."

According to Parish, the last time she saw Tim he had asked her to co-sign a loan so Sean, her nephew, could attend summer camp. She refused. When investigators asked whether Tim was inclined to do drugs, she said she'd never seen him under the influence and he never talked about it.

At one point during the interview, Parish offered one of her most vivid memories of Caroline. At Caroline and Tim's wedding, she said, Caroline had rummaged through the wedding gift envelopes long before the wedding ended. When she finished, all she could do, Parish added, was complain about "not getting enough money" from guests.

For members of the Bureau, that telling little anecdote only added to how much they *didn't* know about Tim and Caroline's relationship—and maybe Caroline hadn't been as forthcoming as she should have been about what else she knew.

Horton and his team of Bureau investigators sat around during late October and brainstormed over what they had learned the past week. Thus far, they had a wealth of information regarding Tim and the days before he went missing. They knew he had called Caroline at 1:03 A.M. from the local Dunkin' Donuts—which was the last time Caroline, or anyone else, had heard from him. They also knew Evans had shown up at Lisa Morris's apartment later at 9:00 A.M. He was dirty, gaunt, sweaty and scared. From there, they picked through the interviews they had done and pieced together the hours and days in between.

"With Tim not showing up for his sister-in-law's wedding on that Saturday after he vanished, and Gary Evans," Horton said later, "showing up disheveled at Lisa's apartment on Saturday morning, Tim's car abandoned at Amtrak, I knew for certain that Tim wasn't being help captive somewhere against his will. He was definitely dead."

CHAPTER 12

A search warrant for the two self-storage units at the Spare Room II that Evans and Tim had rented was issued on October 18, 1997. The goal was to obtain an arrest warrant for Evans, but the Bureau had to first find evidence of any burglaries he—and, possibly, Tim—had been involved in.

Inside the two small storage units Evans and Tim owned was nothing of any particular interest to Horton as members of the Bureau began to search them. There were some old books, a few collectors-edition Beatles records, several ceramic knickknacks and a few pieces of worthless jewelry. Essentially, the last person inside the storage units had, it looked like, taken what he wanted in a frenzy and left everything else scattered about.

Interestingly enough, though, Horton noticed, the unit reeked of stale bleach—and someone had recently cleaned a large patch of cement by the garage door.

Horton ordered everything in the unit bagged and tagged. "Get this stuff out of here," he told several troopers, "and log it."

The storage facility had video cameras set up near the entrance. It was an eight-second-delay device, so the quality wouldn't be that good, but anyone who had entered or exited would be on videotape.

Horton ordered copies of the videotapes from October 3 through October 5.

A day later, after painstakingly watching hours of videotape, there he was, the man of the hour, entering the Spare Room II in his pickup truck. The video was cloudy and grainy, but Horton could see that the bed of Evans's truck was full of items.

How did Horton know for sure it was Evans? For one, the license plate number matched. Second, Evans had a distinctive profile: the crown of his bald head was perfectly round, and he had distinguishable strands of frizzy hair protruding out from the sides of his head, much like Bozo the Clown. Additionally, Evans had shoulder and neck muscles so large they looked deformed. Most important, he had always told Horton he never allowed anyone to drive his truck.

When the Bureau matched up the codes Tim and Evans had been issued by Spare Room II for gaining entrance through the main gate, they found both code numbers had been used throughout the day and night of October 4. But the following Sunday morning, at some point after 2:00 A.M., Tim's code number had stopped being used. Only Evans's number had been accessed after that.

As the reports filed in, it was clear that Tim and Evans had been partners in crime for at least the past seven or eight months and had pulled off several major jobs together. A Bureau investigator in Dutchess County, New York, reported that his team had been looking at Tim and Evans for some time regarding a heist in Great Barrington, Massachusetts. The stolen property had turned up in an antique shop in Cold Spring, New York, and the person who purchased it picked out both Tim and Evans from a photo lineup as being the sellers. A bank video had placed both Evans and Tim in an

Albany bank that same day, cashing three checks written out to Tim Rysedorph from the owner of the same antique shop.

When Evans's probation officer called the Bureau with the news that Evans had failed to report for his weekly probation visit, a judge believed it was enough, along with all the thefts Evans and Tim were now suspected of, to issue an arrest warrant.

Horton then called Evans's probation officer. Evans had shown up for his previous appointment on September 30, the probation officer said (which was a week before Tim had gone missing), but looked totally different than he had the week prior.

"How do you mean . . . different?" Horton asked.

"He was clean shaven." Evans had usually donned a Fu Manchu mustache and goatee. Horton had even photographed him with it. At times, it was hard to keep up with Evans and his subtle disguises, so Horton would "pop in" on him and ask to take his photo. Evans, an "egomaniac," always obliged. Horton would comment on how large his muscles were getting. "You working out hard or what, Gar?" he'd say. "Yeah," Evans would answer, his eyes lighting up.

"He was amazed that someone was paying attention to him," Horton recalled later. "I fed that ego, and by the time I was breaking out the camera, he was happy to strike a pose."

For obvious reasons, Evans hated his probation officer. Whenever he talked to Lisa about him, he always referred to him as "the prick." He also said he was nervous the last few times he had seen him. He talked about a "job" he and Tim had done down in Wappingers Falls, New York, and said he was scared they'd get caught. Being a habitual offender, convicted of several felonies already, he knew the next time he got caught he was facing possibly twenty-five years to life behind bars—which, he said, there was no way he would do.

* * *

A wanted man, there was a bull's-eye now on Evans's back. Multiple photos of him, along with his rap sheet, were sent over the wires to every police department and law enforcement agency in the country. He was considered armed, dangerous and capable of doing anything to avoid capture. Horton had written the Teletype himself:

> *Gary C. Evans, 5' 6"—180 pounds, bald, piercing blue eyes, goes by numerous disguises and aliases, likes to hide handcuff keys all over his body, will try to escape by any means necessary, could be armed and very dangerous.*

It was the beginning of a manhunt for a notorious burglar Horton believed—but didn't tell anyone—was going to be impossible to catch. Additionally, for the first time in the thirteen years since Horton and Evans had begun their game of cat and mouse, Horton believed firmly that Evans was also a serial murderer, which changed everything.

CHAPTER 13

By October 19, 1997, Bureau investigators had interviewed several of Tim's siblings, trying to substantiate what they already knew and, hopefully, develop a few new leads. The case seemed to be running in circles. Every time they thought they were onto something, it turned into a dead end. Sooner or later, someone was going to talk and the case would bust wide open. It was a matter of finding that person and asking the same repetitive questions.

Molly Parish, Tim's sister, had always been someone that interested Horton. When he saw her name on a list of follow-up interviewees, he decided to go see her himself.

A school bus driver and mother of four daughters ranging in age from thirteen to twenty-three, Parish told Horton she hadn't seen Tim since April 1997 when she had stopped at a bar where his band was playing. About three weeks later, however, in May, she said she saw Evans.

Son of a bitch.

"Go on, tell me about Mr. Evans," Horton encouraged, without letting her know why the name meant so much to him.

She explained that Evans had shown up at her trailer unannounced one day. They argued over what they were going to have for dinner and some lottery tickets she had purchased. She said that although she never lived with Evans, she did have "relations" with him from time to time. They had grown up together in the same Troy neighborhood and dated on and off. But whenever she wanted to contact him, she said she would have to page him under the code name "Red."

It was the first time Horton had ever heard the name. "How was he when you saw him last?"

"He had a very explosive temper," she continued, "and hated [Caroline]."

"What about where he is now; do you have any idea where we might find him?"

"I know Gary has a storage shed, but I don't know where it is. I know he stores his 'stuff,' proceeds from burglaries, there."

"What about Gary and Tim; how did they get along?"

"Gary was very angry with Tim. Whenever Gary was in a jam, he expected Tim to help him out. There was some car, drugs, Mike Falco . . . I'm not too sure what it all meant, but Gary never got over it."

There was that name again: Michael Falco. It seemed synonymous with Evans's name inside that small circle of old friends in Troy.

She went on to say she thought Tim's disappearance may have been "revenge" on Evans's part for something that happened a long time ago among Falco, Tim and Evans, but she didn't know the entire story.

"Gary always told me," she said, "that 'people are very easy to get rid of and without a trace.' He once told me, 'Look what happened to Mike [Falco] . . . and there are a couple of other people still missing.' I really feel Gary killed Mike by burying him alive or putting him in a place where he couldn't get out."

After explaining to Horton that Evans liked to confide in a tattoo artist in Troy, she got back on the subject of Tim and Evans's soured relationship.

"Gary never really forgave Tim for being disloyal to him during a time when Gary felt he needed Tim. Gary told me Tim had called one day asking for money, about fifteen hundred dollars. So Gary told Tim he would 'have to do some jobs' with him if he wanted the money."

"If there was one thing Evans was clear about when I interviewed him later," Horton recalled, "it was that he favored working alone. He'd do his best work by himself, he'd tell me, and he wouldn't have to worry about someone dropping a dime on him. He only took along a partner if that person owed him a favor or money. And he made this utterly clear to me: if that person even threatened to go to the cops, he had no choice but to kill him."

A K-9 unit of cadaver-sniffing dogs from the state police searched the area surrounding the Spare Room II self-storage facility, where Evans and Tim had stored their stolen property. Horton felt if Evans had killed Tim, he might have buried him in close proximity of the storage facility.

After searching the perimeter of the facility and the storage units, the dogs found nothing. It was one more in a series of false predictions on Horton's part. He was going on hunches, mostly. Without Evans—without a body—he had nothing but instinct. It was disheartening at times, but it was police work. Not everything worked itself out in sixty minutes, like a television sitcom, and not every lead produced another. Still, most cops believed it took only one arbitrary piece of information and a case could be broken.

Near the end of October, the manager of Spare Room II phoned Bureau headquarters with some rather odd news. He said Tim Rysedorph had called.

"He called you?"

"Yes. This morning."

"What did he say?"

"He wanted information about how late the office was open so he could come in and pay for his unit. He asked if the billing for the month had been sent out yet. He said he wanted to pay his bill before the billing went out so his wife wouldn't find out that he had been renting a unit."

Could it be that simple?

A surveillance team was put together immediately. If Tim—or Evans posing as him—went to the Spare Room II to pay the bill, the Bureau would be there waiting for him.

Horton, however, warned everyone that Evans wasn't that stupid. There was no way he was going to just march into Spare Room II after calling. It was some sort of trap. A way to throw off the scent.

At about 2:40 P.M., as undercover officers from the Bureau, who had been there all day long, stood despondent around the Spare Room II gate thinking that the entire day had been a waste, a 1996 Ford Contour with New Hampshire license plates pulled up to the entrance gate. A female was driving. She was alone. She looked lost. Scared.

But also very familiar.

When officers approached the car and asked the woman to identify herself, she simply rolled the window down and said, "Lisa Morris."

CHAPTER 14

Throughout the years, Evans had juggled scores of women. He liked to brag to Horton about all the women he had slept with. Most of them, he said, were nothing but "whores"—a "piece of ass" he could call every once in a while for some fun. Bedding down with women was a game to Evans, a challenge. There was one time Horton stopped at a hotel room Evans had been renting and Evans handed him a photo of himself and a rather good-looking blonde. They were blasting around the ocean on Jet Skis. "I had that photo taken two days ago," Evans boasted, "in Florida!" He seemed proud of the fact that he could pick up a woman on a Friday night, fly down to Florida for the weekend, "bang her a few times" and return home the following Monday—an all-expense-paid weekend vacation, courtesy of whichever antique shop owner—who had undoubtedly spent his life building his business—Evans had pillaged.

Other times, Evans would show Horton photos of different women and his demeanor would change entirely. He sometimes became docile, as if he had invested his emotions in the woman and she had let him down. One of those women was *Doris Sheehan*, a twenty-six-year-old brunette Evans had dated throughout the years. In one of his letters to Horton,

Evans talked about Sheehan as though she had been the only woman he had ever loved. A bit on the chunky side at five feet three inches, 140 pounds, Sheehan's blue eyes accentuated the beauty of her pudgy yet cute face. She had been arrested for a few DWIs, but other than that she was just a young and naive local girl Evans had won over with his charm and his showering of stolen jewelry.

A local Troy woman who knew Sheehan later said she was "all about material things. She never loved Gary, but loved what Gary could provide her with."

When Horton found Sheehan in late October, after locating her through Evans's prison visiting list, she was apprehensive and unresponsive to most of his questions. She had obviously been trained by Evans to keep her mouth shut if the cops ever came knocking.

"I haven't seen Gary," she said when Horton asked, "since before summer. But," she added, "I spoke to him a few weeks ago."

"What did he say?"

"Not much. I told him to pay me the five hundred he owed me for back rent. He said he was leaving. He told me I could have his truck. A day later, it was parked in my driveway."

Evans had lived with Sheehan in her trailer for a brief period. When Horton found her, she had already hooked up with another man whom she referred to as her "fiancé." They were preparing to move to Florida.

Sheehan had also rented a unit at the Spare Room II back on September 19, 1996, but when the Bureau checked it out, it was empty.

In the end, Doris Sheehan could offer only one more false glimmer of hope.

There was a name on that same prison visitor's list that had been bothering Horton ever since he had seen it. A young kid in his twenties with no criminal record had visited Evans a few times during his last stay in prison. When the

Bureau tracked the kid down, he said Evans had recently been to his house in upstate New York to pay him and his father a visit. The connection between the kid, his father and Evans, Horton soon found out, was work-related. Evans had done some tree work for the family at one time and the three of them had been friends ever since. They liked Evans, the kid and his father said. "He was pleasant. Nice guy. Never bothered anyone. He worked hard."

According to the kid, Evans could scale a tree like a squirrel.

"When he came over the last time, what did he say?"

"Well, he just wanted to stop by to say that he had always liked us and that we would probably never see him again."

"That was it?"

"Yeah. Then he left."

Horton continued to work on Lisa, stopping by her apartment when he could to see if she would willingly volunteer any new information about Evans's whereabouts. When he saw her after she had been identified at Spare Room II during the Bureau's surveillance, he wondered why she had gone there and what her purpose was. Undoubtedly, Evans had put her up to it.

"Were you going to pay Tim Rysedorph's bill?" Horton asked. "I don't understand what's going on here."

"No. I was going to rent a space."

"All right, Lisa, tell me what's going on here. I'm not an asshole."

Lisa paused. Then, "Gary sent me to pay the bill. But he asked me to do it *before* he left. It's not like he called and ordered me to do it."

"That's it? Nothing else?" Horton knew she was lying. He sensed Evans was pulling her strings, like maybe he was monitoring the entire situation from afar.

"Well, I did want to rent a space for myself—I'm cramped here in the apartment, as you can see."

Lisa's apartment was always neat and clean. She had some junk piled in a spare bedroom, but it was nothing overwhelming. What was more, she could barely scrape together eight dollars to buy a six-pack and a pack of cigarettes, better yet come up with $65 or $70 every month for a storage space.

But Horton didn't want to press her. Over the next week, he pestered her about it, but she stuck to her story. He left the subject alone because he didn't want to jeopardize the rapport he had already spent weeks building.

"I wanted her to find Gary for me," Horton said later. "I was using her for that purpose only. The money I was giving her out of my own pocket, the conversations I had with her, acting sympathetic to her situation, was all part of my strategy."

Bureau investigators Chuck DeLuca and Bud York had been on pawnshop detail for a few days trying to locate any stolen property in the region that had been sold recently. Pawnshops were one of the most frequent places Evans liked to fence stolen property. Pawnshop detail included a biweekly filtering of the pawnshops in the area to see if any known stolen items had been bought or sold. Pawnshop owners—although many often find ways to get around the system—are mandated by New York state law to fill out a form for each item they buy or sell. Local police stop by periodically to see if any items on the list match any items reported stolen. All of that information is then keyed into a main database.

Under Horton's direction, DeLuca and York took a ride to the Albany Police Department (APD) to see what they could find out. The APD had a large database of pawnshop information.

With the tap of just a few key strokes, they turned up two names inside the first few minutes of their search: Tim Rysedorph and Gary Evans.

Bingo.

What Horton couldn't believe—when he found out—was that Evans had used his *real* name to sell a pair of gold cuff links to a local Albany pawnshop. Throughout the years, Horton knew of no fewer than ten aliases Evans had used, along with four or five different disguises. But here he was now, just months ago, using his own name to sell stolen property in, basically, his hometown?

It didn't make any sense.

"Later," Horton said, "when I asked Gary about it, he said, 'I can't fucking believe I made that one mistake—I used my own name.'"

Indeed, Evans had never, in about 2½ decades of committing burglaries and selling stolen merchandise to pawnshops, used his real name.

Why now? Horton wondered.

"What I think happened," Horton added, "was that Gary was losing his mind at that point. . . . That certainly became clear after we found out what happened to Tim Rysedorph. But those cuff links were what got the ball rolling for us."

Evans had sold the cuff links, valued at about $1,500, which had been reported stolen from a place called New Scotland Antiques, back on July 18, 1997. He had used his given name when he filled out the paperwork. On top of that, Tim had sold a total of thirty-eight Hummels (extremely expensive statuettes) between April 1997 and August 1997 to the same shop.

The connection between Evans and Tim, it seemed, ran deeper with every stone the Bureau turned. It certainly wasn't a stretch now to believe Evans had felt at some point that Tim had ripped him off or was going to turn him in.

"And if Gary felt threatened," Horton said Evans had told him on numerous occasions, "he said he would have to kill that person. He couldn't risk jail time, he'd say, for what he called 'scumbag criminals worse than [he] ever was.'"

If nothing else, the Bureau now had enough evidence to issue a second "local" arrest warrant for Evans, which would secure his return back to Albany if he was picked up outside the state or county. Troop K in Cold Spring, New York, had already issued a warrant, but, as Horton put it later, "that was two hours away. We wanted Gary here in Albany because, ultimately, we knew we weren't going to find Tim without him."

CHAPTER 15

Pestering Lisa Morris for information now became priority number one for Horton. She was the connection to Evans. It was clear by her showing up at Spare Room II, and then lying about it, that she was Evans's puppet. Getting her to open up was the problem. Horton had been stopping by her apartment nearly every day, sometimes just to say hello. But she wouldn't talk. Within the past few weeks, however, Lisa's daughter, Christina, started warming up to Horton.

Christina said she trusted Evans. He had always treated her well and seemed to make time for her.

As Christina became closer to Horton, Lisa opened up more, too. Because of that, Horton said, he decided to finally explain to Lisa why he was so interested in finding Evans.

"Tim Rysedorph has been missing," Horton told her one night. "We have reason to believe Gary is involved. We have a warrant for his arrest. If you know where he is, you need to tell me now."

Lisa still wouldn't confess to knowing any more than she had said already. But she began to talk in more detail about her relationship with Evans, which told Horton she was beginning to come around.

* * *

October 31, 1997, Halloween, was a dreary day in the Capital Region. With cloudy skies, the temperature had hovered around forty-four degrees all day. There was some fog, but nothing that would hinder the unusual project Horton had on tap for the day. A plus was that it hadn't been cold enough the past few weeks for the ground to freeze, and it hadn't recently snowed or rained, so the ground was in prime condition for . . . well . . .

Digging.

Horton had called his team of investigators together the previous night, shortly before they were about to go home, and explained what they were going to be doing the following day, Halloween morning.

Evans had a fascination for historic graveyards and contemporary cemeteries, Horton explained. An outdoorsman, he would frequently sleep in cemeteries and just roam around at night after the groundskeepers had gone home. For the most part, his interest was criminal. He would study the different statues and headstones, writing down descriptions of them. Then he would go to the local library and look them up in books and magazines to see what they were worth. Then he'd make a few phone calls and find out what the black market was paying. If he found something worth his time and effort, he would steal it. A friend later claimed that at one time he wanted to steal the remains of "Uncle Sam," who was born in Troy and buried in town, and hold them for ransom, but in the end Evans decided the risk was too high.

"Since Gary has a propensity to frequent graveyards," Horton addressed his team, "I want to go to his favorite spot: Albany Rural Cemetery," which was, ironically, only about two miles from Bureau headquarters, "and look up all the fresh graves."

Digging up the fresh graves from the past few weeks and sifting through the tons of dirt and gravel would be time-consuming and expensive. What was the point?

Horton thought Evans might have waited until he saw

that there had been a funeral during the day and, later that night, when no one was around, dig up the fresh grave and dump Tim's body inside it. It was the perfect location. No one would ever look there.

To save time and money, Horton devised a plan whereby investigators would use steel rods about eight feet long to poke down into each new grave site to see if the rod, on its way down, was interrupted by an object in its path. If someone hit an object on the way down, Horton would call in a backhoe and, like an archaeologist, begin excavating the ground. They knew most caskets were, just like the cliché, set six feet underground. If Evans had buried Tim in one of the graves, he would have likely put him on top of the casket as opposed to inside it. One man by himself, Horton figured, couldn't manage digging up hundreds of square feet of earth and then lift up the concrete outer box caskets are placed in. Even Evans, who was as strong as a bull, had his limitations.

When Horton approached the director of the cemetery with his idea, the man was bowled over by the thought, but could do little, in the end, to stop the exploration. It took a while, but after compiling a list of the most recent burials, Horton and his team had about a dozen graves to locate and search.

One grave after the other produced no results. Each time they sank a steel rod into the earth, it slipped through the freshly dug dirt easily, as if it were a bamboo skewer piercing a piece of fish.

"It was worth a shot," Horton said later. "Gary had told me how much he loved cemeteries. I was trying to put myself in his shoes . . . trying to think like him. At the time, I thought if he had murdered Tim, he would put his body in the least possible place I was likely to look. When I found out later what he had actually done to Tim, believe me, it shocked the shit out of me. I thought I knew Evans better than I knew members of my own family—but I would have never guessed he would have taken things to the extreme he did with Tim Rysedorph."

* * *

The month of November turned out to be uneventful as far as finding Evans. Cold leads were followed up and new leads were explored, but the sum total of what the Bureau found was zero. Horton continued to stop by and chat with Lisa and Christina, but Lisa continued to deny she knew anything more.

CHAPTER 16

On some days, Lisa emerged from the shadows of her living room looking weak and pale when she greeted Horton at the door. On others, she seemed flush with the color of life. Horton guessed it was the consequence of a hardened life of booze, poverty and single motherhood. Evans had affected her greatly—and it showed.

Horton was a human being who had feelings like most people, but he also had a job to do. It would have been simple for him to leave Lisa alone so she could work out whatever demons she was fighting. But Tim Rysedorph was still missing and a potential serial killer was on the loose—emotion couldn't become part of it.

By early December, with pressure mounting from the Rysedorph family and Horton at a complete loss for where Evans might be holing up, Horton stopped by Lisa's to explain to her that she needed to come with him to Bureau headquarters to give a formal written statement. Their relationship the past six weeks had been building. They were beginning to trust each other. Horton wasn't denying that. Still, he needed to have most of what they had talked about down on paper in case Evans was picked up. There was no way to know what kind of spell Evans had cast on Lisa and how it would play out if Evans was ever arrested. Moreover, Horton wasn't all that sure Lisa hadn't been in contact with Evans all along. Once the courts got involved and lawyered Evans up, Lisa would be considered a witness. Getting her to agree to give a written statement now would secure her testimony, or at least get her to admit to some things on paper so prosecutors could call her on them later.

There were times when Lisa had been picked up by the local police for getting drunk and harassing old boyfriends with threatening phone calls. Horton had used his pull to bail her out of trouble a number of times. He had even been giving her money out of his own pocket when she had little food in the house for Christina. But those days were over. It was time she came clean with exactly what she knew—no more excuses, no more playing stupid, no more acting as though she were the innocent girlfriend. She knew more than she was saying, a cop with Horton's experience and nearly two decades of service knew better.

Late in the day on December 4, 1997, Horton picked Lisa up at her apartment and drove her to Bureau headquarters. "Trust me on this, Lisa," he said as they made their way. "This will be liberating for you. You'll feel better."

When they arrived, Sully and Horton sat Lisa down in the interrogation room, read her her Miranda rights to her, and began to ask what she knew about Evans. She was fragile and scared, no doubt feeling like she was about to betray Evans.

Horton sat across from her during certain parts of the interview, but would get up occasionally and pace the floor in front of her, while Sully sat directly next to her and wrote down everything she said.

Lisa took sips of water in between talking about her relationship with Evans, and, surprisingly, everything she knew about his "business partnership" with Tim.

"So, you told me you last saw Gary," Horton asked at one point, "on Sunday, October 5, 1997 . . . right?"

Lisa looked away for a moment, paused and took out a

cigarette. "I didn't tell you everything I know about Gary," she said. "I said I *didn't* know Tim Rysedorph."

"Go on."

"I *do* know Tim."

As Lisa spoke, it became apparent that Evans had given her just enough information regarding his latest string of burglaries to flavor what Horton and the Bureau already knew. For instance, they had suspected Evans of a break-in at Jennifer House Commons, an antique-store barn in Great Barrington, Massachusetts. Sure enough, Lisa confirmed that Evans had done the job, but also, she said, burned the place to the ground before he left.

"Gary told me he did that job with his 'partner,'" Lisa said, unwavering in her tone, "who I believe to be Tim Rysedorph."

She was a bit angry with Evans, she continued, for burning the place down because she loved to go shopping there with him. They had frequently taken drives to Great Barrington to scope out antiques Evans would later steal for her. In what sounded like a scene out of a Hollywood movie, Evans told Lisa he simply burglarized the place, poured a few gallons of gasoline on the wooden floor of the barn, dropped a match, and walked away laughing. In minutes, it was engulfed in flames, burning like dry hay.

There was another job Evans admitted he had done by himself. In back of Jennifer House was a green building, sort of a secured storage area where antique dealers kept valuables they were either holding for a particular customer or didn't want to sell. Evans had cased the place for months, trying to figure out how to get in.

The local police were baffled by the job. The thief had tunneled his way through the outside of the building and underneath one of the walls, only to come up on the inside of the building. After stealing the most expensive item he could find, he left a note in place of it: *Thank you, The Mole.*

Lisa confirmed it was Evans.

He had also pulled off a job in Margaretville, New York, near the Catskill Mountains, in late September, Lisa said. This time, instead of going in through a window or tunneling through the floor, he scaled the side of the building next door using a ladder a Chinese Restaurant had left out and entered the shop through an open window on the roof. He justified the robbery by saying it was the owner's fault for leaving the window open.

Then she explained a burglary Evans had pulled off at an antique depot not too far away from the barn he had torched. During that job, he had located a "trapdoor" in the basement of the building and slipped right in one morning when nobody was around. Because there were people roaming around outside the place while he was inside, he said, he put an old phone booth door he had used to get into the building across the window, like a curtain, so no one could see him.

There was an old white house in Hyde Park, New York, Lisa explained, that had caused Evans some trouble. The day after the job, she said, he showed up at her apartment with a scratched-up, bloodied face.

"What the hell happened to you?" she asked.

"As I was going in through a basement window, I tripped an alarm system and took off. Right on the opposite side of the window was a pricker bush. I ran right through it, toward a bingo hall across the street where 'my partner' was supposed to be waiting for me in his car."

"Was he there?"

"No. That fucking asshole split on me."

Lisa said it was Tim. When he heard the alarm, he must have gotten scared and taken off, leaving Evans to fend for himself.

When Evans met up with Tim later that night in a motel room they'd rented, he punched him in the face for leaving him at the scene, screaming, "Don't *ever* fucking do that to me again!"

Horton looked at Lisa as she told the story. *Motive. Gary never forgets.*

* * *

A narrative of certain burglaries Evans had pulled off was, most certainly, good information, and Horton was happy to have it. But as the interview progressed, he wanted Lisa to talk about the last few days she had spent with Evans. It was clear now Evans was the last person to see Tim.

Lisa had been chain-smoking since the interview began. Rubbing her eyes, stirring in her seat, she said she needed a break. So Horton told her to take a walk up and down the short hallway outside the room and use the bathroom if she needed. "But don't get comfortable," Horton warned, "because we still have plenty more work ahead of us."

CHAPTER 17

The second-floor interrogation room inside Bureau headquarters was part of a brick building that looked like an old grammar school. Inside the cream-colored room Lisa was being questioned in was one small window, which looked out across the street at Siena College. Horton kept the shades closed so witnesses and suspects couldn't let their minds wander. The walls were painted a calming hue of vanilla for ambience and mood. Besides a plain metal table and a few chairs, the room sat empty. The mirror on the wall was two-way. There were hidden cameras set up around the room in case the Bureau wanted to videotape an interview.

When Lisa returned from the bathroom, she appeared rejuvenated, refreshed.

"All set now, Lisa?" Horton asked.

"I guess so," she said, running her hands through her hair.

"Tell us about October third. You said you *saw* Gary that day?"

"He stayed at my apartment the night before. I got up about six or six-thirty in the morning," she said as she sat down, "and Gary was already awake, sitting in the living room playing Nintendo. He left about eight and returned about noon. He said he was meeting up with his 'partner' at twelve-thirty."

It made sense that Evans would have waited until 12:30 P.M. to meet Tim, because Tim didn't get out of work until noon. And if there was any doubt that Evans's partner wasn't Tim Rysedorph, Lisa cleared it up by providing details she couldn't have known if she didn't see him. For one, she said she watched Evans leave her apartment and walk over to T.J. Maxx and meet someone who was driving a "light blue two-door car," but had sometimes shown up on a dark-colored motorcycle.

Tim drove both.

Second, Lisa described Tim as if she were looking at a photo of him in front of her: "Same height as Gary, but his build was smaller . . . had darker hair and it was shoulder-length." Then the clincher: "Gary complained about his partner's wife all the time. He called her a 'bitch.' He told me his partner had a job as a garbageman, but was complaining he was always broke because of his wife."

What interested Horton even more, however, was that Lisa said Evans was "afraid" of Tim because Tim had been cashing checks recently, and if they ever got caught, Evans said he feared Tim would "roll over" on him because he had never spent time in prison.

"Gary went south to Wappingers Falls on that Friday," Lisa continued. "He was trying to sell some jewelry with Tim to a dealer he had dealt with before. When he came back later that day, he told me the dealer had tipped him off that the police had been at the shop in regard to some stolen property Gary had sold the guy in the past." Without taking a breath, Lisa then said Evans seemed nervous that night for some reason, and mentioned how afraid he was of getting caught.

"What did he say, exactly?"

"He told me he had decided he needed to leave the area."

"What happened throughout the day?"

"Gary left his truck in the parking lot of T.J. Maxx. About five or five-thirty, Gary and Tim returned to my apartment parking lot: Tim was driving his blue car, Gary his truck."

"Did they come up?"

She said only Evans came inside. "You need to go into the bedroom," he said in a rush of words as he walked in. "Me and my partner have to change clothes."

So Lisa locked herself in her bedroom and waited. As she paced inside her bedroom, wondering what was happening, she glanced out the window. Evans's truck had been parked below. She had a clear view.

She then watched as Evans grabbed some clothes out of the back of his truck and walked over to Tim's car, sat down in the passenger seat and began talking. Tim, Lisa remembered with meticulous detail, looked like he was disagreeing with whatever Evans was telling him because he began to shake his head, indicating no.

Evans, who was raging mad by that point, then got out of the car and walked over to the driver's side, where he began to pull Tim out of the car by his hair.

Tim resisted at first, but then got out.

Then Evans walked back up to the apartment and told Lisa his plans had changed. "We have to go do something," he said.

"Where were they going?" Horton asked, amazed by how much Lisa knew, and the detail in which she remembered it.

"Gary didn't say. I didn't ask."

Evans left her apartment at around 6:30 P.M. in Tim's car, she said, but left his truck in the parking lot.

It made sense—because Tim's car had been found at the Amtrak depot in Rensselaer.

A few hours after that, Evans called Lisa and told her that he'd had "major problems" with his "partner down south," meaning south of Albany. Lisa said she then, under Evans's direction, got into his truck, dropped Christina off at her grandmother's house, drove back to her apartment and waited for Evans to call back. It was about 8:00 P.M. when she returned.

Evans ended up calling at 9:00. "I might need you to pick me up in Troy later tonight," he said.

"Okay . . ."

"Don't turn off the ringer and don't screen any calls," he added. Then, "Answer the fucking phone if it rings. You understand?"

"Yes, Gary."

She said Evans never called back.

Many of the times Lisa provided during her interview were later verified, as closely as they could be, with phone records taken from Caroline Parker's home phone and Evans's cell phone. Horton had no reason to believe Lisa was making any of it up. It was all too detailed and time-sensitive. After all, Lisa had no idea what Horton knew. There was no way she could have coordinated a sequence of events to coincide with the times in question the Bureau had already nailed down.

What Lisa was about to say next, however, would give Horton a better indication as to what happened to Tim Rysedorph and, more important, when and where.

CHAPTER 18

The Bureau knew Tim had phoned Caroline from the Dunkin' Donuts in Latham at 1:03 A.M. on Saturday, October 4, 1997. The Spare Room II storage facility was, Horton had timed himself, a two-minute drive from Dunkin' Donuts. In between both places was Lisa Morris's apartment.

It was all beginning to add up.

Many witnesses had verified Tim's presence at Dunkin' Donuts, and Caroline's phone records reflected the fact that Tim had called from the phone booth outside the front door. At 1:33 A.M., Horton knew, someone had accessed Spare Room II using Evans's code. About an hour later, at 2:30, that same number was used again to depart the facility.

By 2:45 A.M., Lisa was climbing the walls of her apartment with anxiety, wondering where the hell Evans was and what he was doing. Evans had said he would call, but never did. He told her to keep the phone line open, which she did, but the phone never rang.

Suddenly, at 3:00, Lisa heard a car screech its way into the parking lot outside her window. When she looked out her bedroom window, she spied Tim's Pontiac Sunbird, which she immediately recognized. Moving swiftly over to the sliding door in her living room, she then watched as Evans got out of the Sunbird in a hurry and looked around to see if anyone was watching him. Then he ran toward her apartment.

Frightened he might catch her watching him, she rushed over to the couch and acted as if she had been there the entire time.

Evans was clean, she recalled to Horton and Sully, when he entered the apartment. He was wearing blue jeans, a plain white T-shirt and black sneakers. Tim, she realized, was not with him.

"I have a lot of important things to do in the morning," Evans said in a mumble of words. "No matter what you hear this time, it doesn't mean I did anything to your weasel boyfriend, Damien [Cuomo]."

If Evans had a vice besides carbohydrates and chocolate-chip cookies, it was sex. He liked to have it several times a day, Lisa claimed: once in the morning, once in the afternoon, once at night. Lisa had gotten used to having it all the time and, she said without embarrassment, expected it. When Evans showed up at her apartment in the early-morning hours of October 4, she immediately told him she wanted to "make love." Evans, though, who hadn't slept with her for a few days, said he couldn't because he had an "upset stomach," adding, "I have a lot on my mind."

She was shocked.

"Gary *never* had any problems in the past which would preclude him from having sex with me," she explained. "Basically, this was the first time Gary had ever said no to me."

When Evans denied Lisa one of the only true innocent pleasures she had left in life, she began to cry.

"I'm leaving before Wednesday," he said. "I'll make sure I fuck you before then. I can't even begin to tell you how bad things are this time. I can't go back to prison for twenty-five years. I'm not doing that. . . ."

Later that morning, Evans woke up and, over coffee, told

Lisa that "things are really fucked up this time. I am going to be in the newspapers and they are going to say bad things about Falco and Damien. Jim Horton will be knocking on your door. Don't mention T.J. Maxx parking lot, and don't say anything about seeing my partner's car in your lot or T.J. Maxx. Do you fucking understand me?"

Lisa said yes.

After that, they talked about where Lisa was going to spend her morning. Evans suggested she go to a friend's house while he did "some things."

"The worst is yet to come," he added before they parted ways. "But I will tell you before I leave the area for good."

Leaving, Lisa made a mental note of seeing Tim's car in the adjacent parking lot. Evans's truck, she remembered, was parked in front of her apartment.

Tim, of course, was nowhere to be found.

Horton had an admirable capacity for getting people to reveal their innermost secrets. Perhaps it came from his days as one of the NYSP's top polygraphists, sitting all those hours behind a machine, watching a needle flicker back and forth like a metronome, asking questions of people while it judged truth and lies. Perhaps he acquired the skill as a hostage negotiator. Whatever the case, he had an extraordinary talent for empathizing with just about anyone.

There was one time in 1989 when he was asked to respond to the Twin Bridges on I-87 near Albany. A nineteen-year-old kid had scaled a 180-foot trestle of a bridge and was sitting on the edge with one end of a rope tied around his neck and the other attached to the bridge.

He was threatening to jump.

After about ninety minutes of just talking to the kid about life, the kid looked at Horton and said, "Do you have any idea what it's like to be gay?"

"No," Horton said. "But I can see how upset you are and feel your anger."

The kid then admitted he had just told his family and friends he was gay, but they didn't take it so well.

In the end, Horton talked him down.

The next day, he visited the kid in the psychiatric ward and reinforced the advice he had given him the previous day. For years after, the kid called Horton periodically to thank him. The following year, Horton received the Brummer Award, the highest award for bravery a state cop can get.

Lisa Morris's eye for detail, Horton acknowledged later, was exceptional. The last twenty-four hours she and Evans spent together had obviously affected her profoundly.

"Do you need something, Lisa?" Horton asked as they sat together and took a break from the interview. He could tell the past few hours had been emotionally taxing for her. Yet, with the amount of information she had already given up, he felt she knew more. Whether she realized it, Lisa was giving the Bureau a timeline to prove later that Evans was the last person to see Tim.

"You ready to continue?" Horton asked.

"I guess . . ."

At noon, on Saturday, October 4, Lisa said Evans finally called her.

"What did he say?" Sully asked.

"The worst is over. I'll be up in a while."

A short time later, she explained, he showed up at her front door wearing different clothes: jeans, a red shirt, white sneakers. But there was something else.

He was covered with mud.

"You're *not* coming in here like that," Lisa screamed at him as he tried to get into her apartment.

"What the fuck? Let me in!"

After washing himself off with a hose in the laundry room downstairs, she said, he returned.

The first thing Evans asked for, she recalled, was "cookies and milk," as if he were a child who had just completed an enormous chore and wanted a reward.

"I remember," she added, "his hands looking dirty—not greasy, but *dirty*."

Although Evans didn't believe in wearing cologne or deodorant, he was a fanatic when it came to hygiene. He hated any part of his body to be dirty. It was odd that he'd show up looking as if he'd just taken a swim in a mud puddle and it didn't seem to bother him.

He was digging, Horton, pacing back and forth in front of Lisa as she told the story, realized. *He buried Tim Rysedorph somewhere and then drove over to Lisa's house and had milk and cookies. Jesus Christ.*

CHAPTER 19

Cops are constantly put in the position of making moral decisions. Most are compelled, generally by their nature, to do the right thing. Yet the right thing doesn't always produce the results they need—especially when it comes to catching murderers.

A few people would argue later that Horton put Christina and Lisa Morris in serious danger by not telling Lisa he believed Evans had murdered several people, especially Christina's father, Damien Cuomo. Effectively, Horton allowed Lisa to think Evans was nothing more than a burglar, others claimed, when he had every reason to believe Evans was a vicious—and possibly desperate—serial killer who was on the loose.

Did Horton, simply to "get his man," use Lisa and Christina as pawns in what amounted to a human game of chess he had been playing with Evans for well over a decade? In the process, did Horton knowingly endanger their lives by putting them in harm's way in order to flush out Evans from wherever he was hiding?

In order to get Lisa finally to give a statement, on December 4, 1997, Horton later admitted, he had to "drive a wedge" between her and Evans, and make her understand that Evans had possibly killed Damien Cuomo. He did this, he claimed, so Lisa would trust him and begin to push Evans away.

One day shortly before Lisa ended up giving Horton and Sully a formal statement, Horton stopped by her apartment and explained that he honestly believed Damien Cuomo hadn't come home because he couldn't.

"I have a daughter, Lisa. You know that," Horton said. "I don't care who you are, a bad guy or a good guy, it doesn't matter. You are going to try to reach out to your daughter—even if you're on the run. Look at what Gary has done to you! He probably did something to Damien and, on top of that, moved in on you once Damien was out of the picture. He's convinced you that Damien is a terrible father, telling you he took off on you without a word when there's a good chance he killed him. Now Christina has no father. And you, you're sticking up for him?"

They were rough words, and perhaps Horton had crossed a line by making a personal plea to Lisa. But he felt he had to do whatever it took to find Evans.

Crying, Lisa seemed to understand for the first time that Evans had been fooling her for the past eight years.

With Lisa in a vulnerable state, Horton took it a step further just to send his point home.

"We think he's killed Timmy Rysedorph, too, Lisa."

A week later, prepared to talk about everything she knew, Lisa agreed to give a statement.

"Timing was not only crucial, but a huge gamble," Horton said later, referring to the reason why he waited so long to tell Lisa he had a pretty good idea Evans had killed Damien and Tim.

"If I told her too much too soon, I could have blown the entire case. I needed to gain her confidence. She needed to trust me. If she had talked to Gary and he asked if I was coming around mentioning Falco and Tim, he would have had Scotty beam him up. . . . We would have never seen him again, ever. I was sure of that. Throughout the years, he had made me well aware of what would make him disappear forever. And I surely wasn't worried about him coming back and doing something to endanger Lisa or Christina. He was not coming back to the area. Period."

Part of Horton's job was to read people and tweak his style according to the situation.

"I taught 'Interview and Interrogation' in several police academies," he said, "the state police, FBI and Royal Canadian Mounted Police. I had time on my side, so I was able to play Lisa with whatever I wanted. Did I use her? Absolutely. Did I use Christina? In a way, I guess I did. I was very attentive to her when I had the chance—i.e., asking her about school, boys, hobbies—without sounding like a parent. I wanted her to like and trust me so Lisa would, too. People won't tell you anything if they don't like you."

How did Horton figure out Lisa knew more than she was saying?

"Gary trusted her enough for him to go there in the first place with Tim. Why wouldn't he trust her with more intimate knowledge? We were beginning to make a circumstantial case against Gary regarding Tim, even though we had no body. Lisa, as far as we could tell, was one of the last locals not only to see and talk to Gary, but she was sleeping with him and living in between Dunkin' Donuts and the Spare Room Two. Because of what we saw as pillow talk, not to mention the logistics, we felt she had to know more."

And she certainly did.

After Evans washed himself off and returned to Lisa's apartment on Saturday, she said, he sat down on her couch with a bag of chocolate-chip cookies and a glass of milk. As he snacked, she asked him how long he was going to be around.

"I have a lot of things to do," Evans responded.

A moment later, after finishing his cookies, he left.

At about 10:30 that same night, he called.

"I can't stay at my apartment," he said in a whisper, as if

someone were listening in on the call. "I feel like I am going to be ambushed any moment. Can I come back and stay there?"

Lisa not only said yes, but encouraged it.

When Evans returned, he had a box of Freihofer's chocolate-chip cookies—his favorite brand—and a gallon of milk.

"He was clean when he came back; he looked like himself," Lisa explained. "He apologized for having to leave so abruptly earlier that night, and said he was sorry for being in trouble. He wanted to relax. So we watched a movie. *True Romance*."

The next morning, she got up early, about 4:30, and made coffee. Evans, waking up to the smell of the brewing coffee, ran out of her bedroom and yelled at her for stinking the place up. Then he poured the pot of coffee down the drain and sat down on the couch.

Minutes later, after getting dressed, he ran down to T.J. Maxx. On his way out the door, he said, "I have to make a call." When he returned ten minutes later, he seemed fine, more relaxed.

But fifteen minutes after that, he got up and went back to T.J. Maxx to make what he said was "a second call." When he returned this time, however, he was "pale, panicked . . . and visibly shaken. The conversation had gotten him very upset."

"They're already looking for my partner," Evans said, pacing back and forth in Lisa's living room. "I've got to go do something." It is almost certain to assume that the calls Evans made were to Caroline Parker.

An hour later, he returned with a duffel bag and a bag of dirty clothes. His shoes and pants were filthy, Lisa said. "There was dirt and mud in his shoes and on his pants."

Evans then gave Lisa two cell phones and told her to throw them in the Dumpster when he was gone. Then he said he wanted her to drive his truck—"with gloves on"—to a local VFW bar around the corner, leave it and take a cab home.

Before walking out the door, he handed her $300 in twenties. "That's pocket money for you," he said. "I love you. I'll keep in touch with you as much as I can for the next few days. I'm gone for good now." Hesitating, his voice cracked. "You won't see me for a few years."

Taking off down the steps that led up to Lisa's apartment, walking toward Tim's blue Pontiac Sunbird, Evans turned and yelled out for Lisa to come to the balcony.

"Throw me some spray cleaner," he said.

With that, he got into Tim's Sunbird with the spray cleaner and a roll of paper towels and drove off.

Throughout the month of December 1997 and into January 1998, the Bureau followed up on whichever lead it could regarding all the new information Lisa had provided. To no one's surprise, much of what Lisa had said turned out to be 100 percent true.

The one thing that bothered Horton most, despite all the information Lisa had given him, was the fact that Evans hadn't contacted her yet. Evans had said "years," but Horton thought for sure he would have surfaced by the end of January or February. But thus far, at least according to Lisa, she hadn't heard from him.

Because Evans was officially running from the law and considered armed and dangerous, Horton began showing up at Lisa's apartment more frequently and stationed a cruiser nearby whenever the state police could spare one. During some weeks, he'd pop in three, four, even five times, at various intervals throughout the day.

"I knew we had gotten everything we were going to get out of Lisa by that point," Horton later said. "However, I needed to stay in her face and keep reminding her that I wasn't going anywhere. I wanted to believe Gary was going to call her sooner or later and emerge from wherever he had been hiding. I could feel it. I knew Gary. He wouldn't disappear entirely without first rubbing it in my face."

CHAPTER 20

The brilliant spring weather that had fallen on the Capital District during the first few weeks of May 1998 mattered little to Bureau investigators working day and night to find Gary Evans. To find Tim Rysedorph—who had been missing now for nearly seven months—Horton and his team needed to locate Evans. Every lead compiled during the past half-year had been followed up on, but nothing new turned up. Frustration was mounting.

Sitting at his desk one morning, staring out the window at the Siena College green across the street, Horton's growing concern told him that if Evans didn't come forward and contact Lisa soon, they were likely never going to see him (or Tim) again.

"Gary Evans could disappear and, if he wanted to, bleed into the countryside and live off the land forever," Horton said later. "I was worried he had left the country. If he did, we were finished. Or if Lisa had tipped him off about what I was doing, he was long gone."

The reality of police work, though, is this: just when a case seems to be running cold, a lucky break pops up—be it something investigators had missed all along, or a new lead.

The break Horton had been waiting for didn't come in the

form of someone spotting Evans and turning him in, or his getting "stopped somewhere by local cops for a bullshit traffic violation." Instead, it came in an unceremonious phone call to a bar named Maxie's in Colonie, New York. This would lead to a nondescript, small package delivery a few days later by an unwitting UPS driver to a second bar, Jessica Stone's, a hole-in-the-wall not too far from Lisa's apartment in Latham.

On May 12, 1998, Lisa was having a beer at Maxie's when the barmaid took a call from someone named Louis Murray, who said he wanted to speak to Lisa. Murray, the barmaid said, had been calling the bar asking for Lisa for the past few days.

Lisa would drop by Maxie's from time to time, usually in the afternoons. Apparently, Louis Murray knew that.

When she picked up the phone and said hello, she recognized Evans's voice immediately.

First Lisa asked him how he had been traveling without getting caught.

Evans's name and photo had been plastered all over the newspapers and on television. Missing person posters of Tim had been posted everywhere. The newspapers had made the connection between Evans and Tim only recently and were running stories about the Bureau's interest in talking to Evans about Tim's disappearance. Horton had even considered listing Evans on the FBI's most wanted list and appearing on *America's Most Wanted,* a nationally syndicated television show, after it called. However, the fallout from such widespread publicity, he decided, might beckon Evans to sink deeper into seclusion.

Evans admitted to Lisa that he had a full set of identification on him, but said he didn't have a birth certificate.

"How are you traveling?"

"Rental cars. Things are going okay. I'm traveling the country."

"Gary . . ."

"Just listen, Lisa," Evans said at that point. "In a few

days, you are going to receive a package at Jessica Stone's from somebody named Jack Flynn. Make sure you get it."

"What have you been doing?" Lisa asked, ignoring the package remark.

"The fucking package," Evans screamed. "Make sure you get it!"

"Okay. Okay."

Evans then talked about the places he had visited and how he had been financing his trip. But the conversation, at least to Lisa, took a turn for the more serious as he began to discuss a pickup truck he had tried to purchase along the way.

"I had a problem with some guy and a truck I wanted," Evans said.

"What do you mean?"

"Let's just say that that *motherfucker* will never give anybody a problem again."

Lisa was mortified. There were so many thoughts rushing through her mind she didn't know what to do or say next.

"You there, Lisa?"

"Yes, Gary, I'm here," she answered in a broken tone, full of confusion, shock and worry.

"How's that bitch Rysedorph doing?" Evans then asked in a mocking, condescending manner.

"I don't know what you mean, Gary—"

"Has anyone been around . . . you know, cops? What about Horton?"

"No. I haven't seen him for months."

By that response, Lisa had, maybe without even realizing it, come to terms with the reality that she was totally committed to Horton now—frightened and scared to death of the same man she had slept with and let baby-sit her daughter.

Evans didn't say much more during that first phone call, but insisted he would contact her again soon.

When Lisa called Horton shortly after speaking to Evans, she said, "Gary just called me at Maxie's. I happened to be there having a drink."

It's about time, Horton thought.

This was the Gary Evans that Horton had known all those years: a criminal who just couldn't let things be. "An egomaniac," Horton said later. "Someone who loved to show you how smart and deceptive he could be if he wanted to. All he had to do was stay away [from the Albany region] and stay out of trouble. We would have never found him. But here he was calling the one person he must have known I would find sooner or later."

Lisa explained how Evans had told her to "expect a package" delivered to Jessica Stone's within the next few days.

"That's good, Lisa. What else? Did he say where he was calling from?"

"Not sure . . . but he said he had gone to Alaska and found a job on a fishing boat. . . . He also said he went to South America. He was doing 'small jobs,' he said, you know, shoplifting."

"Nothing else?"

"He said he was returning to Albany soon, and for me to expect the package to be sent by someone named Jack Flynn . . . from, I believe, Sacramento, California."

"I need to be there to receive that package, Lisa," Horton said.

Lisa didn't fight the suggestion.

After Horton hung up, he called Sully into his office.

"I want you to find someone named Jack Flynn in Sacramento and see if he knows anything about this package. Who knows? Maybe he's holing up with the guy?"

"Sure, Jim."

"Send a Teletype to the Alaska State Police and let them know Gary might be there. It's a long shot, but what the hell."

When Horton finally had a chance to contain his adrenaline rush, and thought a moment about what Lisa had done, he recognized the fact that she trusted him now completely. If he had ever questioned her loyalty, this one phone call proved she was entirely on his team.

* * *

On May 14, the barmaid at Jessica Stone's, a rather seedy little bar located directly next door to an off-track gambling parlor, called Lisa and told her the package she was waiting for had just arrived. It was a small box, the woman said, sent from someone named Jack Flynn. "I'll hold it here at the bar for you."

Jessica Stone's was Evans's favorite place in the Albany area to eat French fries, another favorite food in his strict high-carbohydrate diet. He loved the way Stone's prepared the spuds. It only seemed fitting he would choose it as a place to make initial contact.

Lisa called Horton immediately. "I think that package from Gary is here."

"Just wait. I'll be right over."

A ten-minute ride under normal circumstances, Horton couldn't drive fast enough to Lisa's apartment. From there, Jessica Stone's was five minutes away.

Inside the bar, which smelled of stale beer and cigarette butts, it was dark and dingy. Horton took a look around and knew right away why Lisa liked it, but couldn't picture Evans rubbing elbows with the barflies who frequented the place. With the exception of the women he dated, Evans hated people who drank alcohol and did drugs.

Observations aside, Horton walked over to the bar with Lisa and asked for the package.

Lisa looked at him as he held it in his hands for a moment and just stared at it. It was a cardboard box, about one foot square. *Jack Flynn, Sacramento, California* was written on the return address, just like Evans had promised.

Placing it on a table, Horton snapped on a pair of latex gloves and grabbed a steak knife from the table next to him to cut the box open.

Inside was a letter Evans had written on May 6, but, for whatever reason, had never sent. There were three small stuffed animals, several brand-new sets of Winnie the Pooh earrings, a few antique vases and a handful of photographs of Evans in various poses and places. In morbid fashion, one photograph showed Evans lying on his back inside a freshly dug grave, the photo of him taken from ground level, directly over him. His fists were clenched, yet both middle fingers were raised and pointed directly at the camera lens.

For everyone who wants me caged or dead, he wrote on the top of the photo. *The free Gary Evans* was scribbled across the bottom.

It was easy to tell he had visited Seattle, Washington, because there was a photo of a dedication that Bruce Lee, the late martial artist and actor, had written to his wife, Brenda, and son, Brandon—a photo that could have been only taken at Lee's grave site in Seattle, where the dedication is set in stone at the foot of Brandon and Bruce's headstones. Evans was consumed by celebrity status and had often talked about his absolute fascination with dead celebrities.

One of the other photos included in the package consisted of Evans sitting in a large tree. He was wearing a tank top T-shirt, his large biceps, triceps and chest muscles easily visible, while his muscular thighs, like ten-pound ham shanks, burst out of the cutoff shorts he was wearing. He was smiling, sporting a full beard and mustache. It was incredible to think he had been on the run for so long but had no trouble maintaining the chiseled physique of a professional bodybuilder.

Several other photos, it was clear, had been taken with a noticeable amount of precision and knowledge of photography. In one, Evans was photographed near a lighthouse Horton would later trace to California. The photos, Horton also discovered, were taken by Evans himself using a tripod and camera equipped with a timer. He had always expressed a love for photography to Horton and had stolen several different cameras throughout his life, and always traveled with them.

By far, the most interesting photo in the bunch turned out to be a headshot of a brown-and-white spotted dog, the eyes of the dog drawn in with pen to look as if they were popping out, large as cue balls. Below the photo, Evans had written: *Lost dog!! Free dog!! Rude dog!!! Shocked and shocking dog!!! Arf, arf, woof and bark.*

The only explanation that one could conclude from the writing was that Evans must have seen himself at the time as an escaped caged animal that had nowhere left to go, and was just wandering around aimlessly trying to figure out his next move. Add to it Evans's monstrous ego, and it seemed that by sending the photo to someone who, he knew, would eventually crumble to Horton, he was making a mockery of the entire situation as if he had planned it all.

Oddly enough, the final photo depicted Evans on a bicycle, just standing, posing for the camera, one foot on a pedal, the other on the ground. Wearing a ball cap, he was half-smiling. On the surface, to anyone who would have crossed paths with him during his journey, he must have appeared to be nothing more than a harmless trail rider out for a pleasant afternoon bike ride. Little would anyone who happened to bump into him know they were staring at a wanted fugitive and dangerous, convicted felon, a man who was being sought for questioning about the deaths of several people.

CHAPTER 21

The letter Lisa received from Evans, for the most part, was an attack on law enforcement, and continued to add validity to what Horton believed was Evans's peculating hatred, in general, toward cops. Additionally, while the photo of Evans lying in a grave, flipping the world the bird, pointed to a direct hatred for all cops, it seemed almost adolescent when compared to what Horton would take from reading the letter.

Don't forget they are all enemies, Evans had written, underlining the entire sentence. *Will say and do ANYTHING to get their goals—and I am their goal bigtime!*

Near the end of the letter, Evans told Lisa not to worry: *I'm on my toes. Kicked into survival mode.* The word "survival" was underlined. *Bigtime. My life depends on no mistakes.*

Evans had, basically, two different sides to his personality: One included characteristics of a happy-go-lucky weight lifter who liked to string along as many women as he could and impress them with stolen jewelry and exotic trips paid for by a life of crime. The other was a professional, sociopath mastermind criminal who would take off into the wilderness if he thought the cops were on his trail and live like a U.S. Navy SEAL, gearing up for what he believed was an approaching war.

During this particular trip out west, Horton would later learn, Evans ran into several problems, which would ultimately force him back east, mainly logistical problems and financial constraints. He was running low on cash. Despite having displayed a "wad" of money to the clerk at Mail Boxes, Etc., in California when he mailed Lisa her package, Evans admitted later he was having a problem finding antique stores to rob. New England, specifically, is a haven for antique shops and barns filled with valuable artifacts. People come from all over the world to travel around New England "antiquing," as they call it. On top of that, Evans had several locations in the Northeast where he could fence stolen property. Out west, he was on his own.

The "jobs" he was pulling out west consisted of breaking into cars, boats and shoplifting small items from department stores. But these were considered "high exposure" crimes that offered little return. A smart criminal like Evans could get caught a hell of a lot easier breaking into a parked car than if he took the time and planned an antique shop burglary, where he was in his element. He simply couldn't find, as he later noted, that "one big score" out west that could have set him up for a few months financially. Moreover, the West was as foreign to Evans as red meat and alcohol; he was out of his league. There were even times when he had become so obsessed with the notion of being caught, he swore in his mind that Horton was stalking him.

"His paranoia snowballed," Horton said, "and he had no escape or release from it—even in his mind. He told me later he mostly camped while out west. He would have crazy dreams at night and wake up in a cold sweat, thinking we were surrounding him. Add to that what he had already told [Lisa]—that he wasn't going to be taken alive and couldn't bear the thought of spending twenty-five years locked up like a 'caged animal'—and you have a desperate sociopath, literally losing his mind, prepared to do anything to survive."

Indeed, Evans's psychological meltdown would never be more evident than when Horton found out what he had done to Tim Rysedorph.

Besides giving an explanation of how scared he was of being caught, and dissing the cops, seemingly, in every other sentence in his letter to Lisa, Evans made a point to say he was concerned about the welfare of Lisa and Christina: *I wonder about you guys all the time.* He encouraged Lisa to date a man she had seen in the past: *For security, even if it's not what you want in your heart. Do the smart thing. . . . My life is fucked.*

The most important section of the letter for Horton was a section where Evans had given Lisa dates when he was going to contact her next: *I am going to try to contact you [at Jessica Stone's] . . . on the 13th, 14th or 15th. I'm traveling on those days.*

Then came the words Horton wanted to hear more than anything else: *I miss you very much and think I can see you somehow. It'll take some doing."*

When Horton read those words, he wanted to pump his fist in the air. *We've got him*. Because if there was one part of Evans's character Horton could count on, it was his stringent practice of keeping his word to his women. He'd lie, of course, where it suited his needs; but when it came to females, Evans meant what he said.

In addition, what drove Evans's desire to reunite with Lisa perhaps more than anything else was his hearty appetite for sex.

Hey, hound dog, Evans wrote at the end of the letter, *I'm super horny. I need your sweet ass for some "marathon sex" like we did so nicely.*

Horton laughed as he finished reading the letter, thinking

that Evans was prepared to travel three thousand miles across the country for a piece of ass.

Or, did Evans know Horton was going to ultimately read the letter? Was the entire event scripted by Evans himself—a setup?

A cautious, if not stealthy, plan had to be put into effect immediately in order to try to trap Evans when, as he had promised, he made contact with Lisa. A phone tap had to be placed on Jessica Stone's and Maxie's, the two bars Horton knew Evans would call. Placing a tap on the line would take time, though, which Horton didn't have.

To think that Evans was just going to hand himself over to Horton seemed too simple. It was more likely he was playing one of his games, strategizing and planning a way to slip into town to meet up with Lisa, turn over a "big score" and zip back out of town without being detected.

Sully found out from the Sacramento Police Department (SPD) that on May 7 a man identifying himself as Jack Flynn had entered a Mail Boxes, Etc. in Sacramento. Pulling a $50 bill out of a "large wad of money," the man paid $44.32 to send four packages to various cities around the country: Voorheesville, New York; Gainesville, Florida; Hoosick, New York; and, as they already knew, Latham, New York. The clerk at Mail Boxes, Etc., described the man as "stocky . . . [carrying] a large army-type duffel bag." When Sacramento police showed the clerk a photo of Evans, he confirmed it was him.

The Florida address turned out to be that of Evans's half sister, Robbie. She had lived in Florida since the early '80s. The Hoosick and Voorheesville, New York, addresses belonged to former friends. Evans had sent them, like he had his sister, worthless books and jewelry. The Latham address was, of course, Jessica Stone's.

It was clear Evans was unloading all of his material possessions so he could travel lightly en route back to the

Northeast. Besides the letter to Lisa, the notes he sent along with the packages to his half-sister and friends were insignificant except for a stark and direct message of desperation and finality, as if he were never going to see any of them again.

CHAPTER 22

Lisa began stopping at Jessica Stone's whenever she had a chance to see if Evans had tried to make contact again. For the past ten days, she hadn't heard a peep: no phone calls, packages, letters. It was as if Evans had abandoned his entire plan—a possibility Horton had worried about all along.

Then, on Wednesday, May 27, after nearly two weeks of silence, Lisa walked into Jessica Stone's and . . .

The bartender, a man who knew Evans because of his affection for Jessica's French fries and the fact that he had been in the bar several times with Lisa, said he had taken a call earlier that day from a guy named Louis Murray. "It was Gary," the bartender said, a smirk on his face, as if Lisa and Evans were trying to pull one over on him. "I recognized his voice, Lisa."

"What did he say?"

"He said to be here at five o'clock tonight; he was going to call back."

Lisa was, by this point, torn in many different directions. She still loved Evans and was beginning to feel as if she had let him down by "giving him up" to Horton. Nevertheless, she also had an understanding Evans had been responsible for the disappearance of her former boyfriend Damien Cuomo, the father of her child. Running on pure emotional adrenaline, medicating any anxiety she felt with booze and marijuana, Lisa began to turn to Horton for support. There was even a thought that Lisa was becoming attracted to Horton in a sexual manner because they had spent so much time together. Horton, of course, always kept the relationship professional, ignoring her advances, writing them off as a by-product of the rapport he had spent months building. Yet, anything could set Lisa off at this point in the game. Horton had to be careful. The stakes were as high as they were going to get—especially since Evans had called and given a specific time when he was going to call back. Everything had to synchronize perfectly. If one part of the plan went wrong, it would fail. If Evans was back in town doing countersurveillance on Lisa, he knew Horton was sniffing around, setting him up.

Leaving the bar and rushing home, Lisa called Horton and told him what had happened. "I'll be there at five," Horton said.

Throughout that afternoon, Horton had every available investigator find anyone named Louis Murray in the Sacramento, California, area. None of the Louis Murrays that Sacramento police found had any ties whatsoever to Evans. He likely had taken on an identity by random. Still, Horton now had a name to alert every law enforcement agency in the country. If anyone named "Louis Murray" was picked up for so much as spitting on the sidewalk, Horton would know about it.

When Horton showed up at Lisa's apartment to meet her, he started talking about the past few weeks, briefing her on what was going to happen next. There wasn't time to place a wiretap on Jessica Stone's or Maxie's. To get a judge to sign a warrant would take a day, maybe two or three. So he had to rely solely on the trust he had built with Lisa. He did, however, have Lisa sign a waiver, giving the state police permission to record any conversations she had over the telephone. Thus, Lisa was given a tape recorder she could easily hook up to any phone she would later use to talk to Evans.

As much as he didn't want to let her go off on her own—particularly on such an important mission—Horton had no choice but to let Lisa drive her own vehicle to Jessica Stone's, while he and two other investigators, DeLuca and Sully, followed at a safe distance—just in case Evans was in town watching them watch her.

At around 4:55 P.M., Horton, DeLuca and Sully, sitting in their car across the street from Jessica Stone's, watched Lisa drive into the parking lot and walk into the bar.

For a few minutes, she waited nervously at the bar, nursing a beer and smoking a cigarette. Evans, Horton knew, was, if nothing else, punctual. If he said he would call at 5:00, he wouldn't make her wait.

At about 5:03, the barmaid, a woman Lisa knew, took a call on the bar phone. A moment later, she said, "Hold on," handing Lisa the phone.

Just like that, Evans was back at the helm, calling the shots.

"Gary?" Lisa whispered.

"Go to Maxie's right now. . . . I'll call you in ten minutes," he said quickly before hanging up.

Horton, Sully and DeLuca then watched Lisa run out of the bar in a hurry, get into her car and take off.

Follow me, she mouthed as she drove out of Jessica Stone's and passed them.

"Go," Horton ordered DeLuca. "Let's go!"

As Lisa pulled into Maxie's, Horton told DeLuca to park the car far enough away so they wouldn't be made if Evans was there waiting for her.

While they waited, DeLuca and Sully told Horton they felt Lisa was nothing more than a barfly who couldn't be trusted to walk someone else's dog, better yet run the entire show, as she was clearly doing.

"Why are we playing this game with her?"

Horton had to depend on his instincts. "She's all we have right now," he said. "We have no choice but to trust her."

Lisa was in Maxie's fewer than five minutes. When she walked out, Horton motioned for her to come over to the car.

"*What* is going on?" he wanted to know.

Lisa was frazzled. Shaking. Anxious. Unsure of herself. "I don't know what . . . the fuck he's up to," she blurted out.

"Start by telling us what he said."

"Now he wants me to drive over to that Irish Pub in Albany. I don't know," she added, brushing her fingers through her hair, looking around the parking lot of the bar, "what the fuck he's doing."

"Let's go," Horton said. "Now."

The Irish Pub was a twenty-minute drive across town. Horton told DeLuca, who was driving, to stay back even farther. "If Gary's waiting for her there . . . Well, I don't know . . . he's . . . Just go."

Lisa drove into the parking lot of the Irish Pub and, wasting little time, hopped out of her car and ran into the bar.

CHAPTER 23

Lisa was in the Irish Pub for only a few minutes when she came rushing back out in a hurry, jumped into her car and sped off.

Horton, parked about one hundred yards down the block, watching closely with DeLuca and Sully, told Sully not to move. "Stay back for a moment. Let her go for right now."

Heading across town, Lisa didn't seem to be driving any faster than she normally would.

"Wait until she gets a good lead on us, but don't lose her," Horton said.

As she worked her way onto the Interstate 787 on-ramp, heading back toward Latham, Sully followed close enough behind to keep tabs on her without making it appear as though they were tailing her.

"When you get an open stretch of road," Horton said as they began to catch up, "pull her over."

Lisa pulled over without incident and Horton rushed to the driver's-side door and motioned for her to roll the window down.

Sitting, staring down at the steering wheel, she didn't say anything.

"What the fuck is going on, Lisa?" Horton asked, leaning down, looking into her eyes.

"Gary's back east!" she said in a panic. "Holy shit. I don't fucking believe this." She started banging on the steering wheel with her fist.

"What makes you say that?"

"He just told me!"

"Okay, relax. Talk me through this. What did he say?" Horton couldn't believe what he was hearing. Evans had not only surfaced, but he was back in the Northeast.

"Gary said he needed my car to do a 'big job' in Vermont because he needs the money. He talked about meeting me . . . having sex . . . some hotel . . . I don't know." At that point, Lisa started to cry. Frustrated and confused by the events of the past hour, she mumbled something, but Horton had a hard time understanding her.

"Come on, Lisa. Calm down. I need to know where he is now."

"He told me to meet him at the McDonald's in St. Johnsbury, Vermont. Tomorrow at one. I don't even know where the fuck that is."

"That's it? He said nothing else?"

"He said he wasn't going back to jail"—Lisa paused for a moment to light a cigarette—"He also said he wasn't going to be taken alive." She took a hard pull from her cigarette. "He's got two guns, he said. I fucking believe him, too. He felt you guys were closing in on him. What the fuck am I supposed to do now, Jim? Huh? Tell me."

Without a second thought, Horton said, "You're going to meet him tomorrow. Go home right now. I'll call you later tonight. If he calls you at home, call me immediately."

"What am I supposed to do, Jim?" Lisa asked again. "I'm scared to death."

When it came down to it, Lisa was setting Evans up. If he had ever found out what was going on, there was nothing stopping him from using her as a hostage to negotiate his release. Was he waiting for her at her apartment? Was he in town? Or was he actually in Vermont?

Nobody knew for certain.

Standing there next to her car, all Horton could think about was the photograph of Evans lying in a grave, sticking both of his middle fingers up.

"For everyone who wants me caged or dead . . . the free Gary Evans."

When Evans told Lisa he wasn't going to be taken alive, Horton knew, perhaps now more than ever, he meant it. Evans had never been known to carry guns. Suddenly he was saying he was armed. Any cop knows a criminal can become the antithesis of his prior behavior; he will do whatever he needs to do to survive; his crimes increase in severity if he feels the jaws of law enforcement clamping down on him. Evans, it was clear in his last letter, had been in "survival mode" for several weeks, trekking across country while thinking of what he was going to do when he got back east. There was no reason to second-guess how serious his intentions were. Horton had to believe he was prepared to do anything.

During a phone call with Horton later that night, Lisa talked about how long a drive it was to Vermont, and the fact that she didn't have any money for gas. Horton promised he would send someone over to her apartment with gas and food money.

"I need to see him, Jim," she said at some point during the conversation. Horton could tell she had been drinking. "I need to have sex. . . . It's been a long time. Let me just meet him and have sex and then you guys can do whatever you want?"

"Lisa," Horton said, "I can't let you do that. Come on. Let's be serious."

Horton had no idea what he was going to do the following day. Here was Lisa worried about getting laid. Was she out of her fucking mind?

"Just go meet him where he said to meet him, Lisa. I need you to do that for me."

"What are you guys going to do?"

"Nothing."

As Horton hung up, he questioned what he was about to do. Was it safe sending Lisa off to meet someone he presumed to be in a desperate frame of mind? Of course not. "It was such a big decision to make," Horton recalled later, "and there I was, making it in what seemed like seconds. Why did I do it? I went through several scenarios later: should I have told her we were going to send a female trooper in her place instead? I realized after hanging up with her that night, I had to truly think things through. In context, I had just sent a woman to meet up with a man I believed to be a serial killer."

The next several hours were filled with making plans and securing the proper permissions from the white shirts in Albany. Horton needed to put together a team of cops to head up to Vermont. Slapping together an undercover operation at the last minute was hard enough, under these conditions nearly impossible. In actual fact, Evans was exhausted. Broke. He had been on the run for months. Now he was back in the Northeast looking to hook up with Lisa so he could pull off one more "huge" score. Horton believed Evans was trying to finance the run of his life. One mistake on Horton's part and people were going to get hurt.

One of the first things Horton did was have Sully secure an order for permission to go out of state. He had to follow procedure by the book. The fallout, after catching Evans, was going to be enormous. There wasn't room for failure. Everything had to go smoothly or it wouldn't work. St. Johnsbury, Vermont, was near the Canadian border heading north. Two hundred miles from Albany, it was a solid four-hour drive. Much of the night would be spent driving.

Horton quickly collected a team of investigators he thought

would best suit his needs. Evans was considered armed and dangerous. *"I have two guns. . . . I am not going to be taken alive. . . . I am not going back to prison for twenty-five years."* Horton needed experience—yet he also needed cops Evans had never seen before. Most Bureau investigators had, at one time or another, spoken to Evans, bumped into him, or arrested him. Moreover, it occurred to Horton that Evans would most likely be at McDonald's in St. Johnsbury by early morning, surveying the layout, conducting countersurveillance. There was also a good chance he would spend the morning traveling around town, looking for recognizable faces.

Horton had DeLuca and Sully already on the team, but he needed two undercover officers who could blend in with the general public in Vermont and walk around town unnoticed, preferably as close to McDonald's as possible.

Undercover officers John Couch and Mary DeSantis had filled a variety of different positions throughout their careers in the NYSP. The one role, however, they fit into like a pair of custom-made shoes was that of Mr. and Mrs. Harley-Davidson. Couch had waist-long hair, a greasy-looking, unkempt beard and mustache, several large tattoos on his arms, and was tall and skinny; Mary, an average-looking gal, could doll herself up in a minute to look like a "biker chick." Horton envisioned them trolling up and down the street in front of McDonald's, holding hands. No one would give them a second look.

A Vermont State Police (VSP) trooper would be the designated walker, pacing up and down the street in front of McDonald's with his dog, a K-9 German shepherd trained to attack on command. He would be dressed in sweats, sneakers, headphones, sweatband. A few local VSP Bureau investigators would be stationed inside McDonald's acting as patrons, reading the newspaper and eating. Since Evans might recognize Chuck DeLuca, he would be set up in a local hair salon next door, while Sully, whom Evans also knew, would be stationed in the bank across the street.

Both would have good views of McDonald's. And both would have shotguns.

Because of his relationship with Evans throughout the years, Horton would have to stay behind—miles away—out on the edge of town near the local VSP barracks. Everyone would be wired with a hidden walkie-talkie device so they could communicate stealthily with one another and Horton. From base camp, Horton would call the shots. No one would move without his order.

Before taking off to Horton's house in Latham to meet before heading up to Vermont, at about 7:30 P.M., Horton called his team together at Bureau headquarters and gave a short briefing.

This was it. It seemed that the past thirteen years had led up to this one chance to grab Evans, bring him in and get him to talk about, most important, Tim Rysedorph. Once Horton found out where Tim was, he could question Evans about Michael Falco and Damien Cuomo.

It was never clearer to Horton as he sat in his office preparing for the briefing that Tim Rysedorph was dead. Evans, certainly, wouldn't travel to the other side of the country with a partner and, most definitely, would have mentioned to Lisa if Tim had been with him. But he never did. Instead, he mocked Tim: *"How's that bitch Rysedorph doing?"*

"Go home," Horton told his investigators, "grab a change of clothes, and meet me at my house. We're leaving in about an hour. Don't be late. We've got a hell of a long drive ahead of us. We need to get up there *tonight.*"

In the interim, DeLuca and Sully had booked a hotel in downtown St. Johnsbury, and had called the VSP to notify them what was going down. Because it was after business hours, Horton had trouble getting cash to finance the trip, and had an even tougher time finding unmarked cruisers.

"I'll fix our cars at my house to look as undercover as I can," Horton said. "I'll go to the ATM and finance the trip myself."

Staring down at his notes, Horton paused before releasing everyone. He wanted to be sure he didn't cause alarm, but he had to make his investigators realize how serious the next twenty-four hours were going to be.

"Everything has to go perfectly," he concluded, "there can be no mistakes."

CHAPTER 24

While on the run, Evans had celebrated his forty-third birthday on October 7, 1997. At that age, he was still, Horton and his team were about to find out, in better physical shape than most twenty-year-olds. Living off Twinkies, one of his favorite foods, Freihofer's chocolate-chip cookies, potato chips, doughnuts, bread, orange juice and milk, one might wonder how he kept himself so fit. To anyone who had known him throughout his life, they were amazed by how bad his diet was but how chiseled he kept his body. It was as if he could eat whatever he wanted and it had no effect on his weight or physique.

There was no magic pill or rational answer Evans could give other than to say he had worked out hard, day in and day out, and had always considered the life he led, and the anxiety and fear that shrouded him, a winning weight-loss program. Always looking over his shoulder, expecting to be "put back in a cage," he felt the burden of that worry helped his metabolism. That, in itself, he later told a friend, was something he believed had everything to do with burning calories at a faster rate than if he were just some worker bee in the cubicle farm, wasting away at a desk, or a factory worker driving around on a forklift all day.

* * *

When Horton and his team arrived at his house in Latham to prepare to drive to Vermont, he explained how they would have to scrape all inspection and registration stickers off the inside of the windshields of their vehicles, exchange license plates with ones from different states DeLuca had taken from the barracks, and remove any radio antennae. There was no room for error. Evans would be looking for any sign indicating cops were in town. He could sniff out the Bureau from anywhere. If he spotted a car in St. Johnsbury that even remotely resembled an unmarked police cruiser, he would abandon his rendezvous with Lisa in an instant.

"There was one hotel in St. Johnsbury, Vermont," Horton recalled later, "which worried me. I knew Gary would scope it out for cop cars. Changing those plates and removing those stickers and antennas seemed a bit overly dramatic and obsessive at the time, I admit. But this is what Gary had driven me to: as he was plotting every single move on his part, I was plotting every move on ours."

Indeed, each brought out the best in the other, despite being polar opposites.

While the team assembled in Horton's driveway and removed radio antennae, registration stickers and changed license plates, Horton retreated upstairs in his house to pack a bag for the trip. Mary Pat, his wife, had been on the receiving end of an often one-sided relationship for the past twenty years. There were times—like tonight, for instance—when Jim would come home unannounced and explain he was taking off on a trip out of state. No warning. No good-byes. Just a peck on the cheek and a promise he'd be home as soon as he could.

Because of the secrecy surrounding some cases, there were even times when he couldn't say where he was off to, or why he was going.

Tonight was different, though. Mary Pat had known Evans on a first-name basis for well over a decade. Evans had called the house for Jim many times during the years and had written him several letters. Mary Pat had read the letters and answered the calls. She had stayed up nights listening to stories about Evans. A petite woman, attractive and motherly, home with two kids for the most part, Mary Pat and Jim met in high school and had been together ever since. A tough woman, thick-skinned, she was devoted to her husband and supported him 100 percent.

Whenever Jim came home and had that focused look on his face, Mary Pat didn't need an explanation, or some sort of glossed-over speech to assuage her feelings of concern. Without asking, she could tell how serious a case was by looking at her husband, and she never once stood in the way of his work. Additionally, she was well aware of the ordeal he had been through with Evans for the past eight months, not to mention thirteen years, and how important this particular event was.

"This is it," Horton told his wife, looking up from packing his clothes into a duffel bag, his eyes bulging with exhilaration and alarm. "I think we've got him."

It was a double-edged sword: both enthusiasm and the gravity of the situation were evident on Horton's face, visible in everything he did. An unwavering sense of determination was obvious in the way he had, over the course of the last twenty-four hours, switched gears into battle mode. Nothing else mattered. For maybe the first time in the nearly eight months since Tim had disappeared, Horton was positive Evans had cold-bloodedly murdered him. That meant Evans was also likely responsible for the disappearances of Michael Falco and Damien Cuomo.

When it came down to it, Evans was a serial murderer. Not just some thief who had become a CI throughout the years and had bartered prosecutors and cops for "good time," using information about other thieves and drug dealers as currency. Evans was a vicious killer who would likely kill again if he felt boxed into a corner. Here now was Horton's chance to sweep Evans up and, with any luck, find out the truth. Evans was considered a habitual offender and was looking at twenty-five years behind bars, at the least. On top of that, his bargaining days were over. The chances of him ever getting out of jail early for turning state's evidence against another felon were nil. When he was caught this time, he was going to rot in prison for what would amount to the rest of his life—which worried Horton more than anything.

In effect, Evans had nothing to lose.

"Jim," Mary Pat said in nearly a whisper, brushing his back with her hand, "good luck. Stay safe, honey. Okay?"

Horton didn't answer. He grabbed his bag and rushed downstairs, throwing it on the kitchen table, and went down another flight of stairs to the basement, where he kept his gun safe.

It is against policy for a cop to bring a personal weapon on the job with him. Horton, though, had little time to follow rules. Decisions were being made on the spot. He would deal with the fallout later.

He opened his safe and took out a sawed-off shotgun he'd had for years, grabbed a box of shells, and ran back up the stairs.

"What are you doing?" one of his investigators asked when he got outside.

"I need it," Horton said. "I don't care. . . ."

Mary Pat had wandered outside into the driveway to see everyone off. As if she were a mother sending her children off to school on a frigid day, making sure they hadn't forgotten their scarves and gloves, she asked, "Does everyone have their [bulletproof] vests with them?"

Jim nodded. "We're all set, Mary Pat. I'll call you when it's over."

CHAPTER 25

St. Johnsbury, Vermont, a Victorian-style village located about forty-five miles south of the Canadian border in the northeastern portion of Vermont, is remarkable for a broad variety of reasons. The land on which St. Johnsbury sits, shaped like an arrowhead, surrounded by the Passumpsic, Moose and Sleeper's Rivers, appears to be untouched by urban revival and contemporary infrastructure. With only eight thousand residents, St. Johnsbury, at one time a thriving industrial monopoly, is today a quiet historic village that travelers pass through en route to Canada. Easily accessible from Interstates 93 and 91, buildings in downtown are a perfect paradigm of the care and eye for detail that builders had put into their architecture centuries ago. The streets are tightly cropped and laden with pedestrian crossing zones, monuments and cobblestone walkways. Buildings are constructed of red brick and century-old fieldstone. Storefronts are archaic in appearance, weathered and falling apart, yet aesthetically attractive.

To a master criminal like Evans, St. Johnsbury was a wealth of potential. Antique dealers and artifact shops dotted downtown and its surrounding boroughs. A small village, with hardly any crime rate to speak of, St. Johnsbury antique shops housed some of the most expensive artifacts and antiques the Northeast had to offer. Evans, who would study antique magazines and take note of particular towns and shops, had recently told Lisa he was planning a "big score." When Horton did a bit of research to find out where the antique trade district was located in town, it didn't surprise him to find shops on just about every corner. It was not a stretch to think Evans had probably been in town for weeks surveying several different locations, maybe even befriending local antique shop owners, building trust and patronage, learning their vulnerabilities, like he had in the past.

For Bureau investigators DeLuca, Sully, Horton, and NYSP undercovers John Couch and Mary DeSantis, the ride up north was deep-sea dark, seemingly endless, and "white knuckle" all the way. They had arrived, in two separate vehicles, at about 1:30 A.M. Tired and worn down by the trip, DeLuca, Sully, Couch and DeSantis were not all that sure of what to expect the following day. They were preparing to face off against a criminal they now understood to be capable of just about anything, banking on the dangers Horton had warned them about during the trip. Still, they didn't understand completely how devious and desperate Evans truly was.

Horton, on the other hand, was in his element, at times expressing the excitement of a kid on his way to an amusement park. For those who didn't really know him, mainly Couch and DeSantis, he gave the impression of a cop much "too excited" for the job, not eating, not talking too much, running on what he later called "contained adrenaline." Horton was on his way to catch Evans after eight months of dead ends and thirteen years of playing cat and mouse. He felt Evans had fooled him all these years. *Burglar? No. Serial murderer.* As a former leader of a major drug task force, Horton—like the others—had been involved in his share of undercover operations, surveillances and break-down-the-door-and-barge-in arrests. Yet setting up an operation to trap Evans was, Horton later admitted, a different type of police work altogether. Evans was not your run-of-the-mill criminal, prone to make the same mistakes cops could usually depend on criminals to make. He was in a class by himself—and now, with nothing left to lose, he was likely ready to go down in a blaze of glory.

"I had been chasing Gary on a full-time basis for eight months by that point," Horton recalled later. "For the first time in the thirteen years I had known him, I now believed he had murdered several people. The stakes had changed remarkably in eight months' time. I wasn't some cop looking for one of my CIs to give up a drug dealer or information about a robbery he might have done—Gary was suddenly this cold-blooded serial murderer we needed to stop before he killed again. I had family members of victims saying some pretty bad things to the press about my relationship with Evans and how they believed I had helped him get out of prison early a number of times—which wasn't true—because he had given me information about other criminals. Subsequently, many believed I had *allowed* him to commit murders."

Horton, who had an untarnished record as a police officer, not only had to clear his name in a sense, but he had to convince Evans—that is, if they could catch him—to talk to him about Falco, Cuomo and Rysedorph. All this, Horton was quick to point out, without having a shred of solid evidence other than a gut feeling Evans was responsible for their disappearances.

"I knew he wasn't going back to prison," Horton added. "The last time I had seen him, he had just gotten out of prison after doing the longest bid of his life. He was crying like a baby. 'I can't do that again. . . . I won't do that again,' he told me. This was an entirely new deal for Gary and me. Whatever friendship we'd had was over. He would have killed me just as he would have killed anyone else—and I knew that going in."

* * *

When the crew arrived at the only hotel in St. Johnsbury, Horton told Mary DeSantis go in by herself, register all of them and check to see if Evans had slipped up and perhaps checked into the same hotel under his own name, or maybe as Louis Murray.

I don't like it, Horton told himself, looking around the parking lot, shaking his head. *This isn't good.*

The hotel was located just outside of town, the only one for miles. If somebody wanted to visit downtown, he would have to pass the hotel to get into town.

Five minutes later, DeSantis emerged, handed out keys to four different rooms and said, "No luck, Jim. No Evans. No Louis Murray."

"I didn't think it was going to be that easy," Horton said, speaking in a more serious, businesslike tone than he had used the entire trip. "Everyone check into their rooms and meet me in mine in ten minutes. I need to go over some things about tomorrow morning."

Horton hadn't expected to sleep. But as he sat on the edge of his bed, watching the sun rise the following morning, he didn't feel the least bit exhausted. He had put all of his resources—not to mention eight months' worth of coddling Lisa Morris, kissing her ass, overlooking petty crimes she had committed—into this one day, hoping it would pay off, and here it was, just like that, game time.

I can't believe this, he thought. *McDonald's . . . full of people . . . high noon . . . the O.K. fucking Corral. . . . A shoot-out in the middle of the day, in the middle of a little town in Vermont, Evans armed and desperate. Is he going to shoot us? Are we going to shoot him? Will a civilian get hurt?*

They were all possibilities.

During a meeting that morning in his hotel room with Sully, Couch, DeSantis and DeLuca, Horton warned them of what he thought Evans was capable of if they cornered him in McDonald's. They weren't dealing with a two-bit druggie who stole car stereos to support a heroin habit. Evans was a professional thief who had killed people, Horton said with stern assertion. He hated cops. He hated the thought of being locked up. He hated, especially, anyone who stood in the way of his freedom.

By 7:00 A.M., everyone was heading toward the local VSP barracks, which happened to be in St. Johnsbury. There would be one more debriefing before everyone took their places in town.

The key to the success of the operation was for each investigator to realize the importance of his or her function in the entire scope of things. Everyone had to work in unison, or it was destined to fail from the start.

"No fuckups," Horton said in the car as he, Sully and DeLuca pulled into the Troop B parking lot. Couch and DeSantis were in a separate vehicle.

As they walked in, Horton first noticed a huge wanted poster with Evans's photo plastered on the front door. There he was: smiling, gloating, full of himself, staring right into the eyes of the man he had called at times "his only true friend," his "brother," someone "I love."

Horton stopped briefly before opening the barrack doors, took a look at the poster, shook his head and carried on without saying anything.

Setting his notebook down on the podium, after everyone exchanged pleasantries, he began by saying how dangerous he believed Evans was at this point in his criminal career.

"If we can, we need to take him alive," Horton advised. "We need him to tell us what he did with Tim Rysedorph, Damien Cuomo and Mike Falco."

After describing what he assumed Evans might look like now, and some of the disguises he may be using, he said, "He's armed. Believe me when I say that Gary Evans would crawl through a straw if necessary. He told a source of mine recently he wouldn't be taken alive."

In all, there were going to be five well-trained cops to take down what Horton described to the team as one of the "most daring, intelligent, athletic criminals" he had even encountered. The odds were stacked in their favor.

"Good, solid police work will prosper."

It hurt like hell to say it, but . . . "I can't be anywhere near the meet. He knows me too well."

Another important decision Horton had made the night before was to not allow Lisa to keep her promise of meeting Evans. There was no way he could take a chance on Lisa's safety. The only problem was, Lisa had already left Latham.

"How are we going to stop her?" someone yelled out.

"I'll take care of it," Horton said.

He then explained exactly how the operation would be handled and where he wanted everyone positioned. One of the VSP troopers got up and sketched out a map of the town near McDonald's on a chalkboard next to where Horton was standing.

Horton took out a pointer and began going through where he wanted everyone positioned. A VSP Bureau investigator would be in a car in the parking lot of McDonald's, sitting, reading the newspaper, eating. "If you spot him when he enters the parking lot," Horton said, staring at the cop, "and he is, as I think he'll be, riding a bike, or on foot, I want you to hit him with your car. Break his legs if you can, then mace him. If *any* of you can take him, I want you to mace him in the eyes."

Bruce Lang, a twenty-year law enforcement veteran, the VSP Bureau investigator in charge, was at first startled by Horton's words. *"Break his legs? Hit him with your car?"*

Horton looked at Lang, "Are you all right with that, Lieutenant?"

Lang shook his head. Smiled. "Cool."

The rest of the team, sitting, listening, began to chuckle.

"I'm dead serious here," Horton reaffirmed. "It's no joke. If one of you can run him down with your car, hit him with the door or drive into him and break his fucking legs, do it. That'll save any shots being fired or Mace flying around."

It was then explained in great detail why Horton wanted everyone in their positions by 10:00 A.M., and why he wanted Evans's legs broken if possible.

"He'll show up early to conduct countersurveillance. He may look different." Horton paused a moment. "Do not make a move unless you are *absolutely* sure you can take him." In as serious a tone as he could manage, he added, "Safety will take place in this order"—he looked down at a note he had written the night before—"Yours first. The public's next. Evans's last." He paused before concluding: "Everyone wears a bulletproof vest."

After he finished, Lang walked over.

"Thanks for your help, Bruce," Horton said, shaking his hand. "Listen, I need an ambulance crew standing by. Where's the closest hospital?"

Lang, surprised by the apparent gravity of the situation, said, "Right near town, Jim. Why? What's up?"

"I want a helicopter ready, too. Just in case one of our guys needs it. I want the best care available in the shortest time possible. Someone may get shot."

Lang took a step back. Raised his eyebrows. *Whoa.* And for the first time, having only hours invested in Evans, understood just how dangerous things could get.

When Horton had a chance to collect his thoughts after the briefing, he sat down and began to worry that, as positive as he had sounded regarding his feelings about capturing Evans, he began to consider the possibility of it not happening. There were too many variables. So many things could go wrong. Evans was too damn smart to walk right into a trap.

What am I missing?

The only hope Horton held on to as he prepared to figure out how to flag down Lisa Morris was that no one would get hurt in the process.

CHAPTER 26

Lisa left Latham at around 8:00 A.M. She was frantic, worried and, she later admitted, excited about the prospect of having sex with Evans one more time before he was taken away from her for good.

I'm going to get laid.

She had made a specific request to Horton that she be allowed to hole up with Evans in a hotel room for "just an hour," so she could have sex with him one last time before they handcuffed him and took him away.

Horton had been firm: "No way!"

But Lisa, driving like an outlaw to make her meeting with Evans, believed she could somehow convince Horton, considering all she had done to help the Bureau get to the point where they had Evans in their sights, to let her have just one last session of "marathon sex" with him.

As planned, by 10:00 A.M., Horton's team was in position, waiting for Evans to make his first move. Horton and Lang drove to the outskirts of town and stationed themselves near the only exit ramp leading into town. With any luck, Lisa would drive right by them as she made her way into town. Horton had Lang drop him off by the exit ramp, and told him to drive about a quarter of a mile up the road and park the car in a commuter lot.

Horton found a good spot near the off-ramp and nestled himself like a mouse down in the brush, radio in hand. Every once in a while, when he heard a car descend down the ramp, he'd peer up and see if it was Lisa.

Luckily, it was sunny and warm that morning and the grass Horton was sitting in wasn't strewn with dew.

Several different scenarios had played out in Horton's mind throughout the past twelve hours, but he never expected to be lying on his back in the brush, staring at the sky, waiting for Lisa to drive into town. The plan had always been for her to meet up with Evans at McDonald's. *But what if she decided to take a different route?* Every local cop had reassured Horton that if Lisa came into town she would have to drive down that particular ramp. There was no other way into town. But what if she and Evans had pulled one over on him? What if Evans planned on doing the same thing: heading Lisa off at the exit ramp?

There is a time in every cop's life when he has to rely on the snap decisions he makes. This was one of those times, Horton said later. "I had to think like Gary Evans. Knowing what I knew about him, I had this gut feeling he was going to do something to Lisa."

Their only chance was to make Evans believe Lisa was going to show up. They had thought about using a Trojan horse method, whereby a cop would hide in Lisa's trunk, or the backseat of her car, and then surprise Evans. But it was too risky, not to mention dangerous for civilians. The only way they would get Evans without hurting anyone else was to make him think Lisa was coming, and then ambush him.

In position near the off-ramp, Horton could radio Lang, who was just up the road, if he needed help.

Any car coming down the off-ramp had the potential to

be Lisa. Within five minutes of sitting in the brush, Horton heard the roar of a car engine and popped his head out of the brush.

As if right on cue, there she was barreling down the ramp in her beat-up old shitbox of a car. Horton, spying her while she was at the top of the ramp, quickly ran into the road, radio in hand, and flagged her down.

Lisa was startled, of course. Reacting instinctively to what was, literally, a man in the middle of the road, she hit the brakes and skid to a stop near a road sign at the bottom of the ramp. With her jaw nearly on the dashboard, she could hardly believe Horton was standing in front of her.

What the fuck?

"You're not meeting him, Lisa," Horton said right away, walking toward the driver's-side window.

"Jim . . . what . . . what do you mean? What the fuck are you doing here?"

Horton ran around to the passenger side and hopped in the car. "Drive up there," he said, pointing to where Lang was parked.

After Lisa parked her car next to Lang's cruiser, Horton said, "It's way too dangerous, Lisa. No way."

By this point, she was ranting and raving, saying how bad she needed to see him, even if it was for only ten minutes. "Come on, Jim. Please," she pleaded.

"No, Lisa. Sorry." Horton grabbed her by the arm and pulled her off to the side so they could talk privately for a moment. She was crying now.

"Please, Jim. I need to see him. Please."

She was, Horton said later, "desperate to have sex with Evans just one last time." She begged: "It's been a long time. . . . Just let us get a hotel room."

To stave off any more problems—". . . the last thing I needed at that point was a hysterical female on my hands"—Horton said, "Okay, Lisa, I'll think about it. Let me run it by the Vermont State Police. Maybe. Maybe."

While they were talking, Lang yelled for Horton.

"What's up?"

Lang pointed to the radio inside his cruiser. "Listen," he said.

It was about 10:30. One of the investigators sitting in his car in the parking lot of McDonald's radioed in a whisper that he thought he had spied Evans pulling into the parking lot.

"Target is here," the investigator finally confirmed. "He just locked up his bike."

Son of a bitch, Horton thought.

Standing about twenty yards away, Lisa was still rambling on about seeing him, but had no idea what was going on.

Horton looked over at her, his ear to the radio. "Lisa, shut up!" Leaning in closer to the radio, he continued listening.

"Target is inside restaurant . . . walking around," someone said.

Evans had pulled into the parking lot, rode his bike—which he had stolen out west—up to the bike rack near the front doors and, in a moment of poetic irony, took out a chain and locked it up.

As any other patron might, he entered McDonald's and proceeded to walk toward the rest rooms in the back of the restaurant. He was wearing blue jeans, an army green lumberjack-type dress shirt, sneakers and a bandanna around his head. Sporting a full beard and pencil-thin mustache, he looked stronger and more muscular than he had at any other point in his life. There was no doubt he had been lifting weights while out west.

Across the street from McDonald's, which was located right in the middle of the town square, was a beauty parlor, a Chinese restaurant and the bank where Sully and DeLuca were stationed in the president's office. There was a stone monument, directly across the street, about five feet high, four feet wide, that looked like a stone replica of a podium.

At the last minute, DeLuca repositioned himself in a house right next door to McDonald's. The VSP had gained access to it by asking the owners if they could use it for the day. He was staring out of the north-side window with binoculars, a shotgun cradled in the crook of his arm.

Evans never went into the bathroom, but instead just cased the entire building and walked quickly back outside, unlocked his bike and began to make his way out of the parking lot. In total, he was inside the restaurant about two minutes. The place had been packed with a breakfast crowd, so it was impossible to mace him or approach him. Additionally, McDonald's hadn't been notified as to what Horton and his team were up to. Horton thought it best to keep the operation as confidential as possible.

DeSantis and Couch, who had a car parked near the restaurant but were on foot, holding hands, walking up and down the street in front, didn't have a clear view of Evans as he began making his way out of the parking lot. The cop with the K-9 walking in front of the restaurant didn't see Evans until he was well out of the parking lot and heading south, away from him. So it didn't make sense to unleash the dog on him.

As Evans worked his way out of the restaurant and onto his bike, no one had said anything over the radio. For about two minutes, Horton and Lang had no idea what was going on.

Back at base camp, Horton began pacing. "Where is he now?"

"Don't know," someone said.

"Come again?"

"We can't find him. Target is gone."

Fuck me . . .

Lang tried to calm Horton the best he could, but Horton, although not surprised, was more frustrated and disappointed than anything else. It wasn't anybody's fault. They were good cops. If they could have taken him, he knew, it would be over by now.

"He'll be back," Horton told the team. "Don't worry about it. Just sit tight."

But he thought differently. *Did we just miss our only chance? Did he make someone? Will he return? Why didn't anyone take him when they had the opportunity?*

Evans had, literally, disappeared off the street. One minute, he was riding his bike; the next, he was gone. It wasn't as if the streets were packed with tourists and townies. It was a normal day, as far as traffic was concerned. But Evans, elusive and slippery, had managed to vanish in front of a team of aptly trained cops who were put in place to catch him.

CHAPTER 27

Horton spent the next hour, like an expecting father, wound up and stressed out. He paced. He sat. He talked to Lang and, at times, went off by himself to go through everything in his head one more time. *Have I done all the right things? What if I missed something?*

Lisa had been sitting in Lang's cruiser, not saying much of anything. She still had it in her head that she was going to meet Evans after they captured him.

Horton's standing orders to the team were to take Evans into custody if conditions appeared safe. The first time Evans showed his face, everyone agreed, was much too dangerous. There were too many people around. But Horton made it clear that if he emerged again, they would have to make a move.

They wouldn't get a third chance.

After a harrowing hour and ten minutes, the call Horton had been waiting for finally came over the radio: "Target once again in sight."

Without Lisa's help during the past eight months, Horton knew he would not be in a position of possibly capturing

Evans. Because of her courage, here they were ready to detain a fugitive suspected of three murders—someone who, just days ago, seemed invisible, "uncatchable."

After some prudent thought on the notion of perhaps letting Lisa meet with Evans one last time, if and when they apprehended him, Horton decided to do what any cop in his same position might do: lie.

"Lisa, listen to me," Horton said, approaching her shortly before Evans had been spotted the second time. "The Vermont State Police will have jurisdiction over Gary if we get him. I've been talking to Lieutenant Lang and there is no way you can meet with Gary, he said. I'm sorry. I have nothing to do with the decision. I thought I did. But we're not in New York."

It was all bullshit. Horton was running the show. If he wanted Lisa and Evans to have one last fling, he could have set it up and nobody could have denied it.

Lisa started crying. "Please, Jim. I just need to have sex with him. When we're done, you can take him."

"Lisa . . . I'm not saying this again. Absolutely not. It won't happen."

"You lied to me, Jim."

"It's too damn dangerous for you. The Vermont State Police don't understand the relationship we've had, Lisa. They laughed at me when I asked them."

What Horton planned on doing, to pacify Lisa's desire to see Evans again, was put a fake wiretap in her car and send her to McDonald's to wait. She had no idea what was going on. She would wait, and when Horton thought she had waited long enough, he would drive there and tell her they had taken Evans into custody—that is, if they caught him.

At 12:55 P.M., an investigator stationed inside McDonald's indicated he had Evans in his sights.

"It's him," another investigator said. "He's here."

Evans had changed his appearance since they last saw

him. Now he was wearing a "wife-beater" T-shirt and cutoff blue jean shorts. He had ditched the bandanna for a hat. It would have been easy to assume that he wasn't carrying a weapon, suffice it to say he really didn't have anywhere to hide it on his body, except he also had a large blue backpack draped over his shoulder, which quite possibly could be full of weapons.

Sitting, listening to the chatter between investigators, Horton felt powerless. He had waited for nearly a year for this day and—at least hands-on—he wasn't part of it.

During his second sojourn into downtown, none of the investigators stationed around town had seen Evans walk in or out of McDonald's parking lot. They weren't sure if he had ever been in the restaurant. Sully, stationed in the bank president's office across the street, looking out the window, had been the first to see Evans arrive. Evans had driven his bike by the window Sully was looking out, rode up a small incline, stopped directly across the street from McDonald's, walked a few yards over to the monument and sat down.

Sully had a clear view of him from the bank window.

Sitting atop the monument, Evans cradled his chin with his right palm, while his large legs hung down off the front without touching the ground. He appeared calm, comfortable, just sitting, waiting, apparently, for Lisa to arrive. Every once in a while, he would look down at his watch and scan the entire area with his eyes.

"I don't even know where he came from," somebody said over the radio.

"Well, he's back."

"Shit," Sully said, "I have him. . . . He's sitting right here."

All of the investigators in the field, Horton later noted, knew exactly what to do and when to do it. They certainly didn't need some overly excited senior investigator barking orders as if he were some taxicab dispatcher, directing their every move. They were professionals. They had all done this before. If there was a chance to grab Evans, they would take it.

As much as it hurt him, Horton could only sit and wait—having no idea what was going on.

Without warning, one by one, each investigator emerged from his or her position and began to move in on Evans at the same time as he sat on the monument.

At first, Evans didn't have a clue as to what was going on. Then, as he "felt everyone closing in" on him, he later told Horton, he leaped off the monument and took three quick steps toward the street, heading for the wooded area behind McDonald's. There were immense pine trees, in perfect rows, like farmed Christmas trees, directly in back of the restaurant. The woods, beyond the trees, were thick and dense. Because it was the beginning of spring, the leaves on the trees and bushes had recently bloomed an army green dark color. It would be impossible for anyone to catch Evans once he bled into the aesthetics of the woods. Further, throughout the morning, it had become increasingly cloudier. The sun was covered by clouds now. Once Evans reached the woods, he would be in his element, the keeper of his own fate. A band of street cops from Albany would be no match.

As Evans bolted across the street, however, the K-9 cop, who was closest to him, unleashed the dog. A large German shepherd, trained to attack a moving target, took one leap and sank his razor-sharp teeth into Evans's calf, tearing a gash in his flesh as if it were a piece of raw beef.

Evans fell immediately to the ground and began fighting off the dog.

Within seconds, every investigator in the field ran toward him and tackled him.

Sully, who had come running out of the bank toting his shotgun, ran up and, along with the others, pointed the barrel of his weapon directly at Evans's head.

Do not move, motherfucker, seemed to be said in unison.

Horton had warned everyone about Evans's penchant for being able to escape while in custody, not to mention the reputation he had for hiding razorblades and handcuff keys all over his body, in every imaginable cavity. The only way to monitor his behavior at all times and be sure he wasn't "up to something," Horton suggested, was to strip him naked.

So, after handcuffing him, two investigators stripped him.

A crowd had begun to swell as people in town began to figure out what was happening. One of the investigators had already radioed for backup and several local and state police cruisers had arrived on-scene, lights blaring, sirens wailing.

Bare-assed and handcuffed, Evans now stood in front of what were scores of onlookers and law enforcement. At first, he tried wrestling the handcuffs off, hopping around, falling down, getting back up again, his right leg bloodied from the dog bite. But then, as he began to realize there was little chance of getting away, he broke into a violent rage, screaming aggressively in what could only be described as one of his Incredible Hulk moments.

Evans would later say he was, at that moment, picturing himself "caged" and locked up again. In his mind, it was over. No more running. No more hiding.

No more freedom.

Twenty-five to life.

Back at base camp, Horton and Lang hadn't heard anything for about eight minutes. The last they had heard was that someone had spotted Evans in town. For all Horton and Lang knew, the entire plan had gone bust and Evans was gone.

Maybe someone had even gotten hurt? Horton thought.

Then, over the radio, came those words cops love to hear during stakeouts and surveillances—which were especially welcomed, Horton later admitted, in this case.

"Target in custody without incident."

Horton looked over at Lang and shook his hand.

"Thank you, Lieutenant, for everything. Your men were amazing."

CHAPTER 28

In the coming months, communities around New England would begin to understand that the stripping of Evans's clothes on Main Street in St. Johnsbury would serve as a metaphor for what was about to happen as soon as Horton was able to secure extradition and bring Evans back to New York State. Evans hadn't said a word to anyone as he was taken into custody. But an hour after he was processed and fingerprinted, he finally opened his mouth.

"Jim Horton. I will only speak to Horton."

He had run out of options. His deal-making days were over. Horton, who still hadn't seen him by 4:00 P.M. that day, had one person on his mind as he contemplated when he was going to visit Evans—Tim Rysedorph.

What Horton was about to hear from Evans in the coming weeks—crimes so horrible in their nature they were hard to fathom—would set Evans on a path of self-destruction, culminating in a series of events that, by midsummer 1998, would devastate anyone and everyone involved.

Before contact with Evans could be established, Horton wanted to find out a few things. Part of figuring out what Evans had been up to for the past eight months while on the run entailed locating where he had been staying while in Vermont.

Since he wasn't talking and Horton didn't want to go in and confront him just yet, it was a guessing game. The most logical conclusion was that he had camped somewhere in the woods near McDonald's. So Horton had a team of troopers begin the time-consuming task of combing the woods. Horton figured if he didn't go in and see Evans right away, Evans would possibly believe Horton hadn't been involved in his capture.

"I didn't want to alienate him," Horton said later. "I wanted him to open up to me when we met later on. I should have known he was a lot smarter than I gave him credit for."

After radioing for a team of troopers to begin searching an area outside of town, Horton and Lang, who were still at base camp, drove immediately to Troop B, where Evans was now chained to the wall, seething like a rabid raccoon.

No one was pressuring him. "Good," Horton said. "Just leave him be. Let him think about things."

"His mind was cranking," Horton recalled. "He was thinking, 'What the hell just happened? How in the hell am I going to get out of this?'"

After Horton explained to Lisa that the wiretap he'd placed in her car was a ruse, she followed him and Lang back to Troop B and waited in the lobby while Horton met with his team. With any luck, Horton told her, she would get to see Evans later that night.

From there, Horton and his team began to go through the items Evans had on him when he was captured. Most interesting was what appeared to be a small, handheld Tech-9 machine gun. At first, it looked as real as the $100 bills Evans had on him, yet ended up being nothing more than a child's plastic toy. Several bus and plane receipts inside his backpack confirmed he had been to Oregon, Alaska, Washington, California, New Mexico, Connecticut and Massachusetts.

Also inside his backpack were maps, brochures, hats, bandannas and several personal hygiene items. Inside his wallet was a stack of paperwork that explained just how far he had gone to conceal his identity. Traveling under the name

"Louis William Murray III," he had managed to obtain four different driver's licenses—two sets under two different addresses—from the state of Washington. In each photo, Evans had altered his appearance just enough so as to look like a different person. In one, he wore glasses, had no facial hair and smiled into the camera; in another, he had a Fu Manchu mustache, wore no glasses and twisted his face muscles enough to appear more serious and academic. Under the Louis Murray name, he had even obtained a Social Security card and enrolled in a food stamp program in Seattle. A tattered and worn Certificate of Baptism, signed by what turned out to be a fictional reverend, was folded and stuffed deep inside a pocket in the bag. On it, he had written his birthplace as Latham, New York—the same town where Horton had lived for most of his life.

Mixed in with a stack of business papers were several business cards from various commercial deep-sea fishing vessels. Later, Horton learned Evans had obtained a job aboard an Alaskan fishing boat that traveled from Alaska into the Bering Strait, finally making landfall in Russia. Evans said he had planned to defect to Russia once the boat arrived, but he had caused some trouble during the trip and ended up locked in the brig.

The Timex Expedition watch he had been wearing when he was arrested had a handcuff key strapped to the back of it. It was a cheap, outdoorsy type of watch one could purchase (or steal) from any department store. As Horton picked it up, held it in his hand and looked at it more closely, he realized it was the exact same watch he had on.

Rusted and slightly bent, a tad smaller than a house key, the handcuff key found strapped to the back of the watch served as peace of mind for Evans. He had escaped from custody before and later told Horton he was never without at least one handcuff key at all times. Yet, as investigators searched further, they found two more keys.

A fourth key, Horton would learn later, was never found.

Whenever Evans went out in public or set out to do a

"job," he hid a handcuff key in his mouth, underneath his tongue. If he ever got caught, he swallowed it. Twenty-four hours later, while in custody, he could shit it out, clean it off and put it back in his mouth. No one knew it at the time, but it was likely that inside Evans's stomach, as he sat chained to the cell wall inside Troop B, was that same handcuff key he had recycled numerous times throughout the years.

Besides finding several more everyday household items, the most telling item investigators found was located in Evans's wallet: a photograph.

Nearly a week prior to his arrest in Vermont, the *Albany Times Union*, a local Albany newspaper, had run a story about cold case investigations. The photo that ran with the story showed Horton opening a filing cabinet. It was a good shot, taken from the waist up. Evans had cut out Horton's photo, folded it neatly and kept it tucked away in a separate pocket in his wallet. If anyone had ever doubted how personal the connection between Evans and Horton was, here was proof: the villain, in all his narcissism, had been carrying around a photo of the cop who was hunting him.

Horton, when confronted with the photo, looked at it and smiled.

"Gary would, even if he was in Vermont, Maine or wherever, order the *Albany Times Union* newspaper so he could keep tabs on what was happening locally. Was I surprised when we found the photo? Of course. But when I sat down later and thought about it, I understood that Gary was, in his own way, trying to prove to himself how much he respected me. The only mistake he made, he told me later, was not leaving St. Johnsbury when he saw my photo in the *Times Union*. That was a sign for him to leave, he claimed, and he didn't listen to it."

An off-duty VSP trooper, who had been out jogging in downtown St. Johnsbury during the morning hours of May 27, had come up on a section of woods outside of town near an underpass and had seen "a man on a bike come speeding out of a culvert" that led into the woods.

Later that day, when the trooper showed up for work and saw Evans in lockup, he said, "I saw that guy this morning coming out of this culvert on the edge of town. . . ."

When Horton got wind of what the trooper said, he immediately ordered a team to the area. Near the culvert, as cops began to search, someone noticed a fresh break in the brush leading farther back into the woods; small trees and bushes had been matted down near freshly cracked twigs along what looked to be a man-made path.

For a few hours, Horton and several troopers searched the area but found nothing. It was rough terrain. Lots of rock ledge. Thick green brush. Blooming wildflowers. Swampland. Hills. Evans's camp could be anywhere inside a two- or three-mile radius.

Realizing it was the perfect spot for Evans to camp, Horton called in a helicopter.

Hours later, the helicopter search team spotted what looked like the top of a tent and directed Horton and his crew into the area.

Sure enough, up in the most mountainous portion of the area, near a waterfall, hidden inside a band of densely overgrown bushes and oak trees, was Evans's campsite.

He had been smart enough to drape a dark green tarp over the top of the small, one-man tent. Not only for cover from the rain, but camouflage.

They could tell he had been camped there for some time. The ground around the tent was worn and well-trodden. There was something about the place, when Horton first arrived, that struck him. It was serene. The air was crisp, fresh, like walking into a greenhouse for the first time. He could understand why Evans chose it.

The campsite itself was homey and peaceful. Evans had apparently planned on staying for quite some time. Throughout his life, one of Evans's greatest pleasures was to camp by himself in conditions other human beings might view as severe. There was one time in 1976 when he camped up north near the Canadian border during winter. Temperatures had fallen beyond comprehension. Later, while in prison, Evans wrote about the experience:

> *I remember in '76 I was camping out alone in the snow . . . on this mountain. It said it was minus 54 [degrees] with the wind chill factor! I was wrapped in sheepskin, inside a down sleeping bag, in a mountaineer tent under a pine tree snow fort. . . . I was freezing!! But it was fun—and one of the last times of freedom I had.*

As Horton began going through the inside of Evans's tent, he uncovered all the basic necessities one might take on a camping trip: water, juice, food, shampoo and soap. Evans had kept several changes of clean clothes stacked neatly in one corner, a stack of books in the other. Among the many books was an old copy of *The Collected Works of Billy the Kid,* a few law enforcement handbooks, and *Criminal Investigation: Basic Perspectives*, a college-level textbook for wannabe cops.

Looking further, Horton found a few rolls of film and a camera.

"Take these down to the lab right away and get them developed," he told one of the troopers.

CHAPTER 29

It had been two years since Evans and Horton had seen each other. The last time they spoke, Horton had told Evans he never wanted to see or hear from him again.

The purpose of any interrogation, most law enforcement textbooks preach, is to "secure a confession of guilt" from a suspect. The notion that someone could be innocent of a crime is not something interrogations are designed to reveal.

Whether it is a hostile—shine a light in the perpetrator's face—type of interview, or a relaxed—"everything will be okay, we are here to help you"—situation, cops who have mastered the art view it the same way: "The better you know your subject, the more you will get out of him."

For Horton, all he wanted out of Evans at this point was the answer to one question: where was Tim Rysedorph?

There was a major problem, however, and it occurred to Horton as he made his way down the long hallway and through the large steel doors that separated him from Evans: In no way could he discuss Tim Rysedorph, Michael Falco or Damien Cuomo, for that matter, with Evans. Studying case law, Horton realized that if Evans had in fact murdered all three men and wanted to admit to it, any tactic Horton now used to obtain those confessions would be scrutinized during trial later on.

"I couldn't blow the case by being overly ambitious. I knew Gary would be lawyered-up within days."

Evans was chained to the wall of his cell when Horton walked in.

In a friendly, mocking tone, Horton said, "Hey, you fuck, what's going on? What did you do now?"

Evans, an embarrassed smile on his face, stuck his hand out, the chains hanging from his wrist clanking and echoing down the long corridor. "Can you believe this shit?" he said, looking at himself chained to the wall.

"What'd you do now, Gar?" Horton was both frustrated and excited to see Evans. "This was a guy," he recalled later, "many of my colleagues told me I would never catch again—especially the way we did. So, some of it was gloating. But my main focus, from the first moment I saw him again, was to get him to give up Falco, Cuomo and, especially, Rysedorph. Before that day in Vermont, I had always viewed Gary as a thief I could perhaps change. But now I saw him as a murderer. Things were different, to say the least."

A few minutes before Horton had seen Evans, he practiced the look and demeanor he was going to use once he got face-to-face with him. It had to be, he said, a "good to see an old friend" type of moment, "particularly for Gary. Any other way would jeopardize any future interviews I was going to do."

Indeed, one wrong move on Horton's part and Evans might decide not to talk to anyone. As it was, he had requested Horton, and only Horton. Which meant he *wanted* to talk.

"I was very nervous, thinking he would see right through me. Here we both were in a strange place (another state), under conditions as stressful to the both of us as they ever were. He is thinking about going back to jail forever. I need to get three bodies from him. There were a million things I could have said to blow it. In a way, that first meeting was phony; he knew I had been behind his capture and I was looking for Rysedorph, but neither of us would broach the subject. On the other hand, we were both, as strange as it may sound, glad to see each other."

Evans was looking at twenty-five to life. He wasn't going anywhere. Horton, however, decided he wanted to have a current photo of Evans to distribute just in case something happened and Evans ended up on the loose again. So he asked if he could take his photo.

"Sure, Guy, whatever you want," Evans said.

Sitting chained to the wall, Evans looked up and smiled as Horton snapped his photo.

"Where ya been, Gar?" Horton asked, pulling the Polaroid from the bottom of the camera and setting it down to dry.

"We meet again!"

"We need to talk about what's going on."

"What's this shit?" Evans asked, lifting up the chains again and rattling them. "Why they got me tied up like an animal, Guy?"

"Let me explain," Horton said, pulling up a chair, taking a seat in front of him. "There's a federal warrant for violation of probation out there for you. You weren't supposed to leave the state of New York, Gar. You know how that shit works. You're a wanted fugitive, for Chrissakes."

The last state Evans should have been in was Vermont. The judge overseeing Evans's last court case for the theft of a rare book of antique bird prints had warned Evans about ever setting foot in Vermont again, or committing any crimes in the state.

"Well . . . ," Evans began to explain.

"Let me finish. Jesus! Of all places, Gar. Why Vermont again? They want your balls here, man." Evans shook his head in agreement. "We've also got a warrant for you in Albany for a pair of cuff links stolen from a shop in New Scotland." Evans bowed his head. "You signed your name, Gar, when you pawned them. You gettin' sloppy in your old age or what?"

"Holy fuck," Evans said, looking directly into Horton's eyes: "What is wrong with me, Guy? I must have been brain-dead on that one."

The one item Horton had promised himself he wouldn't mention was a warrant in Cold Spring, New York. Tim

Rysedorph's name was connected to it. He didn't want the initial meeting to be negative right from the start. Thinking Evans had killed Tim, Horton didn't want to bring up his name. He had to convince Evans he was going to be there for him, like he had been in the past.

"Here's what we have to do, Gar. You can come back to New York . . . waive extradition . . . or fight it here. It's going to take ninety days just to fight it, and you know as well as I do you'll lose."

Evans seemed to lighten up. He didn't want to stay in Vermont; he had no one there. Once Horton went back to New York, Evans knew he was on his own. Additionally, any time Evans spent in jail in Vermont wouldn't count against the time he was subsequently going to get down the road.

Horton got up from his chair, slid it back over near the table in the room and began walking toward the door. "Maybe I'll see you in New York next week, Gar?"

Evans looked at him, but said nothing. His face, however, told Horton he would be screaming to go back to New York by the end of the night.

CHAPTER 30

The newspapers didn't waste any time connecting the dots once word spread that Evans had been captured in Vermont. It had been rumored for years that Evans was responsible for the disappearances of Michael Falco and Damien Cuomo, and now sources inside the state police were telling reporters they were close to solving both cases. With Tim Rysedorph linked to Evans as a childhood friend and, later, what reporters and the Bureau were calling "a string of burglaries," local media began competing to see who could come up with the most eye-catching headline.

The *Albany Times Union* kept it simple, but blunt: FRIENDS VANISH, QUERIES LINGER. The article was accompanied by a familiar photo of Evans, the subheadline a portent of things to come: *A career thief arrested this week will be questioned in the disappearances of 3 associates.*

The pressure was on Horton to produce some sort of confession out of Evans. There wasn't an article written that didn't mention the relationship between Horton and Evans, or the fact that Evans had been the last person to see Tim alive. Horton had made a "courtesy" call to Caroline Parker, keeping her up to speed as to what was going on and the legal issues surrounding how the state police would go about questioning Evans. It involved more than just popping in and asking him where Falco, Cuomo and Rysedorph were, and what, if anything, he had done to them. The legalities were far more complicated than anything Horton had come across in his twenty years as a cop. When it came down to it, besides a bit of chatter among townspeople, there was no evidence linking Evans to any of the disappearances—and no bodies to prove that all three men had been murdered.

In the state of New York, when a warrant is issued against a suspect, counsel automatically attaches to the warrant and a virtual attorney, so to speak, is created. If cops have enough evidence against a suspect to issue a warrant, the court views that suspect as someone who is in desperate need of legal representation. And, more important, if there is enough evidence to issue the warrant in the first place, the court believes law enforcement shouldn't be speaking to that person. Thus, this was the main obstacle preventing Horton from talking to Evans.

In order to be able to discuss matters of any significance with Evans, Horton had to rely on the notion that Evans wanted to get out of Vermont and waive his right to an attorney once he was extradited back to New York State.

By Monday, June 1, 1998, five days after Evans had been captured, word was that he wanted out of Vermont as soon as possible, but the only person he said he wanted to talk to about it was Horton.

In turn, Horton spoke to Evans over the phone and reiterated his prior advice: "Waive extradition."

U.S. Marshals transported Evans back to Albany on Wednesday, June 3. He was placed in custody as a federal prisoner at Albany County Jail—a familiar place he had grown to hate, for obvious reasons, throughout the years. Because of the federal warrants standing against Evans, Horton, a state police officer, still couldn't mention Falco, Cuomo or Rysedorph. Anything they discussed would have to be personal, and Horton was strongly encouraged to stay the hell away from him.

Within a day of Evans's return, Evans called Horton at home, crying. "I need to see you, Guy," he said.

"All right. I'll be over there tomorrow."

Horton set it up where he could meet with Evans in a small, empty consultation room, alone.

Evans was crying as two corrections officers sat him down in a chair next to Horton. The room was noisy, echoey, and cramped. The first thing Horton noticed was how docile and depressed Evans had become. It was quite the change from the cocky, upbeat attitude he espoused in Vermont. The last time Horton had spoken to him, Evans was enthusiastic about the future. He had talked about seeing his nephew, and mentioned a woman in Troy who, he said, had literally raised him.

"Her name is Jo. I think of her as my mother."

But here he was now, unshaven and dirty. He hadn't showered in days. Had he given up?

"You smell. Do you know that?" Horton said as Evans sat down.

"I can't do this," he said through tears, "I can't be locked up anymore. I need to take a fresh-air ride. . . . I need to spend some time with you." He was holding a piece of paper, twisting it, folding it, fidgeting with it.

"We *should* talk, Gar."

"Yeah, yeah . . . I need to tell you —"

"No!" Horton said. "Don't say anything just yet, Gar. There are a few legal matters we have to take care of first."

Evans had let two of his fingernails grow unusually long, and had sharpened them into points.

"What's up with that?" Horton asked.

Looking down, sticking out his hand, Evans began whimpering. Horton recalled later that Evans was "like a baby, crying and breathing heavily. I had never seen him like this."

"With these," Evans said, staring at his fingernails, twisting his hand and curling his fingers up to his face, as if he were admiring a recent manicure. "I'm going to slit my wrists."

"Come on, Gar. Why would you want to do that?"

"I can't do this. I can't be locked up. I need to tell you—"

Horton interrupted again. "Whoa! Don't tell me anything, Gar. Here's what you have to do."

New York had a strange law whereby a suspect with a warrant against him could not waive his right to an attorney and begin confessing to any crimes without an attorney present. It seemed almost ludicrous that a suspect couldn't just sign a waiver and begin talking, but it was the law. Horton wasn't about to waste what amounted to twelve years' worth of work by overlooking it. He was too close. He could feel the energy bleeding out of Evans; he wanted to get things off his chest. He needed to talk. Whatever he was carrying around with him, Horton recognized, was destroying him physically, mentally, emotionally.

"If there was one part of being human that Gary Evans could never handle," Horton observed later, "it was stress."

So Horton explained, as plainly as he could, the law as it stood in Evans's case. He told him he would call the district attorney's office—"Only if you want me to?"—and set it all up on his behalf.

Evans, still crying, mumbling and fidgeting in his chair, began saying how he believed Horton was the only person he had left, the only person he felt comfortable talking to. He talked about Lisa Morris—"I don't ever want to see that bitch again"—and how she had set him up. Then he went into a diatribe regarding Horton's involvement in his Vermont capture. Yet he quickly changed subjects, saying, "You did a good job," as if it were some sort of game between them that Horton had won.

Horton didn't comment. Instead, he listened.

"Why couldn't you have let someone else do it, or go work on another case?" Evans wanted to know at one point.

"Come on, Gar," Horton said. Then he asked, changing the subject, "What should I do for you?"

"Do what you have to. Just get it done."

Horton got up and began walking toward the door. "Hang on, Gar. Don't worry about this. I'll take care of it."

"I won't talk to anyone else," Evans said. "Just you, Guy."

From his cell phone in the parking lot of the jail, Horton called the Albany County District Attorney's Office—specifically, ADA Paul Clyne. Horton and Clyne had worked together on cases in the past.

"Hey, Paul. It's Jim. I've got Gary Evans."

"I've heard, Jim. Good work. Congratulations."

"Listen, he wants to talk to me. Obviously, we want to talk to him. But he has a few warrants on him. He'll waive his rights, but I need a lawyer for him. We need to do it on the record."

This was an unprecedented move all around. It shocked Clyne. Here was Evans, suspected of several murders, ready to waive his rights. In effect, he was signing and sealing a death sentence for himself.

Clyne, a baby-faced man of about five feet eight inches, 140 pounds, wore thick, wired-rimmed glasses. Academic-looking, he could have easily doubled for Ernie Douglas, a character on the hit television show *My Three Sons*. His father, John, was an Albany County Court judge and was commonly called the "hanging judge," or "Maximum John," because of his harsh attitude toward punishing convicted criminals. Clyne, as a prosecutor, had no trouble building the same type of reputation.

"Paul Clyne is honest to a fault," a colleague later said. "Criminals try to stay out of the Capital District because of him."

Clyne explained to Horton how they would have to go about the process of Evans legally waiving his rights to counsel. There would have to be a court date and a judge. Evans would show up with his lawyer and, basically, against everyone's advice—with the exception of Horton, of course—waive his Miranda rights in an open courtroom. He would literally be giving Horton and the state police a free pass on questioning him about anything they wanted.

"Let's get a judge then," Horton said. "Like you said, get it on the record. We'll get him a public defender."

"How 'bout Joe McCoy?" Clyne suggested.

McCoy was a public defender Horton had known for some time. They had always worked well together. Horton would even send McCoy personal business from time to time. As defense attorneys go, cops don't normally associate with them. But Horton trusted McCoy. There was no need getting some young, crass, eager-to-prove-himself lawyer in Evans's camp. As Horton saw it, Evans was ready to admit to several murders. He wanted to talk. Horton needed answers. Family members of Tim Rysedorph, especially Caroline Parker, were back in the newspapers bad-mouthing the police, Horton in particular. Horton needed Evans to confess as soon as possible, before the press tagged him some sort of monster and scared him into silence.

"Joe McCoy sounds good, Jim," Clyne said.

"I'll call him."

"What do you expect to get out of Evans, anyway?" Clyne wanted to know.

"I really don't know," Horton said. "Anything I can, I guess."

When Horton contacted McCoy by phone, he explained the predicament Evans was in, and asked him if he was interested in the case. McCoy, at first, couldn't believe Evans was prepared to waive his rights. It was unheard of. No suspect in his right mind would want to waive his right to an attorney, sit down with a cop and begin admitting to murdering several people. The end result would not be anything that would ever help the suspect.

Despite an overflowing amount of cases on his plate already, McCoy agreed to represent Evans.

* * *

On Friday morning, June 19, 1998, in front of Judge Thomas Breslin, who himself couldn't believe what Evans wanted to do, along with district attorneys Paul Clyne and Sol Greenberg, and public defenders Eugene Devine and Joe McCoy, Evans was brought before Albany County Court. Wearing a lime green jumpsuit, he was shackled from his wrists to his waist to his ankles. He looked tired and beaten down—empty. He had obviously been crying for much of the time he was back in the Capital District. The large bags under the lower portion of his eyelids looked as if they had been painted on with mascara. He sounded weak, frail and confused.

What no one knew at the time was that despite his gutless approach to saving himself and his unreserved "give up on life" attitude, Evans had a get-out-of-jail-free card: a handcuff key, either inside his stomach as he stood before Judge Breslin, or hidden somewhere in his cell.

Right off the bat, the judge asked Evans if he understood what he was doing. "It has been brought to my attention that you have sought an opportunity to speak to the New York State Police. Is that correct?"

In a whisper, Evans said, "Yes, sir."

Horton sat in the back of the courtroom by himself, weighing what was taking place. Like a lot of people in the courtroom that day, he couldn't understand why Evans was so eager to waive his rights, but he wasn't going to argue with him about it.

"He didn't have to do it," Horton said later. "It was kind of surreal. He could have said nothing—and we would have never found anyone. But for some reason—which, of course, I, along with everyone else, would find out soon enough—he decided to make it easy for me."

The judge then stressed the importance of the Fifth and Sixth Amendments to the U.S. Constitution, and how it was designed to protect people in Evans's position. He wanted Evans to understand completely what he was doing.

"Yes . . . yes, sir," Evans responded with assertion, as if he just wanted to get the proceedings over.

To clarify what role Evans would play in the coming weeks and months as he began to talk to the state police, as he so desperately wanted, the judge asked, "Just to put it into context, this isn't . . . 'I want you to question me, members of the New York State Police.' [But,] 'I want to speak to *you*.' Is that a fair statement?"

"Yes, sir."

The judge sat back, looked down at the paperwork in front of him and thought for a moment about what was taking place. For everyone involved, this was the first time they had ever experienced such a thing.

McCoy had one demand. He wanted the court to understand he wasn't going to be accompanying Evans, per Evans's request, during his talks with, as McCoy put it, "Investigator Horton." But if Horton eventually wanted Evans to sign a statement, McCoy wanted the court to recognize that it should first be faxed to him for review before Evans actually signed it.

"You're saying to me, just so that's clear, too," Breslin said, looking up at Evans, "that you"—he looked directly into Evans's eyes—"want to speak to members of the New York State Police in your attorney's *absence*?"

"Right."

"Are you *sure* of that?"

"Yes, sir."

With the legal wrangling out of the way, Horton now had the go-ahead to interrogate Evans about anything he wanted.

Still sitting in the courtroom as Evans was brought back to a holding cell in the same building, Horton began pondering what the next couple of days were going to be like. Once they got going, he expected a long interview session with Evans. Not only would Evans give up Rysedorph, Cuomo and Falco, Horton believed, but probably every other crime he'd ever committed. In the end, what mattered most to Horton was that, for the first time, he was going to hear what had happened to Rysedorph, Falco and Cuomo.

The truth was coming. He could feel it.

Getting up from where he sat in the courtroom, Horton felt a sense of achievement wash over him as he realized that, besides himself, family members of Rysedorph, Cuomo and Falco were finally going to get some answers after all this time. As an added bonus, the press, once he gave them one last good helping of meat to feed on, would get off his back. The Evans saga would be wrapped up, and he could move on to other cases that demanded the time and energy Evans had sapped out of him all these years.

CHAPTER 31

For cops, an unsurprising facet of dealing with criminals on a daily basis is the unpredictability of the people who associate with them and the darkly arousing attraction some of those people harbor.

By the end of June, articles in the local newspapers were speculating that Evans was responsible for not one or two murders, but three. If this was true, and he had killed these men over a period of fourteen years, he was considered, by sheer definition, a serial killer—a brand that would bring a fleeting moment of fame to him almost immediately. Soon, letters from well-wishers—mostly females—came pouring into the jail as though it were Christmas and Evans was Santa Claus.

There was one particular letter that set Evans off on a tangent. It was from a young woman he had dated briefly in 1988. Ten years later, here she was writing to say it had "surprised" her to see his name and photo in the newspaper, but—at the same time—seeing his face had stirred up old memories.

I have to admit, you cross my mind every now and again, she wrote.

They had met at a pool hall. The woman, married at the time, complained she was being abused by her husband.

Being a young mother, she told Evans it was difficult to leave the man because he provided for her and the kids.

Evans's suggestion? A night of sex with him.

They had shared, the woman wrote, a common love for *painting, being creative, the arts and the Allman Brothers Band.* Her fondest memory was of spending a weekend with Evans in Latham at Cocco's Bar. They laughed. They joked. They played pool. They had "marathon sex." Life was good. Exciting. She had forgotten about her abusive husband.

A week or so after that, Evans told her he didn't want to see her anymore. She had become a number on a long list of females he had used over the years specifically for sex.

In her letter, she went on to explain how it had hurt her when he told her he didn't want to see her again. At the same time, though, she wanted to let him know now—ten years later—that she had always thought he was "kind, gentle, understanding, and a great listener." Because of the time they had spent together, the woman wrote, she ultimately developed the courage to leave her abusive husband and had been totally indebted to Evans all these years for giving her the guts to do it.

At the bottom of the letter, in large black scribbling, Evans had written, *Leave me alone! I love [Doris Sheehan].* Then he put the letter back in the envelope and wrote, *Return to sender* on the front. He had told Horton Sheehan was the only woman he had ever truly loved.

The message never reached the woman, however, because it was intercepted by Horton.

Doris Sheehan, a woman Evans had professed his love for throughout the past ten years or more, was someone Horton hadn't thought could help him much. "I considered her just another one of Gary's bimbos. . . . He had lots of them."

Horton and Evans had discussed Doris, and it seemed that whenever Evans ended up in jail, the one person he worried most about disappointing was Doris. In several of the letters he had written to Horton, Evans was always firm about his instructions for contacting Doris.

Tell her I love her, he wrote once. *Tell her not to worry about me. She is the only one I have ever loved.*

Inside the backpack the Bureau found on Evans in Vermont were a half-dozen Polaroid photographs of Doris. Sitting clothed, in various positions on a porch and next to a tree, her long mane of brown hair brushing over her shoulders and rather large breasts, Doris smiled for Evans as he photographed her. She appeared happy and seductive, relishing the attention Evans was giving her.

In the grand scheme of things, as Horton paced the hallway outside Evans's holding cell in Albany County Court, waiting for the marshals to release him, he thought about how he could use Doris as an asset. Bringing up Lisa Morris, Horton knew, was out of the question; she was the scapegoat, the person Evans could place the blame on for being captured. But Doris . . . she could be a bargaining tool; someone Horton could use to make Evans feel more comfortable.

Taking out his cell phone, Horton dialed his office and told Chuck DeLuca to find out where Doris Sheehan was. "I'm going to need her today."

The purpose behind interrogating Evans was to get him to give up Falco, Cuomo and Rysedorph. There was, really, no other reason to speak to him, at least not right away. As an experienced interrogator and former polygraphist, Horton knew he had to provide friendship and comfort to Evans if he expected to get anything out of him. He couldn't just sit him down and begin pressuring him to talk. Evans needed to direct the interview. It was the only way.

Only a few hours after Evans had waived his Miranda rights in front of Judge Breslin, a pair of marshals brought him out and indicated to Horton that he could take him.

Everyone involved, including Horton's own investigators, thought he was crazy for transporting Evans by himself. They were concerned Evans might try something. Branded an escape risk most of his criminal life, Evans was now facing the most serious time of his career. What did he have to lose?

"I wasn't worried, for the most part," Horton said later. "Gary had always said he would never do anything to hurt my career, and I trusted him, as he also trusted me."

Still, it wasn't such a bad idea to bring along someone else for the ride to Troop G in Loudonville, which was about fifteen minutes away.

During the ride, Evans sat in the backseat with one of Horton's investigators while Horton drove. Staring out the window, watching freedom pass him by, Evans whimpered and sulked, as if he were a child on his way to reform school.

"Are you hungry, Gar?" Horton asked at one point.

Evans, shrugging, said, "I guess."

"Good. Let me stop and get you something."

After stopping at a convenience store to pick up a box of Freihofer's chocolate-chip cookies and a gallon of milk, Horton brought Evans up into the "polygraph suite" on the second floor of Troop G, the same room where Lisa Morris had given her statement. There was only one way into the room, through a hallway door, yet two ways out: the door and window.

Playing it safe, Horton left Evans handcuffed.

Approaching a project of such magnitude, questioning Evans about several murders, could only be done in steps. Getting Evans back to Albany from Vermont had been the beginning; putting him before a judge to waive his rights was a good start; while getting him to confess, which could take days, maybe even weeks, was the pot of gold. Horton had waited eight months for this day.

As they were getting comfortable, Evans mentioned that he had one request, and he wasn't prepared to talk about *anything* until it was granted.

"What's that, Gar?"

"I want to see Doris."

Horton, without showing Evans, smiled. Still, it wasn't going be easy. Doris, Horton had found out, was herself doing time in a Troy, New York, jail for a DWI.

"Let me see what I can do," Horton said, leaving the room for a moment.

Horton had to find a second judge, Pat McGrath, and get him to sign an order enabling Doris to leave the jail she was in.

Within a few hours, Horton received permission from Judge McGrath to transport Doris to Troop G, which only added to the public pressure he already faced regarding his getting a confession out of Evans.

Sully picked Doris up and brought her to Troop G, where Evans was now sitting, like a child on a snack break, dunking chocolate-chip cookies into a glass of cold milk.

Dressed in an orange jumpsuit, Doris looked as well as could be expected, considering she was doing time in one of the toughest jails in the Troy-Albany region. She had even managed to lose a bit of weight. Evans, when he first laid eyes on her, perked up.

Horton made it clear he would not allow them to touch each other. There was no way he was going to step out of the room and leave them alone, not with three murders hanging over Evans's head.

After a brief hug, Doris pulled up a chair next to Evans and sat down.

"I'm not going anywhere," Horton said, staring at them.

Evans began pleading with Doris not to worry about him. "I'll be okay," he kept repeating. "Don't worry about me. Please don't."

Doris, who hadn't said much of anything since entering the room, finally spoke up. "I'm *not* worried, Gary."

"She was bland and kind of unemotional," Horton said later. "I had always heard from various individuals that she was nothing but a gold digger and hung around with Gary only because he had always given her expensive gifts.

"I'm sitting there listening to Gary tell her how much he loves her. . . . He's pleading with her, pouring his heart out, telling her not to worry about him. She just shrugged it off, like she didn't give a shit. I'm thinking, 'You bitch . . . at least pretend to be worried about him.'"

For the next three hours, Horton sat and watched Evans talk to Doris. At one point, they asked if Horton could take them outside so Doris could smoke. So he handcuffed them together and took them out behind the back of barracks near a grassy, picnic area. He had two investigators, sporting shotguns, stand nearby, but otherwise let them sit and enjoy what little sunshine was left to the day.

"I was chomping at the bit to get him to talk about Tim, Cuomo and Falco, but I had to play his game."

CHAPTER 32

After Sully took Doris back to jail, Horton pulled up a chair next to Evans. As calmly as he could, he explained the situation. "Look, Gar, we've been here"—Horton glanced down at his watch—"for about seven hours now. We've talked old times. . . . We've had lunch, cookies and milk. I even got Doris in here to see you." While Horton spoke, Evans would look up at him for a moment and then bring his eyes down toward the floor, as if he were being scolded. After mentioning Doris, Horton got up and walked over to the window. After pausing to look out at the setting sun, he said, "We have to talk about Sean, [Tim Rysedorph's son] now, Gar. Do you understand that?"

Seemingly surprised by the name, Evans looked away and started crying.

"Sean, Gar . . . the kid. Tim's son."

"What do you mean?"

"He's had his face pressed up against the glass on Christmas morning waiting for his father to come home," Horton said loudly, walking now toward Evans, "but Tim hasn't shown up, Gar. The kid still thinks his father is going to come walking through the door any day now. We need to give him a sense of closure."

It was approaching five o'clock. Nearly eight hours had gone by since they had arrived at Troop G, almost eight months since Horton had been hunting for answers regarding Tim Rysedorph. Tough questions were coming. Evans couldn't avoid the inevitable any longer

"I put Gary in an antisocial category," Horton recalled later. "In other words, his rules count and mine don't. One thing I knew I had to do was disassociate myself with the police: don't talk police lingo. Don't say 'we,' say 'them.' *They* were bad guys. I was a friend. He had to believe that, or I would have never gotten anywhere with him. When I brought Sean into the picture, I knew Gary would react to it. He loved children—or at least he said he did. Knowing that, I laid it on as thick as I could with Sean."

After letting Evans have a good solid cry, Horton walked over to him, put his arm around his shoulder, and continued. "Gary, you *had* to kill Tim Rysedorph . . . right? It was either him or you? I understand that, man. Come on. This is Jim you're talking to."

Not everyone would have agreed with Horton's tactics. But considering the amount of information and the seriousness of what he believed Evans was going to talk about, he felt the need to try to make Evans feel as comfortable as possible by making him think it was "okay to kill." If Evans had indeed killed Tim, Horton believed he had justified it in his mind somehow.

"I didn't want to sympathize with him," Horton explained later. "Because that tends to put someone down a notch and make them feel like they are below me. It's all technique when you're trying to get information out of someone. Sympathizing with someone makes me sound like, 'You poor son of a bitch. You are so fucked. But *I'm* not. You're the loser, not me.' It makes me sound as if I don't have those problems and I am better off."

Identification and common bonds are two other tactics interrogators use to extract information from suspects. One might say, "You fish? Great, I fish, too!"

"You had to kill Tim Rysedorph. I understand that."

Empathy, however, always produced the best results.

"I would say something like, 'I can feel how bad you feel. I don't *know* how you feel, but I can sense how it is for you.' In Evans's case, I told him, 'Gary, you're in a hole right now. We agree upon that. I can't jump in the hole with you because we'll both be in the hole together. If I get in there with you, neither of us will get out. What I *can* do for you is, throw you a rope and help pull you out—but you have to grab the rope yourself. You have to help yourself first.'

"I couldn't bullshit him and tell him everything was going to be all right . . . but I could let him know I was there to help. If that didn't work, I'd try to distance myself from the cops as much as possible, even though I was a cop. I'd say, 'I'm here to help you, Gary—not *them*,' meaning the good guys on the other side of the door. 'I'll do whatever I can to make this easier for *you*.' It's about offering emotion."

With that, Horton was hoping Evans might say to himself: *I can trust Jim. If he leaves me, I'm stuck dealing with those other cops by myself.*

Evans seemed to latch onto Horton's offering.

"Listen, Gar," Horton said, "I know you killed Timmy Rysedorph . . . and I understand why you did it. But I need to have his body. All you have to do is lead me to it or tell me where it is."

"It's going to be hard," Evans said, bowing his head, talking through tears.

Horton thought about it for a moment: *"It's going to be hard?" What the hell could that mean?*

"Why?" Horton asked. "You mean emotionally, or mentally?" He was confused. What could have been "hard" about it? The most recent, perhaps. But the hardest?

Evans didn't say anything, but continued whimpering.

Handing him a tissue, Horton gave it a shot. "Jesus, Gar, what are you talking about?"

Evans shrugged; he seemed embarrassed.

"You didn't cut him up, did you?" Horton asked out of the blue.

Evans looked up, smiled, and nodded his head up and down.

"Jesus. Is he in one location?"

Evans stuck up his finger: "One."

"How 'bout Falco?"

"In Florida," Evans whispered.

"Fucking Florida? What the hell—did you do him here, or down there?"

"I shot him here and brought him to Florida in the trunk of someone's car."

"Whose car? What kind of car?" Details made all the difference in the world. At this point, Horton wanted to be sure Evans wasn't taking credit for crimes he didn't commit.

"I don't remember," Evans said, losing his patience. "I don't *fucking* remember. It's confusing. I'm confused. It was . . . what . . . almost fifteen years ago."

"Come on, Gar. Whose car? Tell me whose car? You don't kill a guy, put him in someone's car and drive his dead body to Florida without remembering whose fucking car it was."

"Timmy's car. Okay. Timmy let me use his car to transport Michael's body to Florida."

Then it all made sense. Tim had to go because he was, as Horton had thought all along, a liability.

To say the least, Horton was curious about many things now that he knew for certain Evans had murdered Tim Rysedorph and Michael Falco. For one: Damien Cuomo.

"I shot him in the back of the head," Evans said without hesitation or emotion.

"Where is *he*?"

"Can't tell you, Jim. I can't let Lisa and Christina know any of this." Evans didn't want Christina to, of course, know that the same man she and her mother had befriended, the same man who basically moved into their apartment, was in fact the same man who had murdered her father.

"Is he in the Capital District?"

"Yes."

Trying to put his arms around what Evans had just told him, Horton needed specifics before he would allow Evans to take credit for the murders. It was going to be a long, emotional night. Hell, the next few days, Horton understood, were going to be the most productive out of the thirteen years he had known Evans.

"Tell me, Gar, will you take me to where Timmy is buried?"

"Yes. Brunswick . . . Route 2 . . . Eagle Mills."

"Now, let me get this straight: you cut him up?"

"Yes."

"With what?"

"A chain saw."

Horton stopped for a moment and looked away. *Jesus.* "Let me get this straight, you cut Tim Rysedorph up with a fucking chain saw?"

Evans nodded.

"Okay, Gar, you're going to tell me exactly what happened now. . . . I'm talking about Falco, Cuomo and Rysedorph. I want to know every detail. We'll start from the beginning, Michael Falco, and then you can explain to me why you cut Tim Rysedorph up with a chain saw."

Evans looked at Horton for a moment and didn't say anything.

Some time later, Horton met with Evans again. They didn't talk about much. But before Horton left, Evans kind of smirked at him, as if he wanted to say something.

"What is it?" Horton asked. "You're holding out on me, Gar. What's going on?"

"There are others, too," Evans said.

Horton paused. Closed his eyes, dropped his head, and began rubbing his temples. "What do you mean: 'others'?"

PART 2

TWENTY-FIVE TO LIFE

CHAPTER 33

Troy, New York, an industrial town of fifty-five thousand, is located along the Hudson River, which cuts a path through the city near downtown, about fifteen miles north of Albany. For the most part, Troy is a lower-middle-class haven known for the steel mill factories and oil refineries that had, during the 1950s and 1960s, dotted the banks of the river and thrived. Stove manufacturers, textile mills, stagecoach and carriage builders, breweries, bell builders, iron, steel and ore manufacturers, and even the detachable shirt collar were Troy's chief source of pre–Civil War employment up until the 1960s and 1970s. The old saying went, "When the streets [of Troy] are filled with smoke, jobs abound." Today, those same steel mills and factories are desolate and vacant, mere dwellings for rats and homeless people.

Most famously, Clement Moore's "'Twas the Night Before Christmas" was first published in a Troy newspaper in the early 1800s. Since then, controversy has surrounded who actually wrote the familiar story. Yet Troy natives cling to the fame the story has brought them for close to two hundred years.

Undoubtedly, Troy's most famous former resident isn't a politician, writer, actor or sports figure—but a meatpacker.

Samuel Wilson, the story goes, moved to Troy in 1789 with his brother and got a job at a local slaughterhouse. During the War of 1812, when Sam stamped the meat he packed with the phrase "U.S. Beef," soldiers receiving it began referring to the "U.S." portion of his stamp as "Uncle Sam." Still, contrary to the image most Americans have today of Uncle Sam, and the commercialism his likeness has taken on—the cotton white goatee and star-spangled three-piece suit—Samuel Wilson was a plain-looking man, clean-shaven and a bit on the homely side. In his day, Americans paid him little attention.

The buildings in Troy haven't changed much over the course of the past century; the same redbrick 18th- and 19th-century buildings reminiscent of Victorian England still stand tall on city streets and manage to embrace, with a bit of nostalgia, a town that has grown isolated and abandoned throughout the years. Entering Troy from the Village of Menands, the Troy-Menands Bridge, constructed in 1932, crosses the Hudson River at about sixty-two feet above the waterline. About ten minutes from downtown Albany, the bridge, painted a pukey green pastel color with horizontal steel girders and vertical steel beams, looks like a half-circle laid on its side. Traffic moves fast over the bridge that separates Rensselaer County from Albany County. On most mornings, the fog coming up from the river is so thick one might believe the old abandoned oil refineries along the riverbank below the bridge have been fired up again, or the steel mills are once again melting molten ore into bells and iron plates for Civil War ships.

But the reality is, the Troy of today, like a lot of East Coast American steel mill cities, is struggling in a difficult economy, trying to stretch what little work is available and convince people to stay.

CHAPTER 34

The year 1954 was a banner year in American pop culture history. Both McDonald's and Burger King opened their first fast-food restaurants. *Sports Illustrated* hit newsstands. M&M's were launched. Bazooka Joe comics were introduced, as was Trix cereal and Play-Doh. More seriously, Dr. Sam Sheppard was accused of murdering his wife, proclaiming his innocence by telling police a "bushy-haired man" broke into his home and committed the crime. In what would become an issue of heated debate some fifty years later, President Dwight D. Eisenhower signed the phrase "under God" into the Pledge of Allegiance, changing the popular school morning ritual from "one nation, indivisible," to "one nation, under God, indivisible."

On May 17, 1954, the Supreme Court weighed in on its ruling regarding what would turn out to be a landmark case in the civil rights movement. In *Brown* v. *Board of Education of Topeka, Kansas,* the court agreed that "segregation in public schools [was] unconstitutional," which, some say, "paved the way for large-scale desegregation."

For a man who would later develop a deep-seated hatred for African Americans—and have no trouble voicing his bigotry and disdain, routinely calling blacks "niggers" and Puerto

Ricans "spicks"—1954 was, ironically, the same year he had been brought into this world. On October 7, 1954, twenty-two-year-old Flora Mae Flanders Evans, who had lived in and around the Capital District her entire life, gave birth to her second child, a blue-eyed, pudgy little boy of about eight pounds she named Gary Charles. Five years prior, in 1949, Flora Mae had given birth to a girl, Robbie, fathered by her first husband, Ross Edmonds. Ross had abandoned Flora Mae shortly after Robbie was born so he could travel with the carnival. Leroy Evans, Gary Charles's father, came into their lives a few years later and, at the beginning, seemed to be a lifesaver.

Leroy's family of devout Catholics did not approve of the relationship between Flora Mae and Leroy. They felt debased by anyone who didn't follow the family's same strict set of religious guidelines, which Leroy had been set on a path toward from his birth in March 1932. Going to church wasn't an option; it was family law. Like many households back in those days, balancing the effects of the Depression and the fallout of two world wars, life for Leroy became pious, regimented and, in many ways, simple: attend school, church, study the Bible, never miss Sunday school. Poverty wasn't something families complained about; it was a way of life.

Because they had grown accustomed to a hard-knock life, the Evans family ran a tight ship and shunned those who weren't like them.

"We were not really welcomed into Leroy's family," Gary Charles's half sister, Robbie, recalled years later, "because my mom was divorced, already had a child and was Protestant."

Indeed, in the eyes of Leroy's family, Flora Mae was an outcast. If her first husband had left her with a child, there must have been a good reason behind it.

"They went to church all the time," Robbie added. "They were always loving to us kids . . . [but] hypocrites at the same time."

Leroy, Robbie claimed, was always treated like the "black

sheep of the family." His mother and father disowned him after he married Flora Mae.

Not too long after they were married and Leroy and Flora Mae set up a home in Troy on First Street, most of their new friends and neighbors, as well as the kids and Flora Mae, dropped the "Le" from his name and started calling him "Roy." An army air corps pilot in the late '40s and early '50s, by 1957 Roy had grown into a scrappy man with skinny arms and legs, an oval face and patchouli oil slicked-back black hair that shone like chrome. He would later brag to anyone who would listen about his tail gunner days and how he was routinely shot at by the enemy. He had a hole in the side of his stomach, Robbie remembered, but was embarrassed and never talked about it.

The Evans family lived on the bottom floor of a three-story, red-brick-faced apartment building, merely a block from the Hudson. The building had one of those monument-like concrete stairways leading up to the front door from the sidewalk, much like a 1920s-era big-city library. Along First Street, in any direction, were run-down bars and saloons, butcher shops, markets and five-and-dimes. The streets were narrow. When cars parked on both sides, the roads became tunnellike. The street gutters were always full of garbage, cigarette butts, soda pop bottles, cans and dirt. Like most kids in the neighborhood, for Gary Charles and Robbie, summer days revolved around stickball and dodgeball games, hopscotch and jump rope, while winter involved snowball fights and sledding and skating in nearby Washington Park. In between the Evanses' apartment building was an alleyway—or sandlot—where the kids could play tag or just hang out.

"We would just sit on the front porch," Robbie remembered later, "and eat Fudgsicles and drink RC Cola. We'd play games in the alley."

The late '50s and early '60s were prosperous times for Troy residents. With Uncle Sam murals spread about town, the city latched onto what had become an all-American relic and had become known as the birthplace of Mr. America. The city wasn't necessarily devoid of any trouble or social suffering, but industry roared along. There was plenty of work at the oil refineries and steel mills. The schools were respectable. Taxes were fair. There was a sense of community. Neighbors helped one another. There were block parties, PTA meetings, cookouts. People, generally, cared about one another.

With the vast mountains of Rensselaer and Albany Counties a fifteen-minute drive from downtown Troy in any direction, and the abundance of fish in the Hudson, Roy and Flora Mae hunted and fished as often as they could. Roy was a man's man; he liked guns and beer and all things masculine. Together, during the early years of their marriage, he and Flora spent time catching fish and shooting wild game, bringing it home to feed the family. The kids in the neighborhood, including Robbie and Gary Charles, would even get into the act. They'd use chicken scraps they found at the Chuckrow Chicken Plant on River Street, fasten them to safety pins and string and catch carp and eels out of the Hudson River. They would sell them, as Robbie later put it, to "the Jewish and Negro neighbors."

There was one time when a chicken from the Chuckrow plant got loose, Robbie recalled, and ended up in the Evans backyard. In a flurry of physical strength and determination, Flora Mae chased the young bird, cornered it and grabbed it by the neck. After snapping its neck as if it were a brittle twig, she chopped the bird's head off on the back porch in front of all the kids. "Chicken tonight!" she said, holding the headless bird in the air as if it were a trophy.

According to Robbie, life inside the home during those early years was, for the most part, normal and rather mundane. As long as, she was quick to point out, Flora and Roy were working and had money. When they didn't, and they had to depend on free food from nearby churches and warehouses, trouble arose. Additionally, Roy demanded that the kids stay close to the apartment. Robbie and Gary Charles were allowed to ride their bicycles down the block, between Washington and Adams Streets and back, but that was it. If they went any farther, there would be a price to pay. The apartment had a large picture window in the front living room. Roy would sit, chain-smoking Lucky Strikes, drinking Schaefer beer and listening to his police scanner. Every once in a while, he would get up from his chair and check on the children to see if they were abiding by his rules. It wasn't about making sure they were safe, a family friend later said, because Roy never worried about the kids in that respect. It had to do with living under his reign of power. If the kids disobeyed him, as they often did, look out!

Trouble—serious trouble—didn't begin, Robbie said, until after Roy got into a car accident and lost his job.

"He went through the windshield," she said. "Shortly after, he was diagnosed with epilepsy. He had seizures pretty often when he combined his medication with alcohol."

By then, Gary Charles, who had turned ten, was a scrappy-looking kid who wore thick, black horn-rimmed Buddy Holly–style prescription glasses, like his mother and father. As with most boys during those days, he sported a buzz cut, much like the astronauts of the *Apollo*. Neighbors and former friends recall him being "lost and quiet" for the most part, never really saying too much unless he was asked to speak. During his grammar school days, Gary Charles excelled, generally garnering straight A's across the board. He liked to read comic books in his second-story bedroom and watch Robbie and Flora dance around the living room while they listened to Mario Lanza, Hank Williams and Roy Rogers records. One of the more crowning moments in Gary Charles's young life came when Robert Kennedy, on the campaign trail, stopped in Troy and Gary Charles was photographed shaking his hand. The look in young Gary's eyes showed a boy who marveled at the prospect of being able to touch the hand of someone so powerful and famous. The photo appeared in a local Troy newspaper and brought him a meager brush of fame he enjoyed at home and school for days afterward.

Old photos of the family depict a child whose mother took pride in dressing her only boy. In particular, one photo that would resonate later with Gary Charles's life of crime shows a little boy dressed down in a three-piece black suit, black tie and white shirt. He is wearing a fedora, like Dick Tracy or Frank Sinatra. Smirking modestly, Gary Charles is the spitting image of Chicago gangster Al Capone.

CHAPTER 35

Flora Mae Evans, with her bony shoulders and frail arms, large breasts and hourglass figure, had always been an attractive woman in a Jayne Mansfield sort of way. In those early days of her marriage to Roy Evans, she wore taut black dresses and elastic-tight blouses to accentuate her shape. She kept her black hair kinky, in curls. A noted lover of art, she had aspirations of being an artist, and had even displayed her artwork at a Greenwich Village art show one year. She loved to draw pen-and-ink sketches and freehand watercolor paintings. She loved to dance and, at one time, had even wanted to pursue a career as a Rockette.

Former friends, neighbors and even Robbie later agreed, however, that an addiction to alcohol forever stood in Flora's way of ever pursuing a true calling or dream. After she met and married Roy, what had been a mere happenstance relationship with alcohol took on a life of its own. She began going out to bars and drinking around the house. By the time Gary Charles was three, Flora had already made several dramatic attempts at killing herself in front of the kids. As one story went, she was in her bedroom one day cleaning a hunting rifle; Gary was riding his tricycle through the hallways of the apartment; Robbie was in the living room watching television. Roy, sitting in his favorite chair by the picture window, was drinking a beer and smoking a cigarette.

"It's hard to distinguish which happened first," Robbie said later. "Either Gary fell off his tricycle and cried because he heard a gunshot, or [my mother] was distracted by Gary's crying and she missed her mark."

Either way, a shot rang out through the apartment and everyone hightailed it into the bedroom to see what happened.

"I ran into my mother's room," Robbie said, "and saw her lying backward on the bed. . . ."

There was blood sprayed all over the room. Flora had put the gun up to her chest but misfired and nearly blew her shoulder off.

A former neighbor, however, who was also there that day, recalled the incident much differently.

"Gary was all huddled up in the corner," the neighbor said. "I was there . . . in [Robbie's] room. I came out and heard Roy and Flora arguing. Roy shot her in the shoulder . . . nearly blew it off."

Regardless of what happened, after all was said and done, the incident was ruled a "cleaning the gun" accident.

As Flora Mae and Roy struggled to make ends meet, social and domestic pressure to feed the kids and keep the alcohol flowing began to manifest into anger, resentment and violence inside the home. With Roy out of work and home all day long, collecting disability because of the car accident he had been in, Flora had to carry the load. For the most part, she did odd jobs: manufacturing, garment, retail. Her longest run was at a Troy clothing manufacturer, Tiny Town Togs Girl's Dresses. She worked long days in an unair-conditioned sweatshoplike atmosphere, sweating profusely during summer over the shirts she pressed, and freezing in winter. When Tiny Town Togs didn't have work, she would scrub floors and toilets, along with pots and pans, for Jewish families in the neighborhood. Her one source of comfort after a long day of work became Thunderbird wine. The kids would find bottles of it in back of the toilets and in the "wringer washer," hidden from Roy.

"She had to hide [her booze] from Roy," Robbie recalled, "because if he found it, he would pour it down the drain."

Regardless of the chaos that was seemingly getting worse with each passing day, Flora would take Gary Charles and Robbie to the First Presbyterian Church, just down the block. Both kids were often awarded "perfect attendance" pins for showing up at church so regularly. They also attended Sunday school and looked forward to placing their envelope—all ten cents of it—in the offering basket each week.

As the '60s crept along and Roy became more complacent with life due to his being out of work and drinking every day, government assistance became a means of survival.

In his letters to Jim Horton many years later, Gary Charles wrote of a mother and father he utterly despised, and spoke of a childhood rife with violence and abuse of all kinds. Later, he hinted at being abused sexually by Roy, but would never go into too much detail with Horton for fear of, perhaps, having to relive the cruelty all over again.

"My father did things to me," he told Horton through tears, "that I wouldn't wish on anyone."

Evans had also told friends that Flora Mae had abused him sexually for years.

The more time Roy spent out of work—he would sometimes work as a bartender, but it would never last—the more despondent he became. He would sit for hours, on the back porch or in the living room, drinking, smoking and not saying much of anything. When he did speak, a neighbor later recalled, the loudness would seemingly shake the whole apartment complex. When he got mad at Flora Mae, he would chase her around the apartment and lash out at her violently with his hands or his favorite leather strap. Knowing how much Flora enjoyed listening to records, one day he destroyed her record player in front of everyone—possibly just to take away the one last bit of sanity and enjoyment she had left in life.

Jo Rehm had been a skinny little girl, taller than the other kids, with platinum blonde hair, almost white, and the sharp facial features of a bird: pointy nose, thin, caved-in cheekbones and tiny, beady eyes that cut right through whoever got caught in their gaze. Living at 158 First Street, directly next door to the Evanses, Jo later recalled Gary Charles as being a "quiet child" who wasn't allowed to have any friends or, like a prisoner, leave the confines of his bedroom.

"He was kept in the house most of the time," Jo said later. "Locked in his room like an animal."

One facet of Gary Charles's life that became a signature as he grew older was his absolute revulsion toward any type of meat. He hated chicken, pork and beef with a fervor—but especially liver.

"His father," Jo Rehm added, "would make him sit at the kitchen table for hours until he ate his liver. Gary hated liver. . . . We all hated liver."

Jo was seven years older than Gary, and Gary Charles and Robbie looked up to her as a "big sister." Jo said she would spend much of her time in the Evans household looking after the kids when Flora Mae and Roy were either too drunk, or had left the kids at home to go out to the bars. Jo's parents were also heavy drinkers, she readily admitted, and often drank with Flora and Roy.

The drinking in the house became an ordinary part of each day as Gary Charles grew toward his teenage years. He and Robbie awoke each morning expecting Roy and Flora to either spend the day on the back porch getting drunk, or inside the apartment drinking and fighting. As long as the kids did what they were told and kept their mouths shut, there wouldn't be any trouble.

But from an early age, Gary Charles was stubborn. He

did things his way. And when it came to eating liver, he flat out refused to do it as he grew older. When he refused, Roy looked at it as a question of his authority: Gary was being disobedient. It wasn't about the liver; it was about doing what the old man said.

"We used to try to hide the liver in the kitty litter box so Gary didn't have to eat it," Jo recalled.

When that didn't work, and Roy found it, he would beat Gary Charles senseless while the others looked on in horror. Other times, Jo would eat the liver herself so Roy wouldn't have an excuse to beat him.

Roy's weapon of choice was a leather strap he had used to sharpen his straight razor. Whenever he pulled it out—whether to sharpen his razor or begin slashing it lightly in his palm, warming it up for a beating, taunting the kids—they would scramble around the house as if they were playing hide-and-seek, searching for some sort of shelter from the terror they knew was coming.

Despite the beating he knew he was going to get, Gary became steadfast in his decision not to eat the liver. Roy would then break out his strap and whip his son until welts swelled up on his tiny frame. Then he would throw him in his room and refuse to feed him until the next day.

Because the apartment buildings were built so close together, Jo said, she would often open the window in her apartment next door and feed Gary cereal and chocolate-chip cookies through the alleyway.

"Many times," she said, "it was the only way he would get to eat."

Roy—thank goodness—never knew.

Sending a child to bed without dinner was a common punishment parents doled out in the '60s and '70s. If a kid wouldn't eat his peas or carrots, the mom or dad might give the entire plate to the dog and say to the child, "Go to your room!"

For Gary Charles, however, taking a beating and being

starved for twenty-four hours for not eating his liver would have been a reprieve for what some later claimed was one of Roy's most deplorable, violent punishments.

Using a piece of rope or a belt, Roy would strap Gary to a dining-room chair so he couldn't move. When he had him secured in the chair, he would, in between his taking pulls from his seemingly bottomless can of Schaefer beer, shove the liver down his throat until Gary ate every last morsel. Jo Rehm recalled several times when Gary would try to fight off Roy's force-feeding by squirming and twisting his head like a hooked fish. However, he would end up turning purple from choking on the meat and have to give in for the sake of being able to breathe.

"I went over there one time and Roy was nearly choking Gary with the meat, stuffing it down his throat," Jo recalled. "The cops had been called that day because I had pushed Roy when I saw what he was doing to my Gary. They told me I had to go home . . . and didn't even care about the fact that Roy was abusing him."

Robbie, her memory perhaps tempered by time, said she never saw Roy force-feed her brother, but remembered how insistent Roy was regarding the kids eating their liver and "cow tongue."

"Whatever Jo says is . . . true," Robbie said later. "She has a better recollection than I do. I guess my mind just blocks a lot out."

As Gary began creeping up to his teenage years, he began to show an interest in the same things most other kids did: cartoons, comics, sports. Like his mother, he developed a passion for anything having to do with art: drawing, painting, sketching. Roy would quash any fleeting childhood moments of enjoyment for Gary by not allowing him to watch television and refusing to purchase art materials for him. Gary, perhaps beginning to develop a demon seed, began to take it all in and not say anything.

"I remember him lying on his stomach in his room," Jo said, "with his head sticking out of the doorjamb. He was trying to catch a glimpse of television, while everyone else—including Robbie—sat and enjoyed it."

As Jo saw it, Flora Mae was no better than Roy. "She was a whore. A drunk. She didn't care about those kids."

Another childhood friend, Bill Murphy, recalled stories Gary would tell him about Flora Mae taking him as a child to a local "doctor's office," and making Gary wait outside the room and listen to them moaning and groaning their way through an afternoon of adulterous sex. Additionally, while Roy sat at home during those days and drank himself silly, a former neighbor claimed, Flora was also being paid by the owner of a local X-rated cinema to have sex with him.

As the alcohol abuse became more profound as Flora and Roy began spending more time at home, Flora turned once again to suicide as an answer.

For as long as anyone who hung around the Evans household back then could remember, Flora had permanent scars on her wrists from trying to kill herself so many times. Still, whether she was screaming out for help with the failed attempts or not, she tried other means.

One day, Robbie was hanging clothes in the backyard when a neighbor called out, "Robbie! Robbie!" pointing up at the apartment complex next door.

Flora was on top of the three-story tenement across the alleyway, hanging her legs off the side of the building, indicating that she was ready to jump.

As clichéd as it was, Flora chanted unassumingly, "No one loves me anymore. You will all be better off without me. I don't want to live anymore."

Robbie eventually talked her down.

"Mom would walk to the railroad tracks," Robbie added, "and wait for the train to kill her. I had to tell her that Gary and I loved her very much and could not live without her [and] she would come back home."

CHAPTER 36

According to some, Gary Charles began stealing comic books before he had even hit puberty—all with the blessing of his mother.

"Flora Mae was a thief," a close family friend said later. "That's how Gary learned to steal. She taught him."

Jo Rehm recalled a day when Gary was eight and had brought home a "$1,000 ring" for her he had stolen while he was out with his mother. From there, it seemed stealing became an addiction. He started taking whatever he wanted. Neighborhood bicycles became a favorite target. Packs of gum. Food. Car stereos. It didn't seem to matter. As time went on and he grew into a teenager, Evans would even play a Robin Hood role around the neighborhood by stealing jewelry and giving it to the girls. As he grew even older and began stealing from local thugs—drug dealers and other criminal types—the Robin Hood brand became even more pronounced. He wasn't the "bad guy," some said later, taking things that didn't belong to him; he was stealing from "people who deserved it."

Flora Mae and Roy's relationship had been set on a path of destruction, it seemed, since the day they had met back in the early '50s. By the fall of 1967, as Gary Charles turned thirteen, the structure of the Evans household was in a constant state of chaos. The only positive aspect of it all for Gary was that he was getting older—and bigger. Robbie was a sophomore in high school by this point. Albany Business School was beginning to take up much of her thought. She was thinking about moving out and leaving the area, maybe starting her own business someday. While Gary, who was retreating more into a world of solitude and silence, was thinking about traveling the country and "living off the land."

At thirty-five, Flora was still young and attractive, considering the hell she had put her body through due to several suicide attempts and a savage alcohol addiction. If she wanted to, she could certainly leave Roy and start all over again.

Jo Rehm, who had just turned twenty, moved to another neighborhood across town. Suddenly, Flora Mae, Gary Charles and Robbie's life raft, whether they realized it or not, was gone. Jo continued to ride her bike down to First Street to check on the kids—Gary specifically—but she wasn't there like she had been for most of Gary's early life.

"I loved him like a big sister. I worried sick about him and what Roy would do to him once I left."

However, Gary wasn't the boy Roy could manhandle and keep confined inside the home anymore. He was growing into a man, quickly. Still scrawny and shorter than most kids, Gary's body began to change remarkably. His arms and legs, for one, ballooned. He didn't even have to work at it.

Roy, at five feet five inches, about 140 pounds, hampered physically by his chronic use of alcohol and the car accident he had been in, was still a lot bigger and tougher than Gary. Yet Gary was becoming street-tough and fearless. Roy soon would have his work cut out for him if he challenged Gary in any way.

While Gary's body took shape, there were signs his mind was beginning to have trouble processing all the abuse he had been put through as a child. If throwing rocks at the neighborhood kids and beating them up once in a while wasn't bad enough, true signs of the serial killer he would later become began to emerge.

A former classmate and neighbor recalled how he had "been mean to cats." One incident that stood out involved Gary and another neighborhood boy.

"He tied the cat's tail [and] burned him up."

Being mean to cats and neighborhood pets might be part of growing up for some children. But this former neighborhood friend described an utter hatred, which borderlined on psychotic, that Gary displayed for the neighborhood pets. He seemed to enjoy with a certain dark passion the torture he had perpetrated toward the cats and the power he could wield over smaller animals.

For the past twenty-five years, psychologists, sociologists and criminalists have studied how being cruel to animals in childhood affects a person later in life. Many agree that a history of animal cruelty in childhood often leads to criminal problems in adulthood. The FBI, in the '70s, began to recognize, after reviewing the lives of several serial killers, that "most had killed or tortured animals as children."

Flora Mae finally got up the nerve to leave Roy in 1968. Within months after making the decision, Roy granted Flora a divorce and, just like that, she, Robbie and Gary had moved out of Troy and were living on their own just across the Hudson in Cohoes, New York. Gary had moved in with Jo Rehm for a brief period, but she was getting married. He had a home with Flora Mae in Cohoes. Why burden Jo with his problems?

Robbie, now eighteen, had enrolled in Albany Business School after graduating high school. By June, she had married a local man, but quickly divorced him, she said, after the relationship became abusive. For a time, Gary moved in with her after realizing he didn't want to live in Cohoes. Out on his own now, living in abandoned buildings and sleeping in abandoned cars and trucks, eating what little food he could scrounge up or steal, Gary developed a side business. He would do homework for nearby engineering students, providing they gave him a place to stay. When work became slow, however, he would break into Freihofer's trucks and steal chocolate-chip cookies to feed himself.

Flora Mae, as Gary and Robbie made a go of life on their own, married for a third time while living in Cohoes. But, according to some, her new husband was no better than Roy: an abusive alcoholic. After that brief marriage ended, she packed it up and moved to Astoria, Queens, New York, which was south, near New York City. Once there, she met "a man named Jim" and married for a fourth time.

"[Jim] was another drunk," Robbie later said.

While Robbie was pregnant with her first child, she visited Flora Mae in Astoria. She recalled how Flora had taken her to Rockefeller Center to go ice-skating. Life seemed calm for Flora while she was in Astoria. She appeared content for the first time in years. She had even planted a garden in the back of her apartment and grew vegetables. There's a startling image Robbie keeps of her and her mother during those years. They are standing next to a sunflower Flora Mae had cultivated that nearly reached the second story of the apartment complex. Flora appeared seemingly happy for perhaps the first time in her life.

If Flora Mae seemed to be in good spirits and health while in Astoria, it was all a front. She had developed pleurisy. Causes for the disease include a "bacterial or viral infection of the lungs (such as pneumonia), tuberculosis, lupus, chest injury or trauma, a blood clot in the lung, or cancer." An immediate cause, doctors say, is not always found. Generally, one can live a normal life as long as the condition is treated properly. Breathing becomes painful and sufferers complain of "sharp, stabbing" pains in the chest and stomach areas of the body. Flora Mae, who was never one to voice her ailments or problems, became "very ill" while living in Astoria, Robbie said later.

The pleurisy would become, in the years that followed, a subtle premonition of where her life was headed and the tragic way it would soon end.

By 1970, her fourth marriage had dissolved. So she moved north, to Pottersville. Within a year, she would give up on men entirely and begin a lesbian relationship with a woman who, some said later, was "the only person who had ever loved her unconditionally."

But regardless of the new love interest in her life, when Gary found out about the relationship, he disparaged her and told those around him she was "sick." Gary's bigotry was not confined to blacks and Jews and Puerto Ricans; he also claimed to hate homosexuals—but doubts about his own sexuality would later surface and cause one to question whether he actually hated homosexuals or himself.

By the time he turned seventeen, Gary was once again back in Troy, hanging around street corners, stealing food to feed himself, breaking into abandoned buildings to sleep and meeting up with old friends. It was the beginning of the seventies.

Free love. Drugs. Music. Sexual freedom. Vietnam.

Gary wanted nothing to do with any of it. He was a loner. He traveled by himself and worked by himself. He felt people pissed him off and let him down. Still, as he began to think about a career, there was only one vocation that interested him.

"I think Gary had dollar signs in his eyes," Jim Horton said later, "throughout his childhood and into his teen years. He always told me he wanted more than what he had. Instead of settling for what life brought him, he decided, from an early age, to take the 'easy' way out by getting more for less effort."

Early in his life, Gary learned that crime *did* pay. He could get what he wanted and not have to give up forty hours of his week. No boss. No coworkers. No one telling him when to show up, when to leave, what to wear.

After living on the street for what amounted to the summer of 1970, "stealing to survive," he later said, it was around this time when Gary became involved in petit larceny. He had even spent ninety days in a county jail after being caught breaking into a house. The sheriff who had arrested him, perhaps feeling responsible, ended up getting Gary a job at a local cemetery digging holes after he got out of jail. But it lasted only a few days.

"I, too, got him jobs over the years," Horton recalled. "In the early days, when I first met him, I talked a local landscaper into hiring him. But Gary called one day and told me that it was 'too hard' for him. 'I don't like people telling me what to do,' he said. 'I can make more money stealing.'"

By the mid-1970s, Gary hooked up with two old neighborhood friends, Tim Rysedorph and Michael Falco. They ended up sharing an apartment together on Adams Street, down a few blocks from Gary's childhood home. Tim lived inside the apartment with Michael Falco, while Gary lived out back in an old abandoned shed before moving in. Tim, who had spent two years in a Catholic school, a family member later said, "didn't care for Catholic school and went to public." He was a good kid, that same family member insisted. He just happened to fall in with the wrong crowd.

Michael Falco had a reputation around the neighborhood as being a troublemaker. He always seemed to be in the wrong place at the wrong time. Family members and friends later claimed Falco's troubles with the law didn't start until he met Evans. But law enforcement confirmed that Falco had been arrested on numerous occasions before Evans emerged back in town. Born on February 3, 1959, Falco grew into a handsome kid: curly black hair, parted in the middle, a thin face, high cheekbones, olive skin. He was scrappy and petite, about five feet six inches, 140 pounds. He was streetwise and knew the neighborhood.

Evans was four years or so older than Falco. They hadn't really hung around together much as kids, but knew each other from the neighborhood.

As Evans grew out of his teenage body and into his twenties, he became a rather large, muscular man that people around town feared. Because he was short, he was often compared to a wrestler. He began lifting weights obsessively and grew a long, square, wiry beard, much like that of ZZ Top frontmen Billy Gibbons and Dusty Hill. He wore bandannas and large Elvis-type sunglasses. In photos, he rarely smiled. His hair was kept hippielike, par for the times, down to his shoulders. For years, he camped in the woods. But now he was living with Falco and Tim—and beginning to set his sights on the future.

As a thief, Evans's appetite was no longer whet by car stereos, five-and-dime rings and pendants for the neighborhood girls. While studying antiques—reading books, browsing local antique stores, pricing items, disguising himself as a dealer, comparing items with shop owners, learning about expensive artwork and rare prints—he saw a gold mine. It was big-ticket items for Evans now: jewelry, antiques, rare books and pricey artwork. If he was going to take the chance of getting caught during a robbery, it was going to be well worth his effort.

CHAPTER 37

By January 1977, Flora Mae was living in upstate New York with her lesbian lover in what could be called the first "healthy" relationship she had ever been involved in. Robbie, beginning a new life, had moved to Florida. With Roy still living in the Troy apartment by himself, visited rarely by anyone, and Gary pulling off burglaries and robberies with his new pals, Michael Falco and Tim Rysedorph, it seemed as though everyone in the Evans family had gone their separate ways for good this time.

On January 13, Gary went through what can be called a "learning curve" in what had now become his sole passion in life. He had burgled a home in Lake Placid, New York, got caught in the act and was ultimately sentenced to four years in a state prison after being convicted of third-degree larceny. Even more brawny now, at about 155 pounds—all of which was lean, cut muscle—he was getting his first taste of hard prison time at Clinton Correctional Facility in Dannemora, New York. It would be the first of almost two dozen serious arrests and the first of several prison bids.

The prospect of being confined behind bars for so long scared Evans; it was apparent in some of the letters he later wrote to family and friends. The main focus of his insecurity came from doing his time with, he said, "those people: spiks, niggers, faggots and diddlers (child molesters)." Drug dealers were also on his list of "scourge." If he had contained a seed of hatred for anyone he saw as being lower on the food chain than himself because of their color or creed, now he was being thrust into an environment where his life would be centered around those same people.

Evans harbored such a hatred for African Americans that he couldn't as much as look at a black person without saying anything hurtful. There was one time when he and Horton were driving back to his apartment after a meeting and Horton had driven by a few black guys who were walking down the street minding their own business.

"Fucking niggers," Evans said, staring them down as Horton drove by.

"Come on, Gar," Horton shot back. "There's no reason for that shit."

"They are wasting my oxygen," Evans said, shaking his head.

It was, no doubt, a seed that had been planted by his father, who himself was an admitted racist.

The Clinton Correctional Facility in Dannemora, where Evans was being held, had a reputation as a no-nonsense maximum-security penitentiary where the state of New York sent some of its most hardened criminals. Considered a "supermax," Clinton is the "largest and third oldest of New York's seventy facilities." More than 150 years old, it was built as a mining prison back in the 1800s. Located 350 miles north of New York City and seventy-five miles south of Montreal, Canada, it was known as "Little Siberia"—mainly, one would have to imagine, because of its close proximity to Russia, New York and the fact that northern New York generally enjoyed only two seasons: winter and fall.

Not that it mattered to Evans, but six months into his bid at Clinton, his father, at fifty-five, lost a battle with throat cancer and died at an Albany veteran's hospital.

"Roy died a lonely old man," Robbie Evans said later. "His family contacted me a month after his death; he said that's what he wanted. I shed one tear and that was all. I did not mourn his death."

Whereas Robbie had acknowledged Roy's death, Gary never mentioned it.

While confined at Clinton, Evans began to lean on Robbie for support. The tall concrete walls, loud and crowded hallways, outside rifle towers and razor wire kept it real. This wasn't the county jail. It was hard time in a setting Evans had never—and would never—consider himself a violent enough offender to be subjected to.

There is a saying many inmates live by behind bars: "Don't let the time do you; you do the time." As Evans began to count the days until his release, he started writing letters and sending drawings to Robbie. He talked about everything: from what he was going to do when he got out, to the filthy and vile behavior he was witnessing while locked up, to how and why his life had turned out the way it had.

One of his favorite forms of writing became poetry:

Sister Robbin,
Thinking about yesterdays.
Not every day was alone and gray.
The times I wasn't alone, a helper sometimes came to talk. And try to let some sunshine in.

Named for a bird, [you] should've had my eyes.
But brown isn't bad.

A little big sister golden hair.
Nobody knows when nothing shows.
Where will you go from there?

Growing up and sometimes apart.
Still she's one of the few invited to my movie.
Technicolor true-life now time.

At the end of the letter, which was written entirely in verse, he finished by writing, Not *a good time, but rainbows are coming!*

He soon started to include drawings with his poetry. He drew mountains and stars and landscapes. In one, he sketched a naked man sitting on the ledge of a cliff. The man had long hair brushing down his back. He was grabbing at the grass below him and throwing it off the cliff into the wind. Although he had denounced vehemently the lesbian relationship Flora Mae had been involved in now for a few years, the drawing and the accompanying poem had been addressed to her.

I sing now with eyes that rain, Evans wrote. *My freedom and I are back again. I sit on stone and sing of alone. Free.*

Convicts are transferred from one prison to another during their sentences for a wide variety of reasons, largely because of overcrowding. New York State, however, one of the more populated states in the country, had always been in the top five states for housing the most prisoners. Because of overcrowding, New York was constantly moving prisoners from one facility to the other so it could maintain open beds for the flood of inmates it processed each month. When a prisoner became too familiar with a certain facility, or a prison gang began to bulk up in size in one prison, certain inmates were transferred to discourage any behavior that might get out of hand. It is a common part of prison life to wake up one morning in one prison and go to bed that same night in another.

About midway through his sentence at Clinton, Evans was transferred to Great Meadow Correctional Facility in Washington County, New York, southeast of Lake Placid. It wasn't because Evans had become unruly or had joined a gang. In fact, he had done everything by the book and became known, as the cliché goes, as a "model prisoner."

Great Meadow was a facility geared more toward helping inmates acquire an education and deal with the many social and mental problems they either had before they became part of the system or developed as a prisoner. In terms of getting closer to freedom, Great Meadow was a stepping-stone; getting transferred to Great Meadow meant Evans was on his way out the door.

While at Clinton, Evans had developed such a respectable reputation as an artist that inmates began commissioning greeting cards from him. He would draw cards for birthdays, Mother's and Father's Day, along with other holidays and special events, dotting them with an incredible artistic hand that he had likely gotten from his mother. Making just $7 per week working, he would trade the greeting cards for commissary items: Twinkies, doughnuts and cookies.

On the street after serving two years out of a four-year bid, Evans wasted little time going back to his old behavior. Burglary was about the only thing he knew how to do, he would say years later. Burglarizing homes and antique stores came easy to him and he was good at it.

Since his release on March 31, 1980, he went back to living with Michael Falco and Tim Rysedorph. Run-down, seedy and unkempt, the apartment became more of a place to crash during the day rather than anything else. At night, Falco and Evans would go out and commit burglaries—either separately or together—and use the apartment as a place to store their stolen property and set up other jobs. Tim, who, some later claimed, was only dipping his toes into the pond of thievery his roommates were swimming in, began to focus more on his music. Tim, many claimed, was never a guy who had planned any of the crimes; he more or less went along for the ride, at times, to make some extra cash.

Evans and Falco fell into a routine: stealing and fencing

stolen property. Day in and day out, they were either working on a score or setting one up. They had a "fence" in Troy who could turn stolen property over for them quickly, so it became a matter of "don't shit in your own backyard" that initially drove them to commit burglaries in other parts of the state. They would bring the merchandise back to Troy to sell, but would rarely steal anything in town.

In the spring of 1980, Evans was caught with a few hundred dollars' worth of stolen property he had lifted from an antique store in upstate. Already on parole, finishing two years of a previous two- to four-year bid, he was sent directly back to jail to await a court hearing to decide where he would serve the remainder of his previous sentence, along with any additional time from his most recent possession charge.

By May, Falco, now twenty-one, was sentenced to three years' probation for his role in a local bookstore robbery in 1979.

For the time being, their burglary run was over.

Old Rensselaer County Jail, in downtown Troy, where Evans was being held awaiting sentencing, was a nondescript, two-story, white-brick building that took up an entire block. Out in back of the building was a steep incline. The city, on a weekday, bustled with the ebb and flow of daily life around the jail as if it weren't even there. There was a large courtyard on the west side of the building with about a ten-foot-high barbed wire fence surrounding it.

For Evans, doing time in county jails was like living at a shelter, a dormitory atmosphere he could handle. Within days of being at Old Rensselaer County Jail, he befriended several members of the Hells Angels motorcycle gang, who had a large clubhouse in town. The Angels liked Evans. He kept his mouth shut, worked hard behind bars and never gave anyone any serious problems.

Sitting in his cell on Thursday morning, June 12, 1980,

Evans came up with a rather unique—if not ambitious—idea. Because of his size, he figured that if he got together enough Angels—who were big, like NFL linemen—they could hoist him over the fence outside in the courtyard during "rec time" when the guards weren't watching. Two Angels would start a ruckus in one area of the yard, while two others would literally throw him to freedom.

The plan couldn't miss.

Like anything else Evans had ever set his mind to do, he proceeded to wait for the right moment. At about 10:30 A.M., while two Angels began to brawl on the north side of the yard, two other Angels, swinging Evans like a pendulum (one holding his arms, the other his legs), rocked his small body back and forth a few times. With one gust of strength, they heaved him over the fence as if he were nothing more than a fifty-pound sack of potatoes.

Just like that, Evans was on the other side of the fence, a free man.

During roll call later that morning, prison officials realized Evans was gone. Once word spread that he had taken off, guards sent word out and soon a posse of law enforcement was scouring the area.

About five hours later, he was spotted atop the Troy Public Library on Second Street, standing by the ledge.

"I'm not coming down," he yelled as police, armed with shotguns, moved in on him.

"There is no possible way you can get away, Mr. Evans," someone yelled up to him. Onlookers cheered him on as the fire department moved in with a cherry picker.

After an hour-long standoff, cops wrestled Evans to the ground by his hair and brought him back to Old Rensselaer County Jail, where he was put in solitary confinement.

When he was placed back into the prison population some time later, Evans would go on a rant, bragging how he had made a mockery of the guards and local police.

"It was all a joke to him," Horton recalled later. "Gary told me about that day and remembered it with vivid precision. He knew he wasn't going to get far—especially seeing that he had climbed to the top of the library. All he wanted to do was make a laughingstock out of all of them . . . and, in many ways, I guess he did."

CHAPTER 38

September 11, 1980, would be forever etched in Gary Evans's mind as a day his life took a remarkable turn for the worse. After revoking his parole, he was sentenced for the second time in four years to another two- to four-year bid at Clinton Correctional, a prison that had already, in his mind, stripped him of over a year of his life, for second-degree possession of stolen property and first-degree escape.

On October 7, 1981, Evans spent his twenty-seventh birthday behind bars at Clinton. It was the third time in his young life he had celebrated his birthday while incarcerated. Once again, as he settled into a routine of being told what to wear, when to eat, sleep, shit and work, he started writing to Robbie.

For Robbie, the dysfunction she had grown up in as a child and the cold feelings she developed for her father as the years after his death passed were now nothing more than memories. She had set up a rather productive and healthy life for herself in Florida with her boyfriend and son, *Devan*. She was happy. Her only contact with family came in the form of letters from Gary and phone calls to Flora Mae once in a while. Over the years, Gary had taken a particular liking to his nephew, Devan, and talked about him as if he were his own child.

Between April 1981, seven months into his bid, and December 1981, he wrote Robbie about a half-dozen letters. For the most part, he talked about a new passion he had developed while in prison for making stained-glass-window portraits. *I smeared my fingers with shit and drew pictures,* he jokingly wrote. Then, more seriously, he explained in detail to Robbie how to take an everyday piece of glass and turn it into a "new art medium," always reminding her that there was "money" to be made in doing it.

Prison life was rough for him this time around. He couldn't "practice martial arts," he said, because "stretching and kicking" weren't allowed. In fact, at one time he had been locked down for two weeks for doing what he called "kung fu–looking" moves.

In some respects, the bigotry he had fostered throughout most of his young life began to dominate the tone of his letters.

I could trade three cartons of cigarettes ($15) and have a homo visit my cell for a few hours, but I'm not into that.

In the same letter: *There's a nigger fag all my friends are busting on me about, because he always says "hi" and goes wiggling by me when we're lifting weights.*

Throughout the letters, it was clear that the time was once again "doing" Evans.

I've gotten no mail at all! Doing ok. . . . I hate this place and wish I could go someplace nice.

Robbie wasn't writing back to him on a regular basis. She would answer some of his letters, but not within the timeframe he would have liked. In just about every letter he wrote, he began by asking her why she wasn't writing back.

The further into the bid he got, the more he began thinking about parole: *In nine months I'll see the parole board . . . and in 22 they* have *to let me go!! That's in 684 days—I did 433 so far!!*

Then, *I'm wheeling, dealing and stealing anyway I can. . . .*

By November, now a year into his sentence, the regimented

structure of prison life had taken its toll. His interaction with other inmates, the surroundings and being confined nearly twenty-four hours a day began to wear on him.

Robbie, in the few letters she had written, encouraged him to move to Florida when he was released. Start fresh. Begin a new life. She was family. He loved his nephew. Why not, Robbie kept insisting, move to Florida and start from scratch?

Just back from talking to [Devan], Evans wrote. *The more I talk to you guys the better an idea it sounds to go there. I just hope they'll parole me this coming spring. . . .* Later, in the same letter, he added, *Sometimes I feel like I'd just like to get a shotgun and payback about a dozen people, but I know I'd have to go back to living on the road.*

There were certain people in Troy, he insisted, who had "rolled" over on him and traded information about crimes he had committed to save their own ass. Enemy number one was Michael Falco, he said, who, he believed, had given him up in trade for a lesser sentence.

I know if I end up staying in New York, I'm not hanging out with anybody. *I'll be thinking real hard if I feel I have to do something—it won't be just any "random" quick-money thing. I can't stand being in jail anymore. I'm falling apart physically & mentally. . . .*

And then came the most disturbing section of the letter: *The Civil War against the niggers will be happening soon—and I'm going to be a hero in that. I'd like to have a place in New York for all of you guys to come because there's bad odds in Florida.*

Ending the letter with his standard phrase, *write soon,* he added, *I just read that Florida is 8th city [*sic*] for crime, Miami first, West Palm Beach 3rd . . . full of niggers + spiks. I hope there's places where they ain't. And if I have to cut my hair for a job, that's out!*

Life for Gary Evans was about living under *his* rules. If whatever happened to him didn't fall under a set of guidelines he had constructed, he blamed everyone but himself. In all the letters he had written to Robbie throughout his first year back behind bars, he never once took responsibility for any of the crimes he committed. It was always somebody else's fault.

CHAPTER 39

Gary Evans hadn't planned on being in prison for much of 1982. But as February came and went, he was still wondering when the parole board was going to hear his case and release him.

On March 19, a Friday, the parole board finally called him in. That night, he sat down and explained to Robbie in a letter what had happened.

The reason why he was refused parole, he claimed, was because it had been his second time upstate and he was still on parole from a previous sentence: *They want me to speak to a counselor regularly regarding my anti-social behavior.*

To him, it was all a joke. He said he would do what he had to do to make parole, but refused to admit there might be something wrong with him. He viewed everyone around him as "lowlifes" and "scumbags." He saw his future as being no different from his past. He was in prison not because he was a criminal, but because he had gotten caught.

There's a lot of things I have to do in N.Y. and I know it'll be stupid of me, but I can't help it—I'll end up coming back. . . . I'll never return to jail again—I couldn't do that to myself. This one here has totally wrecked my head. I have to try everyday not to let myself come out of this shit too vi-

cious, but it's hard when I think how I got fucked over by all those people. And it's still continuing.

Flipping back and forth, he would say how much he wanted to move to Florida when he was released, but then explain how *Florida is really getting overrun by all those stinking spiks. . . .*

One of the more bothersome aspects of doing time, he said, was that he wasn't allowed to lift weights or work out regularly: *I trimmed off a lot of excess weight. I lost some muscle, too, because I don't have weights. But when I get into lifting my bag of books or my bed, I tighten up again.*

If there was one dominating characteristic that seemed more evident as Evans's time behind bars accumulated, it was his remarkable nerve. Whether he was building it up more for his big sister, he made it clear he wasn't afraid of anyone: *I have a lot of serious problems with the Hell's Angels [*sic*], but I ain't worried about them on the street.*

Indeed, his problems with the Hells Angels had only just begun.

By September 12, 1982, the New York State Department of Corrections (DOC), knowing Evans would be getting out on parole within the next few months, transferred him nearly four hundred miles west to Attica State Prison, one of New York's most feared, legendary and hardened institutions, where the worst of the worst were housed. Serial murderers. Serial rapists. Child killers. Mobsters. Black Panthers. Deviant sexual predators. And high-profile criminals of all types.

Attica had a history fraught with blood and violence. Back on September 13, 1971, after what amounted to a four-day "revolt," NYSP troopers stormed the prison and ended up killing thirty-two inmates and eleven corrections officers. Since then, the prison was reviled as a place of bigotry and hatred toward African Americans and Puerto Ricans, who had staged the "revolt," demanding to be heard about their concerns for "poor living conditions" inside the prison.

The DOC, in sending Evans to Attica, was perhaps sending him a message—because in all actuality, he had never committed a violent crime. He was a burglar who had, by that time, never been involved in an armed robbery. He had, however, been arrested eight times (burglaries and petit larcenies) within the past ten years, which made him a habitual offender. On top of that, on September 8, 1981, just a few days before he had been sentenced, he had threatened a few inmates he was being corralled with at Albany County Jail and had to be isolated from the general population. A few months in Attica before he was released, many were saying, might just teach him a lesson.

As soon as he arrived at Attica and got settled, he began writing to Robbie: *Well, if you got the telegram, you know I've been sent to Attica. I got a real Shanghai job! It was done just to spite me, also with the hope that some harm would happen to me here. I'm now in protective custody because there are too many Hell's Angels [*sic*] here. . . .*

Isolated by himself, letter writing became Evans's only way to vent his frustrations. He wasn't allowed into the general population of the prison, and the time he spent by himself, alone, cut off, insulated, began to weigh on him mentally: *I* cannot *do anymore time in a* cage! . . . *There's a lot of people who would love to see me . . . hurt or dead, and I'm not going to please anybody by letting any of that happen to me.*

As the time beat him up, Evans started to mention a former girlfriend, *Stacy*. He hadn't seen her in years, but a tattoo of her name on his chest indicated he'd had a rather intimate relationship with her at one time. From his viewpoint, one would guess they were long-lost lovers, involved in perhaps a ten-year relationship. But, in truth, Stacy had been one of his high school sweethearts. Anyone who knew Evans had gotten an earful of Stacy at some point. He was obsessed with her. Sitting in his cell, confined twenty-four hours a day, Stacy became the object of his affection—someone with whom he could create a fantasy world around. And so, as he fixated over her, obsessing over her in letter after letter, he began making plans to see her when he got out: *I believe that I'm going to begin looking for [Stacy] and there's going to be some obstacles to that. I haven't figured out what I'll have to do about that.*

Stacy had moved out of Troy years ago. She was married. Had a family. Lived a normal life with her husband and children. It was a good bet she hadn't even *thought* about Gary Evans since leaving Troy: *A lot of things concern [Stacy]. . . . I don't want to ruin my life for some bitch, but I* will *see her again, and if I have to force the info out of somebody where to find her, that's what I'll do. . . . There's a lot of people who deserve some bad deeds after all they've done to me.*

It was clear that his main source of vitality became revenge as he plotted and planned what he was going to do when he got out of prison. In one breath, he would talk about finding a job and settling down to a normal life, and then go on about getting back at every person who had ever, in his opinion, done him wrong.

Time and again, he blamed his burglary colleagues for his being locked up: *Man I hate this place more than anywhere or anytime in my life. I'd strangle the bastards responsible for sending me here if I could.*

Then, in the same letter, *That asshole in Troy . . . is doing eight months in the county jail, but he gets out in March. If I get free before him, I'm going to spend some time with his girlfriend, sell everything he owns, and visit him in the county jail.*

Later, *So many people owe me money that haven't done anything to help me out, they're going to pay when I get in their face!*

Again, anyone who had ever crossed paths with Evans and not served his needs was to blame for his most recent incarceration. In his clouded mind, it had nothing to do with his own behavior: *Sis, Do you think you can imagine how much I want those scumbag lowlifes in Troy who got me busted, beat me for my money? I get the chance right and*

I'm going to drink their blood, and I'll take pictures when I'm doing it. . . . These people are paying!

He went on to talk about a "shitlist" he had developed while isolated in his Attica cell. Some thirty-seven names were on the list, he wrote, but *I left a lot off!*

Later, Horton would agree that as Evans sat isolated in Attica, he began talking himself into becoming something he hadn't been up until that point in his life: a murderer. There he was—alone, angry, disconnected from the world—focusing on anyone who had ever looked at him the wrong way.

I don't think I can manage them all, he wrote, again referring to his "shitlist," *but the important ones will definitely see my smiling face some dark night, and there's going to be some screaming, begging, crying snake bastards when that time comes. . . . I feel like making headlines as a vampire mass murderer. I feel like filling up a private graveyard.*

Then, *Just six-and-a-half more months.*

CHAPTER 40

Confined to his cell at Attica, counting the days until parole, Evans was living the life of a "hermit," he opined in a letter to Robbie on September 29, 1982, merely a day after he had written his last letter. There were times when he was so lonely and unable to do anything else, that he would begin a letter in the morning and continue writing all day long. Some of the letters were set up in the form of a journal. Morning, noon, night. He would leave his cell to eat, then return and write to Robbie what had happened during dinner. A guard would come by and give him a hard time, and he would write about it.

By this point, his beard had grown about eight inches below his chin. He had even drawn an "actual size" picture of it in one letter. The picture looked more like Jesus than perhaps Evans resembled, and what he wrote underneath it certainly didn't have any pious connotations: *I still want to fill a private graveyard.*

The more he wrote—almost daily—the more concerted an effort it became to plan his future. Job? Home? Going clean? None of it seemed to interest Evans. Moving out of the country? Hooking up with old crime cohorts? Finding those responsible for his latest incarceration? This was what fed his motivation to survive. He had lost a considerable amount of weight and had been skinnier than he had ever been in his life. Unable to lift weights and eat a regular diet of what he liked—cookies, cereal, milk, doughnuts, Twinkies—he was forced to eat loaves of bread and cake that "taste like shit."

In every letter he wrote from October to December, he insisted that it would only take "$200" to get him out of prison. He begged Robbie for the money. He was also furious, he said over and over, because she rarely wrote back. The parole board wanted to be certain, he explained, that he had money and a place to stay when he got out, or it wasn't going to release him early. The $200 could pay off the debt he had accumulated while in prison and leave him enough cash to get on his feet. Every day, it seemed, became his last day behind bars.

I should be out in a week!

A week would go by.

I should be out next week.

Another week would pass.

Maybe next week.

In a November letter, he talked about Flora Mae for the first time since being behind bars: *I don't know, I think something happened to mom. I haven't heard from her yet, and she was all happy that I let her visit me . . . 1rst [*sic*] time in 5½ years, and I gave her a painting + she said she'd write.*

When Thanksgiving 1982 came around, he floated the idea of leaving Troy when he was released and never seeing "anyone" again: *I know I cannot be around ANY people. I don't need any girl around except rarely (and don't really need them then); I've done without for six years now, 3 months in between. I don't trust anyone, male or female. . . . I can go weeks without saying a word. . . . I'd make a good monk, wouldn't I?* Then he sketched out a plan for himself if he were to ever receive a sudden windfall of cash. The entire plan centered on material possessions: boats, cars, motorcycles, houses and land. Interesting enough, at the end of the list he indicated how, in fact, he might go about getting his hands on the cash: *I also know [someone] that put a gun to [someone's] head + took a few lbs. of coke. . . . There's ways and ways and ways. A lot of things I won't do but a lot I will do. I'd rip off a crook in a minute, that shouldn't be illegal to do!!*

On December 13, 1982, he wrote what would end up being his last letter for a while. He seemed upbeat and happy. Parole was in reaching distance now, he had been told. Robbie had, after weeks of his begging and pleading, scrounged up the $200 he needed to pay off his debts. The only obstacle standing in his way now was where he would be going when he was released. His parole officer wanted him to go back to the Capital District, find a job and live at the Salvation Army until he could find a "room" of his own. He, in turn, said he couldn't because there were Hells Angels "after him." He wasn't, he explained, going to get killed "that easy."

In any event, he promised he would move back to the Capital District. Once there, he figured he'd explain to his parole officer the dilemma he was in with the Angels and was convinced parole would allow him to move to Florida.

Be it the elation he felt after hearing he was going to leave prison any day or the fact that he didn't want to end up right back in prison, he wrote, *I have thought more often of just leaving the assholes I don't like alone. Not all of them, but most of them. I'll just leave [them] to their shitty lives.* But near the end of the letter, he couldn't resist: *I have to have a couple [of them], though.*

Many of Evans's burglary victims would later pounce on the New York justice system for continually allowing him to walk away from his prison bids early. Some would even claim he was trading information about drug deals and weapons and other crimes he learned about while in prison for time.

His letters, however, proved otherwise. According to his own words, Evans was merely a product of the DOC. He was just another number on a list of inmates who could get paroled early as long as they stayed out of trouble while in prison and told their parole officers what they wanted to hear.

Hitting the brick on December 29, 1982, for the first time in nearly two years, Evans began looking up old friends immediately—specifically Michael Falco, who himself had just been released after doing a brief bid for burglary.

Within weeks of hooking back up, Evans and Falco pulled a few small jobs together and then parted ways. By January 1983, Evans had found his way to Florida: the beach, the sun, the women.

Robbie was living in Lake Worth, Florida. She had been doing pretty well for herself. Mainly spending time at a trucking business she had started, Gary was Robbie's only connection to back home. Since his release, he had bulked up bigger than he had ever been in his life. Photos from that era show a man with legs like tree trunks, rippled with muscles. His arms were close to seventeen inches around. His neck and shoulder muscles bulged inside his clothing as if he had stuffed padding underneath. His ZZ Top beard, now nearly reaching the tip of his heart, was always groomed well. Obviously, he took pride in his body and loved to show it off.

Flora Mae hadn't been keeping in touch with her children all that much throughout the past few years. She was living in Pottersville, New York, with her lesbian lover, in a trailer owned by a bar that was also on the same premises. Her alcoholism had taken on new heights. She was drunk all the time.

On February 6, 1983, Gary, Robbie, Devan and Robbie's new husband took a drive from Lake Worth to Tampa to visit Robbie's in-laws. It was a beautiful day: blue skies, turquoise water, lots of skin and sand.

When they arrived back home later that day, the NYSP called to inform Robbie that Flora Mae had been found dead.

Robbie, though, was too overtaken with emotion to continue the conversation, so she handed the phone to Gary.

Flora Mae had, according to Robbie, cashed her Social Security check that day, paid what little rent she owed and then went to the bar to have a few drinks.

"When she left the bar," Robbie added, "she slipped on the ice as she was about to put her key into her car door . . . and hit her head on the bumper of her car."

Doesn't make much sense, considering the bumper and the car door on any vehicle are at least five feet from each other. Nonetheless, because there was no one around—it was near midnight—Flora Mae, lying unconscious from the blow to her head, froze to death "in a fetal position" near her car.

The next morning, a neighbor found her. Only a few months before her fifty-first birthday, Flora Mae Flanders Evans was dead.

Later, as the years wore on, the story behind her death took on a life of its own. "She was a drunk," some said, "who passed out in a snowbank and froze to death."

There was even one story that tagged Gary as her killer. Yet it was impossible, unless he flew to Buffalo, New York, early that day, drove to Pottersville, murdered his mother and flew back to Florida that same day.

Gary and Robbie took a train to Albany the same day they got the call and had Flora Mae cremated so they could "take her with them always," Robbie said. Gary didn't want anything to do with his mother's ashes. Robbie scattered some of the ashes in a reservoir where Flora Mae liked to fish and threw some on a parkway in North Carolina "so she could fly with the birds and be at peace with nature."

CHAPTER 41

As the lilacs began to bloom and the ground thawed in the Capital Region during spring 1983, Evans was back on the streets of Troy running with his old "business partners," looking to set up a few jobs. It had been only months since Flora Mae's death. But Evans was never one to dwell on pain. His mother and father were gone. His sister lived in Florida. Alone now, he pondered his own misconstrued notion of what the future held. He didn't want to find a "real" job, or even begin to think about going straight. He had made quick money in the past burglarizing homes, businesses, antique shops and jewelry stores. He had done hard time in the nation's toughest prisons and survived. All he wanted now was the perfect score. Once he had enough money, he was taking off on what he referred to as a "tour."

Still, there were some loose ends in Troy he had to clear up. Either while in prison or shortly after he had been paroled, it was never made clear, Evans found out that a few Angels had roughed up a judge's son pretty bad. *They broke his face . . .*, he later wrote.

Because of what he knew about the incident, a district attorney in Troy had been encouraging him to testify before a grand jury. His testimony could help put the perpetrators behind bars for a long time.

For Evans, nothing he ever did came without a price. In fact, in some of his later letters to Robbie, he claimed that the DA's office in Troy had even promised to trade his testimony for a few charges he was facing regarding a "market [he] tried to hit."

There was one problem, however. Word among criminals on the street traveled like junior high gossip. No sooner had Evans begun talking to the DA's office, then he developed a reputation on the street for being an informant. Interestingly, he had chastised and threatened some of his old business partners in letters to his sister for the same reason, yet here he was doing it himself.

On another level, Evans looked at the Hells Angels situation as a "get out of jail free" card. He felt that if he got caught doing another burglary, he could simply float his grand jury testimony and walk—that is, providing the Angels didn't get him first.

With Easter, 1983, fast approaching, Evans was back in Troy living with Tim Rysedorph and Michael Falco on Adams Street. Since Evans's departure, the apartment had become, not only a place to sleep, but a storage facility for stolen merchandise, according to law enforcement. A favorite spot was in the floorboards.

Evans's latest run with Rysedorph and Falco, however, wouldn't last long, because on April 22 he was picked up for burglarizing a home. While out on bail for that charge, he was picked up *again* on May 10 for grand larceny and burglary.

At the time, he still owed the New York parole department sixteen months from his previous two- to four-year bid, for which he had been released twenty-four months early. Even if, by some mere happenstance, he beat the latest charges, he was still looking at a year or more for violating his parole.

After he spent a few days behind bars in Saratoga County Jail, where he had been picked up, Evans's court-appointed attorney visited him to discuss what—if any—options he had.

"You can't beat this case," his attorney insisted.

"I'll plead guilty to two misdemeanors," Evans said, "as long as I get sentenced to sixteen months and do the time here!" He could have agreed to a lesser sentence of twelve months, but the time would have to be served in a state prison, something he wasn't prepared to do. The last bid had broken him. State prisons were "hell," he said later. They hardened people.

"I'll see what I can do."

Evans was always thinking ahead. In Saratoga, a county jail that generally held people awaiting sentencing, he knew he was safe from the Angels. Out in the state prison system, there was no telling where he would end up, or who he would run into. Doing an extra four months in a county jail would be far easier than facing a pack of Hells Angels in Attica or Clinton.

Within a week, his lawyer returned with some good news. The DA agreed to the sixteen months in county. He ran the risk of getting transferred, but he would never see a state prison, at least that's what the DA promised.

According to Evans, he had set up his latest burglary so he could secure enough money for a piece of property he wanted to buy in his sister's name in upstate New York or Vermont. Sitting in jail once again, counting the days until his release, he realized his dream would have to wait for at least one more year.

You were almost a property owner in N.Y.! Evans jokingly wrote to Robbie on May 10, 1983, just days after he began serving his sentence. *I thought I'd be making some decent money. . . . Oh, well, have to cancel that one for a while.*

Talking about an appearance he had made in court to seal the deal with the DA's office, Evans carried on about the behavior of some members of the state police he had witnessed while in court: *You wouldn't believe the way [they] were lying. Under oath even. And trying to look all righteous and truthful. Man it got me pissed.*

It was around this same time that members of the Bureau began showing up at the jail to talk to Evans. They were fishing, trying to see what he knew about certain people. Evans had no trouble giving up information when it served him. There were times when he would brag about major drug deals he had heard about in Troy and Albany on "such and such" a day. He hated drug dealers. He believed a drug dealer was no better than a child molester or rapist. Stealing from them, in his mind, wasn't a crime; he was doing the public a service. Furthermore, giving up information about drug deals was a bartering tool. He could have cared less if word ever got out and he became a target.

By July, he had been given a release date: September 16, 1984. What made this date special was that not only would he become a "free man" once again, but he would no longer be on parole. To Evans, parole was bondage. It was like being held hostage by the system. It had nothing to do with his paying back society for his crimes; to him, it was "the man" holding him down. In September 1984, he would be clear to go wherever he wanted, do whatever he wanted, without being tied to a parole officer.

A short time before the Fourth of July holiday, 1983, Evans penned a succinct letter to let Robbie know where he was. After explaining briefly that he was clear of any "problems" with the state police, he wrote, *A guy I do things with got busted and bought his way out by telling on me. He knew about music equipment I got because he helped me sell it—guns also. . . .*

A few weeks later: *The State Police brought a fed to see me. I arranged to have my nice gun dropped off. No charges against me. No problems. My whole troubles started when a guy I have known for years, and have done a lot of things with, got caught in Vermont. He started telling on me to get out of charges he had here in New York.*

Members of the Bureau later confirmed that the "guy" Evans was referring to in that letter was Michael Falco: *Anyway, I gave back my gun and a $900 power saw I got for cutting safes.*

Regardless of how hard he tried, Evans couldn't get over the fact that he was playing a game of "you tell on me/I tell on you"—a game he and Falco had been ostensibly playing with each other for years. The old cliché, Bureau investigators later acknowledged, was true: *"There is no honor among thieves."* They give up one another on a routine basis. It's just part of who they are.

The DA in Troy who had been pursuing a case against a few Hells Angels had begun to finalize his plans for putting Evans in front of the grand jury. The pressure was on. A judge's son had been beaten severely. Someone was going to pay. In August, Evans would be expected to tell the grand jury everything he knew about the assault.

But first [the DA's office] had to agree not to try to charge me, Evans wrote, *with the market I tried to hit.*

Once again, Evans had escaped any real hard time behind bars. He would be out of jail in September 1984 and, most important, totally liberated from parole. Nevertheless, with two felony convictions under his belt already, if he got caught and convicted of a third felony (any serious crime punishable by more than one year in prison), it was possible he would be branded a persistent felon and face twenty-five years to life. This scared Evans. The thought of being locked up that long shook him up. Still, as he began to make plans for his release, he couldn't comprehend that it was his own behavior that had put him behind bars to begin with. He repeatedly blamed anyone but himself for being locked up—and continually vowed to pay each and every one of them back after he got out.

There's people in Troy that have to pay, and people that

jammed me up . . . and I know enough now not to do anything with anybody. I should have known before!

Whenever he was locked up for more than a night or two, Evans would begin to obsess over what he was missing on the outside, fantasizing and dreaming about the most obscure things. His latest pipe dream included building a "dream house" in the woods when he was released. He said he "deserved" it after all he had been through in life. Where he was going to get the money was never an issue. He just assumed a "big score" was going to fall in his lap one day.

He also mentioned a "para-plane" he desperately wanted to buy when he got out, and even drew a picture of it. It was a helicopter about the size of a large lawn tractor. It had a parachute attached to the back of the seat. The propeller was in the back of the vessel as opposed to on top. Most interesting to Evans as he explained it was that there was no way it could crash. *It goes 35 MPH, but will climb to 6,000 feet (over road blocks!). Only needs 50 feet to take off or land. Folds up into a car trunk!!*

He called himself "Evans the air pirate." He talked about traveling around the country, apparently committing burglaries at will, but being able to avoid police as if he were some sort of superhero.

In August 1983, Evans finally went before the grand jury and implicated members of the Hells Angels in the beating of a local judge's son. The way he saw it, because of what he had done for the DA, his record would be wiped completely clean. He was under the impression that when he was released in September 1984—one year away—he would be an absolute free man—"no parole"—for the first time in seven years.

CHAPTER 42

The next year was a cakewalk for Evans as he finished his sentence. He had been transferred to Warren County Jail, north of Albany near the Vermont border. A new program had been initiated at Warren whereby inmates who had proven they could stay out of trouble and act reasonably sane were afforded the opportunity to work outside the prison grounds on the interstate picking up garbage. Surprising to Evans, he had been chosen to participate in the program shortly after his arrival. What's more, when he wasn't outside soaking up the sunshine between 8:00 A.M. and 4:00 P.M., he now had access to weights and a gym. He had put on about fifteen pounds of muscle since he had been incarcerated and was bench-pressing, he claimed, about 120 pounds more than his own body weight. His ZZ Top beard had grown long and thick and now nearly reached his nipples. It was clear in his letters that he was happy for the first time in years. The only real trouble he had gotten into while at Warren was a scuffle with a "child molester," whom he had pummeled one night after the guy began pestering him.

As he counted the days until his release, Evans trumpeted the idea to his sister that any future "jobs" would have to be done alone if he wanted to avoid prison in the future.

"No partners" became his mantra.

One of the downsides to doing a longer sentence in the county jail system was the anxiety of knowing you could be transferred at any moment. Just when an inmate might get comfortable and develop some sort of routine, a transfer would undoubtedly come through. Thus, by the end of February, Evans had been moved to Montgomery County Jail, about one hour west of Troy. But a month later, he was back at Warren. The main reason inmates were moved around like checkers while in county jail was the need for beds. As the mid-1980s progressed, cocaine distribution became the number one source of income for drug dealers, and the drug of choice for buyers. Troy was known as a refuge for hard-core drug users and drug traffickers. Logistically, it was the perfect location for major dealers in New York City, where the mother lode of cocaine generally came in, to traffic the drug throughout upstate New York, New Hampshire, Vermont and even Canada.

Dealing drugs wasn't something Evans had ever wanted to get involved with. He had always said how much he hated drugs and drug dealers. But robbing big-time dealers of their cash became a potential new business he began to think about pursuing after his release.

A big shipment of coke came up to Troy (with a wimp!), he wrote, *from Hollywood, Florida. But I found out too late to ambush it.*

In that same letter, he spoke of an "Italian friend" whom he was going to hook up with when he was released. *But no felonies till I'm ready. Just lil' stuff.*

That Italian friend, he promised, was going to introduce him to a new line of work, which could, he insisted, yield huge amounts of cash quickly.

Long before the Bureau's senior investigator Jim Horton had ever considered becoming a cop, Albany native Doug

Wingate was chasing down bad guys and working cases as an investigator for the Bureau in Loudonville. Wingate had joined the NYSP as a trooper in 1968. He was asked to join the New York City division of the Bureau as a narcotics officer in 1972, but he declined the position because of what he described later as a serious "cut in pay." Wingate had a part-time job on top of working a lot of overtime as a trooper. Working in New York City would have meant being away from his family for long periods of time. He would also have to put the brakes on his part-time job, which he didn't want to do.

"They held that against me," Wingate said later, laughing a bit at how ridiculous it seemed that because he had turned down the NYC offer he wasn't offered another position with the Bureau for almost ten years. "Back then," he continued, "the test question was: 'Would you like to go into narcotics?' If you said no, they held it against you."

Either way, Wingate never looked back, and had "no regrets," he said, about a career that would ultimately span some thirty-six years.

By 1979, he was working in Loudonville, Troop G, as a Bureau investigator, for the most part looking into burglaries, robberies, rapes, sexual assaults and murders.

At five feet nine inches, 195 pounds, Wingate was cookie-cutter perfect when matched up against the rest of his Bureau counterparts. He was garrulous and conniving when he needed to be, friendly when the job called for it, and even crass, authoritative and brassy when he felt a suspect had information he needed.

The perfect cop, in other words.

Wingate had met Evans a few years before Horton walked into Troop G as a green investigator. It was spring 1981. At the time, Wingate was stationed in Brunswick, a little town in the mountains just north of Troy. Each Bureau barracks had what investigators called a "Back Room"—an in-house nickname for a group of investigators that, basically, investigated anything that fell under the heading of "crime."

In those days, Brunswick was a bit of a reprieve from the hustle and bustle of Troy. There were large, stately homes with well-manicured lawns and expensive cars parked in three- and four-car garages. Ten-story pine trees—faultless triangles of nature—dotted the countryside. A hilly town, with streets snaking and twisting around valleys, mountains and streams, Brunswick was scenic and hunter-friendly. People moved to Brunswick to get away from the confines of city life. It was quiet. Private. People kept to themselves.

For Evans and his cohorts in Troy, however, Brunswick became a treasure trove of potential merchandise to steal. Most people didn't equip their homes with alarm systems back then, or didn't feel the need to, so breaking and entering into homes for Evans and his cronies became as easy as walking through the door.

One characteristic that had set Evans apart from those with whom he burgled was his cleverness. He was always looking for the perfect way to steal.

"Gary was very intelligent," Doug Wingate said later. "I'm not talking just as a thief—but an intellectual. He would read books, cover to cover. Study those areas he wanted to excel in."

When Evans realized what Brunswick could offer him as a thief, he didn't think twice about focusing on the town as a place to turn out quick, small-time jobs that would ultimately finance the bigger jobs in other parts of New England he had always dreamed about. Further, Wingate explained, Evans had an astute quality to the way he spoke and could carry on an educated conversation about anything. This impressed Wingate. He had become used to dealing with criminals who were, for lack of a more appropriate term, "stupid," he said. Many had chosen a criminal life because they couldn't make it in the real world. But not Evans. He could have done anything he wanted, Wingate was quick to point out, and been successful at it. When he applied that knowledge and general intelligence to turning jobs in Brunswick, he realized quickly the windfall the town offered.

Evans had always viewed burglary as a full-time job. When he applied his smarts to it, he came up with several unique ways to steal that simply amazed cops when they found out later. One of his favorite things to do, for example, involved scouring parking lots of five-star restaurants, jewelry stores and antique outlets for luxurious vehicles: Mercedes, BMWs, Jaguars, Cadillacs. Once he found a vehicle that interested him, he would look inside the car to see if the owner had left his or her garage door opener clipped to the sun visor or somewhere out in the open. Then he would break in, steal the opener and rummage through the glove compartment, hoping to locate the car registration to find out where the person lived. Once he had the address, he would write it down and literally walk into the home after opening the garage door.

"I knew the person wasn't home," he said, "because they were at the restaurant eating dinner. It was the perfect score."

In 1982, Wingate was investigating a string of burglaries throughout the upper north country, which included Warren County, Essex County and Hamilton County. During that investigation, he had developed a contact in Troy by the name of *Tyler Jacobs*, a two-bit thief who had a reputation for beating up people. Jacobs was a "strongman," known more for his ability to break legs than anything else.

One day, Wingate got a call from the state police in Bennington, Vermont. A trooper explained that Jacobs and another notable Troy thief, *Raymond Bosse*, a guy Evans knew pretty well, had committed a burglary. Jacobs had been caught in the act and was locked up in Bennington. Bosse had escaped when the cops showed up, took off for Troy, but was caught by two Back Room troopers in Brunswick.

"Bosse was a pretty tough kid," Wingate recalled. "There

was a whole crew of these guys who were burglars. Really tough kids. They did not do drugs. They did not drink. When they went out to do a burglary, they were stone-cold sober. Professionals all the way."

Bosse was, indeed, no slouch. He had arms on him almost as big as Evans's, but he was taller and heavier. When Wingate went in to talk to him, he wouldn't say a word. Because he wouldn't talk, and he had committed a crime in Vermont, Wingate had him shipped back to Bennington to face charges there.

Throughout the years, Jacobs had become one of Wingate's informants, and always had information about what was happening on the street. As a criminal, though, one of his downfalls was that whenever he had his back against the wall, he talked.

"Before I left to go to Bennington," Wingate said, "I got clearance from the DA to give Jacobs carte blanche on any burglaries or larcenies."

After getting hold of Jacobs's attorney, Wingate set up a meeting.

Over the next two days, Wingate and Jacobs built a rapport and talked about several different unsolved burglaries in and around the Capital Region.

"Tell me about some of the *other* burglaries," Wingate said, just to see what Jacobs was willing to talk about.

"Am I home free on those, too?" Jacobs asked.

"I'm sure I can take care of that."

"There's a meat market in Guilderland. I did that job with Raymond Bosse."

"You're a codefendant; how can I get Bosse?"

Raymond Bosse was someone the DA's office, Wingate and other members of the Bureau were looking at for some time. He was a "tough guy," Wingate recalled, "a wise guy, in the sense that we wanted to get him on more than what we had."

"Well," Jacobs said, "I know he's just a codefendant, but

if you really want Bosse . . . talk to this guy named Gary Evans."

Wingate had never heard the name before.

Puzzled, Wingate asked, "Who is Gary Evans? Why would he want to talk to me?"

CHAPTER 43

Over the next few days, Tyler Jacobs, looking to trade information for jail time, continued to talk to Doug Wingate about Gary Evans and, moreover, the burglaries Jacobs knew Evans had been involved in.

This, of course, piqued Wingate's interest. Perhaps Evans could shed some light on some of the Bureau's unsolved burglaries. In particular, there was a jewelry store heist in Oneonta, New York, Jacobs said Evans had masterminded. The Bureau had been trying to solve the case for nearly a year.

"Gary went down there one day with a kid named Mike Falco," Jacobs said, "and they cased the place out. They went back there that night and, for whatever reason, Mike chickened out."

"What happened then?"

"Well, they took off. But Gary went back the next day with Raymond Bosse."

"You didn't go with them?"

"No. Evans decided they should take a Greyhound bus to do the job," Jacobs continued. "They wouldn't be noticed that way."

"What?"

"Yeah, a fucking Greyhound. Gary is smart."

"What's he look like?"

"He wears a bandanna all the time. You can't miss him. Once you see him, you won't forget him."

Wingate began by running Evans's name through the system. After a quick search, Evans turned up at Saratoga County Jail. He was halfway through his most recent bid, with a release date set for September 1984.

When Wingate showed up at Saratoga, he and Evans had, what he called later, a "standoff." Evans just stood there, sizing Wingate up. Then, after a few moments, asked, "Why the fuck would I *ever* talk to you?"

Wingate said, "I don't know much about you. But my goal right now is to do Raymond Bosse. I need help on a couple of cases he was involved in. One is a meat market job in Guilderland . . . you know all about that, don't you?"

Evans became enraged. "I didn't do that!"

"Well, I know you didn't."

"I don't do anything in Albany County."

"You do know about it, though—"

Evans wouldn't let Wingate finish a sentence without interrupting.

"Still, why the hell am I going to talk to *you*?"

"Look, if you're just going to stonewall me," Wingate said, "fuck it. I'll just go to Ray and we'll talk about going to Oneonta on the bus and . . ."

That seemed to lighten Evans up some. Wingate hadn't given up Tyler Jacobs as his informant, and wasn't about to. But he wanted Evans to know—without coming out and saying it—that he wasn't just dangling a carrot. He was working with solid background information.

As Wingate continued, Evans stared at him in disbelief: *How do you know so much about this job?*

"I know you went down there with Mike Falco. I know he chickened out. And I fucking *know* you went back with Bosse."

"Wait a minute," Evans said.

"You know, Gary, when you take a bus to a little town like Oneonta, you really shouldn't wear that bandanna. You went in and cased the place. . . . Who is going to forget you? Just look at yourself!"

"Okay . . . okay," Evans said. "What do we need to do?"

"You need to start by telling me all about the meat market job."

In the end, Wingate and the Albany County DA's Office used Evans and Jacobs to nail Raymond Bosse on the meat market heist, and within a few months, Bosse was indicted.

That one chance encounter Wingate initiated with Evans, however, would turn out to be much more. It was, for Evans, the first time in his career as a thief he had truly trusted law enforcement and wasn't burned.

What was odd about Doug Wingate and Evans's first encounter, and the fact that information Evans provided ended up putting Raymond Bosse behind bars, was that Evans, in his letters during that same period, blamed Bosse for his latest stint in prison.

I talked to the state police investigator, Evans wrote on September 29, 1983, *that (so far) hasn't lied to me (that I know of, anyway). He says I have no problems anywhere. . . .* Later, in the same letter, he added, *I positively learned one thing: Don't ever let anyone know what I'm doing. [Raymond] got talkative to the wrong people and here I sit.*

CHAPTER 44

The closer Evans got to his release date, the more he began to focus on revenge. It was clear that prison life, once again, was getting to him. He complained about "authority having a hold on" him. About being confined "like an animal" when there were serious criminals walking the streets, committing evil acts and getting off. Yet, regardless of what he talked about, Evans always brought the subject back to what he was going to do to those people who had, in his mind, been responsible for every day he spent behind bars.

You know I have a lot of hate, he wrote, *for a lot of people—and eventually that will be straightened out.*

A few months before he was released, he came up with a rather unique plan to avoid capture when he got out and inevitably he promised, started a new reign of burglaries—a plan, indeed, straight out of a spy novel.

After talking about the serious money he was going to be making with the Italians he met recently, he wanted to have the Italians point him to a "crooked doctor" so he could "get skin grafts" on his fingers. His reasoning behind the painful surgery? In what sounded like a child's voice, he wrote, *So I can't never be proved to be me.*

Evans insisted he was going to stay in the Northeast when he got out of prison, because it was "where [he] wanted to be." But in his next letter, he changed his mind and began talking about moving to West Virginia. Houses and land were cheap there, he said. Then, in typical Evans fashion, a week after that, he was thinking Connecticut, Maine or New Hampshire: *I'm getting the hell out of New York.*

Those last letters written before he was released were shrouded with paranoia: *I think how easy it would be for a parole officer, a cop, or a Hell's Angel [sic] to plant something on me and get me busted—like a gun or drugs. . . . It'd be my third felony, twenty-five to life. There was this nigger that had two felonies. The Angels were looking for him. So he started keeping a pistol in his car. They found out and told the cops, and the cops stopped his car. He got twenty-five to life.*

Like he had in the past, Evans began setting goals for himself that were entirely unattainable. The amount of money, for example, it would take for him to give up burglarizing, he said, was an enormous figure he could not possibly have ever made. *I figure if I make a minimum of $500,000 I won't have to rip-off again.*

During the summer of 1984, he began talking about someone he called his "best friend."

He doesn't do any criminal shit. . . . He's like me, stays alone, no drugs or drinking. He's just into bands.

It had to be, law enforcement later said, Tim Rysedorph. According to Evans's letter, "Tim" had been laid off recently. This bothered Evans. He wrote if it had been him, he would have *burn[ed] the place down after [stripping] it.*

Evans's developing psychosis of shedding blood when he got out of prison was, one might argue, directly related to his upbringing. The rage and anger he voiced in his letters had always been flavored with anecdotes about his childhood, interwoven with stories of getting back at those who, he believed, had turned on him.

For example, as he battled with himself, debating on paper whether to kill when he got out or not, throughout his prose were memories of the hell he had gone through as a child: *I didn't really grow up with anybody when I think of it. I never went outside thanks to that dead asshole [Roy Evans] who I plan blowing out of his grave sometime in the future.* And it wasn't enough for Evans that his father had died an early, horrible death; he wanted to kill him all over again. *Maybe I can talk myself out of my bloody plans afterwards. I don't know. Only time will tell. Probably can.*

Doug Wingate, as he got to know Evans throughout the years, pointed out later that Evans's father was, indeed, one of the main sources fueling Evans's violent behavior.

Whenever Evans had been picked up, the police had always found several handcuff keys on him.

"I asked him one time why he carried all those handcuff keys," Wingate recalled later.

Besides the obvious reasons, Evans said his motive was much deeper emotionally, and far more personal.

"He said to me," Wingate added, "'I was handcuffed long before I was ever arrested.' So I questioned him about it. I wanted to know what he meant by that."

Evans then began to talk about his childhood. He said his father would handcuff him to a post in the basement of their First Street apartment and savagely molest him in the most vile ways.

This deep-seated hatred for his father undoubtedly played a part in his behavior later on. In 1984, as freedom drew closer, he projected that "hatred" he often spoke of in his letters toward those people he thought had been responsible for his incarceration. *I think sometimes if I could buy some land in the mountains and go away by myself for a long time I could get all the hate out of me, but now I know it's too late.*

A death wish began to materialize as the months and weeks until his release turned into days and hours.

As far as becoming a mellow old artist in a stone home in Vermont, which he had often written about, *that's a fairytale. I'll never be old, and I really don't care. I know who I am. I hate all authority. Respect none. I live for revenge and that's all.*

CHAPTER 45

Be it overcrowding, or the fact that Evans never caused that much trouble while in prison, he was set free on March 31, 1984. What he had dreamed of all along (getting out of jail without the umbra of parole hanging over him), however, wasn't going to be a reality. Because he was being released early, he was placed on a "conditional release program," which simply meant he was on parole until his sentence was exhausted. For the next nine months, he would have to be on his best behavior, once again reporting to a parole officer.

With no direction and absolutely no intervention with any sort of postrelease program to set him on the right track, Evans went back to committing burglaries right away.

On January 10, 1985, Evans's conditional release expired. He was totally free now, unconstrained from any type of parole.

Since his release almost a year ago, he had again been living with Michael Falco and Tim Rysedorph. Although Tim had devoted himself to his music and rarely—if ever—participated in any of the jobs Evans had been doing at the time, Falco had become, in many respects, Evans's partner.

Near the beginning of February, a friend of Evans's told him about a flea market in East Greenbush, a little town just southeast of Albany, where there was a lot of "gold and valuables." This interested Evans. He loved stealing gold and jewelry; both were easy to pawn and hard to trace.

A few days afterward, Evans confided in Damien Cuomo, a known thief in the neighborhood, someone with whom he had just met, and asked him if the flea market in East Greenbush was worth the effort.

Cuomo, Evans said later, agreed it was a good location to burgle. It was set back from the road and no one was ever around at night.

With that, Evans went to Falco and asked him if he wanted to do the job. "Go check it out first," Falco suggested. "See if they have anything worth our time."

East Greenbush, New York, a mostly white, middle-class suburb of Albany, presented Evans and Falco with a plethora of potential targets. Most notably, the large flea market on Route 9 that Damien Cuomo had sanctioned. Flea markets were a common faction of Albany County's culture and economics. With large strip malls spread about East Greenbush, many antique dealers set up circuslike tents and offered customers a wide variety of items. From simple 99¢ knick-knacks to $5,000 and $10,000 paintings and statues.

What interested Evans most as he walked around, casing the place one afternoon, was the setup of the place. He and Falco, he realized, could get in and out quickly, and take with them plenty of gold.

The East Greenbush Plaza Flea Market, as it was called, located at the intersection of Route 20 and Route 9, was always a favored spot for "antiquers." A one–story building, antique dealers could rent out spaces along an arm of the mall. It was a fairlike atmosphere, vendors and customers bartering and trading, trying to get the best price.

On February 16, a Saturday, Evans and Falco loaded up Falco's brown Plymouth Satellite with a rope ladder, some common burglar tools, two empty duffel bags and a police scanner.

"You ready, Mikey?" Evans said as they took off.

"Let's do it."

At thirty, Jim Horton was a young and eager Bureau investigator working for the East Greenbush division of Troop G. By February 1985, Horton had hit the year mark as a Bureau investigator. He had been married to his high school sweetheart, Mary Pat, for five years. His son, Jim, was four years old, and his daughter, Alison, had just been born on February 3.

Horton was hungry. He needed to make his mark as an investigator and prove himself worthy. For the past three years, he had been literally working double duty. For the most part, he was a "road trooper," chasing speeders on the interstate. But on an "as needed" basis, he was also part of an elite team of troopers who had been chosen, after a rigorous set of tryouts, for the dive team. They were called out at various times to search lakes, ponds and rivers for dead bodies. It was rewarding, Horton, an admitted thrill seeker, said later, but at the same time caused him some problems at home.

"My wife was against it because of the danger involved and the fact that our job centered on finding dead bodies."

As the years passed, and Mary Pat realized how much it meant to her husband to be part of the group, she accepted it. Yet it still didn't make it any easier.

"There is always some fear in the back of your mind when you are married to a cop," Mary Pat recalled later. "You think of things like him being left bleeding on the side of the road after a routine traffic stop goes awry. . . . These images pop into your head. You can't prevent them. But as an optimistic person, I have always felt we were decent people and that God wouldn't let anything that horrible or tragic happen to us. Maybe that is naive. But it sure helped me get through each day."

Since joining the Bureau, Horton hadn't been involved in too many cases of any merit. He had investigated burglaries and robberies, larcenies, sexual abuse cases and rapes, but nothing that put what his superiors knew were his expert investigative skills to the test.

The East Greenbush Bureau didn't operate as a twenty-four-hour, around-the-clock police force. Because of the type of work involved, investigators were split into two shifts: 8:00 A.M. to 4:00 P.M., 4:00 P.M. to midnight. Since the East Greenbush division didn't have a cop at the station all the time, they would trade off on being what Horton later referred to as the "call guy."

The call guy would take a beeper home with him and be on call for the night. If any crimes that needed intervention by the Bureau took place throughout the midnight to 8:00 A.M. hours when no one was around, the call guy would be asked to begin an investigation immediately, while the remainder of the shift showed up in the morning.

Evans and Falco took off at about 11:00 P.M. on February 16—Falco drove, Evans road shotgun—with the thought that the flea market in East Greenbush would be vacated for the night.

When they arrived, Evans suggested they park around in back of the building. It was dark. There were woods on the opposite side of the back of the building. For a person to see them, he or she would have to drive around back and literally look for them.

Evans, always thinking, noticed right away when they got out of the car that there was a portable toilet standing directly next to the building about one hundred yards from where they had parked.

"Let's hop up on top of that," he whispered to Falco. "It'll put us right on the roof!"

"Looks good."

The building they had climbed up on top of wasn't the

flea market section of the building, so they had to walk along the roof until they found what Evans described later as a "hatch door" leading down into the flea market section of the mall.

Within a few minutes, while Falco acted as lookout, Evans slipped the pins holding the hinges of the door out, lifted the door up and hung a rope ladder down into the building.

Just like that, they were staring at well over $30,000 in merchandise they could take without stirring a field mouse.

For the next fifteen minutes, smashing jewelry cases and breaking open boxes, they loaded up two large duffel bags with all the gold and jewelry they could find. Evans took one side of the building, while Falco took the other.

Back at Falco's car a bit later, after getting out of the building the same way they had gone in, they piled the duffel bags into the trunk and took off slowly.

As Falco made his way around the back of the building toward Route 9, a local East Greenbush cop making his nightly rounds hit his lights and stopped them along a dirt road leading to the main road from the back of the building.

"Shit," Evans said. "Just play it cool, Mike. He didn't see anything."

"What's going on?" the cop asked as he approached Falco.

"Not much . . . ," Falco began to say.

"We just stopped to take a piss," Evans said, leaning over to look at the cop. He had a police scanner hidden under his left leg. Most everything else was in the trunk. Falco had cut out the side panels near the backseat of the car so he could hide stolen merchandise down inside, and they had loaded some of the more expensive jewelry inside. Smart enough to know better, they had nothing in sight that would indicate they were burglars.

"What are you doing coming out from behind that building?" the cop wanted to know.

"Well," Evans said, "we didn't want to piss here . . . out in the open."

By this time, Evans had his hand on the door handle. "I

was ready to split at that moment," he said later. But just as he was going to make a break for it, the cop said, "Okay, but just get the hell out of here. Don't come back here again. Piss somewhere else."

After writing down their names and addresses, the cop got back into his cruiser and took off.

Gary Evans took this photo of Timothy Rysedorph, 39, who went missing on October 3, 1997. *(Courtesy of Robbie Evans, "Little Big Sister")*

Gary C. Evans is shown leaving a self-storage unit parking lot in Colonie, New York after cutting up the body of his final victim with a chainsaw and placing it in garbage bags. *(Photo courtesy of the New York State Police, Troop G, Identification Bureau)*

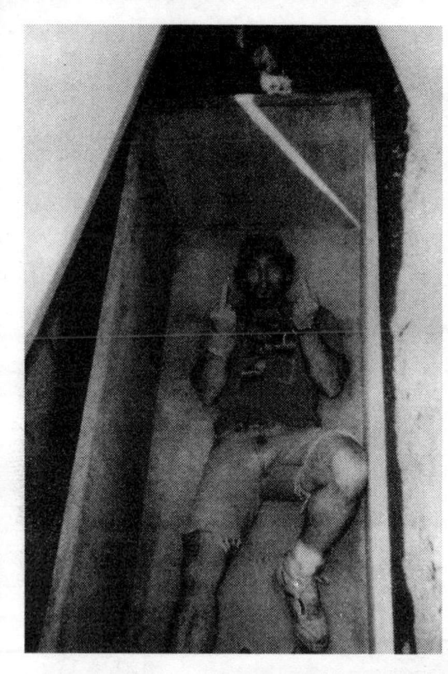

May 1998: Evans lying in a freshly dug grave after fleeing New York and leading Investigator Jim Horton on a multi-state manhunt. *(Courtesy of Robbie Evans, "Little Big Sister")*

After murdering his final victim, Gary Evans fled to the west coast and used several different identities to avoid capture by Jim Horton. *(Photos courtesy of the New York State Police, Troop G, Identification Bureau)*

In early 1998, Evans eluded capture by taking work on an Alaskan fishing boat and also posing as a tourist. *(Photo courtesy of Robbie Evans, "Little Big Sister")*

Evans in 1998, on the run, stopped to photograph himself at Bruce Lee's gravesite in Seattle, Washington. *(Courtesy of Robbie Evans, "Little Big Sister")*

While fleeing Horton, Evans spent time in Washington state and Oregon. *(Photo courtesy of Robbie Evans, "Little Big Sister")*

Evans in 1987, shoulder-to-shoulder with one of his heroes, David "Son of Sam" Berkowitz.

The game of cat-and-mouse that had gone on for 12 years between Gary Evans and Jim Horton came to an end on May 27, 1998, when Horton captured him in St. Johnsbury, Vermont. *(Photo courtesy of Jim Horton)*

Investigator Jim Horton began his career with the New York State Police on February 20, 1978. *(Photo courtesy of the New York State Police Academy)*

Born on October 7, 1954, Gary Evans grew up in this apartment on First Street in Troy, New York.
(Photo courtesy of the author)

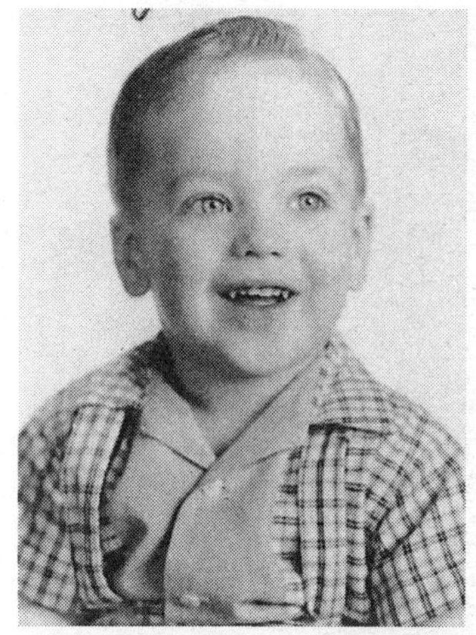

Even when he was two, Gary Evans's family and friends were already talking about his striking blue eyes. *(Photo courtesy of Robbie Evans, "Little Big Sister")*

Evans's father, Leroy Evans (shown here with Evans's sister, Robbie), would, among many other abusive punishments, strap his only son to a chair and force-feed him.
(Photo courtesy of Robbie Evans, "Little Big Sister")

Although Evans later said he loved his mother, Flora Mae (shown here with Evans at Pine Lake, New York), he often blamed her for not protecting him from Leroy.
(Photo courtesy of Robbie Evans, "Little Big Sister")

Little Gary Evans standing next to his sister, Robbie, before heading off to church. *(Photo courtesy of Robbie Evans, "Little Big Sister")*

A straight-A student during his grammar school days, Evans hated having to wear thick, horned-rim glasses, because he was often picked on by the other kids. *(Photo courtesy of Robbie Evans, "Little Big Sister")*

Obsessed with the outdoors, by the mid-1970s Evans was already burglarizing homes and living in the woods to elude police. *(Photo courtesy of Robbie Evans, "Little Big Sister")*

As Evans started to bulk up by the late 1970s, he grew a beard that draped down below his chest. *(Photo courtesy of Robbie Evans, "Little Big Sister")*

Awaiting sentencing on a burglary charge, Evans escaped from Rensselaer County Jail in downtown Troy *(shown here)* on June 12, 1980, with the help of four Hell's Angels. *(Photo courtesy of the author)*

The downtown Troy apartment where Gary Evans lived with Michael Falco and Tim Rysedorph. *(Photo courtesy of the author)*

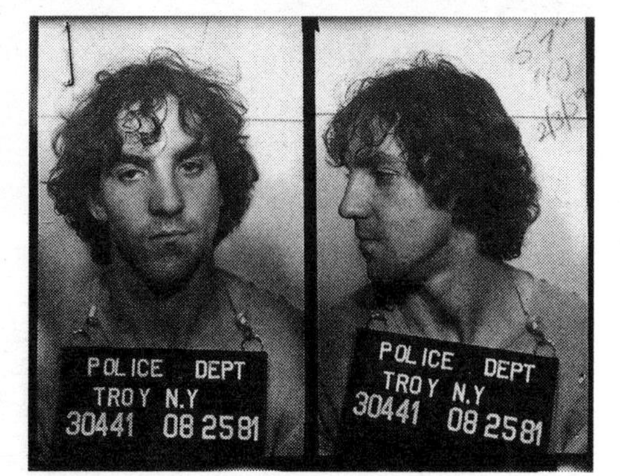

Michael Falco (shown here) and Gary Evans were partners until Evans murdered Falco in 1985. *(Photo courtesy of the New York State Police, Troop G, Identification Bureau)*

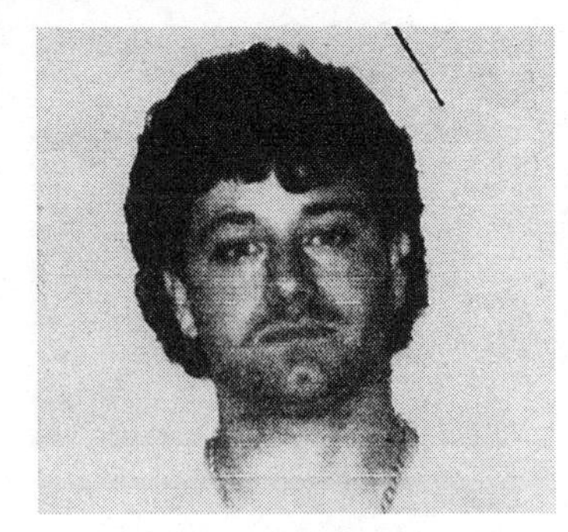

Twenty-eight-year-old Damien Cuomo became what Evans would later call "a liability" who "had to be killed." *(Photo courtesy of the New York State Police, Troop G, Identification Bureau)*

Evans and Cuomo broke into the Square Lion Jewelry Store in Watertown, New York, and Evans then murdered store owner Douglas Berry. *(Photo courtesy of the New York State Police, Troop G, Identification Bureau)*

Evans took this photo of Damien Cuomo while they were doing burglary jobs together in the mid-eighties. *(Courtesy of Robbie Evans, "Little Big Sister")*

In the fall of 1989, Evans took this photo of Damien Cuomo a few weeks before he killed him. *(Courtesy Robbie Evans, "Little Big Sister")*

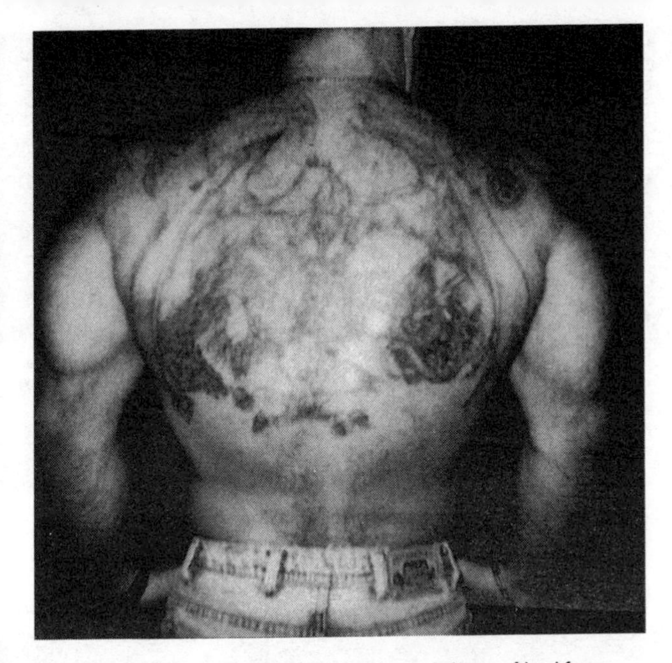

In 1992, Evans was in the best physical shape of his life.
(Photo courtesy of Jim Horton)

Investigator Jim Horton would stop by Evans's apartment and photograph him. *(Photo courtesy of Jim Horton)*

Troop G in Loudonville, New York, where Senior Investigator Jim Horton worked during his thirteen-year ordeal with Gary C. Evans.
(Photo courtesy of the author)

Senior Investigator Jim Horton eventually got Gary Evans to admit to killing five people in the span of nearly fifteen years.
(Photo courtesy of J. Jevons)

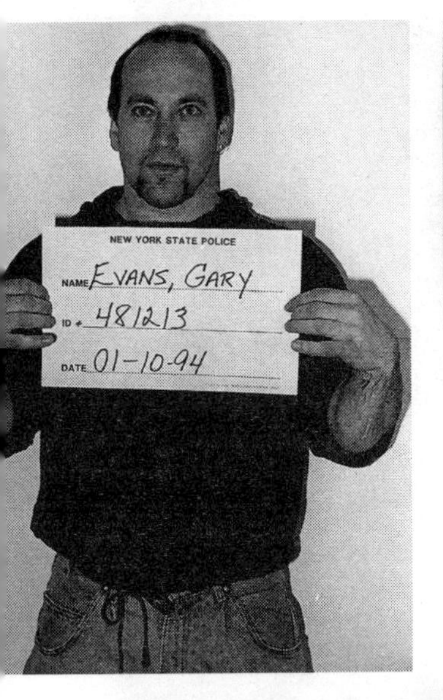

Investigator Jim Horton arrested Evans on January 10, 1994, for stealing a 1,000-lb. marble bench out of a local cemetery. *(Photos courtesy of the New York State Police, Troop G, Identification Bureau)*

Evans took this photo of himself in the early nineties. Some would later ask if it showed a secret life he had been leading for years or if it was a simple Halloween costume. *(Photo courtesy of Robbie Evans, "Little Big Sister")*

In 1998, shortly before his escape, Evans led Jim Horton to this field in Brunswick, New York, where he buried his dismembered final victim.
(Photo courtesy of the author)

Evans buried his first victim, Michael Falco, in this shallow grave in Lake Worth, Florida.
(Photo courtesy of the New York State Police, Troop G, Identification Bureau)

Handcuffed to Jim Horton, Evans searches this wooded area in Troy, New York, where he buried his second victim, Damien Cuomo.
(Photo courtesy of the New York State Police, Troop G, Identification Bureau)

On August 14, 1998, Gary Evans escaped from federal marshals by jumping off the Troy-Menands Bridge, which spans sixty-two feet above the Hudson River, near downtown Troy, New York.
(Photo courtesy of the author)

The area near the Troy-Menands Bridge where Gary Evans landed after escaping from the federal marshals who were transporting him.
(Photo courtesy of the New York State Police, Troop G, Identification Bureau)

Federal marshals were driving this Astro minivan when Evans retrieved a handcuff key from his sinus, unshackled one of his wrists, kicked out the side window, and escaped.
(Photo courtesy of the New York State Police, Troop G, Identification Bureau)

This fully intact razorblade *(left)* was found secured to Evans's ankle; this smaller blade *(right)* was found tucked up and underneath his upper gum, behind a molar.
(Photo courtesy of the author)

Evans lodged this handcuff key deep up into his right sinus.
(Photo courtesy of the New York State Police, Troop G, Identification Bureau)

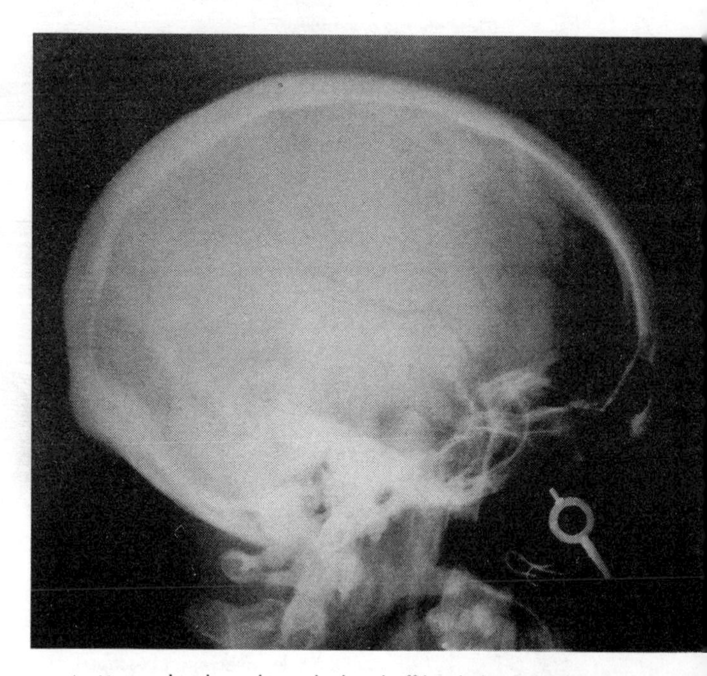

An X-ray taken later shows the handcuff key lodged in Evans's sinus cavit
(Photo courtesy of the New York State Police, Troop G, Identification Bureau)

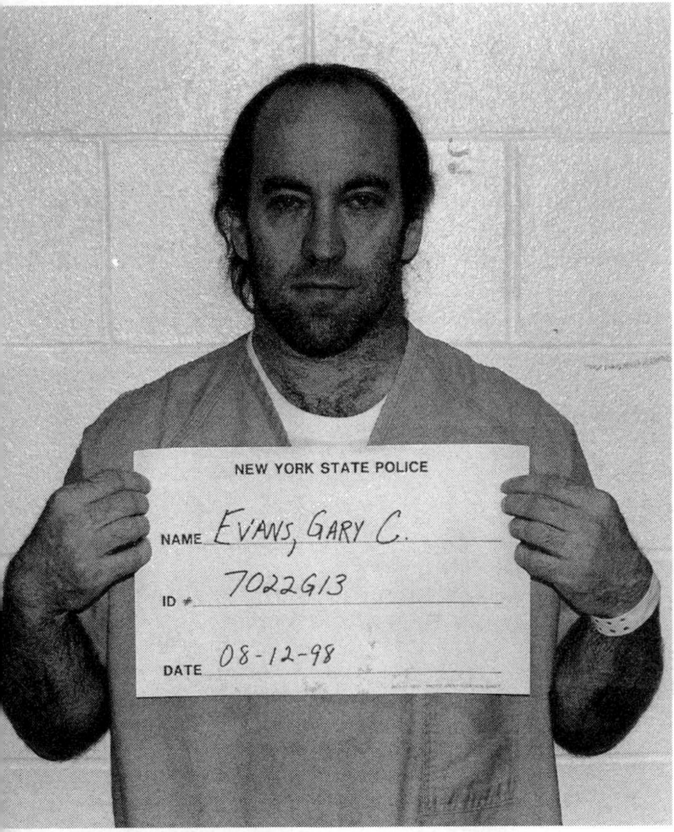

This was the last photo taken of Evans before his escape on August 14, 1998. *(Photo courtesy of the New York State Police, Troop G, Identification Bureau)*

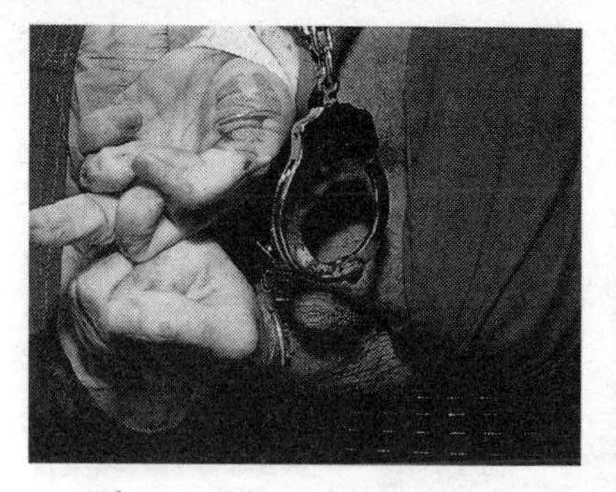

Defiant until the end, Evans was found with his middle finger sticking up. *(Photo courtesy of the New York State Police, Troop G, Identification Bureau)*

Jim Horton in 2004, with Gary Evans's ashes. *(Photo courtesy of the author)*

HARD AND MY FINGERS ARE COLD + CRAMP
BETWEEN CLOUDS way BELOW, CITIES. IT KEE
TURNING AND
I CAN HEAR IS
THAT IS TRYI
OFF, AND
CRUMBLIN
IF I LOOK
LOSE MY
LOOK UP
CAN'T SHUT
AND I'M

A portend of things to come, Gary Evans drew this picture of a man flying through the air, shards of glass around him, and sent it to Horton on August 9, 1998. *(Letter from which photo is taken courtesy of Robbie Evans, "Little Big Sister")*

Life-long friend and Gary Evans supporter Jo Rehm *(left)*, and Evans's sister, Robbie Evans Stowe *(right)*, during happier times. *(Photo courtesy of Robbie Evans, "Little Big Sister")*

CHAPTER 46

The owner of the East Greenbush Plaza Flea Market called the state police as soon as she opened the doors the next morning and realized it had been burglarized.

The trooper who showed up to take her statement figured out immediately that whoever was responsible had gained entry from the ceiling—the hatch door on the roof had been left pried open.

After surveying the point of entry, the trooper took a walk out back and noticed two sets of footprints in the dirt leading to a set of tire tracks.

Initially this ruled out drug addicts and amateurs. It was clear the job had been done by thieves who, at the least, knew something about burglary. Thus far, though, all the state police had were a few smudged footprints and a list of about one hundred missing items valued at approximately $15,000.

Not exactly a lot to go on.

A few days later, on Wednesday, February 20, the East Greenbush police officer who had stopped Evans and Falco back on the night of the burglary notified the state police what had happened and told the Bureau investigator working the case that he had written down Evans's and Falco's names and addresses.

Just like that, the Bureau had two suspects.

Bill Morris, a Bureau investigator with more than a decade on the job, kept a desk directly next to Jim Horton's at the Bureau's East Greenbush barracks. It was Morris who had been given the flea market case first. So on that Wednesday afternoon, after the East Greenbush police officer had come forward with information about stopping Evans and Falco, a Teletype went out explaining that the Bureau was looking to question Evans and Falco about their possible involvement in the burglary.

Now they were wanted men.

Approximately one week after Falco and Evans burglarized the East Greenbush flea market—Evans wasn't sure of the exact date later when he explained the event—Tim Rysedorph told him that while Evans was in jail, Falco had "ripped him off" by taking some "jewelry they had hidden underneath the floorboards" in their apartment on Adams Street.

This infuriated Evans. There was nothing worse, he had always said, than one of his "partners"—and they were always referred to as partners, never friends—stealing from him.

When he confronted Falco about it later, Falco insisted they had lost the jewelry during the heist. "Where is it?" Evans asked. "Somebody said they saw you take it!"

Faced with that, according to Evans, Falco changed his story and said the jewelry had been stolen, but not by him. Evans then dropped the subject and walked away without saying another word.

"The old cliché," Jim Horton said later, "is true: 'Thick as thieves.' But also thieves among thieves. There is no honor among thieves. They steal from one another as well as stealing from anyone else."

As Evans stewed over the next few days about what Tim had told him, he became increasingly worried that Falco would give him up for the East Greenbush job if the cops questioned him. He knew that when people felt backed into a corner, they did things to protect themselves. Evans was sure Falco would "roll over" after he had accused him of stealing from him.

That fear of going back to prison for twenty-five years to life was driving Evans's every move now. It was all he thought about.

The next time he saw Falco, he confronted him about it again. They were loading clothes into the trunk of Tim's car, which was parked in back of the apartment they shared.

At first, Evans offered Falco a chance to admit he had in fact stolen the jewelry from him. But Falco, Evans later said, wouldn't go for it.

Tim was upstairs in the apartment. He had no idea what was going on.

After a few minutes of what Evans later described as typical yelling and screaming and threatening each other, the argument turned into finger-pointing and pushing.

"Calm the fuck down," Falco said. "We'll figure it out. Let it go. It's only a fucking piece of jewelry."

But Evans couldn't. It wasn't about the jewelry; it was about honor. He was full of rage. Someone had ripped him off—a partner, no less—and that person had to pay. Like he had written to his sister while doing his last bid in prison, it was payback time.

"Fuck *you* . . . ," Evans shouted as Falco was lifting a box of clothes, getting ready to put it into Tim's car.

With Falco standing there, staring at him, Evans began breathing heavily, making loud grunting noises. He rarely carried a gun with him at any time. But tonight was different. He knew he'd need it. So as Falco turned and bent down to place the box of clothes into Tim's trunk, Evans reached into his pants and took out a .22-caliber pistol that he'd already armed with a homemade silencer made from door screen and duct tape.

You son of a bitch! Evans raged.

Then, without warning, he placed the barrel of the gun to the back of Falco's head as he leaned down into the trunk.

Pop.

It was over in a flash: one round fired into the back of Falco's head at point blank range, by a man who acted with heartlessness, as if he had killed people professionally his entire life.

After killing Falco, Evans pushed his body into the trunk and ran upstairs to get Rysedorph.

In the apartment a minute later, out of breath, Evans said, "Come with me. I need your car."

After grabbing a sleeping bag from his room, Evans bolted back downstairs, Rysedorph right behind him.

Looking to see if anyone was around, Evans opened the trunk and pointed to Falco's body.

"What the fuck?" Tim screamed, looking away.

"You shut your mouth," Evans said, waving his gun in the air. "Or you're fucking next."

Evans then grabbed the sleeping bag and ordered Tim to help him wrap Falco's body in it.

When they were finished, Evans said, "I'm taking your car."

Evans later claimed he had planned the murder days ahead of time. He knew he was going to kill Michael Falco that night, he said, and he knew he was going to take Tim's car to dispose of the body. It was never a spur-of-the-moment crime. He had planned it the moment after Tim had told him Falco had ripped him off.

But Rysedorph's entire story was a lie.

Some time later, Evans ran into a woman he, Tim and Falco knew fairly well. While they were talking, Evans noticed she was wearing the infamous missing piece of jewelry he had stolen during the job with Falco.

"Nice necklace," Evans said in a patronizing tone.

The woman looked down at it, then lifted it up off her chest and stared at it. "Yeah . . . it's beautiful," she said. "Tim gave it to me."

Evans paused for a moment. "You mean Timmy Rysedorph?"

"Yes!" the woman said, smiling.

Evans didn't say anything. Instead, he walked away mumbling to himself. *That lying motherfucker*.

For two months, Bureau investigator Bill Morris had searched the entire Albany region for any sign of Evans or Falco. Every lead Morris followed turned up nothing. He would get what appeared to be a break and it would turn cold. He would hear from a source that Evans had been seen around town, but Morris always seemed to be one step behind him. Finally, word on the street was that Falco and Evans had split up and taken off: Evans to Colorado; Falco to California.

CHAPTER 47

Evans left Troy immediately after wrapping Michael Falco's body in a sleeping bag and placing it, he later claimed, with the help of Tim Rysedorph, in the trunk of Tim's car. At that point, as Rysedorph and Evans loaded Falco's body into the trunk, Tim wasn't going to argue with Evans about anything. In fact, when Evans told Rysedorph he was taking his car to dump Falco's body, Tim said, "Hey, man, whatever the fuck you want."

From there, Evans took off to the one place where he thought he was safe from the world: Lake Worth, Florida, where his half sister, Robbie, lived.

The one aspect of the trip that interested Jim Horton later when Evans sat down and recounted the entire ordeal was how Evans hid out while transporting the body. Along the way, Evans would stop at a rest stop every ten hours or so, park Tim's car near the woods and camp out about two hundred yards away from the car in the deep brush.

"Why would you do that?" Horton wanted to know.

"Just in case," Evans said, "the cops were watching me. If they had ever searched the car while I was sleeping in the woods, they would have nailed Timmy Rysedorph"—Evans began laughing at this point—"for the murder. That's why I took his car to begin with."

As to why he would bury the body only miles from Robbie's house, Evans said he knew the area. Florida seemed like the logical next place to go. He could bury Falco and then go visit Robbie, his nephew and her new husband.

Evans lasted about six weeks in Florida and decided to drive back to Troy to face his demons. No more running. No more hiding. If the cops had anything on him, he surmised, they would have shaken down Rysedorph and eventually found him.

While in prison, Evans had learned that the best marks to rob were drug dealers. They always carried a lot of cash and were reluctant about calling the cops if they had been robbed.

Trying to lay off burglaries for a while, Evans hatched a plan when he got back to Troy in April 1985 to rob one of the most notorious drug dealers in town.

If there was one mistake Gary Evans continually made throughout his prolific career as a professional thief, it was thinking that he could get away with almost anything and, while doing it, rub the noses of the cops who were chasing him in the muck he left behind. He constantly put himself in a position to get caught—especially when he knew the cops were already after him.

Just about every investigator who had ever crossed paths with Evans said the same thing about him: "He liked to mess with your head and believed, without a doubt, he was smarter than anyone."

"And in many ways," Horton recalled later, "he was—but only up to a point."

On April 21, 1985, Evans set out for the night with his latest plan to score a large amount of cash. He had managed to convince a local drug dealer he had stolen some marijuana from another drug dealer. He said he wanted to turn it over as soon as possible. The drug dealer, after listening to Evans, said he would pay him $12,000 for it, and they set up a meet that same night at a local commuter parking lot by the Hudson River in downtown Troy.

It was about 10:30 P.M. when Evans showed up in his Saab. The other guy, along with a friend, showed up minutes later. After the guy showed Evans the $12,000, counting it in front of him, Evans took the cash and said, "We have to do this fast. It's in my trunk."

While the two men got out of their car and walked over to Evans's Saab, Evans took off down a nearby alley.

Both men, as they realized what was happening, started chasing him—one of them, according to Evans, had even fired several shots at him as he ran away.

If there was anyone in Troy who knew the neighborhood, its back alleyways and hiding places, it was Evans. As a young boy, to hide from his abusive father, he would take off and hop from rooftop to rooftop, sometimes even camping out on the roofs of abandoned buildings.

After he ran through what he later said were "gangways and backyards," he found himself back at the same commuter lot where he had started. He had lost both drug dealers during his getaway and was now staring at the drug dealer's "brand-new car," which, he said later, he "hopped in . . . and got away."

The drug dealer and his partner then walked to the Troy Police Department and reported that they had picked up "a guy named Gary Evans" hitchhiking and, as they were driving around town, he carjacked them and robbed $12,000 in cash.

The Troy PD immediately sent out an all points bulletin with a description of Evans, his arrest record and a description of the car he had "stolen at gunpoint."

Meanwhile, Evans had driven from Troy to Cohoes, a little mill town just outside of Latham.

According to police, as Evans pulled into town, he ran a red light.

A Cohoes police officer, just bouncing around town patrolling the same neighborhood, spied Evans as he ran the light, popped his lights on and began to pull him over.

Evans panicked. Thinking he was being stopped for the robbery, he decided to try to outrun the cop. As he was driving speedily through town, he started throwing things out the window: his fake identification, the gun and anything else he thought might be used against him. The only thing he didn't toss, however, was the cash.

After being cornered near the edge of town by several Cohoes police officers, Evans stopped his car and gave himself up without a fight. As one of the police officers was handcuffing him, reading him his Miranda rights, another cop told several of the other officers that Evans had been throwing various items out his window as he was being chased. A few cops soon retraced the route and ended up finding the gun and his fake identification.

With Evans locked up in a three-by-six steel cell in the basement of the Cohoes Police Department (CPD), awaiting arraignment on several charges, including resisting arrest, possession of a weapon and first-degree armed robbery (two felonies), his name turned up on a state police register as "wanted in questioning for a burglary in East Greenbush in February 1985."

Cohoes Police, not having any choice in the matter, then put in a call to the Bureau, alerting them that they had Evans in custody.

At about 2:00 A.M., on April 22, Horton received a call at home from the state police dispatcher. "Cohoes PD has a guy named Gary Evans in custody," she said. "He's wanted for one of your burglaries."

Horton was the call guy that night, responsible for answering any calls that came in during off-shift hours. Evans was, of course, Bureau investigator Bill Morris's man. But since Morris had already gone home for the night and Horton was on call, it was his responsibility to head over to Cohoes to speak with Evans.

Evans had developed a rather unique relationship by this point with Bureau investigator Doug Wingate. They had seen each other on numerous occasions, not always in connection with crime. Evans would even stop by Wingate's house when he was in the neighborhood just to say hello. He would stop by Troop G in Loudonville, whether he had information or not, just to, Wingate said later, "shoot the shit" and talk about life.

So when Evans found himself locked up in Cohoes, he knew his only chance of leniency from the DA's office was to begin talking to the Bureau.

At this point, Horton had never met Evans. He'd heard about him around the office and had, like a lot of cops, developed an impression of him, but he had never actually taken part in anything the Bureau was doing with Evans.

Cohoes was about three miles from Horton's home in Latham. It was late. Horton had been called out at all hours of the night in the past for various reasons, so it was no surprise. Nonetheless, a call in the middle of the night from a local police department regarding a burglary was, he said, "a pain in the ass."

As he drove, Horton mulled over what he had heard about Evans. He had convinced himself that he was going to interview some sort of cultish icon of a criminal who had a reputation as a notorious thief of antiques. Evans was, if nothing else, infamous around the Capital Region. He was viewed as a hardened, seasoned ex-con other criminals feared. This all weighed on Horton as he contemplated what he would say to Evans and, better yet, how Evans might react when he arrived.

The CPD holding cell, which Horton had never seen before, was dank and dark, and smelled of bodily fluids and mold. The paint on the walls of the cells was chipping off in sheets. The beds were nothing more than a thick, mattress-less sheath of steel with a hard pillow no thicker than a pack of cigarettes. The toilet, set in the corner of the cell, visible by anyone from anywhere, was stainless steel, even the seat.

Cohoes, nicknamed the "Collar City" because it was, at one time, the top manufacturer of shirt collars in the region, had run itself down throughout the years. The police department was a brick-and-mortar building in the center of town that included the city's only court. Driving into town, Horton could have easily looked around and thought, *Mayberry, R.F.D.* Smalltown, USA: a general store, post office and diner. Not much else.

In Horton's opinion, the state police, especially the Bureau, were pretty well-respected throughout the state by local police departments. Members of the Bureau usually got the "royal treatment" when they showed up at a local PD to interview a suspect, he said. Even being new to the job, having only logged about six months by this point with the Bureau, Horton knew that local cops looked up to Bureau investigators. Evans would even say later that he would "never fuck with members of the state police or the BCI—you guys don't mess around."

"That's not the case," Horton said later. "But if people think that, what the hell. We're no better than anybody else. But local police and criminals see us as the 'big shots,' so to speak."

The anticipation Horton felt as he drove into town seemed to build as he parked his cruiser downtown and walked into the CPD.

"Here was the 'infamous' Gary Evans," Horton recalled. "He had escaped from jail. He was a notorious burglar. He was this and that. . . . As a cop, you get a picture in your mind of this monster figure."

More than that, though, this was one of the first times Horton had been called out as a Bureau investigator to interview a suspect in the middle of the night.

"I was thinking, 'Should I call Bill Morris?' It was kind of his case. 'What am I going to say to him (Evans)?' I was green. I just didn't know what to expect."

When Horton walked into Evans's cell, he was shocked to see this "small" man with a beard and thick glasses staring back at him. Horton was, then, at thirty, in perfect physical shape, having just come from the diving team after spending years as a trooper. He was young. Strong. Much taller than Evans.

That first meeting between the two men was rather cordial, Horton explained later. There was no strong-arming or pushy talk on Horton's part; it was more of a "how can I help you?" meeting.

If Horton had one skill as a cop that not many other cops could match up against, it was his ability to talk to people rationally, without being an overbearing authority figure. He never talked above anyone, nor did he ever make a suspect feel like he or she was below him.

"I'm Investigator Jim Horton from the Bureau," Horton said nonchalantly as he walked into Evans's cell and stuck out his hand.

"Glad to meet you," Evans said, extending his hand.

It was the beginning of a relationship that would last almost thirteen years.

CHAPTER 48

The uniform cops hanging around the CPD holding cell area while Horton was inside Evans's cell were beside themselves, Horton said later, with what he believed was "envy and fascination" as he began talking to Evans about his role in the East Greenbush burglary. Evans's reputation had seeped down into local police departments all over the Capital District. He was, to many cops, "the catch." The Cohoes PD had scored a home run in nabbing him, even if it was by Evans's own doing.

So as Horton and Evans talked, the local cops paced outside Evans's cell, making snide remarks and staring at them as if they were zoo animals on display.

Horton became increasingly uncomfortable as he and Evans talked. Immediately he felt there was some sort of connection between him and Evans; perhaps a sense of comradeship, as if they had known each other for years.

"Listen," Horton whispered at one point, "you're going to be shipped over to Albany County Jail in the morning after seeing a judge here in Cohoes. Let's talk there," he added, looking at the Cohoes cops peering into Evans's cell, "we'll have more privacy."

"Sounds good," Evans said.

"I'll see you there tomorrow."

As Horton left, he glanced over at the table on the opposite side of the holding cell area and saw Evans's belongings sitting on a table. Stopping for a moment, he took a look at the money Evans had stolen from the drug dealer, which had been spread out on the table in piles of $1,000.

Without making too much of it, Horton then walked slowly by the table and, perhaps out of sheer police instinct, counted the piles.

Twelve, he told himself as he left. *Twelve thousand dollars.*

At one o'clock in the afternoon on April 22, 1985, Horton, after not sleeping much, kept his promise to Evans and drove to Albany County Jail to sit and talk with him. Before they got started, Horton said later, he wanted to make it clear to Evans that this was going to be a formal interview. He told him he needed to get a written statement regarding anything he knew about the East Greenbush burglary. It wasn't a courtesy call, or a friendly visit to find out whom he was going to give up to save his own ass; it was an interrogation about a burglary the Bureau suspected Evans had been involved in.

Without balking one bit, Evans agreed to cooperate.

So Horton took out a notepad and began what would turn out to be the first written confession Evans had ever given to police.

Evans, who had blasted his crime partners in letters to his sister over the years for rolling over on him, marked Damien Cuomo and Michael Falco right away as Horton began asking questions about East Greenbush. He gave Horton a detailed, step-by-step account of how the job was set up, by whom and how it had been carried out. He acted as if he were enjoying snitching on his colleagues.

Because Falco hadn't been heard from in months, and every source the Bureau contacted on the street claimed he had taken off out west, Horton posed the question to Evans to see what he knew.

"I think he's in California," Evans said without hesitation, "using the name Ian Patrick Phibes."

"Thanks. We'll check it out."

Shortly before the end of the interview, Evans indicated he had one more important statement to put on record.

"What's that?" Horton asked while packing up his things.

"Me and Mike [Falco] were tipped off about how to enter the flea market from the roof by a guy Mike knows whose father works at the flea market."

"This was," Horton said later, "a significant day for Gary Evans and me. He had never given a confession to anyone in law enforcement before. For some reason, he latched onto me that day and began trusting me. I had no idea what this one 'chance' meeting would end up becoming in the end. But it was clear to me on that particular day that Gary thought of himself as better than all the criminals he had ever known or given up. In his criminal mind, he justified his crimes by noting that the guys he was giving up were ten times worse than he ever was."

When it came time for Evans to sign the confession and date it, he looked at Horton and said, "I can't believe I am signing up for prison."

While Evans awaited a court date on several charges, which now included criminal possession of a weapon, first-degree armed robbery, grand larceny and burglary of a jewelry store, he began doing what he had always done when he found himself, in his words, "caged up, like an animal": he wrote to his sister.

On May 1, he sent a brief letter explaining his latest predicament. Yet, through his obvious embarrassment of doing the same things and getting the same results, he found a bit of solace in the fact that he did a "favor" for the state police.

He wrote: *They're trying to get the counties to drop charges and let the feds take me on a weapons charge.* That meant a lesser sentence.

It was also clear he had put his trust now in the state police and was depending on "certain" Bureau investigators to bail him out of what amounted to the worst possible situation he could have found himself in with the law: twenty-five to life.

At the end of the letter, he advised Robbie not to write to him: *. . . because it hurts. I know you love me and I love you. I'm OK. Don't worry, I'll see you.*

A few weeks later, on May 27, he wrote again, explaining exactly what he had done and how he got caught. He maintained that "the Cohoes cops stole $3,000" of the $12,000 he had stolen from the drug dealer. The next day, when Horton stopped by the CPD to pick up an arrest report, he, too, became suspicious that a Cohoes cop had taken $3,000 from the $12,000 they had found on Evans when they arrested him. Horton, of course, knew there was $12,000 because he had counted it himself the night he interviewed Evans at the Cohoes PD.

But when he went back to the records room to get a report, he asked the cop, who was sitting in front of a pile of reports, which one was "for the guy who ripped off the drug dealers in Troy for $12,000?"

"It was only nine thousand," the cop said.

"What?"

"Yeah," the cop continued, "we have nine thousand all bagged up."

Shell-shocked and a bit confused, Horton didn't say anything. Instead, he grabbed the report and immediately drove to Albany County Jail to talk to Evans about the money.

"Hey," he said after the guards brought Evans to him, "I just came from Cohoes PD. There was only nine thousand dollars there today. . . . There was twelve thousand last night."

Horton said later that Evans then "got this cat that swallowed the canary look" on his face and said, "Well . . . what are you going to do?"

"Well . . . what?" Horton demanded.

"It's fucking drug money," Evans said. "Who really gives a fuck?"

"I care!"

"A guy I went to high school with," Evans said, smirking, "took it. He's got kids. He's a good fucking guy. It's just fucking drug money. What do you care?"

"Who was it?" Horton wanted to know. He was getting upset. "Tell me right now who fucking took that money!"

Evans turned and walked away.

"Hey, I'm asking you a question."

Turning around, in a whisper, Evans said, "I'm not going to tell you, Jim. Not ever."

Over the next ten years, Horton would routinely ask Evans who the corrupt cop was, but Evans would always go off on some tangent, explaining that loyalty was one of the only pieces of himself he had left. Horton would say, "Come on, Gar. Just tell me who it is?"

"He's a good cop," Evans would say. "He has kids. It was drug money. Who fucking cares?"

Years later, while Horton was using Evans as an informant to gather information about a serial rapist and murderer, Evans's and Horton's names and photos were in the newspapers whenever news broke about the case. In fact, throughout the twelve-plus years they knew each other, not six months would go by without at least a blurb being written about them in the newspapers.

One day, Horton had to go down to the Cohoes PD to pick up some paperwork about a prisoner they had in lockup, who would ultimately turn out to be the same serial rapist and murderer he had been investigating.

As he was gathering the reports, a Cohoes detective walked

up to him and said, "Hey, how are you? I see you guys are using Gary Evans in that [serial rapist] case we've been investigating."

"Yeah," Horton said, forcing himself to sound cordial and polite, mincing words until he located the report. "He's been helping us out, providing some solid info."

"No shit," the detective said, "you know, I went to high school with Gary Evans."

And there he was: the cop who had stolen the $3,000 some ten years earlier.

"Oh, you did, huh?" Horton said.

Because it had been so long and Horton knew Evans would never testify against the cop, he decided not to pursue it.

"It wasn't worth jeopardizing the case we were working on with the Cohoes PD at the time," Horton recalled later with a tinge of frustration and discouragement in his voice. "We were in the process of getting a serial rapist and murderer off the streets. Evans would have denied everything. It would have been my word against the detective's. I had no proof. I was told to drop it."

Whenever Evans found himself confined to four walls and a barbed wire fence, he was faced with the prospect of doing an internal inventory. Having nothing but time on his hands to think about his life, he would always look back and contemplate where he had gone wrong.

Sis, I really don't know what to do . . . , he wrote near the beginning of June, while waiting to be sentenced. *I have a problem with time—I've had it as long as I can remember. That's the problem, remembering things when I don't want to.*

From there, he went on a diatribe regarding, of all things, "taking showers." He listed all the different places he had ever taken a shower and equated each with a bad memory of childhood. He mentioned "Canada, Colorado, Florida, prison, friends' houses, etc." Anywhere, in other words, but home.

In the same breath, however, he talked about sleeping in a field by himself. He recalled "eating cookies and milk kept cold in a stream."

This was euphoria for Evans: living alone in the woods. And the idea of it being a possibility, he claimed, was always something that kept him from going totally insane while locked up: *All these thoughts and memories come into my head without me trying. How would you like to have thirty years of bad memories flashing through your mind all day? There's so little good ones.*

After that, he refocused his obsession back to his high school sweetheart, Stacy, whom he hadn't seen for ten or more years by this point: *Everything reminds me of her. We spent so much time together. There's nothing in the world that doesn't connect with her in my mind. . . . After I was sick a few months ago, I was really in a bad mood, felt like going skydiving and not pulling the chute open. The only reason I didn't was because . . . I haven't found [Stacy] yet, and some people have gotten away with doing rotten shit to me and I want to pay them back. So I do illegal stuff to try to get enough money to do the things I want.*

CHAPTER 49

By the time the June flowers were in full bloom, Evans was in county lockup stewing over the "deal" he had supposedly made with the state police—a deal that would send him back to maximum-security prison for yet another two- to four-year bid. Any pipe dreams he had of getting out sooner with the help of the state police was a figment of his imagination. Members of the state police, specifically Jim Horton and Doug Wingate (the two Bureau investigators Evans was referring to whenever he mentioned "favors" and "state police" in the same sentence), had never promised him such a thing. Trading information for time in prison wasn't something Horton or Wingate could do. They could "put in a good word" for somebody. But that was it.

To no one's surprise, in early July 1985, Evans was sentenced to two to four years. In truth, it was a gift, considering his criminal history.

His time would be spent, at least until a more permanent bed could be found, at Clinton Correctional, a prison with which he was already very familiar.

It probably seems to you, Evans wrote on August 11, 1985, *(like it does to everyone else), that the solution of staying out of jail is easy—just stop illegal activities and get a job. But whenever I do work or have to be around people (which really* bothers *me), I have strong feelings of wasting time not doing what I want.*

The statement made no sense. Anyone that wanted to live an honest life had to work for a living. But Gary Evans didn't view life in that manner. In his mind, he deserved wealth without sacrifice. A home without a mortgage. Cars. Vacations. Diamonds and jewels for his women. All because of the "rough upbringing" he had been put through by his "horrible parents." He was "forced" to steal in order to get the things he wanted. Time and again, faced with what he knew was the worst possible environment he could find himself in, he did nothing to modify his behavior to avoid it.

Because Evans had planted the seed in the minds of just about everyone who had ever known Michael Falco that Falco had run off to California after burglarizing the East Greenbush flea market with him, Horton had no reason to believe otherwise. So Horton obtained a warrant for Falco's arrest and made sure every California police department understood the Bureau was looking for him. Of course, weeks and months went by and no one heard from Falco.

As the summer of 1985 drew to a close, Horton tracked down Falco's common-law wife, *Tori Ellis*, the mother of Falco's kids. She, too, was under the impression Falco had split to California after hearing it from several people who had, in turn, heard it from Evans. When Horton confronted Ellis and asked her about Falco, she ended up turning over several pieces of jewelry from the East Greenbush flea market job that Falco had given her.

"Where is he?" Horton asked. "Have you heard from him at all?"

"No," Ellis explained. "He took off on me and the kids. . . . I heard he was in California."

* * *

Sing Sing Correctional Facility, located in Westchester County, New York, in Ossining, was built more than 160 years ago, and is probably the most famous New York prison. Movies have been shot at Sing Sing, books have been written about the place and several notable prisoners have spent the bulk of their time there. On top of its dark and violent history of riots and prisoner takeovers, about six hundred convicts have been executed at Sing Sing throughout the years. The criminal makeup of it is, without a doubt, among the toughest in the United States. New York courts send hard-core rapists, murderers, thieves, gang members and child predators to Sing Sing, either to teach them a lesson they will likely never learn, or to send them a message.

By late August, Evans was on his way south to do his two- to four-year bid at Sing Sing. For Evans, remarkably, he viewed going to Sing Sing as some sort of step up from where he had spent most of his time in other upstate prisons. To him, Sing Sing wasn't as bad as it sounded. Most important was the fact that he could add another famous feather to his criminal cap. Once people heard he had done time at Sing Sing, Evans knew, they'd view him differently. An immediate respect, at least in the criminal world, would be there waiting for him when he got out.

There was never "one specific reason" Evans ever gave for latching onto Horton during the fall of 1985. Horton later admitted that a statement Evans made to him shortly after they met offered some insight as to why Evans perhaps trusted him so earnestly.

"You treated me better than any other cop," Evans said one day when Horton asked him why he was always calling and asking for him.

"I like to treat people as people," Horton told Evans that day. "Without you, I wouldn't have a job."

For Horton, getting Evans to confess to the East Greenbush flea market burglary was a watershed moment in his career.

He had been a new investigator and here he had solved a major burglary case. Evans had been, at the time, a Bureau target for years. The old-timers, Horton recalled, would always taunt him about getting Evans: "You'll never catch him! He's too good a thief."

With Evans away in prison, Horton assumed he wouldn't hear from him. By this point, Horton had been transferred from the Bureau's East Greenbush barracks to the Loudonville Bureau, Troop G, which was closer to his home and more action-packed. The only reason he would have for contacting Evans would be if he had a case and wanted to use Evans as an informant. Other than that, he had little use for him.

On September 25, 1985, as Horton was working a murder case unrelated to Evans, he received a letter from him.

How many other S.P. do you know who get mail from Sing Sing? Evans opened the letter with. Referring to Horton as "Guy," a name he would commonly use as the years progressed, he began talking about the "fake" drug deal he had been involved in that had gotten him locked up this time around. He wrote: *Word is . . . [the drug dealer I ripped off] will get me killed when I get out (he'll have to stand in line). I have thought a lot about how easily his brother . . . could do it. (And if he does, please try to get him for it, okay?)*

There was a sense of camaraderie in the letter that struck Horton. He didn't expect, for one, to ever hear from Evans again, nor did he imagine Evans to sound so calm and fixated on himself as a criminal who was, in his twisted mind, "working" with the state police.

"I think that first letter served two purposes for Gary," Horton commented later. "One, I think he found a cop who he knew would treat him decently. . . . Remember, we had no idea he was a murderer. We believed he was a prolific burglar who could help solve an endless array of local burglaries. Two, he thought he had a cop he could bring in to his twisted fold and make him an ally."

On the second page of the five-page letter, Evans began once again to dangle Michael Falco from a stick, rubbing

Horton's face in the deceitful fact that Falco was still alive and on the run. He talked about a guy he met in prison who knew Michael Falco: *I came upstate in August, but spent July in Rensselaer County Jail. While there, [a] weird guy that Mike Falco sold jewelry to came in for traffic or drunk or some bullshit. While there, he told me he talked to Mike at a concert. Said he kissed off [Tori Ellis] + kid. Which is typical Falco family sentiment, and went west again.*

He next wrote he had spoken to Tori, too: *"Fuck Mike," [he said she told him,] since he threw her away. . . .*

Throughout the letter, he gravitated toward giving Horton names of potential informants who could help him solve cases. Then he talked about the two drug dealers he had robbed, and ended up giving Horton several names connected to the main source of drugs in Troy. At the end of a long paragraph, after laying out the entire drug operation the two guys ran in Troy, he wrote: *You're welcome!*

It was as if Horton had thrown Evans a bone by treating him like a human being and now he was bringing it back.

Then it came time, in his characteristic way of just coming right out with it, to talk about payback.

Anyway . . . how can you guys sleep at night knowing I'm rotting in Sing Sing?! Clean up Troy, I won't be back there but I'd like to see [the] hometown stand straight.

The very last line of the letter was, perhaps, Evans at his best, taunting Horton, as he would for the next thirteen years: *Write this infamous person at infamous Sing Sing. What the hell. It'll look good if you ever write a book.*

CHAPTER 50

During the early days after they first met, Evans saw Horton as an inexperienced investigator, still wet behind the ears. Horton was "the new guy" at the Bureau. Because of that, and the fact that he wholeheartedly believed he was smarter than Horton, Evans tried to shape and mold him into the type of cop he needed on his side. Horton, admittedly, was eager to prove himself as a young Bureau investigator. In a sense, he later said, he fell for Evans's charm, at least in the beginning.

After talking to Evans several times throughout September after receiving that first letter, Horton went to his Bureau captain and told him what was going on. "Captain, I got this Evans guy talking about all kinds of burglaries and drug deals and—"

"Kid," the captain said, interrupting, "leave it alone. Let Troy take care of those drug dealers. Worry about your job. Murders. The bigger fish."

Horton felt discouraged. He thought he had accomplished what other Bureau investigators had tried for years to do but couldn't: penetrate the armor of the abominable Gary Evans and get him to open up.

Horton would understand later that his captain knew a lot more about law enforcement than he let on.

"Gary Evans was playing me," Horton said. "He was throwing me things: drug dealers, robbery suspects, et cetera. But he was also giving me bullshit names and crimes that never happened. My captain knew I was being played."

Evans believed he was controlling Horton. He thought he could pull a string and Horton would rush right over to console him and grant his every wish.

But Horton was also using Evans. He knew Evans could further his Bureau career. He knew Evans would eventually cough up important names. And he knew he ran a risk by befriending Evans—that it could all backfire on his career if he wasn't careful.

Throughout the remaining few months of 1985, and well into the beginning of 1986, as Evans continued to do his time at Sing Sing, he became one of Horton's top CIs. Every cop has a few on a string—some with good information, some not. Most of the information Evans provided, Horton said later, was either impossible to back up, or totally spot on. Evans knew exactly what he was doing. In the years to come, Horton would realize that the main thrust fueling Evans's desire to give up only certain bits of information was to throw Horton off the scent of Michael Falco. Evans would later admit he believed that if he kept Horton busy with other crimes and criminals, he would never suspect—and he didn't until years later—that Evans was involved in Michael Falco's disappearance.

Indeed, both men were using each other—and both thought he was smarter than the other.

In October, Evans sat down and sent his sister a letter and, with one stroke of his pen, explained how he'd figured out his life. He finally realized why he had spent the better part of the past ten years behind bars: *I can't believe I'm here again. But I know what did it: that guy not wanting the painting and I was trying to get [my last girlfriend] as a replacement for [Stacy], which is impossible.*

Evans had, during the first few months after he had been released from prison the last time, tried to sell some artwork he had made while in prison. But the first person he tried selling it to brushed him off. Then he went out and found a steady girlfriend. Because he had failed as an artist and tried to replace his beloved high school sweetheart with another woman, he now figured out that his way of dealing with those failures was to turn to a life of crime. It was as if he couldn't look at his own behavior, and his refusal to admit the truth about his life was just too overpowering.

In that same letter, he talked about spending his entire twenties in prison. He didn't recall much of it, he said, because most of it had been spent behind bars.

By December, Evan had been transferred to Dannemora. This didn't sit well with him. He said he was "slowly and fastly going crazy." What angered him most was that he was put in a cell next to the first cell he had spent time in back in 1977. It was a constant reminder of how his life had spiraled in a complete circle. With twenty-four months left on his most recent sentence, he realized, his life was heading nowhere . . . fast . . . and there was nothing he could do to stop it.

Then something odd took place. Robbie wrote to him, explaining how she had received a phone call from someone who sounded like him. The person—and Robbie had wholeheartedly believed it was Gary—had mentioned something about a fetish with animals, bestiality. Someone had called and, disguising himself as Evans, bragged about having sex with animals, or something to that effect.

You're fucking up my head saying somebody is doing my voice perfectly, Evans wrote, the anger and hate evident in his penmanship, which was sharp, clear and direct. Evans generally had a soft approach to his writing: light and fluffy, sometimes cursive and other times print. He was always gentle in that respect. But this letter was all business.

Over the course of the next few weeks, his letters focused

exclusively on the "caller." He believed, about a week after the incident, he had figured out who it was and swore, even without any proof whatsoever, to wreak havoc on that person when he got out of prison: *And right now I want this motherfucker worse than I want [anyone, even those] who put me here.*

By the end of the letter, it didn't matter to Evans that he had no evidence to support his claim of who it was, but he had made a decision, nonetheless. There would be no more discussion about it: *He's my pick for the guy behind this shit. And that's enough for me.*

On January 2, 1986, he wrote again and, after talking to Robbie earlier that day by telephone, convinced himself to drop his pledge to destroy the guy he "thought" had made the call. Robbie had, apparently, figured out through phone bill records that the guy Evans had suspected couldn't have been the person who made the call. It was impossible.

I thought I had it solved. I don't know any other asshole that you know, so you'll have to figure it out! And just like that, as quick as he was to put the guy on his grand hit list, he let it go and never brought it up again.

CHAPTER 51

As he celebrated yet another New Year holiday—1986—behind bars, Evans's appearance began to change. He was losing his hair now by the handful and his teeth, which he blamed on the "fake Bangladesh" dentists in prison, were rotting because he was too afraid to get any work done. Nearly completely bald, except for a frayed ring of hair encircling the lower portion of his head, he yearned for contact lenses. Not only would he "look good," he said, but he wouldn't have to worry any longer about the guards who were teasing him because of his thick "Coke bottle" prescription glasses.

During the late seventies and into the early eighties, Evans could have cared less what his ZZ Top beard looked like. But now, he was obsessed about keeping it neatly groomed and much shorter. Instead of it reaching his belly button, he had groomed it only inches long, hugging his jawline.

Still, the most noticeable part of his transformation was his body. For years, he had fought with his weight, struggling to get above 175 pounds. But now, it seemed overnight, he had gained about ten pounds—all of which was, he claimed, lean muscle. Photos from that era show a massive man, bulky and wide; his shoulders seemingly ran from the top of his neck down below his biceps.

Although he still bounced back and forth between high and low moods, he was beginning to embrace the time in prison, saying that being incarcerated for so much of his life "would have killed your *ordinary* human being years ago!"

Taking responsibility for his actions, however, wasn't on his agenda.

He wrote: *Everything should've been so* different. *I should've had [Stacy], never came to prison.*

He also talked about what he called a "major event that changed" his life. It was back in 1975 when he bought his first vehicle. He was twenty-one years old. He spent $700 on it—money, he said, he had earned from "working" a "real" job. Three days after he purchased the vehicle, though, while driving home from Stacy's house, the engine blew.

Now that pissed me off. No money. No car. So I stole one just like it and painted it and put stickers and plates and [the] I.D. [tag from my other vehicle] on the engine. I was going to sell it fast but got stopped by the cops. I think someone told on me, he wrote.

This one event, he now insisted, was the turning point in his life. And it all revolved around his "precious" high school sweetheart, Stacy: *People are going to pay for any obstacle placed in front of me when I get out and go find her. I am sick of "half-stepping." That's slang for not doing the full, complete act that should've been done. . . . I am going to see her again. Any fool who gets in the way to prevent that will get out of the way much faster.*

Over the next few months, the tone of his letters varied among three main themes: revenge, racism and Stacy. He'd talk about a group he called the "White Survivalist Road Warriors." They looked out for one another. If there was ever a "race riot" in prison, he said, the group was ready. Eating "no meat, fish, birds, eggs or vegetables" for "17½ years," he claimed, had made him into a powerhouse of a human being. His biceps were seventeen inches in diameter now. He was solid as stone. Ready to take on anyone who "fucked" with him.

In early March, he wrote he had *a visit from a guy in Troy—one of the [Harrington] twins [Steve & Bob]. [Steve] is an outlaw. His brother is a guard in a prison camp. They're both okay. [Steve] is a friend (business acquaintance, I mean). He knows everything leading up to me getting busted. He did a few things for me.*

Steve Harrington and Evans had a long history together, yet none of it could qualify as a friendship.

According to what Horton and Doug Wingate later found out, Evans and Steve hated each other.

"That's probably why he never killed him," Horton said later. "Because he talked so much about how he hated him all the time, we would have known right away who had killed him if he ever turned up dead."

Knowing he could never kill Steve, Evans still felt the need to do *something*. So he tormented him. In some respects, Steve and Evans *were* partners. They didn't commit burglaries together, but were involved in other illegal activities. One day, they bought a tractor trailer loaded with fireworks from out of state. Fireworks, in New York, are illegal. Evans would never say exactly what happened, but he ended up stealing the entire load from Steve, selling it and not sharing the money.

On different occasions, Evans and Steve would call Horton and other members of the state police and try to set each other up. Or, as Horton told it, they would "just provide intelligence on each other in an effort to get the other arrested. It got to the point where no matter what each one said, it was either not taken seriously or we knew what they were doing and disregarded it altogether."

There was one time when Evans called Horton and said Steve had tried to kill him; and he wanted him arrested for attempted murder. So Horton ended up meeting Evans in an abandoned parking lot in Menands, near Troy. Evans was driving a Toyota pickup truck at the time.

"He was livid," Horton recalled. "He gave me a three-foot piece of heavy-gauge pipe that was about two-and-a-half inches in diameter. It was huge, and capped at each end with a fuse coming out of it. It was a serious-looking bomb, but a shitty try at the fuse. Evans told me he had come out of his motel room and found it wired up under his truck with hanger wire. The 'fuse' was wrapped around the exhaust. He said it was full of gunpowder, which he had emptied prior to meeting me."

Horton checked inside the pipe and found remnants of gunpowder on the inside walls.

There was another time when Evans said there was an aluminum packet of cocaine hidden in the door of the gas cap of his truck.

"I quickly realized," Horton said, "after a few weeks of this, that it was a personal battle between them and I didn't want to get involved unless it became criminal. I took the pipe bomb from him. Mostly so he wouldn't use it against [Steve] himself. I know he could go buy the same ingredients, but took it anyway. I didn't log it in as evidence because there was no case."

At one point, the feud between them had become so heated and routine, they had run out of ways to attack each other. So Evans decided to begin messing with Steve's head, in a psychological manner.

Back when Jason, the mass murderer from the *Friday the 13th* movies, was popular, Evans went out and bought a white hockey goalie mask. At the time, Steve lived on top of a mountain on the New York–Massachusetts border. Some people later claimed Steve had put surveillance cameras along his driveway and in the woods around his house because, for one, "he was dealing drugs," and two, he was scared shitless of Evans. At night, Evans would skulk around the woods in back of Steve's house with the Jason mask on and make howling noises. One night, feeling brave, Evans placed the mask on a tree branch along Steve's driveway so it would spook him when he drove up the driveway. Apparently it worked—because a few days later, Steve ran into Evans and threatened to kill him if he continued to "fuck with" him. He was raging mad and embarrassed, but wouldn't say why.

A short while later, Evans sneaked up behind Steve's house as Steve was lying in his bedroom, and began tossing stones at the side of the house. Fed up, Steve took out his gun and emptied it through the wall of his bedroom.

Evans said later he took cover on the ground, but couldn't stop laughing because he had gotten Steve to "shoot up" his own house, which was what he had planned.

"I verified all of this," Horton said later, "because I had interviewed [Steve]. He was truly paranoid of Evans. He had a legitimate pistol permit and carried it everywhere he went in a shoulder holster. He even told me that he slept with it, fucked his girlfriend with it on, and even went to the bathroom with it—all because of Gary Evans."

Whenever Evans did something—be it burglary, lifting weights, not eating certain foods, obsessing over Stacy—he took it to extreme levels. There was no middle ground or "happy medium" that could ever satisfy him.

By all accounts, Steve, Horton said later, wasn't the type of guy cops cared all that much about. "He was a scumbag, to be honest."

Although Steve had never been arrested for any major crimes, Horton and Wingate later said they knew he was involved in everything from drugs to robbery to the disposal of a body.

Two guys from Troy had killed, in savage fashion, a sixteen-year-old pregnant girl by cutting off her arms, legs and head. They knew Steve and got the bright idea to take the body parts out to his mountaintop home and dispose of them in the woods. It was winter. The ground was frozen and covered with snow. So instead of digging a ditch and burying the body parts, they put the girl into Hefty bags and threw her over a snowbank along Steve's driveway. Afterward, they went up to Steve's house, told him what they had done and, according to Horton, "had a party."

Steve never called the police. But Horton and Doug Wingate, who were investigating the disappearance of the girl, were told by an informant that the body "may be up there in the woods near" Steve's house.

After the Bureau caught the killers and located the body, Steve was never charged. Instead, the state decided to use him as a witness in the murder trial against the killers.

With news of the arrests and upcoming trial in all the area newspapers, Evans figured out Steve was going to testify and devised a plan to mess with him one last time.

While Steve was on the stand testifying, Evans showed up in the courtroom and sat directly in his line of sight. "Steve went bullshit on the stand while Evans just sat in the courtroom and smiled at him," Horton said later. "At one point, Steve began screaming, 'I can't concentrate with him here!' pointing at Evans. 'Get him the fuck out of here.'"

The judge ultimately had to stop the trial and have Evans removed from the courtroom. For years afterward, Evans bragged about how screwed up Steve had become after the incident. To top it off, months later, Steve's father died, and Evans sat out in front of the funeral parlor in his truck smiling and staring down mourners as they entered and exited.

CHAPTER 52

Horton thought he was making some progress in finding out where Michael Falco had supposedly run off to after committing the East Greenbush burglary with Evans. He had no idea, of course, that Falco had been wrapped in a sleeping bag like a mummy and had been buried in a shallow grave in Florida. Thus, he had no reason *not* to believe Michael Falco had pulled off the burglary and relocated to California, like mostly everyone on the street had been saying.

By the fall of 1986, what at first seemed like a break in Falco's whereabouts surfaced. A Bureau investigator had heard that Falco had been seen in Troy. So two investigators went out and swept the neighborhood, looking for anyone with information about his whereabouts. After talking to a few people, the investigators were led to the one person they knew who could either dismiss the rumor that Falco had returned, or back it up: Tori Ellis, Falco's common-law wife. If Falco had come back to the area, they believed he would have certainly made contact with Ellis.

She immediately admitted that if he had been back in town, she would have seen or, at the least, heard from him.

She claimed she hadn't. "I believe . . . and I am just speculating," Tori Ellis told police, "that Michael is dead."

"Well, ma'am," the investigator said, "if he does return, you need to call us."

"I'd encourage him to give himself up," Ellis said. "I won't be involved with a wanted man."

The Bureau conducted a nationwide search for any vehicles registered to Falco or any of his known aliases, but came up with nothing. A few weeks later, they tracked down one of his brothers. But he, too, said he had no idea where Falco was, and hadn't seen him in almost a year.

Over and over, as reports filed in, Horton began to realize Falco was either extremely good at ducking out of sight, or something was keeping him from contacting anyone. Whatever the reason, Horton promised himself, he was going to find Michael Falco.

It seemed like an odd thing for Steve Harrington, Evans's archnemesis, to do, but after visiting Evans in prison on a few occasions, Steve promised Evans a job working on a construction site after he was released from prison. Horton later speculated that there could have been only one reason why Steve would have done that.

"Evans must have had something big on Steve and was threatening to drop a dime on him. There is no other explanation. They hated each other. It was well documented."

Not sure about what he was going to do when he was released, Evans told Steve he'd think about the job offer. But when it came down to it, there was no chance in hell Evans was ever going to earn an honest living. It just wasn't part of his makeup. He had made it perfectly clear in his letters that he was not someone who could take orders from another human being. More than that, he had a new plan now for when he got out of prison—and it hardly included working on a construction site with a man he hated.

Whatever Evans did while in prison—be it painting, drafting classes, or just sitting around thinking about how his life should have turned out—he couldn't get over the fact that Stacy was someone he would never see (or have) again. He just couldn't let her go. And as his projected release date drew closer, he began to focus on Stacy more than he ever had. The poor girl was living on the West Coast somewhere with a husband and kids, and had no idea a murderous sociopath was spending his days and nights in prison plotting and planning how he would win her love once he was released. It was a good bet that Stacy, in all her days since she had last seen Evans, hadn't thought about him more than in passing. While Evans, on the other hand, was consumed with the notion of finding her and living out some sort of twisted fairy tale.

On . . . the day before [Stacy's] birthday, I drew a picture of her, he wrote in spring 1986. *Then I drew a bunch of crows and told them to find her for me.*

He went on to explain how he had gone out in the yard of the prison one day and "made a crow noise" back at a crow he believed was "talking" to him. *Sounds like bullshit, right? But I have a thing for crows that I don't talk about,* he wrote. Continuing, he said that he was planning on getting a "crow tattoo" when he was released because he had "promised" the crows.

Whether it was the crows talking to him, or thoughts of Stacy, Evans continued to have delusions of grandiosity as his release date neared. He had been locked up for so many years that whenever he began a bid, he tended not to look ahead for fear of having to face the extent of his stay. Yet, whenever it seemed like he could put his arms around a release date, he relished in finishing the time.

Most sociopaths display the same set of common characteristics. Among the most universal: a manipulative and conning manner, shallow emotions, incapacity for love, lack of empathy, impulsive nature, lack of any realistic life plan, paranoia, repressive control over most aspects of their victims' lives, a way to justify the means to every end and a goal of enslavement for some (or all) of their victims.

At various times, Evans displayed all of them.

With parole less than a year away, it seemed—at least from the memories Evans was recalling about Stacy and their childhood romance—that perhaps he had reached a point of no return.

I drew a picture of [Stacy] on a stone bridge. . . . She lived in the country and we built a bridge over a stream out of old barn wood. She used to sit there playing melodie songs on her guitar and singing for me, and she used to wait there for me when I'd come through the woods to her house, he wrote.

This was, of course, a fantasy. It had a fable, visceral quality to it. The story lacked reality and resolve. He was picturing what the relationship could have been, not what it was. Because as quick as Evans could paint a picture of the perfect romance, he could, in the next sentence, turn vulgar and callous: *The only thing I hate myself for is not putting all my efforts into finding her right away. Because she's the most important thing in my life. . . . But there's only one way to find her and that requires hurting 1 or 2 people and I was trying to avoid that. But now I see there is no other way.*

He added, before ending the letter: *As soon as I get released . . . I'm beginning. I know just what to do. And when I finally arrive at wherever she is, what a meeting that'll be. It's scary thinking about it.*

In his next few letters, he didn't let up about Stacy. In one sentence, he would say he had abandoned the idea of finding her, and in the next talk about how he was going to end up back in jail as he began trying to track her down by "making" certain relatives of hers talk: *I fantasize talking to her. Seeing her smile at me. . . . And I know I am going to shoot every asshole that puts an obstacle in front of me. There's an asshole in Troy that married her sister. They split to California. If he doesn't know where [she] is, I'll make him tell me where she is. . . . They were afraid of me when I was comparably harmless, wait till they meet me now. I'm through with these fools blocking my wishes, and for no reason except for they want to.*

Evans could be melodramatic in his writing, especially when he allowed the more psychotic side of his character to take precedence over what amounted to superficial charm. *I'm going to be all nice and humble and polite,* he wrote, talking about when he showed up on the front doorstep of Stacy's brother-in-law's house to ask him where she was, *and they're going to give me that polite 'no' shit. . . .*

Then, as he began to talk about what he was going to do to Stacy's brother-in-law, he related the situation to Hollywood. He said if her family gave him any trouble, they would be *starring in a private* Halloween, Friday the 13th Part 5, Nightmare on Elm Street *movie and I'm the fucking producer and director.*

Here was a maniac coming apart at the seams, centering his obsession on a group of people he hadn't seen in well over fifteen years. These were harmless people going about their normal lives. Yet, unknowingly, they were the focus of a madman's torment, lust and uncontrollable urge to blame anyone and everyone but himself for the life he had created.

As time moved forward, he became even more paranoid over the things in his life he had little control over. He believed, for example, "someone on the street was screwing" with his mail. He thought people he hadn't seen or heard from in years were out to get him. He thought the prison guards were zeroing in on him and watching him because of what he "knew" about other inmates. And he wholeheartedly believed there was some sort of conspiracy between Stacy and her family to keep him locked up and away from her.

By Christmas, Evans was thinking seriously about his release date, which he had been told was now a little over a year away. Still, he continued planning what he was going to do when he got out. Thus, as the Christmas season approached, he started once again writing to Horton, all for the purpose of setting up a relationship with him he would need to cultivate and exploit once he was released. Indeed, a relationship that turned both bizarre and violent as the years passed.

CHAPTER 53

Entering the Capital District of New York from Massachusetts on Interstate 90, at times an eight-lane roadway that cuts a path through the Berkshire Mountains, one gets a sense of how vast, immense and spread out the land truly is. Homes are out there, nestled among the millions of pine, oak and maple trees, but they are hard to spot from the road, only their snowcapped roofs and smoking woodstove pipes visible from ground level. Along the edge of the interstate, deer graze in herds like cattle on the wild grass and berries, seemingly undisturbed by the noise pollution the interstate produces. Christmas season in the region, like much of the Northeast, is straight out of a Hallmark greeting card: lustrous, charming, elegant.

As Horton took in the 1986 holiday season surrounded by family and friends, he began thinking about how his career had progressed since he joined the state police back in 1978. Inside just eight years, he had accomplished more with the state police than most do during their entire careers. He had gone to interrogation school and ended up getting an offer for a job to teach; he had been one of the NYSP's top divers; and now he was beginning a career in the Bureau that had already produced positive results as far as developing sources and arresting, as Horton liked to put it, plenty of "the bad guys."

Shortly after Horton and Mary Pat sent family members packing after the holiday season, he received a letter from Evans. Looking at it as he walked from his mailbox down the long driveway to the spacious contemporary home he had built himself on family-owned land, he developed a feeling the letter was perhaps only the beginning of a relationship that might surpass any other cop-source relationship he'd had.

Well, guy, Evans opened the letter, *I was . . . afraid mostly that the DA . . . had cooked up some bogus shit on me. . . . I really don't know what to do when my release date comes, I can be set up so easily. . . . Even my release date I'm getting fucked out of: it's supposed to be next December, but now they are saying it's March of '88, which is bullshit.*

Horton could only shake his head while reading the opening line.

"Here you have a repeat offender upset over the fact that he is going to do extra months on two years, when he should have been serving four years to begin with," Horton said later.

In some ways, Horton wanted to scold Evans and tell him to wake up and do the time without bitching about it and blaming everyone else for the misfortune he had brought on with his own behavior. Yet, he knew Evans was—and would become—an asset to the Bureau. The situation had to be handled delicately. Unprecedented was the fact that here was a career criminal, which most cops in the Capital District wanted to put on the trophy stand, writing to him, giving up drug dealers and thieves. Horton couldn't alienate Evans. He had to play the game, and make him believe he was on his side.

Since the last time they had spoken, Evans had been transferred to Clinton Correctional. He said he had been transferred because there were still a few Hells Angels after him. His counselor had put him under protective custody.

Someone was screaming at me out of the window. . . . Turns out it was [Michael Falco's brother], Evans wrote. He had told scores of inmates that Evans was a snitch.

Then Evans applauded Horton for his efforts in keeping "quiet" about any *leaks from developing about our talks. I was worried about that,* he wrote.

Next he talked about allowing the Bureau to use him as an undercover to nail the same drug dealer in Troy he had himself robbed—the crime, in fact, for which he was doing his latest bid: *I wouldn't mind playing bait to the scumbag if I knew the Calvary [the Bureau] would prevent me from getting my head shot off. It's something to think about, anyway, and I don't have anything better to do.*

Throughout the remainder of the three-page letter, Evans drew maps and pointed Horton to locations where he could find jewelry he knew other burglars in Troy had stolen and hidden. He also listed the names and places where Horton could find fenced jewelry: *Anything I can ever do to aid in sweeping these people out—let me know.*

There was Evans again trying to place himself morally above the same group of individuals for whom he could have been considered their ringleader.

At the end of the letter, he focused his attention on the person he knew Horton would be asking questions about once they got a chance to sit down again and talk—Michael Falco: P.S.: *I had [Tori Ellis's] address but some of my papers got lost in this shuffle. If you have it and want to send it, I'll write and ask for any info on Mike.*

It was Evans's way, he later admitted, of baiting the hook.

Evans viewed the dawn of the New Year, 1987, and all those years before it where he had spent his days and nights locked up, as "stolen from him." It was the same old story.

He wasn't paying a debt to society or accepting responsibility; he was complaining that the system had been set up to "screw" criminals like him. He couldn't decipher the difference between those who didn't commit crimes and weren't locked up and those—like himself—who were habitual offenders and locked up all the time. Any time taken off his sentences for good behavior or overcrowding wasn't enough; he thought he deserved more, especially since he was now sending Horton a wealth of information regarding some of Troy's most notorious offenders.

"Gary Evans was greedy," Horton recalled later. "Even though he got caught and arrested many times throughout the years, those arrests pale in comparison to the number of crimes he committed. He worked his job—which was burglary and murder—twenty-four hours a day, seven days a week. Whether casing a place to hit, committing the crime, fencing the merchandise or simply looking over his shoulder and planning ahead. There were even times when he was well off financially but would never turn down an opportunity to steal."

Horton was an expert at profiling criminals. Perhaps as obsessively as Evans dedicated his life to crime, Horton spent his time studying people like Gary Evans, their movements, behaviors and minds.

"Gary was a classic antisocial personality. He took no responsibility for his actions. Our rules weren't his rules."

He was selfish, Horton added, and cared only about his own well-being. He had no close friends. He was lazy and flat out refused, under any circumstances, to take orders from anyone.

When it came to women, be it Stacy, Lisa Morris or even his own mother, he showed no respect and, some later claimed, despised their very existence.

"He hated my mother," Robbie Evans recalled later, "for being such a weak person throughout her life and ours. He hated her lover, too. Gary thought all women were, in his own words, 'snakes,' and could not be trusted."

In a certain way, Evans's assumptions regarding the females in his life perhaps held some truth—because, in the end, it would be the one woman he put the most trust in who would ultimately turn on him.

CHAPTER 54

Throughout the next year, Evans obsessed over the same things he had focused on whenever he was in prison: Stacy, revenge against anyone he thought had ever crossed him and the status of his physique. He was lifting weights harder now than he ever had, getting results like never before. The more growth he saw, the more he wanted.

A recurring theme in his letters over the past ten years became clearer as he grew older: narcissism. The world revolved around him. Whether he was talking about his body or his crimes or why he was in prison, the center of the universe was Gary Charles Evans.

I'm getting so big! he wrote in late 1987. *Biggest I've ever been. Hard as a rock!!* He carried on about his arms, legs, biceps and triceps. *Lots of people want to work out with me but I work alone. Everybody asks me for advice. I see guys copying exercises I made up!! I feel like a superstar.*

The man was in prison—one of the toughest prisons in the country, no doubt—yet he felt "like a superstar" because other inmates were paying him a bit of attention by copying his exercises.

That being said, however, he felt life had been hard on him: *I deserve such nice things.*

He believed Stacy had tried to contact a former friend of his years ago, but that friend was part of a larger conspiracy to keep her from him.

I want to drink his blood, the piece of shit, he wrote. *He is VERY high on the list. Number 4, in fact, but maybe number 1, depending on the circumstances.*

Evans's sexuality had never been disputed among certain friends, relatives, the females he dated or even Horton, who had been trained to dissect criminals' deepest secrets. Evans, though, would drop faint hints every now and then of what could be considered, at the least, a sexual confusion on his part. For example, he drew a picture of himself as a female, yet he wrote, *But love you [Stacy]* underneath where he placed the name Gary next to the drawing. It was on a scrap of paper he meticulously used to count the number of days he had left behind bars using straight lines and X's, as if he were on a deserted island.

It was apparent, too, that he was more fixated on celebrities than he had ever been. But instead of admiring them from afar, he felt a desire to get closer to them, and often kicked himself for not acting on his impulses: *I saw Joan Jett a couple of weeks before I got busted [the last time]. I wish I could've kidnapped her. There's a girl back home who looks like her.*

Robbie had offered to help him find work if he moved to Florida after his release, and for a fleeting moment, he seemed to float the idea: *Hey, the nursery thing you mentioned sounds good. If it's going to happen, let me know. The guy may just be talking. I've seen so much bullshit, I don't deserve anymore.*

As the notion of being around other people began to fester in him, even as a truck loader at a Lake Worth nursery, he couldn't help but put the focus back on himself. Within the next paragraph of the same letter, some fifty words long, he had written the pronoun "I" ten times. It was all about Gary Evans.

He often compared Stacy to the other females he'd dated, and none measured up: *Even someone as beautiful as [Deirdre, a former girlfriend] couldn't get [Stacy] out of my mind. I want her too much! And knowing she's* somewhere *is ruining my every day and night. . . .*

By October, with only months to go on his sentence, the focal point was back on Horton, whom he had recently described to a friend as his "puppet." He was trying desperately to convince Horton to believe that he was going to be a huge asset to the state police when he got out. He talked about death threats made against him by several people in Troy. He named five people who were involved in the fencing of stolen goods and the drug trade in Troy. He even mentioned Michael Falco's name in terms of his being part of the same group.

But the most telling part of the letter to Horton came in the form of the punishment those people he was giving up deserved: *I'm in favor of the death penalty. I've seen some truly evil people who should be executed. I can't understand New York not having it.*

The most famous person he had met while behind bars, he said, was David "Son of Sam" Berkowitz: *I lifted weights with [him] for about a year. I never used to go near him because that's fucked up, killing innocent girls. . . .*

But as quick as Evans tagged the Son of Sam a psychopath, he changed his opinion and described him as "a likable guy, really": *He never talked about the killings. I used to kid him that he should've shot niggers or rapists and he'd laugh. I had a brief look at that new book about him,* The Ultimate Evil, *by Maury Terry, and the guy was claiming Berkowitz was with a satanic cult and he had proof. I asked Dave and he laughed it off.*

By the end of the letter, he promised Horton he would send copies of the letters between him and the Son of Sam. Horton eagerly waited, of course, but never received them.

Instead, Evans sent them to a childhood friend.

His relationship with the Son of Sam was far more personal—not to mention bizarre—than he had explained to Horton. Throughout their friendship, Evans and the Son of Sam wrote dozens of letters. The Son of Sam would get sent to solitary confinement and he and Evans would swap letters via another inmate as if they were e-mailing each other.

The language was quite cryptic. At times, they wrote in medieval dialect: *Take care, White Knight of the Dunes,* the Son of Sam would sign off, or *Dear, The Barbarian . . . Sir Gary* or *Sir Lancelot Evans.* It was as if they had their own language. For the most part, the Son of Sam thanked Evans for sending him magazines, books, tapes—he favored Bob Dylan over Loggins and Messina, he said—and food. Other times, they discussed weight lifting and general life behind bars.

As one might imagine, the Son of Sam was a target in prison. Because of his celebrity status, other inmates gunned for him, and he often described to Evans the notes and threats he would routinely receive.

Interestingly enough, in one letter, the Son of Sam wrote that he had run into "two Puerto Rican friends" of Evans's and was *sending them over . . . a gift from Big Dave.*

This wouldn't mean much on the surface, but taken into context with what was later learned about Evans's alleged attraction to transsexuals, one might wonder if the Son of Sam was acting as some sort of pimp, repaying debts of food and books with sexual favors?

One of Evans's favorite books, he explained, was *Red Dragon*, by Thomas Harris, the prequel to Harris's blockbuster best-seller *The Silence of the Lambs*. Evans insisted the Son of Sam read the book. He did, he said, but didn't much care for it. It was "fair." Ironically, he said he didn't "like psycho stories."

The AIDS crisis had just been made public that year. The Son of Sam said it was "a lot of shit" and "media hype." Evans, though, was worried about it affecting the world, while the Son of Sam said it would stay confined to the "inner cities . . . prostitutes and junkies. . . ." He then went on to list which states had reported cases, along with how many in each state.

The Son of Sam continually fed Evans's ego, complimenting him on his muscles and addressing him in a way he must have known would cater to Evans's grandiose thoughts of himself. One time, he told Evans there were "lots of Little Gary's," yet "only one Big Gary." He also called him the "Great Tricep King."

Evans, at one point, told the Son of Sam how much he missed seeing him. *I miss visiting you, too,* the Son of Sam wrote back. In the same letter, he thanked Evans for supplying him with what was an endless array of fruit cocktail, juice and other snacks.

One note that somebody had slipped into the Son of Sam's cell had frightened him, and he expressed to Evans that he was afraid to "go to sleep at night." The guy had called him a "cheap cocksucker" for not having snacks in his cell to steal, then went on to say that if the Son of Sam didn't fill his cell with doughnuts, oatmeal pies, nutty bars and chocolate, he was going to "rip" the "veins out of" his neck while he was sleeping.

Evans was totally absorbed by the stories. He felt important that *the* Son of Sam was sharing it all with him.

In his final few letters, before getting out of solitary, the Son of Sam talked about collecting mouse droppings on his cell floor. He'd shoot the "shit pellets," he explained, using a slingshot, at people who walked by his cell. He promised to bring a bag of shit pellets with him so he could show Evans how to do it.

You'll be impressed, he wrote.

The Son of Sam had sent Evans a copy of *Muscle & Fitness* magazine one day, but Evans sent it right back. To Evans's sheer horror, the editors had chosen to use an African American bodybuilder in an article, which turned him off.

I forgot, the Son of Sam wrote, *how prejudiced you are.*

According to Evans, the relationship he had with the Son of Sam ended when he called him "David Berserk-o-witz" one day while they were lifting weights together. *He got really pissed,* Evans wrote to Horton. Then Evans came up with a rather bizarre theory regarding the Son of Sam's pedigree. He claimed a new article he'd read said the Son of Sam was really adopted: *His name at birth was . . . are you ready? Richard Falco, son of [Michael Falco's parents]! I almost shit reading that!! I haven't said anything to him because that's personal and I don't want him catching an attitude at me.*

Asked later about the connection between Berkowitz and the Falcos, Horton said, "I do remember [Evans] telling me that. But I didn't take it any further. I really had no reason to at the time. It was meaningless to what I was doing with Gary. And, to be honest, it was one of those Gary statements that just seemed to be so far out there, I didn't put much credence into it."

Certain people behind bars scared Evans, and he was quick to point out who they were: *Baby fuckers; half-man, half freaks; guys with tits and no balls who would be glad to give you AIDS in a minute; three big, black ugly fuckers . . . with big tits.* He was "scared one of them" would "beat the shit" out of him and "suck [his] dick!"

Horton would later speculate after learning of a proclivity Evans had for transsexuals that this was perhaps his way of further trying to disguise who he truly was. Otherwise, why mention it at all?

In his letters, Evans also claimed that Michael Falco was going to give him trouble when he got out of prison. Again, he was thinking ahead, subtly dropping Falco's name to continue the facade of Falco's being alive and well and hiding out.

Near the end of the letter, Evans asked Horton to voice his opinions: *Do you have any suggestions? Can you see any solution? You know my situation, what do you think?*

Then came the same role-reversal ploy Horton had heard from scores of hard-core criminals over the years: *Your almost job of a criminal profiler sounds interesting! I wish I could've gone your way instead. I'd like hunting people down, surveillance, and the excitement involved, spying on shit and having access to all kinds of great stuff, and getting PAID for it! I'd shoot all the sex criminals, too, that'd be the best part.*

It was almost too much for Horton to swallow. Evans was buddying up to him more than he ever had—something Horton had never seen from a hardened criminal in his nearly ten years behind the badge. He now felt Evans was going to be hard to get rid of once he was released. There was no way to avoid it.

Just before Christmas, 1988, merely weeks before his release, Evans had a brush with violence. He had gone into a child molester's cell and, he claimed in a letter to Robbie, *body-slammed [him] all over. . . . Got some good shit off. [But] also got locked in for fifteen days (very lenient).*

By Christmas, he had made a decision about what he was going to do when he got out: *I think I'm going to end up renting a room in Troy while looking for work/$/ apt. . . . Yeah, right! I can see trouble coming. Scumbag Jew parole officers are waiting for me again.*

Days before his release, he wrote one last letter. He seemed excited to be getting out. He was going on three years behind bars with this latest bid, and it was obviously wearing him down. *I have a ride out of here,* he wrote, *not a bus like a lowlife.* Then, in true Evans racist fashion, he took the opportunity to berate his parole officers at the expense of an entire race of people: *The 3 I've dealt with were all N.Y.C. Jews—the scumrace of the world, ranked right down with niggers!*

Every day Evans spent behind bars seemed to harden him. Instead of teaching him the age-old lesson that crime didn't pay, prison allowed him time to plan what crimes he was going to commit when he was released. Yet no one, perhaps not even Evans himself, could have foreseen the horror he was about to bestow on the people he saw as mere obstacles in his way toward a better life.

CHAPTER 55

The state of New York paroled Gary Evans, who was already a murderer, hell-bent on murdering again, on March 1, 1988. As Evans hit the street as a free man, Horton was digging his feet even deeper into his work at the Bureau, juggling no fewer than two hundred cases that year: murders, rapes, burglaries, drug deals and assaults—anything and everything.

In early March, Evans called Horton at his home to let him know he was out. "Hey, Guy! What's going on?"

"How are things, Gar?"

Whenever he called Horton, Evans would open the conversation by telling him stories about prison life, which generally led into a rant, whereby he ridiculed every criminal in Troy whose name he had given Horton, always ending with the question: "Have you arrested any of those fucking assholes yet?"

He was frustrated with Horton for not going out and arresting people on every single piece of information he had given him. Although he never told Evans, Horton was fed up with a system that seemed to, at times, favor the criminal.

"Gar, I just can't go out and arrest people on what you tell me," Horton told him. "I need proof. I need a case."

"You gotta arrest those motherfuckers, Guy. They're bad people."

"So, you want that job I promised you, or not?" Horton said, changing the subject. "Forget that criminal shit. Let's focus on your life."

"What is it?"

"I have a friend at a local nursery who needs help. Lots of heavy lifting. Meet some people. Show off your muscles. It's perfect for you."

"Sounds pretty good."

In the course of a few months leading up to his release, Evans had turned the tables on Horton. "People ask me why I got him jobs and became what some said was 'friendly' with him," Horton recalled later. "Well, when he befriended me, I believed, perhaps very naively, that I could change him. I tried to talk him into a life of good things because I saw good in him. He was smart. Articulate. Well read. I wanted to help him."

A few days later, Horton met with Evans in the parking lot of Troop G. Evans seemed seriously interested in pursuing the nursery job. It was not only two city blocks from Horton's home, but it was right around the corner from the motel where Evans had been living since getting out of prison.

Evans had what Horton later called "prison muscles." He was extremely beefy, and wasn't afraid to show it off by wearing tank tops and tight-fitting shirts. When he walked into the nursery around mid-March, the owner saw someone who could possibly lift shrubs and small trees onto customers' vehicles without any help.

When it came down to it, however, Evans was never one to be bossed around by anyone; he just couldn't stand someone telling him what to do. On top of that, his boss at the nursery turned out to be a female, who managed the place, and not the person who had hired him, a male.

After two weeks, he called Horton and told him that "it was way too hard. Anyway, I can't work for a dyke," he added. "It's too busy a place. They push me and push me to do more."

"Come on, Gar. Tough it out."

Evans paused. Then, "I can make more money doing what I do!"

Horton wasn't going to give up on Evans that quick, however. So he called a good friend who managed a local depot in town.

"Listen, I have this buddy of mine who needs a job," Horton told the guy. "He's a hell of a worker. He's big, muscular. He can be a loader."

At the time Horton was working to find Evans a job and keep him focused on an honest life, Horton's family—his wife, Mary Pat, and kids, Jim and Alison—began to get to know Evans more personally. Evans would call and say hello to anyone who answered the phone. He would carry on conversations with Mary Pat as if they were old friends.

As Horton continued to work on his friend at the warehouse to hire Evans, he came up with an idea. "Listen," he said to his friend one day, "Gary is a convicted felon. I know it's hard to trust someone like that. But why don't we have him act as an undercover while he's working? He can keep an eye out for those workers who are robbing you." There had been a rash of larcenies at the plant in recent months. Horton knew Evans would jump at the opportunity to act as a cop.

"Okay," Horton's friend reluctantly agreed. "That might work."

Because Evans was a felon, the warehouse agreed to hire him—but only under a pseudonym.

It had taken Horton three weeks to convince his friend at the warehouse to hire Evans. It took Evans three days to decide that the work wasn't for him. Again, he went back to his old way of thinking, and spared no words when giving Horton an explanation.

"You fuck," Horton said when he found out Evans had quit, "you screwed me!"

"Come on, Guy, that shit was rough. Lifting boxes, loading trucks under the crack of a whip. It's too hard. I'm not taking orders from those fuckers. I can make better money and not break a sweat doing what I do."

Point in fact, he had never stopped stealing. Although Evans was complying with Horton's suggestion to try out the high road, Evans was committing more burglaries during that time than he ever had, Horton found out later.

CHAPTER 56

Gary Evans had heard the name Damien Cuomo in the past and had run into him once in a while, but he had never considered working with him. During the early part of the summer of 1988, Damien was living in an apartment on Industrial Park Road in Troy with his longtime girlfriend, Lisa Morris, and their daughter, Christina. Damien loved the place, mostly because it was located just behind the old-fashioned red-brick home where he grew up.

Around town, Damien was known as a "good thief," a former friend later said. He was small—"about 130 pounds soaking wet"—and could scale walls and fences like a cat. As a teenager and into his early twenties, he would show off by shinning his way up two adjacent walls as if he were Spider-Man. He could get in and out of houses quickly, without waking anyone up. For years, police had suspected an African American man of being what locals had dubbed "the hillside burglar," because several burglaries had been committed in one "hillside" neighborhood in Troy. But Horton and friends of Damien's later said the hillside burglar was Damien Cuomo.

Born on September 10, 1961, Damien was almost seven years younger than Evans. When they hooked up in 1988, Damien had just turned twenty-two. At five feet six inches, he was nearly as tall as Evans, but Evans had close to sixty pounds—all muscle—on him. Standing next to Evans, Damien looked scrawny, frail.

Where Evans excelled at burglarizing antique stores and jewelry stores, slipping in and out seemingly at will, Damien was a professional residential burglar. He had broken into homes since he was a teenager, some claimed. It started, according to an old family friend, with bicycles.

"As a kid," a friend later recalled, "Damien would steal bicycles in the neighborhood. His parents were really strict. His father, who went to church, I think, every single day of his life, would lock him in a back barn whenever Damien got into trouble.

"They had this [water] well in the front yard that had dried up. Damien would steal the bicycles and put them in the well so no one could find them."

Evans just showed up at Damien's apartment one afternoon and knocked on the door. Lisa Morris was home at the time. Damien was gone. She had never seen Evans before, nor had Damien ever mentioned him.

"Me and my girlfriend," Lisa said later, "were sitting behind Damien's parents' house one day [not too long after that] sunning ourselves when Gary came up. He was looking for Damien and then he said something. After they met, he was always pulling Damien out of the house. They would be gone for a long time. I didn't like him. He took Damien away from us, his family."

The hatred Lisa had for Evans began after Lisa and Evans "had words" one afternoon and Evans threatened to "throw her off the balcony if she gave him any more trouble." Lisa was working two jobs at the time, trying to make the best of what she saw as a pretty good life with Damien and Christina. She knew Damien was a thief and took off to commit burglaries, but she was determined, she recalled, to have a family with him and Christina.

Throughout the next year, Damien and Evans became inseparable. They hung out together. Traveled together. Committed burglaries together. And enjoyed what had become a rather reclusive life as two of Albany's most notorious, and successful, burglars. Other thieves in town envied their successes.

While Evans worked on his relationship with Damien Cuomo, he still kept his eye on Horton. At one point, he went to Horton and explained how he could set up a sting to buy two stolen weapons from a local Troy burglar.

"What do you want, Gar?"

"Nothing! I just want to fuck this guy hard."

So Horton gave Evans the money and told him to set up the deal.

A day later, Horton had two stolen weapons off the street and a local burglar in jail, and Evans was back on his way.

"He would come to me and talk about what was going on in Troy," Horton recalled. "He needed to stay in touch with me. Keep me thinking he was doing good things for me—which, in many ways, he was. But it was all a ruse."

On June 28, 1989, Cuomo and Evans were driving north on Interstate 87 from New York City in Damien's Chrysler Fifth Avenue. They had just finished meeting with someone who was going to start fencing stolen merchandise for them when a state trooper pulled them over for speeding.

"Fuck," Evans said. "We've got the trunk full of shit."

"Relax," Cuomo said, slowing the car down. "Let's play it cool."

While the trooper was asking Damien for his license and registration, Evans began to shuffle in his seat. Trained to snoop out any suspicious behavior, the trooper had enough sense to ask Damien Cuomo and Gary Evans to get out of the car. Then, "Pop the trunk," he said as another trooper pulled up. "We're going to have to take a look."

There on the floor of the trunk were several items one might use during a burglary, kidnapping or both: three black ski masks, two stun guns, a police scanner, two walkie-talkies, a slim jim, crowbar, screwdrivers, duct tape, rope, two sets of handcuffs, two sets of thumbcuffs, a plastic Uzi machine gun, gloves, hats, several maps of the Northeast and a book of police radio frequencies.

Looking at everything, the trooper assumed Evans and Damien weren't heading to a masquerade ball, but were perhaps either coming from a burglary or en route to committing one.

The stun guns was Damien's, Evans said later. Cuomo had a habit of breaking into homes when people were asleep, and would often use the gun to put people down who woke up. Evans hated him for it. If there was one thing Evans never did, he claimed, it was break into homes while people were inside. He found it too risky. Not to mention there were plenty of homes where people weren't home.

"'I'm the good burglar,'" Horton recalled later in a sarcastic tone. "That's what Evans always wanted me to believe. He'd tell me that he was a better person than Cuomo or Falco because he never did what they did. The truth of the matter is, Gary would break into homes if people were home *if* he thought he could get away with it."

In a scene straight out of the children's classic *How the Grinch Stole Christmas,* Cuomo once broke into a home while a family was sleeping, a former girlfriend of Damien's claimed, and woke up a small child, who ended up walking down the hallway and staring at him as he rummaged through the home looking for items to steal. Upon seeing her, Damien told her to scoot back to her room without saying a word.

The child said she was thirsty.

So Damien got her a glass of water and sent her off to bed before cleaning out the house.

* * *

After spending nearly the past year turning dozens of jobs together—homes, businesses, antique shops, jewelry stores—Evans and Cuomo had become good friends. When they committed burglaries, one of their favorite ways to throw off authorities was to wear sneakers three or four sizes too big. This way, any footprints left behind wouldn't match. By all accounts, they were good at what they did. Professionals. Where one man lacked a certain flair for climbing walls or cutting a hole in a window without being heard, the other made up for it.

It was common knowledge inside the confines of the state police that Horton and Evans had a relationship that perhaps stretched a bit over the cop-informant line. So with Damien and Evans in lockup at the Albany Thruway State Police barracks, just outside downtown, it was no shock to Horton when he got a call at home alerting him that Evans and his "partner" had been pulled over for speeding, but were suspected of possessing burglar tools.

"Jesus," Horton said mockingly, "what a shock that is!"

When Horton arrived at the barracks, Evans looked embarrassed, as if he had been scolded by a teacher and sent to the principal's office. He was both humiliated and disappointed that he had let himself get caught for something so seemingly inconsequential. The last thing he wanted was to look bad in front of Horton.

Cuomo, never one to talk to cops, said nothing when Horton introduced himself. Turning to Evans after not getting a response from Damien, Horton said, "I can't help you much. This is your mess. Stay out of trouble and this won't happen." He could tell Evans didn't want to talk.

"I'll try," Evans said.

"Yeah, right . . . just keep me out of it from now on," Horton said, and left.

Years later, Horton would find out that Evans and Cuomo had the entire inside of Damien's car lined with stolen merchandise, but the cops never found it. It was in the side panels and underneath a rug in the trunk.

"That day was a turning point for Gary Evans," Horton recalled later. "He had been arrested for something trivial . . . in a sense, making a stupid mistake. He realized he was getting sloppy in his work. It upset him. But little did I know then, of course, what was going to happen next."

CHAPTER 57

Located in the upper northern part of the state, hugging the northeastern tip of Lake Ontario at the mouth of the St. Lawrence River, Watertown, New York, is just over two hundred miles—a 3½-hour drive—from Albany. A melting pot of mostly Irish, German, Italian and French immigrants, crime in Watertown is something residents worry little about. One murder in town per year is, generally, a shock to the nearly twenty thousand residents who call Watertown home.

As the fall of 1989 brought thousands of tourists from all over the Northeast to take in Watertown's wonderful views of the foliage, Evans and Cuomo targeted the town as a candidate to do some business. An added bonus, it was almost as far away from Albany as one could get in the state, offering isolation, yet easy accessibility to the interstate.

One of Damien's best friends had joined the military after high school and had been stationed at Fort Drum, an army base directly north of Watertown. The guy knew the area well. He called Damien one day and told him that there was a small coin and jewelry shop in downtown Watertown run by one man. It would possibly be an easy target to hit. The way Evans explained it later, Damien's friend called and said, "I know of a perfect place for you to rob. There's an old man there. No alarm system. He sleeps in the back on a cot with a gun."

Indeed, sixty-three-year-old Douglas Berry, owner-operator of the Square Lion Coin and Jewelry, located in the center of downtown Watertown, directly across the street from Public Square, was an unassuming businessman who had opened the shop back in the mid-1970s with hopes of leading a quiet New England life. Berry couldn't afford an alarm system, so he occasionally slept in what Evans called a "loft," which was in the back of the shop, and, for protection, kept a handgun underneath his pillow. Berry had been married for what seemed like forever and lived in a small single-family home in town with his wife. Some who knew Berry spoke highly of him for the fact that he didn't much bother anyone. He kept to himself and was, more than anything, determined to succeed in business. He worked long hours and often ran the shop by himself. At six feet two inches, about 225 pounds, Berry sported a thick shock of brown hair he kept greased back in a '50s fashion.

Attached to a beam near the loft where Berry slept was a mirror. If he happened to hear something while in bed, he could look up at the mirror and see what was going on in his store without getting out of the loft.

When Cuomo heard about Berry's shop, he immediately called Evans and, excited, told him about it. Evans liked the idea of the location and the accessibility. Berry not having an alarm system was, of course, also a plus.

Evans, however, was never one to take things at face value; he knew any job that sounded too good to be true probably was. "Let's go up there," he suggested to Cuomo, "and take a look before we do anything."

Damien was, Evans admitted later, always ready to jump in the water without first getting his toes wet, whereas Evans liked to scope things out and take his time, making sure there were no obstacles in his way he couldn't overcome. Contingencies meant getting caught. In this case particularly, Evans wanted to be certain the information they were getting was solid. More important, he wanted to be sure they weren't being set up.

Throughout the summer, Evans and Damien drove to Watertown several times to check out the Square Lion. They had even walked into the shop and sold Berry a few pieces of gold they had stolen.

On the morning of September 7, 1989, they once again headed north to Watertown in Damien's car to check out the Square Lion and bounce around town to see how things looked. For the hell of it, they brought along ski masks, a crowbar and two handguns, a .38-caliber pistol Cuomo always carried with him, and a .22 automatic Evans had at times packed.

Evans said later he made a point to bring along his .22 "because of the information we had gotten earlier [from Damien's friend] about Berry possibly being armed."

The Gary Evans motto: "Kill or be killed."

Along the way, just outside of Watertown, Damien was stopped by a trooper for speeding. After getting a ticket, which "pissed him off," Evans said, they pulled into the center of town and parked near the Square Lion.

Evans explained to Damien on the way up north that they would drift into town, park near the shop, and hang out across the street for a few hours so they could watch the place. Damien was a bit antsy to get the job done, but agreed.

While they were in town, Evans explained, Cuomo became "too anxious . . . pacing up and down the sidewalk, chain-smoking cigarettes." Evans, who was methodical when it came to planning burglaries, tried calming him, he said, but it didn't do much good.

"Let's just sit and watch, Damien," Evans said at one point. "Let's see what kind of traffic goes in and out, and what kind of business this guy does."

"I want to get this over with," Cuomo said.

"Just fucking relax."

Throughout the afternoon, they walked the streets of Watertown and got something to eat. It was a quiet town, for the most part. Evans liked that. It told him they could move around town stealthily without standing out. If they looked out of place for any reason, someone would remember them when it came time for the cops to interview people.

Evans later said that he and Damien, months before they went to Watertown to burglarize the Square Lion, came up with what would turn out to be a brilliant idea—that is, if one is a thief.

"Come on, Damien, we're taking a drive up north."

"Where we goin'?"

"Just get in the fucking truck and shut up."

The Canadian border was about 240 miles northwest of Albany. In what turned out to be a three-hour trip, by the end of that morning they were inside the borders of Canada shopping at a local convenience store.

Damien bought Canadian cigarettes; Evans purchased snacks and several other items branded with Canadian price tags and bar codes.

"We're going to need this stuff when we do that Watertown job," Evans told Cuomo as they left the store. "Hang onto it. Don't fucking lose it."

Behind the Square Lion was a large parking lot, partially secluded. The entrance to the store was in front, on the first floor of the building, street level, leading out to the sidewalk. In back, there was a second-story picture window with two side windows that cranked open from inside. Berry's loft was just inside the window to the right.

As night fell on Watertown on September 7, Evans took a look at the window and figured they could pry it open easily and probably get in without being seen or heard.

After casing the back of the shop, they took turns going into the store to check it out. Evans had even made it into the back room, where Berry had his loft, and saw the cot Berry slept on, he later admitted.

Undeniably, Damien's informant had been spot on with his information, which pleased Evans considerably. He now believed for certain it wasn't a setup.

Damien was an expert at scaling walls and getting into buildings through windows and small crevices. Evans assumed Damien could walk up the fire escape in the back of the shop, then crawl along the building, balancing himself on an electrical wire hugging the wall, until he reached the window. Once he shimmied the window open and got inside, Evans could climb up the same way and follow him in.

In the back of the building, just below the window, was an office, Bear Construction Company. It was around 4:30 P.M. when Evans and Cuomo began scheduling the break-in, they figured workers in the building would be gone by 5:00, 6:00 P.M. the latest. They also knew from Cuomo's informant that Berry generally closed the shop at about 6:00 and retreated to his loft after getting dinner.

Sitting in Damien's Fifth Avenue later that evening, parked in the back parking lot, waiting for Berry to lock down the shop and turn off the lights, Evans noticed something while staring at the building.

"What is it?" Cuomo asked as Evans went quiet.

"I bet that motherfucker won't even lock the window."

CHAPTER 58

Contingencies are an unpredictable part of even the best-laid plans. Where burglary is concerned, the unexpected always happens. Throughout Evans's career as a thief, whenever he set out to burgle, he rarely took into account the nature of the people he was stealing from. He generally took people for granted and believed he was smarter than everyone else—including law enforcement, Horton especially. Innocent people were, to Evans, merely obstacles. He believed he would always escape the jobs he did unblemished because he had thought every aspect through in detail. As for the Square Lion in Watertown, because of the uncontrollable greed he harbored, Evans was about to break one of his golden rules of never entering a building while someone was inside.

Douglas Berry, for some reason, still had the lights on in the Square Lion as 9:00 turned to 10:00 P.M., and 11:00 crept up on midnight. He was either watching television or working late. Either way, as Evans and Damien waited patiently for the signal—lights out—to go in, they wondered whether the opportunity would ever arise.

"What the fuck is this guy doing?" Evans wondered out loud at one point.

Then, at about midnight, Berry emerged from the shop and walked up the street to Mr. Sub, a local grinder shop. Inside, he chitchatted with the girl behind the counter about collecting baseball cards. After about twenty minutes, the girl finished making Berry's favorite grinder, a turkey sub, handed him an orange soda, and, after Berry paid, before he left, he said, "Stop by the shop tomorrow about ten A.M."

"You'll be there?"

"Yes, I'm sleeping there tonight."

As Berry left, four white males, who had been hanging around inside the sub shop while he had been talking to the clerk, followed him out. The clerk recalled later that there were two more white males waiting outside. And they "might have overheard her conversation" with Berry about the baseball cards.

Seeing that Berry wasn't going to be going to sleep any time soon, Evans and Damien decided to go out and get something to eat.

By 12:30 A.M., September 8, Berry finished his grinder and nestled himself up in his loft to watch television and fall asleep.

At about 4:30 A.M., nearly daylight, Evans recalled later, he made a decision that Berry had been sleeping long enough for them to get in without being heard. But there was a slight change of plans, he mentioned to Cuomo. Evans said he would now go in first, but he wanted Cuomo right behind him. As soon as Evans got inside, as Damien Cuomo crawled through the window, Evans explained, he was going to sneak up behind Berry while he slept, hold his .22-caliber pistol to Berry's head and watch him until Damien zipped around the shop and collected what they wanted.

If Berry so much as twitched, Evans promised, he was going to shoot him in the back of the head.

"Sounds good, Gar," Damien said.

With that, Evans remembered later, he "grabbed the fire escape and got a good hold . . . then reached down and pulled

Damien up." From there, they walked across the piping the electrical wire was housed in and made it to the window in under a minute.

Looking at the window, Evans whispered, "It's fucking open! I told you."

Not a few minutes after they had emerged from Damien's Fifth Avenue, Evans and Damien were standing inside the Square Lion Coin and Jewelry, and no one—including Douglas Berry—had seen or heard a thing.

Once inside, Evans pointed to where he wanted Cuomo to begin. Then he sneaked up behind Berry, who had shuffled a bit as he approached but didn't wake up, and knelt quietly behind him, the barrel of his .22 pointed directly at his head.

Don't you fucking move a muscle, old man.

CHAPTER 59

Evans had always kept a copy of *Criminal Investigation: Basic Perspectives* throughout most of his criminal life. He valued greatly what the book offered him as a thief. If cops studied the book to learn more about their prey, Evans pointed out later, why couldn't he study the book from a criminal's standpoint? It seemed only logical that he could stay one step ahead of law enforcement if he knew what they were doing.

Found later, the copy Evans owned was marked up with notes he had handwritten. He had also highlighted portions of text he wanted to remember. The most tattered and worn pages were from a chapter titled "The Investigation of Burglary." He had studied this section, obviously, more than any other. He wrote notes, circled phrases and words, underlined pieces of text.

The method Evans and Damien had used to gain entry into Douglas Berry's coin shop, according to *Criminal Investigation: Basic Perspectives*, was called the "stepover or human fly move."

Authors Paul Weston and Kenneth Wells wrote, "The burglar is an aerialist. The 'stepover burglar' steps from a fire escape, balcony, or other building to a nearby window. . . ."

This was the exact procedure they had used to gain entry into Berry's shop. In the book, Evans had underlined the passage, seemingly pushing down hard with his pen, indicating to himself, perhaps, that he would ultimately run across this exact situation at some point during his career.

"There is no doubt that Gary Evans was a professional thief, burglar, arsonist, murderer," Horton recalled later. "He knew his 'trade' very well, and would tell me that he spent hours and weeks and months studying crime and how to be the most effective criminal he could be. But his weaknesses, in the end, overcame his strengths. I wouldn't realize it until years later, but while committing that burglary in Watertown with Damien Cuomo, he crossed a line I never thought he would."

Once Evans crossed that line, Horton acknowledged, there was nowhere left for him to go but further down.

Damien had taken an "army zip-up type of bag" with him into the Square Lion. He planned on filling the bag with as much jewelry, gold, coins and rare baseball cards as he could find while Evans watched over Berry.

"When we got into the place," Evans said later, "we tried to be real quiet, but the floors were squeaky. Damien went toward the front of the store and started putting stuff in the bag."

That was when, he added, things took an unexpected turn.

Evans had hopped up on top of a glass jewelry case to get up where Berry was sleeping in his loft. The jump up was noisy, but not enough to wake Berry.

Squatting at the "head end" of Berry's cot, Evans held his .22-caliber pistol an inch or so from Berry's head.

If the motherfucker moves, he's done.

As Damien tried desperately to be quiet, the floorboards, squeaking and squawking, refused to cooperate. Every step produced a tired-sounding, slow and loud creak in the floor, like the whine of an old screen door closing.

As Berry snored, he began to shift in his cot as Cuomo moved about the shop.

"Keep fucking quiet," Evans whispered.

Cuomo then took a tray of diamond rings, gold chains and necklaces and dumped it all at once into his bag. This startled Berry, Evans recalled later, and he "seemed to be waking up. He stopped snoring and started to move around a bit."

After Cuomo finished dumping the load into his bag, he took another tray and did the same thing.

This time, Berry woke up and began looking around.

I had my gun pointed right at his head, Evans wrote in chilling detail, *[when] the guy definitely woke up and picked his head up and turned towards me.*

When Evans saw that Berry was slowly waking up and, perhaps still half-asleep, figuring out what was going on, he "shot him once in the head."

There was no blood, struggle, or loud popping sound. After Evans fired the shot, Berry simply fell back down on his pillow, as if he had been knocked unconscious.

Even though Evans had equipped his .22 with a homemade silencer, the gun still produced a muffled sound that startled Damien.

Hearing a quick *pop*, Damien rushed toward the loft, looked up and said, "What the fuck was that?"

Evans didn't say anything at first. Instead, he looked into Damien's eyes and, ignoring what he asked, said, "Are you finished?"

"No. There's more."

"Fuck it, we're leaving right now."

By the time they were finished burglarizing the Square Lion, and Evans had murdered Douglas Berry, daylight had arrived. When they made it to the back window to get out, Evans spied a street sweeper working in the parking lot over near where Damien's car had been parked. Lucky for them, the guy hadn't heard a thing because the sweeper was so loud.

Before Evans and Cuomo sneaked out the window, Damien took the pack of Canadian cigarettes he and Evans had purchased in Canada out of his bag, crumpled it up and threw it near Berry's body.

With over $30,000 worth of jewelry, baseball cards, coins and gold loaded in Cuomo's bag, he and Evans drove back to Troy without a problem.

Once they got back to town, they made a date to meet in three days. It was agreed that Damien would hold on to the stolen merchandise. He knew someone who would buy most of it, he said. "I'll get rid of it," he told Evans, "and pay you when I see you in three days."

"I'll be there."

At about 10:00 A.M., on September 8, Shirley Berry, Douglas Berry's wife, decided she'd drive down to the Square Lion after trying unsuccessfully to reach her husband by phone all morning. Something, Mrs. Berry thought, was wrong. It was out of character for Douglas not to answer the phone.

When Shirley entered the shop at a few minutes after ten that morning, she saw a few of the jewelry cases opened. It appeared as though some items were missing, but she wasn't sure. Confused, she said loudly, "Douglas?"

After not getting an answer, Mrs. Berry then went up to the loft, where she found him lying on his cot, seemingly still asleep.

Her first thought was that he'd had a heart attack in his sleep. He looked so peaceful just lying there. With a .22-caliber weapon, the hole it leaves in the human body is so small that if the wound isn't on an easily accessible part of the body, it is almost impossible to see.

With her husband dead, Mrs. Berry phoned the local Watertown Police Department (WPD) to report a possible break-in, and what she now believed was the murder of her husband. "It's suspicious," she told the dispatcher, "because I noticed diamonds and gold coins missing from one of the display cases."

By 2:20 P.M. that same day, state police investigator Keith Fairchild from Troop D in Oneida, New York, was on the scene. After some preliminary interviews with Shirley Berry, the medical examiner and a few other local law enforcement, all he could come up with was one .22-caliber spent projectile found near Berry's head, a "fired bullet casing" by his right elbow, a crumpled pack of Canadian cigarettes and a size-ten "latent footprint" found on a piece of glass in the back of the shop.

CHAPTER 60

As they had planned earlier that week, Evans and Damien met in Troy on September 11, 1989, to decide what to do next. Damien had—as he promised he would—sold all of the merchandise stolen from Berry's Watertown jewelry shop. "Here," Cuomo said, handing Evans a wad of money. "There's about fifteen grand there."

Evans smiled. "Not a bad day's work, Damien, huh?"

"I guess," Cuomo said. He was still a bit shaky, Evans said later. Acting anxious. Not himself. Whereas Evans had killed before and the murder of Berry, an innocent victim, didn't seem to matter much to him, Damien Cuomo was a burglar. The idea of killing a man had never been part of who he was or what he did.

"You can never tell anyone about that job, you fucking understand me?" Evans warned, changing his tone from casual to serious. "Never."

"I know, Gar. I understand."

Evans later explained to Horton what he was thinking as he and Damien parted ways after their brief conversation. "I really didn't trust Damien. I knew that motherfucker had been ripping me off little by little the entire time I knew him."

You'll get yours, too, you little fucker, Evans thought as he watched Cuomo drive away. *Real fucking soon.*

Gary Evans and Lisa Morris, Damien's longtime girlfriend, the mother of Damien's child, had always hated each other, Morris explained later. "He took a lot of Damien's time from me. They were always taking off."

Sometimes it was a day, maybe two, perhaps even three or four. Damien would always return, though, bearing gifts for Lisa. But she still couldn't stand to see Evans. Lisa had dreams of marrying Damien, she said. But at the same time never mentioned it to him for fear of scaring him off. "If it happened, great. I had my heart set on it. I loved Damien. He was a *great* father. He loved his daughter."

Still, as well as Lisa and Damien were getting along, everything changed after Evans started showing up. Damien wasn't focused on family as much. He became, Lisa insisted, more interested in "the next job" he was going to pull off with Evans.

There was one time when Evans showed up at the apartment after he and Cuomo had burgled the Square Lion, and Lisa told him to "stay the fuck away from Damien." Evans had, as he often would, shown up out of the blue. Standing in front of Lisa on the second story of the apartment porch, listening to Lisa bellyache about taking Damien away so much, Evans stared at her and said, "You shut the fuck up or I will throw you off this balcony."

"You don't scare me," Lisa said.

"Just tell your little fucking boyfriend that I was here."

As Evans drove away, he began laughing. *I'm going to fuck her someday*, he told himself. *She doesn't know it yet, but I'll have her wrapped around my finger.*

As the weeks passed after the Watertown job, Evans began showing up at Cuomo's nearly daily. He became like a stray cat they had fed one day, Lisa joked later. And because he was there so much when Damien wasn't around, Lisa said she was forced to "leave Christina," who was three years old at the time, with him. "I had been working two jobs," Lisa recalled. "Because Damien was away so much doing his thing, I spent a lot of time with Gary. Although we didn't like each other all that much then, I felt I could trust him with Christina. Damien felt the same way."

Lisa began to drink much more heavily, she later said, around this same time. She had always indulged in "a joint once in a while and maybe a beer or two," but now she was drinking and smoking pot almost daily. "It was Damien not being around and me knowing what he was doing."

She later denied knowing anything about the Watertown job and murder, but she readily admitted that she knew Damien Cuomo and Gary Evans were burglars, and chose to look the other way.

By November 1989, Watertown detectives had a suspect in the murder of Douglas Berry. A "white male, age thirty-one," with an "extensive arrest record in New York and New Jersey." The guy was a Watertown loner who had, two years prior to Berry's murder, "bragged about killing [Berry] . . . and taking his gold."

When detectives tracked him down, he denied any involvement. Several days later, detectives asked him to take a polygraph.

"Sure," the guy said, "I have nothing to hide."

Most people, when faced with the grim prospect of a murder hanging over their heads, will, uncontrollably, harbor some sort of anxiety about the crime, even if they weren't involved. It's human nature. This particular guy had already bragged to his buddies at a local bar that he was going to kill Berry and rob him.

Faced with what was beginning to look like an entire town ready to tar and feather him, the man agreed to the polygraph, yet failed the test horribly. So, as the public demanded an arrest, he left the state.

Weeks later, detectives failed to put together enough evidence to prosecute him and the case was reopened and sent back to the state police.

It appeared that Evans had committed the perfect murder. As he watched from afar, keeping tabs on what was going on in Watertown, he realized how easy it was to get away with murder. He had killed two men with no ramifications.

Why not try it again?

CHAPTER 61

Before the first major snowfall of the 1989 winter, Evans decided he needed to do something that would ultimately be of great importance to him in the coming weeks. Near the end of November, a day or two after Thanksgiving, he drove down to the local nursery in Troy and purchased three bags of topsoil and about nine feet of chicken wire fencing one might use to protect a small vegetable garden from rabbits.

After grabbing a saw and shovel, Evans drove up in back of Damien Cuomo's apartment on Industrial Park Road in Troy. Pulling up in the back of the apartment complex, he parked his truck off near a wooded area out of view. From there, he walked about a half-mile into the woods and began looking for an area less accessible from the apartment complex's driveway.

Walking up and down steep inclines and small hills, he located a young tree about four inches in diameter and began sawing away at the bottom of it. Sweating, stopping every so often to take a breather, in minutes the tree was lying on its side, on the floor of the woods. Heading north from where he was standing, Evans began walking in a straight line.

"One . . . two . . . three . . .," he said to himself as he counted off sixty paces. Once there, he began digging.

After breaking through what amounted to an inch or two of frost, he hit sand and ended up digging out a three-foot-deep, three-foot-round hole. Then he lined the hole with the chicken wire so it wouldn't cave in on him, placed the three bags of topsoil inside the hole and covered it with a piece of wood he found nearby.

Walking away, he realized that if any of the neighborhood kids came up on the area, they might spot the piece of wood and, out of curiosity, lift it up to see what was underneath. So he grabbed as much mulch, leaves and whatever else he could find on the floor of the woods and spread it over the top.

Later, Evans explained to Horton that he believed Cuomo had shorted him on the Watertown job. He thought Damien had sold the merchandise for far more money than he had claimed and pocketed the extra cash. Plus, he added, "I had an arrest record. Damien didn't. That made it easier. He would roll over on me in a minute. He had a wife and kid. It was time for him to go. That little weasel fuck was the hillside burglar and they arrested some nigger for it who probably did one or two burglaries in his life while Damien was laughing his ass off."

When Gary Evans made up his mind, facts didn't matter. If he believed Damien Cuomo had ripped him off, in his mind it had happened.

It was time for Damien to go.

PART 3

EN PASSANT

CHAPTER 62

Gary Evans wasn't the only full-time criminal Jim Horton had been investigating since his arrival at the Bureau in 1984. By the end of 1989, Horton was quickly rising up through the ranks of the Bureau, well on his way to becoming one of its coveted senior investigators. During each year, he and other Bureau investigators had worked dozens of murder cases, often juggling many of them at the same time. As a father and husband, the cases that haunted Horton most involved young women and children: sexual molestation, rapes, abuse and murder. He brought that type of work home with him and spent many nights tossing and turning, trying to figure out that one missing link in the chain of evidence that could solve a particular case.

One case in particular that bothered Horton and his longtime partner, Doug Wingate (who was, in many ways, Horton's mentor), involved a local Filipino housekeeper, Rose Tullao, who had gone missing in early 1986.

Horton and Wingate had it on good information that a local repeat sexual offender, Jeffrey Williams, a bushy-haired loner who "liked to hurt women," was responsible for Tullao's disappearance and, ultimately, had murdered her in an act of evil so chilling it was hard to stomach, even for two seasoned cops.

In October 1987, Tullao's skeletal remains were found in a park in Cohoes. As soon as Horton and Wingate learned the details of the crime, they saw Jeffrey Williams's trademark all over it.

"A pillowcase was involved," Horton noted. "Jeff Williams had used a pillowcase before to subdue and sodomize a woman."

What's more, two local cops had spotted a car late one night down by Peebles Island State Park in Cohoes and went down to check it out. Touching the hood of the car, it was warm. After observing Williams walking out of the woods near the car, one of the cops asked him what he was doing.

"Taking a piss," Williams said.

The cops then took his name, wrote down his license plate number and let him go.

Two years later, when Horton found out that someone fitting Williams's description had been questioned by local cops down by "a wooded area" in Cohoes, he ran the plate number of the car. When it turned out to be Jeffrey Williams's car, Horton knew he was close to getting him.

By the end of the day, they had found was left of Tullao's decomposed body.

"He must have just finished killing her," Horton recalled later, "when those local cops spotted him emerging from the woods. Doug Wingate and I had made it a priority to keep Jeff Williams on our radar. We knew he had killed Tullao, and suspected he killed others."

Born on July 8, 1960, Jeffrey Williams, with his boyish-looking face, thick, dark black eyebrows and bone white, perfectly straight teeth, could have doubled for Peter Brady, one of the characters on the popular '70s sitcom *The Brady Bunch*. Yet, at six feet five inches, nearly 235 pounds, the women Williams preyed upon were no match for what was a monster of a human being. His criminal background dated back to his early teens when he was arrested for stealing a car. A few years after that, at nineteen, he was arrested for "sodomy, robbery and burglary" after he attacked a Clifton Park, New York, woman who later identified him. Realizing prosecutors had a rock-solid case against him, Williams pleaded guilty to "attempted sodomy" and ended up with a two- to six-year sentence.

"That first woman Williams raped, he didn't kill her and she identified him," Horton said later. "That's what these rapists learn—that killing their victims is the only way to be certain they won't be identified."

After serving time on the sodomy and assault conviction, shortly after being released from prison in 1983, Williams pleaded guilty to shoplifting, which placed him under what New York State called its "second felony offender" status. He ended up doing almost three years for, essentially, no more than lifting a pack of gum.

In 1987, the Bureau began focusing on Williams in the disappearance of Diane Deso, a local girl whose body was found washed up on the banks of the Hudson River that summer. She had been strangled and possibly raped. There was also Karen Wilson, a twenty-two-year-old local girl who had been missing for years but whose body had never been found; and a seventy-eight-year-old woman who had been raped and robbed in 1986.

Horton and Wingate felt Williams was responsible for all three crimes.

"He's an animal," Horton said later. "He hates certain types of women."

Indeed, somewhere along his sociopathic jaunt through life, Williams had, according to Horton and Wingate, developed a burning hatred toward a certain cluster of females. In a statement to police, Williams once said he "had problems with women" and admitted there were "certain types" he despised and, more important, "there were certain types . . . [he] wished to injure." Reading aloud the police report during one of Williams's many court proceedings, Justice Joseph Harris added that Williams especially hated women with "large buttocks, women who wore short skirts, women who were old or over forty years of age and women who tried to look young."

This didn't sit well with Horton, whose wife, Mary Pat, at a mere five feet, one hundred pounds, couldn't, in any way, be put into Williams's "big butt" category (nor was she over forty at the time), but she liked to "dress young" and fashioned her clothes by trends set by younger women.

Perhaps more frightening than that, though, was the hatred Williams harbored for Horton himself, who, with Doug Wingate, had pursued him vigorously since 1987. It was no secret Williams had told other inmates that Horton was enemy number one on his list. And some prison rumors had it that he had even mentioned Mary Pat and Alison, Horton's daughter, on occasion, threatening to grab one of them as soon as he had the chance.

Obviously, this scared Mary Pat, seeing that Williams lived five miles from Horton's home. At one time, they changed their phone number because they thought Williams was calling the house.

"I knew he didn't live far from us," Mary Pat recalled later. "I knew he was a *really* big guy. I knew he once said he didn't like women who tried to dress 'young.' I almost always shop in the junior department. I'm petite. I like to wear current fashions. I knew he could easily overpower me. I asked Jim to show me pictures of him. I wanted to know *exactly* what he looked like. I wanted to study his face."

Mary Pat, a dental hygienist, described Williams as having a "big lower jaw, like Jay Leno," a feature she would notice right away on any person.

"If he ever came to our door, or approached me in a parking lot, I wanted to know that it was him. . . . I was worried he would try to 'get even' with Jim by raping and then killing me or Alison, our daughter. I felt this was a real possibility. He was huge, frightening, and he had killed before and gotten away with it."

After Williams's release from prison in 1986, he met—

and eventually married—a local girl, who was only sixteen when they met, while he was twenty-six. When they married the following year, the girl became pregnant and ended up having the child while Williams was in Albany County Jail waiting to go to prison on a twenty-five to life bid for, of all things, stealing a rocking chair out of a garage. Shortly before that, on January 23, 1988, Karolyn Lonczak, a beautiful eighteen-year-old from Cohoes who worked as an "overnight monitor" for Residential Opportunities Inc., a group home in Cohoes for mentally challenged adults, was abducted in the middle of the night from the living room inside the group facility. Two months later, her nude body was discovered about twenty miles north of Cohoes on the banks of the Tomhannock Reservoir. She had been strangled and stabbed several times. Because her body was so decomposed, an autopsy failed to determine if she had been raped.

At the time, Williams had lived only blocks from the group home. Needless to say, he became one of Horton and Wingate's main suspects.

After Lonczak's body was found, Horton and Wingate decided to put Williams under a twenty-four-hour surveillance. There were too many girls turning up dead. Too many attempted abductions. And way too many pieces of evidence pointing directly at him.

One night, two Bureau cops tailing Williams spied him breaking into a garage and stealing a rocking chair. A day or so later, he was seen peeping into a window, watching a young woman while she readied herself for bed.

"When they saw him doing that," Horton recalled, "we realized he was getting closer to doing what he did best: rape and murder. We knew he had killed before. So we grabbed him."

Horton ended up interrogating Williams for seventeen hours that night. Taking three separate statements from him, Williams confessed to killing the Filipino girl, Rose Tullao, during his final statement.

"The second statement he gave me," Horton said later,

"showed more culpability on his part. An hour later, during his final statement, he admitted everything. He said he burglarized Tullao's place. He piled some things up under a window to get in. Then he chased her throughout the home, tackled her, punched her, knocked her unconscious, knocking out several of her front teeth, put a pillowcase over her head and strangled her with a phone cord." When Williams was finished killing Tullao, he told Horton, he had sex with her corpse.

Admitting to knocking her teeth out was important, Horton added, because only Tullao's killer and the police could have known that detail.

After a lengthy trial, Williams was found innocent of murdering Tullao, but was convicted of stealing the rocking chair. When the jury read the "not guilty" verdict, Williams turned around and looked over at Horton, who was sitting in the back of the courtroom. *Fuck you,* Williams mouthed with a smile. *Fuck you . . . Horton.*

I beat you.

The smart judge, perhaps believing Williams was guilty, sentenced him under a persistent felon guideline to twenty-five to life for stealing the rocking chair, noting that Williams had "confessed to Horton that he had killed Tullao."

"It kept him in prison until we could build our other murder cases against him," Horton recalled. "Williams and his team of defense attorneys beat us fair and square. The jury was concerned about the seventeen-hour interrogation; Williams's lawyers argued that I had 'coerced' a confession out of him by depriving him out of food and water and a bathroom. It wasn't true. But the jury believed it was. In retrospect, seventeen hours was a long time to interrogate someone. But I was ordered to do that. The DA was there. The entire interrogation was bugged. Two-way mirrors."

In the criminal justice system, Horton added, it is, at times, "a game of wins and losses. On that day, the bad guy won."

Leaving the courtroom, Horton was conflicted, confused, angry and depressed. He questioned the criminal justice system, how it worked, how it protected criminals and his role in it all.

"I was so disappointed after that, I felt like quitting the job," Horton remembered later. "I did everything by the book . . . everything I was told to do. The system let me down. I pushed the envelope a little, I suppose, with that seventeen-hour interrogation. But this guy was bad."

Horton knew that not only had Williams murdered the forty-year-old Tullao, but he'd also murdered and possibly raped Karolyn Lonczak, who was only eighteen. To let a murderer like that go free, it was all too much for Horton to stomach.

A competitive person by nature, having competed as a downhill skier for years with a wall filled with medals and ribbons, Horton had never really been on the losing side of anything so important. It was his first major homicide case with the Bureau—and he lost.

To make matters worse, the rocking chair theft conviction was eventually overturned. Then Williams was released from jail for "time served," but ordered by the court to wear an ankle bracelet and serve out the remainder of his sentence at home.

"I was devastated and embarrassed by the entire incident," Horton said. "I couldn't believe the jury let this guy get away with it. Some members of the jury were crying while walking out of the building. I hoped they were crying because they had made a huge mistake."

What bothered Horton most was that Williams targeted truly innocent, defenseless females. They were powerless against him. He could strike now at any time. The judge had even called him a "walking time bomb."

Horton didn't know it in 1990, but Gary Evans would be one of the key factors involved in bringing down Jeffrey Williams—and the fact that Williams had chosen young women as his victims was the bait Horton would use to attract Evans.

CHAPTER 63

Damien Cuomo lived with his girlfriend, Lisa Morris, and their three-year-old daughter, Christina, on Industrial Park Road in South Troy. Taking a left off Spring Avenue, Industrial Park Road runs straight up a brief incline and turns into Colleen Road. On the left is the large apartment complex where Damien and Lisa lived.

On December 26, 1989, Evans called Cuomo and told him he wanted to meet up with him to discuss "some things." Damien had just spent a pleasant Christmas with his family.

"What's up?" Cuomo wanted to know. "It's the holidays, Gar."

"I need to talk to you, Damien. It's important."

Evans had been upset for weeks over what he believed to be thousands of dollars Damien had kept from him after fencing the merchandise they had burgled from Douglas Berry's Watertown shop. He couldn't let it go. One day of anger turned into two, and before he knew it, his feelings of aggression became uncontrollable.

I have to act on them.

Lisa had, she recalled later, drunk heavily the night before, so she slept late on the morning Evans showed up at the apartment to pick Damien up. Christina was in the living room watching cartoons when Evans knocked on the door.

"Tell Mommy when she gets up," Damien told his daughter, lifting her up and kissing her on the cheek, "that Daddy will be back in a half hour."

Evans was waiting by the door, listening, watching.

"Where are we going?" Cuomo asked when they sat down in Evans's car.

"Just up the road here . . . we need to talk privately."

Evans took a left out of the parking lot and headed straight up Industrial Park Road toward a dirt parking area by the woods. The drive took all of about sixty seconds.

As soon as Evans pulled out of view near the edge of the woods, in one single motion he shut the car off, took out his .22-caliber pistol and pointed it at Damien's temple. "You thieving . . . fuck! You stole from *me*? And you thought you . . . you could get away with it?" Whenever Evans got excited, friends later recalled, he spoke with a noticeable lisp and stumbled over his words.

Cuomo didn't say anything, Evans explained later. He just sat there, "scared like the weasel fuck he was."

Evans then got out of the car, keeping the pistol pointed at Cuomo the entire time as he walked around the front of the car over to the passenger side, where Damien was sitting. He then reached into his back pocket and took out a pair of handcuffs.

After handcuffing Damien's hands behind his back, Evans, without saying a word, shot him three times—*pop, pop, pop*—in the back of the head. Then he took out a white plastic shopping bag and placed it over Damien's head.

Asked later why he did that, he said, "'Cause I didn't want to look at his face after I killed him."

With Damien Cuomo slumped over in the front seat of his car, Evans went inside the trunk and took out a shower curtain, blanket and some rope.

"I wrapped him in the shower curtain and blanket," Evans

described later, "and dragged him through the woods to the hole I had already dug."

Once he arrived at the hole, he lifted the wooden makeshift door he had placed over it weeks before, removed the three bags of topsoil and dumped Damien headfirst into the hole. Then he covered him with topsoil, broadcasted some of the remaining soil over the top of the hole, shimmied some of the brush over it and drove back home.

Horton wouldn't find Damien Cuomo's body for ten years.

At about eleven o'clock on the morning of December 27, 1989, Evans called Damien's apartment.

"Hello?" Lisa said in her smoker's scratchy voice.

"Where's that fucking weasel boyfriend of yours, Lisa? He's supposed to take me to the airport."

"I have no idea. . . ."

"Well, he's supposed to take me—"

Lisa cut him off. "I can take you, Gar."

"No. Fuck it. I called a cab. But you tell that little fuck when I catch up with him, he owes me."

Lisa said she would and hung up.

Whenever Damien left town—which he often did—he would always let Lisa know when he was coming back. There wasn't a time Lisa could later recall when Damien had left without first giving her a date of his return.

Damien Cuomo was never known as a person to stay in one place for very long. His being gone, at least in the early part of 1990, didn't exactly stir up any type of worry among his family or friends. But when he failed to contact anyone after a few months, rumor began to circulate that Evans, who had been overheard by several people saying he was going to kill Damien, had made good on his promise.

As for Lisa, she had heard that Damien had begun "ripping off" local drug dealers lately, so she surmised, when Damien never came back and never called, that he was "hiding out."

"I didn't know if he robbed a drug dealer or whacked a drug dealer," Lisa later said. "I thought maybe he did a burglary and the cops knew about it, so he took off."

At one point, Lisa called Damien's brother and mentioned that she thought something was wrong. It was unlike Damien to run off without any word whatsoever. She wanted to know if the Cuomo family had heard anything.

Damien's brother said he knew nothing.

Then Damien's car turned up.

"People started blaming Gary when Damien's car showed up abandoned," Lisa recalled. "But I thought then, as I did for a long time, that [an old neighbor of Damien's] had something to do with [his disappearance]."

After murdering Damien, Evans headed south to Florida so he could "lay low for a while." He had been sleeping with Lisa's neighbor for a few weeks by then, so he brought her along to make it seem as normal as possible, like he wasn't running from anything.

After two days, Evans said later, "she ended up getting on my nerves, so I left her ass there and took off to my sister's."

He wasn't gone long—because by the middle of January he was back in town, beginning what would end up being a full-time job of working to convince Lisa that Damien was still alive; that he was nothing more than a deadbeat dad who had taken off on his family.

As soon as Evans got back, he called Lisa. "Have you heard anything? What's going on? Is he back yet? How are you holding up?"

By this point, Lisa was a mess. Crying all the time. Thinking the worst. She was drinking heavier, knocking back vodka by the glassful to deal with what she firmly believed was the loss of her boyfriend, whom she had dreamed of "marrying and having five kids with," she later said through tears.

On the other end, Evans was plotting and planning his every move where Lisa was concerned, setting up not only an alibi for himself, but for Damien Cuomo, too.

On January 25, Evans went down to the post office in Troy and changed Damien's address. He didn't invent some address in another state, but simply filled out a change of address form and put down Damien's mother's address in Troy and signed Damien's name.

With that done, he began working on Lisa.

Showing up at her apartment nearly every day, Evans began telling her that he believed Damien had taken off to North Carolina to live with one of his brothers.

"He left you and Christina," Evans would say. "He's not coming back."

One day, Lisa had overdosed on "some pills and alcohol" and ended up in the hospital. The thought, she said later, of not having Damien around any longer was too much. The pills and alcohol helped her forget.

When she got out of the hospital and returned home, she found a note on the door to her bedroom, which was locked: *I'll be back to talk to you tomorrow . . . the babysitter.*

"It looked like Damien's handwriting," Lisa said later. "I believed it was."

Note in hand, Lisa ran to the phone and called her neighbor. "The little bastard is here. I just found a note," she said frantically.

"Gary's here," her neighbor said, handing him the phone.

"Don't go in the bedroom," Gary said. "I'll come over and check it out."

Cuomo had installed a special door to his bedroom. It was solid oak, designed to keep people out. He generally kept all of his stolen merchandise in the bedroom.

Lisa knew Damien wasn't inside the bedroom, she recalled. "But I thought he had come home and was trying to keep me out of the bedroom for some reason."

So Evans came over and kicked the door open. Inside the room, she and Evans found a suitcase of Damien's spread out on the bed, clothes hanging out of it, a sweater of Damien's on the bed beside it. The window in the room was open. There was a balcony and staircase just outside the window leading to the street.

"It looked like Damien had come home and was packing," Lisa said. "When he heard me come in the apartment, he left abruptly."

Watching Lisa looking over the suitcase and staring at the window, Evans cracked a devious smile behind her back.

"Jesus," Evans said, looking at everything, "he *was* here, wasn't he, Lisa?"

Lisa started crying.

CHAPTER 64

Weeks prior to what had now been a month since anyone had seen or heard from Damien, January 27, 1990, he had made plans with a few friends to fly out to Nevada for a few days of skiing. The Troy Police Department, however, after a preliminary investigation into his whereabouts, figured out that the tickets they had purchased were never used.

After talking with a former girlfriend of Lisa's, the police in Troy found out that Damien and Lisa didn't have the perfect relationship Lisa might have led them to believe. Damien was, the police reported, having "problems with Lisa" and had even talked about leaving her.

When police dragged Lisa in to ask her about it, she said she wouldn't "sign a statement until she talked with a lawyer." A friend of Damien's family had told police she had overheard Lisa talking on the phone one day asking someone "how much it would cost to kill Damien."

In his report, the Troy cop noted that Lisa had become "very upset" when he approached her with that specific bit of information. The cop claimed he had never told Lisa who had given him the information, but that Evans and Lisa showed up at the woman's house the following day demanding she never speak to the police again.

I wanted to arrest [Lisa] and Gary [Evans], the cop reported, *but [the friend] did not follow up. I tried to make an arrest, but [the friend] refused to prosecute because she is afraid (harassment).*

It seems a bit odd in retrospect, but on Super Bowl Sunday, 1990, a little over a month after Damien's disappearance, Lisa had a Super Bowl party at the South Troy apartment she had shared with Damien. It wasn't a large gathering of friends and family, but more of an intimate get-together among Lisa's closest friends, which now included Evans.

By the end of the night, with everyone having gone their separate ways, Evans asked Lisa if he could stay.

"Sure," she said.

Within an hour, Evans had Lisa in bed, on her back, she later recalled, having sex for "hours on end."

From that day on, they were an item—at least in Lisa's alcohol-induced, bereaved state of mind.

Evans had a crop of women he was bedding down at any given time. Each woman later had her own story to tell as far as what type of relationship she'd had with him. Where one woman might act as his friend, allowing him to talk about his childhood and how much he hated his parents, another might act as a mother figure, calming him, babying him, telling him everything was going to be all right. Evans would never, of course, tell his lovers about the murders he was committing. But he would divulge secrets about his life that he had told no one.

One woman Evans had carried on with for well over a decade was *Deirdre Fuller*, a New Hampshire native Evans had met during one of his many jaunts up north to burglarize, pillage and torment antique shop owners.

Deirdre was only sixteen when she met Evans in 1977. He had just gotten out of jail and went up north to do a job when they were introduced through a common friend.

Reared in a middle-class family, Deirdre saw Evans as a "quiet guy" who was, she said years later, "gorgeous and larger than life," especially in her youthful eyes. She knew Evans had been in trouble and he never lied to her about his time in jail or problems with the law. Young and, perhaps, naive, she wanted to flirt with not always doing the right thing in life. Although her family shunned Evans, in the beginning she saw the relationship as nothing more than a way to rebel against what was expected of her.

Over the years, they developed a relationship that consisted of Evans showing up in her life when he felt like it. Deirdre even reckoned it was a "friendship" more than a relationship in terms of sexual intimacy. "I was less of a lover to him and more of a . . . Well, he became my family," Deirdre said later. "He had nobody. I was very lonesome at that age. Although we were from entirely different worlds, we sort of found a common ground."

Evans would call Deirdre. They would talk for hours. A good listener, she said she became his therapist in many ways, helping him sort through whatever quandary he found himself in at the moment. Other times, they would share the same dreams and goals and talk about the future.

Throughout their relationship, Deirdre had always had a boyfriend, a man whom she went out with, slept with, and considered her mate. Evans didn't mind, she said. He even encouraged her to meet a good guy—a doctor, lawyer, some sort of professional. "Get married and have kids," he'd say.

"Gary was an organic guy; he lived for camping and skydiving. . . . I had no idea the extent of his violent side; I never saw it."

They liked to listen to classical music, she added, or maybe Elton John. To her, Evans was this "wonderful" person she felt safe and comfortable around. "He wasn't my boyfriend; we connected on a deeper level than that."

As the friendship grew throughout the years, Evans would make things for Deirdre and give them to her as gifts. Like with most of his women, he showered her with jewelry and gold, but she often pushed it aside, knowing where it had come from.

She couldn't go out in public with Evans, she recalled, because he was like a "child in a man's body." There was one time when they had gone to a local retail store and Evans wanted to buy her something. He was so engrossed with the process of purchasing the gift, that when they got up to the cash register, it was as if no one else were in the store. He made a fool out of himself and Deirdre by pushing his way through an "old couple" who were in front of them in line.

They would go months without speaking or seeing each other. But Evans would always call and ask Deirdre whom she was dating. He was genuinely interested in how she was doing, she claimed. He wanted to be sure she was always taken care of.

As the summer of 1990 began, Evans and Lisa Morris were seeing each other almost daily, having sex as often as they could. Evans had even won Christina's love by drawing her pictures and spending time coloring and playing with her. Lisa said later that Christina and Evans shared a genuine love for each other that no one could take away. Regardless of the person he was, he treated Christina, Lisa said, "like a queen."

During pillow talk, Evans would open up and tell Lisa about certain apsects of his life. One of Lisa's most vivid memories of that time, she recalled later, was a story about Stacy. One night, while they were in bed, Lisa noticed a tattoo on Evans's left breast. In prison ink, Evans had Stacy's name written in rather large font just above his nipple. After that day, Lisa added, Evans began to focus his energy on once again locating Stacy.

While doing his last bid in prison, he had pledged to Robbie several times that the day would come when he would set out to find Stacy and, if he had to, would convince her to love him again. It had been two years since he last spoke of Stacy, but he was ready now, he claimed, to fulfill all those promises he'd made of finding her, regardless of who stood in his way.

He had tracked down Stacy's number, one former friend later said, by breaking into Stacy's parents' home in Long Island and rummaging through the family desk. But when he called her, she barely remembered who he was.

"We were kids," Stacy said after Evans said hello and reintroduced himself. "I have my own family now. Why are you calling me?"

"I'd like to see you again."

"I enjoyed the time we had together and respect you, Gary, but I can't see you. I don't know you."

She lived, Evans soon found out, in California.

Hanging up, he became despondent and morose. He realized Stacy wanted nothing to do with him. His dream of the two of them riding off into the sunset together was nothing more than a fairy tale.

Days later, he confided in Lisa that he "had to see Stacy. I need to see her. If she gets alone with me, sees me again, maybe she'll fall in love with me."

Lisa told him that it wasn't meant to be. "Leave it alone, Gar. Forget about it."

A sociopath, by clinical definition, "feels entitled to certain things as 'their right.'" Stacy was one of those "things" in Evans's twisted mind. Sociopaths never "recognize the rights of others and see their [own] self-serving behaviors [as] permissible."

It was obvious Evans was determined to put Stacy back in his life—whether she, or anyone else, agreed with his plan.

CHAPTER 65

Shortly after telling Lisa he was planning on kidnapping Stacy, Evans took off to California to find her. He had made up his mind. Stacy was his. No one could deny him that. He was going to rent a van, wait for her to walk out of her house and snatch her off the street. He had always prided himself in the fact that he would "never hurt a child or a woman," but this was different, of course. It was about love. He hadn't seen Stacy for nearly fifteen years, but she was going to love him again—she just didn't know it yet.

Before he left for California, Evans called Deirdre Fuller and told her a similar story.

"Don't go," Deirdre pleaded with him. "Don't do it." Evans had told Deirdre about Stacy and had spared no detail regarding how much he loved her and why they had to be together. Deirdre, perhaps like Lisa, never thought he would act on his impulses, yet here he was focused now on the notion of taking her against her will.

"How did you get her address?" Deirdre asked.

Evans explained how he had burglarized Stacy's parents' house in Long Island. Then, "I'm going," he said before hanging up.

A few days later, he called Deirdre again. This time, he

said he was in California ready to carry out his plan. He had a pair of handcuffs, a rope and a van. Nobody was going to stop him.

"I'm going to force her to spend time with me," he said. He had a place in "the mountains" all picked out. There was no one around for miles. He could tie Stacy up, feed her and convince her to love him again. "If I could persuade her to stay with me," he insisted, "and get her away from her life, maybe she will fall back in love with me."

While out west, Evans found out where Stacy worked and decided to show up unannounced. She spoke to him, Deirdre recalled him saying, and was rather courteous, but said she couldn't see him. It had been too long. She had a life now—a life away from Troy that didn't include him.

The following day, Evans drove to Stacy's home and had words with Stacy's husband. Stacy became upset and totally rejected him. Sensing how much she didn't want to be with him, Evans abandoned his elaborate plan of kidnapping her and flew back to Albany.

After that call, Deirdre realized there was another side to Evans she had never really known throughout their many years together—and it scared her.

"I was frantic [when he called me from California]. What do I do?" Deirdre recalled later. "I think a crime might happen . . . and I don't want to put my life in danger by reporting him. If I decide to turn on [him], maybe my life is in jeopardy."

And that is how Evans worked. He scared people into being quiet. Not by making idle threats, but by taking action.

If the incident with Stacy wasn't enough to prove to Deirdre how insane Evans truly was, at one point later in 1990, after what was almost thirteen years of seeing each other occasionally and speaking over the phone routinely, Evans and Deirdre's relationship ended abruptly one afternoon.

Evans showed up at Deirdre's apartment just to say hello—at least that's what she thought initially. On her dining-room table was a tourist brochure for Belize, a popular vacation spot in the Caribbean.

"Oh, are you going away somewhere?" Evans asked, picking up the brochure, flipping through it.

"Yeah," Deirdre said. She could tell something was wrong from the tone of his voice. He was digging for information.

"Where?"

"Belize."

"Oh, who you going with?"

"A guy I'm dating."

"Really," Evans said. "How come you didn't tell me about this guy before?"

"I don't know . . .," Deirdre said. She was being evasive, she recalled later. She could tell Evans already knew the answers to his questions.

"Why didn't you tell me about him?"

"I don't know."

"What . . . Is he *black*?"

"Yeah, he is, Gar."

"It's over for us, you know that. As friends. Lovers. *Anything!* I don't know you anymore." Evans was fuming by this point. He began breathing heavily. Pacing. A lover had violated one of his most sacred rules. Deirdre had already lost a relationship with her father over the guy, an honorable man who attended medical school. He was going to become a doctor. Like Evans, her father had given her an ultimatum: the African American or me. But not quite in those words.

Evans then demanded she give him back every last item he had ever given her, dating back to 1977 when they first met. He wanted it all: the knickknacks, letters, cards, jewelry, jackets, antiques, a TV stand, chairs and desks. Everything. He said he would be back with his truck to pick it all up.

"If I can have it all," she remembered him saying before he left, "I won't hurt you."

"Here was this 'secret friend' I had for thirteen years," Deirdre said later, "and now I was *his* enemy. I was fearful that he was going to hurt the guy I was seeing."

Evans's face, while he was leaving, became "flat," Deirdre recalled. He grew cold-looking. ". . . Like no expression at all. It was as if our relationship was a business transaction to him."

Over the next two days, Evans filled his truck twice and brought the items to a friend's house. Out in the parking lot, while loading things, he was "mumbling" to himself. "If there's anything worse than a nigger," the nosy neighbor upstairs heard him say just before he left, "it's a nigger lover!"

Deirdre never saw or heard from him again.

CAPTER 66

As Evans continued to cultivate an intimate relationship with Lisa Morris, succeeding in convincing her that Damien Cuomo had been living large in South Carolina, basking in the sun, soaking up the good life without her and Christina, Horton and Wingate worked doggedly to build a case against Jeffrey Williams. They conducted interviews, tracked leads and kept a close eye on Williams as he finished his current sentence at home under the guard of a plastic anklet. For this simple reason, Horton and Wingate lost touch with Evans for a while, yet he still seemed to show up in their lives, Horton admitted later, to "keep an eye on us."

By June, it was no secret around town that, although it had been only six months since Damien's disappearance, Evans was shacking up with Lisa. According to an interview that the Troy PD gave to a local newspaper, they had interviewed "one hundred" of Damien's closest "friends and acquaintances" and still couldn't find him.

Since Damien had been gone, his father had taken very ill. The Troy PD assumed that "he would have come to see his father" if he was able to. On top of that, Cuomo had not tried to make contact with his daughter, Christina. This, particularly, seemed out of character for him.

* * *

Although Evans spent a considerable amount of his time at Lisa's apartment, he kept a room at the Coliseum Hotel, which was—not by coincidence—only about a mile from Jim Horton's home in Latham.

This was Evans's office. He used it as a place to keep only certain items: his answering machine, a caller ID, phone and some toiletries. He would also keep an alarm system on the floor. So whenever he had the chance, he could dissect it and study how it worked.

For Evans, the past few months had become a constant routine of looking over his shoulder. Word around Troy was that he not only killed Michael Falco, but Damien Cuomo, too.

To keep on good terms with the Bureau, Evans would periodically stop by Troop G and offer up someone. At some point in 1990, he had convinced a local guy from Troy to sell him a .44 Magnum. After making arrangements with the guy to meet him, Evans called Horton and Wingate and told them about it.

"Gary Evans always claimed he wanted to get guns off the street," Doug Wingate said later.

Later on, Horton and Wingate found out that it was all a ruse to keep them focused on anything besides Damien Cuomo and Michael Falco.

"I received a call from Damien," Evans told Horton one day. "He wants me to go into his parents' house and remove several boxes of stolen goods that he had hidden in an old shed behind the house. He told me he wanted me to move the boxes because he thought the police were onto him."

"Sounds good," Horton said. "Let's do it."

Evans drove up and got permission from Damien's parents to go into the shed and retrieve the boxes. When state police opened the boxes, they found coins, stocks, bonds, passports, personal papers from several area homes Damien had burglarized and an empty bank bag from Capital Tractor.

Tucked down underneath everything was a .22-caliber Ruger—the same gun that Evans had used to murder Douglas Berry.

Wingate and Horton weren't naive, so they continued to question Evans about Falco and Cuomo.

"Gary weighed every word you said," Wingate recalled later. "You couldn't say a sentence where he didn't see where every single word was going. If you don't have Gary, you *don't* have him!"

"The word is," Evans said when they pressed him about Michael Falco, "he went to California. Damien went south."

Horton was, many of his former colleagues said, an extremely "creative cop, who did whatever he had to do to get the job done."

By the fall of 1990, at thirty-five, Horton was considered an experienced investigator who was going places in the Bureau. Most didn't understand his profound desire to help Evans turn his life around. Of course, Horton had no idea Evans was a serial killer. He saw him as a career thief who needed some direction in life—maybe a guy who perhaps had a rough childhood, but could turn his life around if he only applied himself.

"The problem was," Horton said later, "that every time I tried to help Gary, he let me down."

Still, whenever Evans found himself in trouble with the law, he depended on Horton (or Wingate) to get him out of it.

There was one time when Evans needed to replace a mirror on his truck. Like any good thief, he decided there was no way in hell he was going to pay for it, so he drove up to Brunswick and found a car dealership.

While unscrewing the mirror off a brand-new truck, a security guard spied him on a television monitor and phoned police.

After being taken into custody by Brunswick State Police,

Evans started barking Horton's name to the judge during his arraignment. "I help Horton. He's a state police investigator. I want to talk to him."

Horton got a call from the judge, who happened to be a former trooper and one of his ex-bosses. "We've got Gary Evans on a petit larceny over here. He said he'll 'trade information . . . do something for you.'"

Horton, by mere happenstance, had just been promoted to the federal drug task force as supervisor.

"I'll go over and see him," Horton told the judge.

Later that day, Horton took a ride to Brunswick to see Evans. "What the hell, Gar," he said, laughing, "you let some fat, five-dollar-an-hour security guard catch you? I thought you were better than that?"

"Fuckin' shit . . . I can't fucking believe that I got caught stealing mirrors by a motherfucking security guard." If there was something in the room to destroy, Horton recalled, Evans would have probably given it a good beating.

Horton continued to laugh. He couldn't get over it. Evans had broken into some of the most secure antique shops and jewelry stores in the Northeast without as much as disturbing a mouse, yet he had been caught by a security guard? It didn't make sense.

"What are you, some petty thief?" Horton continued. "Are you going to start shoplifting candy bars next?"

"Fuck you! I'm a better thief than that. I just needed the stupid fucking mirror. Can you help me out of this, or what?"

"This is going to cost you," Horton said with a quip of sarcasm. "You *will* owe me."

CHAPTER 67

After Horton spoke to the judge on Evans's part, Evans was given a $240 fine and cut loose. Not two hours after he was released, he called Horton at home. "Let's go. What can I do for you?"

"That was fast."

"I pay my debts. I don't go back on my word."

"Well, Gar, you're famous for ripping off drug dealers. . . . Why don't we try to figure something out."

In the federal system, a CI can do what is called a "reversal." Simply put, the cops can have the drugs and the bad guy can have the money; thus, a CI can solicit the dope deal. In the state system, this can't be done; it is considered entrapment.

Horton continued: "Here's what we'll do. I'll assign you to an agent. We'll provide you with a thirty-pound bale of marijuana. Who can you get to buy it from you?"

Evans shot right back without missing a beat. "*Archie Bennett.*"

Bennett was a neighbor of Damien Cuomo's, known around town as a "big-time" drug dealer. Evans had always hated him. He said he would enjoy "fucking him" and not lose a minute's sleep over it.

A few days later, Evans called Bennett and told him he had robbed a drug dealer in New York City and wanted to dump a bale of pot as soon as possible. "I want thirty-four thousand."

Bennett said he would get back to him.

Within days, Bennett called to say he had the money.

"Good," Evans said. "Meet me at the parking lot near the Laundromat by the river." It was a popular spot in Troy down the street from Bennett's house. Bennett knew exactly where Evans was talking about.

He and Evans then set up a time for the following day.

Evans called the agent Horton had assigned him and explained what was going on. When Horton heard, he immediately began wondering if Evans was telling the truth. It seemed too easy.

"I need to be there," Horton told the agent. "Nobody knows Gary like me. I trust him, but I don't trust him."

In all, there were about ten agents set up in every nook surrounding the area near the parking lot. Horton stationed himself in a convenience store diagonally across the block.

Evans pulled up about 1:30 P.M. An agent met with him and gave him the bale of dope while Horton sneaked around to the front of his car and unhooked the coil wire so Evans couldn't act on any strange impulses he might have of taking off.

At 2:00 P.M. sharp, Bennett walked into the parking lot and sat in Evans's Saab.

Under normal circumstances, a CI would be arrested along with the target to make it look like a normal grab. That way, the buyer wouldn't suspect—at least not right away—a setup.

Evans, however, told Horton he wanted Bennett to know he was being set up. Horton didn't have much of a problem with it. If Evans wanted to show Bennett he wasn't scared of him, so be it. But Horton said they wouldn't make an issue out of it; they just wouldn't cuff Evans and lead him away with Bennett.

As Horton took a crunch out of a hot dog while standing in the window of the convenience store across the street, he watched as Bennett gave Evans a brown paper bag, which contained the money.

Within a few seconds, all of the agents "swooped in and grabbed Bennett." Evans, turning to Bennett, mouthed, *Fuck you, asshole,* and walked away from the car.

As Bennett was being put into one of the cruisers, Evans began mumbling and skulking about, noticeably upset at something.

"What is it, Gar?" Horton asked.

"Fuck, fuck, fuck!" Evans said. "Damn it all. Son of a bitch. Motherfucker."

"What *is* it, Gar? Talk to me?"

"Bennett never even asked me to see the drugs!"

"Yeah, so. Big deal. We got him."

"I could have pulled this shit off without you assholes and pocketed the thirty-four thousand myself. Motherfucker, I didn't need you guys."

Horton started laughing.

In the end, Evans received about $2,500 for his role. A confidential informant, under the federal system, is entitled to a percentage of any take he is involved in.

After working with Horton on nailing Bennett, who was basically given a slap on the wrist and released, Evans became engrossed in the excitement of working with Horton on that level. He envied Horton in many ways, and made no secret about telling him how much he wished he could have been more like him.

"My way of thinking was to always make Gary feel like he was doing a good thing by me," Horton said. "He believed that I was totally taken with him—and that was part of my wanting to know things about him he just wouldn't come out and tell me. I began to suspect that he'd had something to do with the disappearance of Damien Cuomo and

Michael Falco, as we became closer. I still had no proof, of course, but I felt I was getting somewhere."

Indeed, once Evans got a taste of police work, he wanted more—like an addict.

Months after the Bennett job, Evans phoned Horton and told him he needed to talk to him about another "job." Horton was never one to pass up an opportunity to hear Evans out. So he agreed to meet him.

"We met in the parking lot of a grocery store in Watervliet, New York, across the Hudson River from Troy," Horton recalled later. "I parked away from most of the shoppers, in an area where most people wouldn't want to park."

Evans showed up on foot, which was pretty standard for him whenever he and Horton met. "He had his vehicle parked nearby, but was probably doing counter-surveillance on me, like he always did."

After sitting down in Horton's car, Evans began to talk about an idea he had to purchase a few guns. As he talked, a car pulled up, nose to nose, to Horton's.

"With all these places to park, this guy comes way over here?" Horton said aloud.

"That motherfucker," Evans said in agreement. Then he opened a newspaper and pretended to read it to block his face so the people in the car couldn't see him.

Within a few moments, a red Chevrolet Camaro pulled up next to the other car. Neither driver had noticed Horton and Evans sitting in front of them.

Horton couldn't believe his eyes, but both men got out of their cars and began to make an exchange.

"Drugs for money," Horton recalled. "Right in front of me. Gary and I couldn't believe it. As the deal was going down, I'm laughing, explaining to Gary what I'm seeing because he's still covering his face with the newspaper."

"Look at these two guys," Horton said to Evans. "I can't believe it. They're doing a drug deal not ten feet from me. Isn't it obvious that I'm in a Bureau car?"

Evans couldn't help himself. He had to peek around the newspaper to see it for himself.

"Motherfucker," he said.

"Quick, get out of my car," Horton said at that point. The men had completed the deal and were getting into their cars to leave.

"Let me go with you," Evans pleaded. He had a noticeable hint of excitement in his voice.

"Get out of my car," Horton said again, with a bit more authority.

Evans began begging. "Please let me go, Guy. I want to bust them with you. Come on, it'll be fun. The two of us working together like cops."

"Get. The. Fuck. Out. Of. My. Car." Horton wasn't kidding now. Both cars were approaching the parking lot exit. He had to take off at that moment or the chance of catching one of them was gone.

"Come on, Guy?" Evans asked again.

"I'll physically throw you out of the car, Gar. Now get out."

As Horton opened his door to walk around to the passenger side to pull Evans out, Evans took off.

"The cars went in different directions," Horton added. "I chose to stop the first car, thinking that he was the buyer rather than the seller, because the seller would have more money. He ended up being the buyer. He had an 'eight ball' of cocaine on him. I had gotten the plate number off the Camaro and went and picked up the seller later that night. Gary called me the next day at my office and wanted to know what happened."

"I wish I was a cop so I could do that," Evans said before they hung up. "I wish I was like you, Guy."

CHAPTER 68

Not long after Horton and Evans had worked together on the Archie Bennett drug bust, Evans began showing up, it seemed, wherever Horton went. By early 1991, Horton was bumping into Evans routinely in Latham. Near his home. At the market. The local sub shop. The diner. Wherever Horton went, Evans was right behind him.

"Hey, Guy," Evans might say, coming up from behind. "What's going on?"

"What are you doing here?" Horton would ask.

After Horton realized it wasn't a coincidence, he started to turn the tables and "pop in" on Evans wherever he was living. Evans would be sitting on the floor in his hotel room, studying alarm system manuals, browsing through antique magazines, reading astrology books and true-crime books and magazines.

"What's up, Guy? Come on in."

Horton tried to center his conversations on why Evans couldn't focus his passion on something legal. But Evans would always spin the discussion back to burglary, so Horton learned to play into it.

"Tell me about burglarizing homes, Gar? What is a good target?"

Evans perked up. "I would never hit a house with an alarm system sticker on it, or a house with a Beware of Dog sign."

Horton made a mental note: *Get alarm system stickers.*

"What about those manuals . . . why study them?"

"Most antique shops have alarm systems; they help me understand how they work. I've never been caught inside while doing a job."

Then Horton found out Evans had camped out in the woods in back of his house. "He was watching me watch him," Horton recalled later. "Both of us had our own agendas by that point."

It was no secret that Horton and Doug Wingate were investigating Jeffrey Williams. Local newspapers and television had covered the Williams case extensively.

Evans would raise the subject once in a while, but Horton was careful about what he said. It was an ongoing investigation. Sharing information with anyone—better yet a convicted felon—would jeopardize the case.

"Let him [Jeffrey Williams] get out," Evans said one day to Horton and Wingate, "and your worries are over!"

"You let us take care of Williams, Gar. Don't worry about it," Horton said.

This seemingly casual conversation planted a seed in Horton's mind, however. "I knew then that the day would come where I could possibly use Gary to help me with Jeffrey Williams. We just didn't know how at that point."

The relationship between Horton and Evans began to work its way to the Horton family dining-room table.

"Jim and Gary's relationship never bothered me," Mary Pat Horton recalled later. "After all, Jim and I thought he was just a local thief—a guy, according to Jim, who didn't have a favorable childhood or solid role models, a guy who 'never had a chance.' I knew Jim was developing a rapport with him and that Gary trusted him because Jim treated Gary like a human being during their encounters. I felt sorry for Gary—because of what I knew about his childhood. As the calls by Gary became more frequent, it just reinforced to me that this guy really had no one else he could turn to. The kids and I started to refer to him as 'Uncle Gary,' because he called the house much more often than any of our real uncles."

CHAPTER 69

By Farmer's Almanac standards, October 17, 1991, was a typical fall day in New England. In Albany, temperatures had hovered around fifty-nine degrees, while the sun set under the moon phase of Waxing Gibbons at 6:10 P.M.

Moon phases were important to Evans; and he would make note of it later in his life. A lot of his paintings and drawings had always centered on the rise and fall of the moon. The Waxing Gibbons, which is nearly full, rises during the day when most people cannot see it. Some historians claim the Italians attacked the Albanians during World War II by the light of the Waxing Moon because it had illuminated the night sky as if it were daytime.

Evans would never say that he chose the night of October 17, 1991, to act out on his bloody impulses because he favored the Waxing Moon, but his love for astrology might make one wonder if, perhaps, like a wolf, he allowed the moon to guide him on that night.

Little Falls, New York, is a ninety-minute drive from Albany, conveniently located in the middle of the state. With a population of just over five thousand, Little Falls is about as "small town" as it gets in New York: old-fashioned cafés, low-rise commercial buildings, a few retail outlets and one small coin shop on Main Street, run by thirty-six-year-old Gregory Jouben, a black-haired, good-looking local who had worked hard most of his life trying to survive as a small business owner. Beside his coin shop, the seven-story office building where Jouben rented space was vacant.

Evans loved Jouben's shop because it was far enough away from Albany where he could come and go without being noticed.

"I had brought some stolen property/jewelry there a couple of times and got to know [Jouben] a little bit," Evans said later. "The first couple of times he didn't ask for any ID or my name. But the last time I went there, he asked me to sign my name, so I made one up."

Two weeks before Evans went into Jouben's shop for the last time, on October 3, 1991, he began camping out on the top floor of the mostly abandoned building.

"I was short on money and was scoping out [Jouben's shop] to later rob it," Evans recalled.

Cops later found holes in the concrete walls where Evans had practiced shooting his .22-caliber pistol. He had even spray-painted graffiti messages on the walls: *This is my fucking bank!* and *Stay the fuck out of my bank!*

The other reason for moving into the building two weeks prior to the night he chose to burglarize Jouben's shop was that he wanted to watch Jouben's movements, Evans said. He knew Jouben had some rather expensive jewelry, but he didn't know exactly where he kept it, he said. So at night, shortly before Jouben closed the shop, Evans would watch him by crawling around the ceiling tiles and peering at him from above. Within a few days, he found out that he was putting all of his most expensive merchandise in a state-of-the-art floor safe. There was no way, Evans realized that night, he could get into the safe without the combination.

"But I thought I would watch him for a few weeks and pick a night when he forgot to lock the safe."

By the end of the second week, he became frustrated; he later admitted he couldn't wait any longer.

That afternoon, he went to a local hardware store and purchased an Open/Closed sign: orange lettering, black background, the same as any For Sale sign.

After returning to where he was living on the top floor, he stuffed the sign down the front of his pants, underneath his shirt, stuck his .22-caliber pistol in a bag—"I had the gun inside a bag secured with duct tape, so when I shot him, the brass shell casings would stay in the bag"—and put it, along with a few other items, in a large duffel bag. In his front pocket, Evans placed a gold medallion with the word "bitch" etched across the front of it.

By 5:00 P.M., he was ready to go to work.

At about the same time, Jouben closed his shop and set out across the street to make a deposit at the local bank. A local Watertown police officer even watched him make the drop.

The cop was traveling southbound on Ann Street, going toward East Main, when he saw Jouben heading back into his shop. "He was wearing light-colored clothing and . . . looked happy at the time," the cop reported later.

Evans left the top floor at approximately 5:00 and worked his way downstairs to approach Jouben about buying the gold BITCH medallion.

Jouben was sitting at his jeweler's table near the cash register when Evans walked through the front door, the bells hanging off the doorknob rattling as if it were Christmastime. Jouben couldn't see Evans from where he sat. But by the time he got up to check who had walked in, Evans had already locked the door from the inside and placed the Open/Closed sign, with the Closed side facing out, in the window.

"Can I help you . . . ?" Jouben asked as Evans approached him.

"How are you?" Evans said.

It took a moment, but Jouben recognized Evans. "Hey, how have you been? I'm closing in a few minutes."

Evans reached into his pocket and pulled out the broach. "Can you check this out for me real quick?"

"Sure," Jouben said as they walked back to his desk. Then, as he slipped on his eyepiece and jeweler's lens, Evans reached into his bag and placed his hand on a .22-caliber pistol he had purchased recently.

"Greg [Jouben] took [the broach] from me, sat down at his desk," Evans recalled later, "and began to look at the piece through his eyeglass."

Viewing the piece, Jouben could tell immediately it was worthless. "The diamonds are ACZ . . . worth maybe ten dollars," he said, still gazing at it.

Next, as Jouben lifted the piece up to the light for a better look, Evans shot him once in the back of the head.

Jouben then fell onto his desk, his body convulsing and shaking. . . . Blood ran down the back of his head, across his shoulder and onto his forearm and thigh.

Evans quickly walked to the front of the shop and checked to see if anyone had heard the shot. Confident no one had, he shut the lights off and grabbed a handful of diamond engagement rings—the items he'd had his eye on for the past two weeks—and put them into his duffel bag.

Jouben, however, wasn't dead; Evans heard him stirring at his desk and immediately ran toward him.

Reaching him a few seconds later, Evans later said he saw Jouben, barely able to move, reaching for the phone.

Motherfucker . . . you're still alive?

As Jouben, grunting and struggling to take a breath, lifted the phone receiver, Evans pumped two more rounds into the side of his head. At that point, blood splattered across Jouben's desk, clothes and face as the shots tore through his skull. He fell back in his chair; his head hanging off the back headrest, a trail of blood dripping . . . pooling up on the floor.

Scared he had made too much noise, Evans then grabbed a few more items and took off. Inside the back of the shop was a door leading to other sections of the building. Knowing the layout of the building, he worked his way through the labyrinth of doors and hallways and found the main stairwell leading up to the roof.

Running up to the fourth floor, Evans fled out the door and ended up facing "a lower roof on an adjacent building."

Like a teenager acting on a dare, he hopped from building to building, crossing over alleyways about fifty feet below. He had parked his truck just down the block earlier that day.

"As I was going out of the building and across several roofs, I heard stuff dropping out of the bag all the way."

When he reached the fourth roof, he shinned down a set of drainpipes attached to the side of the building, like a fireman, and found himself standing in an alley staring at his truck.

CHAPTER 70

The Little Falls Police Department (LFPD) received a call around 8:49 P.M. from Constance Jouben, Gregory Jouben's seventy-seven-year-old mother. She had been working with her son that day and left the shop, she said, at about 3:30 P.M.

"My son," Constance told police over the phone, "failed to come home from work at his usual time. I've called and called over there . . . but haven't gotten an answer."

"Okay, ma'am," the dispatcher said. "And you're worried about him?"

"Yes. I don't know. This is unlike Gregory. He's usually home by seven."

"We'll check it out."

Within minutes, three Little Falls patrolmen were dispatched to the scene.

One of the officers tried the front door, but it was locked. Evans had locked it himself. Walking around to the side-street entrance, where a window looked into the shop, the cop then tried the side door, but it, too, was locked. Peering into the shop through the window, the cop could see Jouben slumped over backward in his chair, in front of his desk.

"Hey, can you hear me?" the cop yelled, banging on the window to see if he could get Jouben's attention.

After walking around and kicking open the bottom portion of the front door, the same cop crawled in and found Jouben's "stiff and rigid [body]. . . . He had blood on his face and all over his body . . . a pool of blood on the floor."

A fourth cop had been dispatched to the scene while the others were already inside. When he arrived minutes later at the front door, he saw Constance Jouben milling about, wondering what was going on.

Two "young girls" were outside the building on Ann Street, around the corner. As the cop approached them, one of them said, "You can see him. He's slumped over."

With the front door now open and cops wandering around everywhere, Constance Jouben walked in and followed one of the officers toward the back.

"Someone killed him," she blurted out when she walked around the corner and saw her son sprawled out on the chair, blood all over his face, clothes and floor. "Why did they have to do this? He's dead. . . ."

Evans left Little Falls and drove directly back to his motel room at the Coliseum Hotel in Latham. The following day, he boarded a bus to Colorado and met up with a fence he had used from time to time.

The total tally from the Little Falls job was just a hair over $60,000.

Blood money—all of it.

When he returned to Latham two days later, Evans buried the gun he had used to kill Gregory Jouben, along with a second gun he had been carrying with him, in a metal box in the back of Albany Rural Cemetery in Menands.

The LFPD, along with the local state police, conducted an investigation into Gregory Jouben's murder and immediately found several items that Evans had left behind. In all of the planning he had done, Evans had forgotten to clean up the abandoned section of the building where he had been living. Cops found an "oily rag" he had used to keep his gun from rusting, empty water and juice bottles, various snack wrappers, the graffiti on the walls and one size-8½ sneaker footprint.

None of it would be enough to connect Evans to the crime, or even send cops in his direction, but all of the evidence would later place him at the scene and confirm his statements.

Although Horton was working officially for the DEA, part of the deal between the feds and the state police was that he could also be used for homicides. Busting drug dealers and drug addicts wasn't exactly how Horton preferred to spend his time. By 1992, he had put together nearly fourteen years with the state police, and his record spoke for itself. He felt his talent for catching murderers, thieves and rapists was not being utilized in the DEA.

"I was a polygraphist, a homicide cop. . . . I did not care for narcotics," Horton recalled. "The honest truth is, arresting dope dealers wasn't a challenge. Some guys are very good at narcotics. Undercovers, especially. I wasn't an undercover. It didn't do anything but discourage me. We'd get a guy for selling dope, roll him; then we get the next guy, roll him, and he'd give us another name. It was a cycle."

The relationship between Horton and Evans had become more personal and regular by 1993. Evans continued showing up around town wherever Horton was and Horton continued to "pop in" on Evans at the various hotel and motel rooms he rented around the neighborhood. Horton knew Evans was burglarizing the entire time, but he never caught him with any stolen property or burglar tools. Evans was smart to burglarize businesses and homes outside Albany, for fear of Horton.

"He would never, in all the years I knew him, shit in his own backyard," Horton said later. "He knew I wasn't only stopping by his room to talk. He never lost sight of the fact that I was a cop doing my job."

Throughout the entire time Evans was burglarizing and murdering people under Horton's nose, he had lifted weights religiously. Bigger now than he had ever been, Evans would flaunt his muscles in front of Horton whenever they saw each other. Horton would flatter Evans by commenting on how good he looked.

"He would even pose for me," Horton said, "and allow me to take Polaroids of him. He'd flex his muscles, screaming like the Hulk, and I would take photos of him."

Part of it, Horton admitted, was to feed Evans's immense ego; but much of it had to do with keeping tabs on his different appearances.

"I would leave his hotel room after taking five or ten Polaroids of him and drive back to the office and fax the photos to every law enforcement agency in the Capital Region. Gary liked to wear disguises. Having an up-to-date photo of him was helpful to everyone."

Early in 1993, Evans took off to Vermont to go live in the woods for a while. He had yearned to buy some land and build his dream home. But the money he had been making off burglaries wasn't enough. There were several antique shops in Vermont he had been eyeing for years. The time was right, he decided, to pillage them all.

Back home, Horton and Wingate had their hands full with Jeffrey Williams, who had recently tried to pry off his court-appointed anklet. A judge, realizing how dangerous Williams was, put him back in prison to serve out the remaining portion of his sentence. Yet as Horton and Wingate continued to build a case against him for the murder of Karolyn Lonczak, the clock ticked. He would be out of prison a free man in a matter of weeks. They were sure he would kill again.

CHAPTER 71

At thirty-one, Kathy Alexander was a young and eager entrepreneur looking to fulfill a dream of owning her own antique shop. She had been around the business since the early '80s. Her parents had owned shops all over the Northeast. By 1991, armed with what she saw as enough experience to make a go of it, Kathy opened the Thompson Mills Antique Center in downtown Bennington, Vermont, with the notion of living a carefree, quiet life in what is essentially the epicenter of New England antiquing.

The Thompson Mills Antique Center housed tens of thousands of dollars' worth of antiques, fine china and other valuable collectibles. Vermont is "antique central." People come from all over the country to drive around the state in search of that special something. Kathy felt she had a little slice of heaven, which was all she had ever really wanted.

Evans walked into Kathy's shop, she later recalled, only a few weeks after she opened. "He came into my shop under the guise of being a collector," she said, "and became a friendly repeat customer."

Kathy saw this "nice-looking guy" in great physical shape. At about 350 pounds herself, Kathy had battled a weight problem much of her adult life. What struck her right away about Evans was that he treated her as if she were a runway model. Evans always wore tight-fitting shirts and tank tops, Kathy said, to show off his muscles. Befriending him immediately, she fell for that charm Evans could lay on people with flawless ingenuity. At one point, she had even floated the idea of fixing him up with her girlfriend, but she decided against it after he walked in one afternoon with Lisa Morris on his arm.

By all accounts, Evans seemed like the perfect gentleman. There was one time when Kathy sold a rather large bookcase to a woman while Evans was browsing the store, and he ended up loading it into the woman's car without being asked. He'd always ask intelligent questions about antiques, Kathy said, and make idle conversation about newsworthy topics.

It was, however, all part of a sociopathic magnetism Evans had developed and cultivated throughout the years to get what he wanted. He was playing Kathy from the moment he met her—and she never had a clue.

Within months, Kathy had moved her shop up the road from where she had first opened. Unlike her former shop, she didn't install an alarm system, however. Bennington, Vermont, didn't seem like the typical mark for thieves. Very rare was it that a shop was burglarized. An alarm system was just one more nuisance, she insisted. Another hassle she didn't need while struggling to make a living.

In March 1993, Evans started showing up at Kathy's shop more frequently. He and Kathy would chat for longer periods. She trusted him. He gave her no reason not to.

After opening the shop one morning in late March, Kathy noticed that a few items had been moved around, but not really disturbed. Taking a closer look, she realized someone had broken in through the bathroom window and stolen what amounted to approximately $20,000 of her most valuable merchandise. The thief, she figured out, had handpicked the items he stole: priceless diamonds, some gold and a rare pocketbook (handbag) collection.

When she got over the shock of being violated, Kathy sat down and told herself that whoever had broken into the shop "had been nice about it. I knew that whoever it was would end up being someone I knew." Not once, though, did Evans's name ever cross her mind. "I just never considered him. He didn't seem like that type of person."

A few days later, after Kathy had phoned police and an investigation was launched, Evans dropped by to say hello. "Hey, Kathy," he said with a touch of concern in his voice, "I heard you were broken into."

"Yes," Kathy said. "It's devastating."

"I bet. I heard that there were other break-ins, too."

Evans knew firsthand, of course, because he had hit three other shops in Vermont besides Kathy's that same week for a grand total of about $85,000. All of the merchandise was sitting safely in the woods where he had been camping for the past month.

"I know that whoever broke in," Kathy continued, "liked me."

"Really . . . you really think that?"

"Yes. The place was undisturbed, except for the missing merchandise. The thieves were actually neat about it."

The other shops had been trashed from top to bottom. Evans had ransacked one place after pillaging it and smashed a bunch of items in another. For some reason, he left Kathy's shop clean except for what he took.

"So you have any suspicions about who did it?" Evans asked.

"I had gotten into an argument with another local antique dealer," Kathy explained. "Some people around town say that I had something to do with it for insurance reasons."

She laughed. Evans laughed. It was an absurd accusation.

"Good luck," Evans said, leaving the shop. "I'm sorry about what happened."

It would be two years before Kathy found out that it was Evans who had burgled her shop. While talking to him during the afternoon of the burglary, Evans had asked Kathy if he could use her bathroom. Once inside, he simply unlocked the window in the bathroom and literally crawled in through it later that same night.

When Evans arrived back in Albany, he kept a low profile, while managing to pull off a few residential burglaries. But as the weeks and months wore on, he began running low on cash and needed to pull off what he later called a "big score."

Where had all his money gone?

"Gary loved to spend it as soon as he got it," Horton said later. "He showered the women in his life with gifts and trips and anything else they wanted. I also believe he bought some land in Vermont right around this same time."

In any case, Evans was broke. So he camped out at the Albany Rural Cemetery on Route 378 in Menands, just a few miles from the Troop G barracks in Loudonville. Horton, who was finishing up his stint with the DEA and also working homicide cases for the Bureau, and Wingate were hoping to secure a new arrest warrant for Jeffrey Williams. Neither Horton nor Wingate had seen Evans all that much over the past year.

That night, Evans slept in the cemetery near a marble bench he'd had his eye on for quite some time. A rare piece of art, a bit smaller than a casket, the bench weighed about one thousand pounds. Evans had already lined up a buyer for it in New York City—that is, if he could find a way to hoist the granite relic onto the bed of his truck by himself in the middle of the night without getting caught.

Mr. Ingenuity, Evans went out and obtained an engine hoist and hooked it up to the bed of his Toyota pickup truck. Back at the cemetery hours later, he had no trouble strapping a rope around the bench and lifting it onto the bed of his truck without being seen or heard.

Within three hours after stealing it, he was in New York City unloading it.

Horton or Wingate had no connection to the marble bench theft. They worked homicide. But a Bureau investigator working on the case, by the end of March, had enough evidence against Evans to pull him in for questioning. Evans's fence apparently had sold the piece to a legitimate antique dealer and the guy traced it back to Albany. Scared he had purchased stolen property, the guy made a few calls. When the fence was brought in, he gave up Evans right away.

Any Bureau investigator knew that there was only one cop who could find Evans. So the investigator contacted Horton and told him what was going on.

"Let me and Doug take care of it," Horton said. "We'll find him."

Because Horton was busy working a case for the DEA, Wingate decided to start looking for Evans himself. If he found him, he would call Horton and the two of them, together, would question him.

Evans had not only rented hotel rooms and slept in the woods, but he also kept an apartment in Troy.

In 1814, the Emma Willard School, on Pauling Avenue in the north end of Troy, opened. It was the first school in the Northeast to offer the same curriculum for females as it did for males. More than 175 years later, Hollywood used it as a location to film portions of *Scent of a Woman,* starring Al Pacino. Three houses away from Emma Willard, on the same side of the street, Evans rented an apartment on the third floor of a two-family house. He had always loved the idea of being around famous people or places. Living on Pauling Avenue, on the grounds of Emma Willard, as he later explained, gave him a narcissistic satisfaction of being able to touch the hand of fame. Although it wasn't much of a big deal to anyone else, he felt as if he, too, was famous in some way for living on the same grounds that Hollywood had chosen to shoot a film.

* * *

It didn't take Wingate long to find Evans. But instead of confronting him, he shared the information with Horton and they decided to wait until they knew for certain Evans was going to be home.

Wingate lived only a few miles from the apartment. Every day, on his way to work, he would drive by to see if Evans's Saab or truck was parked out front.

Finally, on the third day, he radioed Horton.

"He's there!"

That year had been one of the worst on record for snowfall in the Northeast. Certain parts of New York had logged several feet by Christmas.

After hearing from Wingate, Horton said, "Wait for me, Dougie. I'll be right there."

Trekking through the waist-high snow out front, Horton and Wingate noticed one set of footprints leading up to Evans's apartment, but none going out.

"He's in there," Horton whispered as they approached the door.

Days before, they had been given some information that Evans was telling people he was not going to be taken alive again by the cops. Regardless of the close relationship they'd had with him over the years, they assumed he meant business. It wasn't going to be a friendly visit. Evans had grown considerably more paranoid since killing Douglas Berry, Damien Cuomo and Gregory Jouben. Unbeknownst to Horton, back in the late '80s Evans had what looked like a prehistoric pterodactyl tattooed on about 85 percent of his back. Throughout the tattoo he'd had skulls etched inside the animal's wings and body. He had been telling people the skulls represented "notches in [his] belt."

He was keeping a tally of the people he had murdered.

CHAPTER 72

"Gar, you in there?" Horton said while knocking on the door. Wingate stood on the opposite side of the doorway. Both men had their weapons drawn.

"Who is it?"

"Gar, it's Jim and Doug."

Evans, without hesitating, opened the door and invited them in. The apartment, Horton and Wingate noticed, was completely empty except for a phone, answering machine and caller ID.

Horton walked over to the picture window and looked down. "We were on the third story," he recalled later. "It got pretty heated right away. Doug and I thought for sure we were going to tussle with him."

Evans later told Horton he was thinking of fighting his way out. Wingate said he and Horton would have "kicked Gary's ass all over the apartment."

Horton disagreed. "Gary, at that time, was fighting for his life. We were merely doing our jobs. When you look at it from the standpoint of a fight, Gary had nothing to lose."

Finally, after some small talk, Horton said, "Gar, listen, we're here to arrest you for the marble bench."

Evans stared at Horton and then looked toward the window. There was a good two-foot cushion of snow on the ground. Evans later said he thought seriously about diving out of the window and taking off, but decided against it only because he knew it would cause a lot of problems for Horton and Wingate, two cops he respected probably more than anyone else in his life at the time.

"Knowing Gary," Horton said, "if he jumped, he would have landed on the ground like a cat and disappeared."

Evans was facing some serious time for the theft of the marble bench. A repeat felon, he was looking at likely two years, maybe more depending on the judge.

"Let's see if Gary," Horton said to Wingate one day shortly after they arrested him, "will agree to befriending Jeffrey Williams. Maybe he can get us something?"

Wingate smiled.

Since trying to cut his anklet off, Jeffrey Williams had been locked up in Albany County Jail, yet he was going to be released in a matter of weeks. In the interim, Wingate and Horton had gotten lucky when two inmates came forward and claimed Williams had admitted that he had "fucked up and left a medallion [of his]" on Karolyn Lonczak's body. With that new information, Horton and Wingate reinterviewed dozens of people involved in the case and ended up getting enough information to send the case to a grand jury.

As Williams sat in jail under the notion that he was going to be getting out in days, the grand jury returned two indictments: second-degree murder and first-degree kidnapping.

With Williams set to get out of jail at midnight, Wingate and Horton showed up at the prison unannounced with a new arrest warrant.

"The jailers called up to the tier," Horton recalled later, "for Williams to be sent down. Doug and I stayed out of sight, but could see him coming."

Williams believed he was being released. But when he reached the lobby, Horton stepped out and said, "Remember me?"

Horton recalled that "he turned grayish white. I actually remember the color draining out of his face at the moment when I said, 'You're under arrest for the murder and kidnapping of Karolyn Lonczak.' I then read him his Miranda rights out loud in front of the jailers so there would be witnesses."

While Horton finished reading Williams his rights, Wingate cuffed him at his wrists. Horton then bent down to put leg shackles on him.

"He must have literally shit his pants," Horton said, "because I nearly passed out from the smell when I bent over. I wanted to be as professional as possible, so I didn't say anything."

Horton and Wingate's case centered on, basically, circumstantial evidence. They needed more to seal the deal—ideally, a confession.

Evans was thrilled at the prospect of helping Horton nail Williams. Williams preyed on children and women. Evans said he hated that about him.

"Will you help us?" Horton asked.

Evans stroked his chin and thought about it for a moment. "You want me to kill him for you. . . . I'll strangle the motherfucker!"

"No, no, no!" Horton said. "That is *not* what I am asking you to do, Gar. Come on, let's be serious here."

A moment later, Wingate came into the room and they explained to Evans what they wanted him to do. "We'll put you in a cell next to him," Wingate said. "Just talk to him. Maybe he'll tell you things about any crimes he committed . . . just anything he would say."

It didn't take long for Evans to realize that, either way, whether Williams coughed up any information or not, he could manipulate the situation in his favor.

"Let's do it," Evans said. "I'll get the motherfucker."

CHAPTER 73

On January 10, 1994, Evans was placed in a cell directly next to Jeffrey Williams. At first, Williams seemed a bit scared of Evans, but Evans became pushy. Within a few days, they were talking regularly and, according to Horton, playing chess.

If there was one thing Evans did well, it was the way he methodically went about the tasks set in front of him. When he set his mind on something, he kept at it until he was satisfied with the outcome. Those first conversations with Williams consisted of the two of them just talking about "different jails and prisons" they had done time in. Evans would bring up different people he met along his incarcerated path to see if Williams knew any of them.

As the days passed, Evans became more ambitious with his comments. While watching *The Getaway*, a movie starring Kim Basinger, on television one night, Evans leaned over to Williams and whispered, "How nice it would be to have a partner like that Kim Basinger."

"Yeah," Williams said, "that would be good: having a woman like her who would keep her mouth shut and not talk to the police about anything, no matter what."

Evans had followed Williams's case in the newspapers. He knew he had been convicted of stealing a rocking chair and had been sentenced to twenty-five years to life for it. He saw an opportunity to bring up the Lonczak murder by mentioning the rocking chair. Laughing, he asked, "What the fuck is your girl going to talk about—you stealing a fucking rocking chair?"

"There's a lot more to it than that," Williams snapped. He seemed, Evans recalled later, a bit upset by the question, making it seem like the only notch in his belt was the theft of a rocking chair.

After the movie, they walked back to Evans's cell and continued talking, discussing different enemies they had each accumulated throughout the years.

"I'm having a lot of problems with some fuck in Troy," Evans said. "I'd like to see something done to that motherfucker."

"I understand," Williams said. "I'm having problems with this guy, Mr. Lonczak. I have a huge beef with him."

"What's it about?"

Williams explained that Karolyn Lonczak's father wouldn't let the case against him go. "He thinks I killed his daughter," Williams said. "If he keeps this fucking case going . . . well . . . I might do something to that fucker."

Evans got the impression from Williams that he was afraid of what Mr. Lonczak might do because he believed Williams had killed his daughter.

"No shit," Evans said.

"What would you do," Williams then asked, "if somebody killed *your* daughter?"

"I'd kill him myself. But why are you so scared of this guy? Can the police get you for the killing?"

"I don't think so. . . . They were supposed to think retards killed her."

It was apparent to Evans that Williams was somehow alluding to the fact that in some way he had botched the murder.

"Retards?" Evans questioned. "What the fuck do you mean—'retards'?"

"Yeah. She worked with retarded people. . . . But I fucked up."

"Huh? . . . I'm confused."

"I fucked it up because a retard wouldn't have had a license to bring her where she got —"

Evans interrupted, "A license?"

"A fucking driver's license. A retard wouldn't have had a driver's license. A retard would have left her there. I should have left her there."

Karolyn Lonczak worked at a rehabilitation home in Cohoes. She had been abducted out of the home in the middle of the night and found eight weeks later in a snowbank about twenty miles north.

From that, Evans assumed he had gotten out of Williams what Horton and Wingate were after. So, good to their word, after Evans reported back to them and explained what Williams had said, Evans was released on February 12, 1994. To make things appear more legitimate, Evans went back to Albany County Jail a week later and visited Williams. Horton and Wingate wired him to see if they could perhaps get Williams to implicate himself further, but he didn't say anything more about the murder.

On the street now, Evans was grinning from ear to ear at being able to manhandle Jeffrey Williams like a puppet and get what he felt was a confession out of him. It had all been a challenge to Evans. He felt good about himself. He had not only helped Horton, but in his mind a "scumbag who killed women and children" was going to prison for life. If for some reason Williams got off, Evans told Wingate one day, he would see to it that he never hurt another human being again. "Let that fucker get out," Evans said, "and your worries will be over, Doug."

Horton met with Evans at the end of February to discuss what would happen next. There would be a trial. Evans would have to testify. "You can't fuck up, Gar," Horton warned him, "and get into any trouble before this trial. Your credibility is shit already. If you show up in leg chains and handcuffs, Williams's attorney will destroy you."

"Come on, Guy. Don't worry about it. Trust me."

Leaving Troop G in Loudonville after talking to Horton, Evans headed north to Vermont. Nestled comfortably in the Norman Williams Public Library in downtown Woodstock, Vermont, was the James Audubon book of rare prints called *Birds of America.* A large book, about the size of an average wall painting, Evans had put it on his list of items to steal long ago. It was worth nearly $100,000. He figured he could get in and out of town in one night with little problem. Slipping in through a back window and stealing the sixty-pound, leather-bound book, he figured, would be no harder than walking into a department store and lifting a pair of slacks. The only glitch in his plan, which Evans didn't know, was that on the board of trustees of the library was a federal judge who took a considerable amount of pride in having *Birds of America* displayed in the library.

CHAPTER 74

Light snow fell on the night of March 20, 1994, a Sunday. It was cold, even by New England standards, for that time of year. The temperature had never risen above twenty degrees.

The Norman Williams Public Library on Park Street near the green in Woodstock housed more than thirty thousand books and periodicals. It was closed on Sundays, like many libraries in the United States. Evans had been inside the building, scoping it out, on several different occasions. He understood security in the place was lax.

Arriving in the middle of the night, he simply went around to the back of the building and removed the hinge bolts holding the irons bars on one of the windows in the basement. Within fifteen minutes, he was in the library and out—the James Audubon *Birds of America* book in hand.

Later, he said it was one of the easiest burglaries he had ever pulled off, and laughed at how naive conservators of the book had been about protecting it from people like himself.

When the clerk came in the following morning and discovered the theft, word spread quickly that one of the library's most valued possessions was gone. The federal judge on the board of trustees was livid. The book had been the library's crown jewel, often bringing people to town specifically to see it.

"Once the judge became involved," Horton said later, "he literally"—Horton laughed at the cliché—"made a federal case out of it."

Indeed, by midmorning, FBI agents from all across New England had arrived in town to work on the case. Days later, agents from across the country were involved.

By this time, Evans was back in Latham. The book, he later said, was on the Canadian-Vermont border, sealed in a plastic bag, buried underneath the home of an old woman who had no idea he had even broken into her house and hidden it there.

As the FBI began its hunt, Evans started looking for a buyer.

Horton had finished his stint with the DEA around this same time and was now back working full-time for the Bureau in Loudonville. It felt good to be back in the captain's chair. Narcotics had been a bore since the first day.

His reputation as having a relationship with Evans was not only common knowledge among state police, but the FBI was fully aware Horton was the one cop who knew more about Gary Evans than anybody else.

Near the latter part of March, the FBI contacted Horton about Evans. A federal informant in prison had come forward and said his brother had been contacted by Evans, who was looking for someone to buy a book he had stolen in Vermont. Evans had made the mistake of giving the informant his real name.

The FBI invited Horton and Wingate to its main office in Albany to debrief them about Evans. The head of the task force in charge of getting the book back had already set up a meeting between Evans and the informant to discuss the possible sale of the book.

"There had to be thirty agents involved in this case," Horton recalled later. "When we walked in, it was like a Hollywood movie."

FBI windbreaker jackets. Earpieces. Attitudes.

Horton and Wingate weren't asked to participate in the investigation, but were there to more or less hand over whatever information they had that could be useful in capturing Evans.

"Don't underestimate Mr. Evans," Horton, standing, explained to the eager crowd of agents. "He may be armed. He will use countersurveillance techniques. He won't have the property [book] with him." A line that Horton had used numerous times throughout the years meant more now than it ever had: "He'll crawl through a straw if he has to."

As Horton and Wingate viewed the situation, the entire meeting seemed more like a political move on the part of the FBI. There were so many agents involved, none of which had any idea with whom they were dealing, or how well Horton knew him.

"It was funny, actually," Horton said later. "Here was this big room. All these agents were standing around . . . all for Gary Evans."

Just a couple of days after the meeting, the agent-in-charge called Horton and invited him and Wingate to a stakeout he had set up. Evans was scheduled to meet the FBI's informant at 6:00 P.M. in a parking lot on Wolf Road in Colonie, which was not too far from Horton's home.

"Sure," Horton said. The agent made it clear, however, that they weren't part of the team, necessarily, but could sit in on the arrest and watch.

There will be no arrest, Horton mused to himself.

At about 4:00 P.M., Horton and Wingate showed up at a hotel in Colonie that the FBI had set up as base camp. When they walked into the fourth-floor room, they couldn't believe their eyes. Agents wore night vision goggles. There were telescopic lenses, tape recorders and several other pieces of

James Bond–type equipment spread about the room. Agents were coming and going, talking on walkie-talkies as if they were about to make the arrest of their careers.

"Doug and I," Horton recalled later, "we kind of looked at each other and whispered . . . 'They're fucked.' We told them what to do and they totally ignored all of our advice."

Not only hadn't the FBI taken Horton and Wingate's advice, but they disregarded a couple of key factors. For one, Horton had been adamant about setting the operation up twenty-four hours in advance. The FBI, he learned when they got there, had been at the hotel for only a few hours. Second, Horton told them to "keep it simple . . . a few undercover agents, no more." By 5:00 P.M., there were about twenty agents spread all over the place, some of whom were walking in and out of the building while wearing those loud blue-and-gold FBI windbreaker jackets that screamed FEDS.

Evans later laughed about the ordeal when he explained to Horton what he was doing while the FBI were setting up. "I counted sixteen agents," Evans said, "in the diner, walking around the hotel, in cars, on the street."

Evans was on foot when he showed up to meet the informant. He had parked his truck about a mile away and walked to the parking lot. An undercover agent and the informant met with him, but he said absolutely nothing about the book. He let the informant do most of the talking and never once mentioned that he even had the book. At one point, he said, "I may know someone who knows someone who has the book. . . . What if I did?"

Generally speaking, if a thief smells something funny while meeting with a fence, he will take off and never contact the fence again. Evans, however, viewed the entire operation with the FBI as a challenge and yearned to see how far they would take it.

Ten minutes into the conversation, Evans decided he wasn't interested in talking anymore. The FBI had nothing to arrest him on, so it had to let him go. He had never mentioned the book specifically, nor had he said he could get it. Even if he had, the book was nowhere in sight.

As he took off on foot, the FBI scrambled for position. With a plane already waiting, it was decided a tail would be put on him for the night to see where he went. Perhaps he would lead them to the book?

From there, Evans left in his truck and, realizing he was being followed the entire time, took the FBI on what he later called a "joyride" for the next six hours.

"All he did," Horton said, "was drive around in a huge circle while twenty FBI agents wasted the night watching him. It was typical Gary Evans all the way. . . . He was in charge from the moment he set up the buy."

CHAPTER 75

The FBI's informant made contact with Evans a few days later and said he wanted to set up another meeting to discuss buying the book.

To make sure he had all bases covered, Evans had Lisa Morris, with whom he had been living on and off since killing Damien Cuomo, move the book from place to place while he dealt with the FBI. Before the meet at the hotel, Evans had driven up to the Canadian border to get the book, just in case the buyer was legit. But when he found out he was dealing with a snitch, he gave it to Lisa and had her move it from state to state while he met with the informant.

To say the least, the FBI highly underestimated Evans. And there was certainly some type of power struggle going on between it and the state police. Egos aside, if the FBI wanted the book back, they must have known there was only one cop who could get it for them.

Still, before handing the case to Horton, the assistant special agent-in-charge, Joe Flynn, whom Horton described later as "a good guy who knew his job," decided to take one more chance with his informant, who was able to renegotiate another meeting with Evans in the parking lot of a restaurant in Lake George, New York.

The FBI decided to show up in Lake George in a recreational vehicle. A team of agents pulled up in an RV several hours before the meeting was to take place. At least this time they had taken some of Horton's advice.

According to Evans, he had been camping out in the woods near the parking lot of the restaurant for three days. That morning, he later said, he looked through a set of binoculars as the RV "pulled into the parking lot and the agents got out, stretched and went into the restaurant to get breakfast and go to the bathroom.

"I watched the entire operation," he added, "laughing my ass off."

Around the time of the meet, with agents nestled in the RV waiting for Evans to show up, Evans got on his mountain bike, strolled into the parking lot and, he later claimed, approached the RV slowly. After scoping out where the informant was located, he then began circling the RV on his bicycle, knocking on the windows, banging on the sides. "I know you're in there. . . . Come on out," Evans said as he drove around the vehicle a few times.

Playing out his hand, he then rode up to the informant and told him to "go fuck himself."

"He was lucky I didn't kill him right there in the parking lot in front of all those federal motherfuckers," Evans explained to Horton later.

"With their tail between their legs," Horton said later, the FBI called after the incident in Lake George and "asked for my help in getting the book back."

Horton told them, "I can get it back, but I really haven't had much contact with Gary lately." Then, without saying "I told you so," Horton said he would do it, but it had to be done on his terms.

The FBI, perhaps just wanting to get the book back any way it could, agreed.

Months went by before Evans contacted Horton. And

that's the way it had to be, Horton said. "He had to come to me. It couldn't be the other way around."

Horton was already looking to rip into Evans because of the deal they had made after Evans made bail and said he would stay out of trouble so he could testify with a clean slate against Jeffrey Williams. Now Horton was looking at not only bringing a convicted felon into court to testify, but he would be dressed down in shackles and an orange jumpsuit.

The exact situation he wanted to avoid.

As patient as a fox, when it came to capturing criminals, Horton rarely gave up. His days as a polygraphist and interrogator had taught him that to try to predict a criminal's behavior was impossible, but allowing him the space to conduct business his way was essential.

After a few anxious months of not hearing from him, Evans finally called Horton at his home during midspring 1994. "It's the Unabomber," Evans said, laughing. "What the *fuck* is going on, Guy?"

"How the hell did you get my phone number?" Horton asked right away. He had changed his phone number for about the third time in as many years because of Jeffrey Williams. Mary Pat had been getting hang-up calls. The press had been bothering him about Williams and Evans.

Evans laughed. Then, "Your wife gave me the number." He said he had followed Mary Pat into a local photo shop one day. While inside the store, he heard her tell the clerk her phone number.

"You bastard," Horton snapped. "You following my wife around now?"

"I would never hurt her, Jim. You know that."

"You screwed me," Horton said. "You promised me you would not get into any trouble. We have the Jeff Williams case coming up soon. I need you to testify."

Evans became quiet. "Sorry, Jim. I am what I am."

"Well, how are we going to fix this?"

"I can't go back to prison, Guy. I can't. I'll get twenty-five to life. No motherfucking way I am doing that."

"I need the book back. Where is it?"

"What are you going to do for me?"

Horton told Evans he would look into talking to the judge about going easy on him for the theft of the book if he turned it over, but it was going to be difficult. "You really pissed that judge off, Gar. He's on the board of trustees of that library."

"Do what you can."

"Where are you?"

"I can't tell you that, come on. I should go now."

"You better call me back. You promised to help me out with Williams."

Evans said he would call back in a few weeks. Meanwhile, he suggested Horton talk to the judge and come up with some sort of deal. "See what you can work out."

The judge wanted Evans bad. It wasn't only the book. But Evans had also burglarized several antique shops in Vermont around the same time. Local shop owners were calling for a stiff sentence. He was a repeat offender.

Horton's job, however, was to get the book back and prepare Evans for the Jeffrey Williams trial. So he and Wingate made several trips to Vermont to curry favor between U.S. attorneys from Vermont and New York and the federal judge. Evans said he would do two years at the most. The judge, after carefully analyzing the situation, perhaps realizing that if the library wanted the book back he was going to have to cave into Evans's demands, made an offer of twenty-seven months. Looking back, Horton explained how it was the only way the feds could get the book back. Evans was in control of the situation; he could destroy the book and never set foot again in the Northeast.

Of course, no one could have known it at the time, but they were cutting a deal with a serial killer.

When Evans called Horton back, Horton explained the situation. Evans wasn't all that thrilled—he had put a cap on twenty-four months—but agreed, nonetheless, to turn himself and the book in.

The Monte Mario Motel, only one mile from Horton's home in Latham, was a ramshackle, weekly rental that derelicts from all walks of life frequented. Weather-stained white stucco on the exterior bore traces of grime and dirt collected from the years of neglect, while the inside of the rooms would have likely offended homeless people. Evans had been staying at the hotel on and off for years.

By the middle of June 1994, Horton and Wingate had made plans with Evans to meet at 8:00 one morning in the parking lot of the Monte Mario. Evans was reluctant, of course, but at the same time ready to go to jail and fulfill his obligation to Horton.

"Just have the book!" Horton told him when they spoke a few days before the meet.

CHAPTER 76

As Horton and Wingate pulled into the Monte Mario, they saw Evans standing in the parking lot with a bag of toiletries in his hand, smiling.

"What's up, Gar?" Horton said as he and Wingate got out of the car.

"We meet again. . . ."

"Listen, I have to search you. I'm not going to be made to look like a fool for turning you over to the FBI and you're packing all kinds of 'goodies.'"

"Go for it."

The plan was, Horton and Wingate would arrest Evans and drive him to Rutland, Vermont, to meet with the FBI. Once there, he would become federal property.

As Horton went to pat Evans down, Evans handed over three handcuff keys: one underneath his watch, another in his shoe and a third tucked inside a hand-made seam in his belt. He had a fourth key, however, Horton never found. Years later, he explained how, as Horton and Wingate pulled into the parking lot, he swallowed the fourth key. He figured once he had a chance to get settled into his cell up north, he could recycle it through his body and hide it on his body or in his cell.

Horton and Wingate had such a respectful relationship with Evans that they decided against handcuffing him. It was a long, dull ride up to Rutland. Why make things more tense?

So, like three buddies on their way to a weekend of drinking and fishing, Horton, driving, Wingate, riding shotgun, and Evans, alone in the backseat unhandcuffed, began their journey up to Vermont.

"I wasn't upset at the fact that he didn't have the book on him," Horton recalled later. "In fact, if he'd had it on him, I would have thought differently about him and even lost some respect for him."

The drive was unremarkable. They talked about their lives, television, sports—and how Evans had let Horton down. Along the way, Horton stopped and bought Evans cookies and milk, doughnuts and potato chips.

"You are unbelievable," Horton, shaking his head in disgust, said at one point after stopping at a rest stop. "You couldn't just stay out of trouble until *after* the Jeffrey Williams trial?"

"I left the area, didn't I? I didn't do anything around here."

"You didn't go far enough away. . . . You really pissed that judge off. You are not going to be welcomed with open arms up there. I hope you realize that."

At any point, Evans could have jumped out of the car, or taken off during one of their many stops.

"Doug and I figured that he had turned himself in and wasn't interested in running."

Horton had made earlier plans to meet several FBI agents at a local Denny's restaurant in Rutland.

"We bought Gary breakfast, told him to be a good little boy for the feds, turned him over and drove back to Albany."

The FBI then shackled Evans, put him in a cruiser and drove north to where he had hidden the book.

In true bureaucratic fashion, the FBI gave the New York State Police no credit for getting Evans to turn over the book. On June 22, 1994, the *Rutland Herald*, a local Vermont newspaper, ran the headline: FBI RECOVERS AUDUBON BOOK; MAN ARRESTED.

According to Evans later, not only did the FBI not want to admit that Horton and Wingate had been instrumental in the return of the book, but one agent mocked Evans's relationship with them, saying, "You don't have your 'friends' from the New York State Police here to protect you now."

Evans hadn't been locked up in nearly seven years. Now a product of the federal system, he was at the mercy of overcrowding and available bed space and thus shipped frequently around the Northeast, from prison to prison, like a box of documents.

Horton and Wingate went to see him when they could, but months would go by without any contact. When Evans felt they were blowing him off, he'd dash off a letter. It was clear that prison was turning an already paranoid deviant into an insolated sociopath who began to allow the demons that had controlled him periodically throughout the years take full control over him.

I hope you can come soon, Evans wrote to Horton in early 1995. *I'm not doing too good. . . . I'm talking to a doctor here. Can someone talk to me?*

The remainder of the letter, which was brief, consisted of Evans begging for some sort of attention from Horton. His handwriting had changed; it was unsteady, scribbled and almost unreadable.

After receiving the letter, Horton went to see him.

"All he did was cry," Horton recalled later. "He was in the worst state of being I had ever seen him."

The Jeffrey Williams trial was slated for summer. Horton needed Evans in good emotional health, but the next letter, written a week later, proved he was, perhaps, beyond that point now: *I am very fucked up. I'm going to be OK for trial. . . . I'm just . . . I just get scared in these places. I'm not OK.*

His sentences, at times, made little sense: *I love [Doris Sheehan] so much everything gone I can't I'm not doing good. Can you come and talk to me please or call me because I'm not doing good at all.*

With the Jeffrey Williams trial looming, Horton once again went to see him.

"Gary Evans had turned into a different person. . . . He was losing his mind, literally," Horton recalled. "His entire look had changed from bad to worse. He was now nearly completely bald. That bothered him. He wasn't showering."

Indeed, Evans had realized too little too late that it had been a mistake to turn over the book. Two years behind bars was like a life sentence.

The changes Horton had seen in Evans by the summer of 1995, however, were nothing compared to what Evans had been doing shortly before he had turned himself in to Horton and Wingate.

CHAPTER 77

Gary Evans had always referred to Bill Murphy, a Troy native he had met in the fourth grade while they were classmates at School Ten in Troy, as the "only honest friend [he] ever had." Throughout the years, Evans turned to a life of crime while Bill got married and divorced, remarried, worked an honest job in a factory and lived a secluded, family life in South Troy before moving to the country.

Evans would show up at Bill's house at about 8:00 on some mornings and just shoot the shit with him over a workout. Bill had a gym in his house. He worked third shift. Evans would never tell Bill anything that would get him into trouble with the law or make him an accessory to a crime, but Bill had no trouble reading between the lines and drawing conclusions of his own.

Over the course of the past ten years—1985 to 1995—Bill had watched his childhood friend change from a hotheaded young kid who wasn't afraid of anyone, someone who kept scores of girlfriends, to an introverted loner who became relentlessly paranoid and, Bill later admitted, strangely "afraid of people."

There were times when Bill would complain to Evans about a boss or neighbor. Evans would get an evil look in his eye and say something frightening: "I'll take care of it for you, Bill. Don't worry about it."

"No, Gary," Bill would tell him, "don't do anything! Let me live my life and deal with people my own way."

Bill simply wanted to be there as a friend for someone he saw as never having had a chance in life.

"I don't condone what he did," Bill said later, "but I understand how he turned out the way he did."

Bill had seen it firsthand. Evans's father would beat Evans savagely and, after kicking Bill out of the apartment, stow Evans away in his room for days at a time.

"He would even take the lightbulbs out of Gary's room so he couldn't see anything. And he would starve the poor kid. That's how Gary learned to be a sneak—he was forced into it."

Bill also saw some of the violence Evans's mother's boyfriends and husbands seemed to direct toward Evans, who was much smaller than the other kids. Some of Flora Mae's boyfriends and husbands used Evans as a whipping post, Bill recalled, often beating him for no particular reason in front of Bill and other neighborhood kids.

One of Evans's favorite things to do as a thief, Bill recalled, was to "hit the same place twice." Evans had done it several times. He relished the emotional high he got out of burglarizing an antique shop or jewelry store and then going back a few weeks later and hitting it again.

One time, Evans pulled up to Bill's house with a load of bedding and large, bulky items in the back of his truck. Bill asked him what he was doing.

"I need it to cover me," Evans said. He wanted to burglarize a particular jewelry store—he never told Bill the name or location—in broad daylight. He was excited. The thrill was in getting away with it in front of a crowd of people. He would hit the place on a Sunday afternoon while patrons in the bar across the street were getting drunk. He explained that the mattresses and bedding were going to block the view from the bar. He would park his truck in front of the building and be in and out within fifteen minutes.

At times, Evans would just stop showing up at Bill's, and Bill understood that if he didn't hear from him for a period of time, he was either on the run or in prison.

"Each time he came out of prison," Bill explained, "he was harder." Oddly, Evans had always told Bill he was terrified of growing old. "Old people creeped him out. He hated wrinkly skin and just about everything about them." For that reason alone, whenever they'd discuss it, Evans would suggest that he would never make it beyond fifty.

There came a point during their relationship, however, when Bill became terrified of his longtime friend.

"Gary started to become more paranoid over the years. He began scaring me. Talking really crazy. He had always said he wanted to kill a 'woman and a nigger.' I don't know that he ever did, nor did I want to [know]. I could have gotten him to open up more, but I just didn't want to know about certain things. And he respected that."

Bill was intrigued, he said, by the stories Evans would tell him. After a night of slaving in the factory, Bill would sit attentively and listen to Evans spin one yarn after the other. But as the years passed and Evans became more engrossed in a life Bill felt involved more than simple burglary, his behavior became more bizarre. Once, Bill went out into his barn and noticed several coffee cans along the side of the back wall. They were full of human fecal matter. It wouldn't be until years later that Bill found out Evans was defecating in the cans so he could sift through the waste and find a handcuff key he had swallowed after the cops had pulled him over or he had spent the night in jail.

Yet, if that wasn't strange enough, something Bill found one day inside a dollhouse Evans had been building in Bill's garage affected Bill enough to where he began to put as much distance between him and Evans as he could without offending him.

Evans would stop by from time to time and work on the miniature dollhouse. Like his paintings and stained-glass designs, he relished the tranquillity of creating something from scratch. One day, though, when he wasn't around, Bill went out into the garage just to take a look at the miniature house. Underneath it, he discovered a trapdoor. Inside the trapdoor was a smattering of rather odd items Bill would have never figured Evans to own: several transsexual and homosexual magazines, along with dildos and other sexual toys one might use for gay sex.

Could Evans have been a closet bisexual? Bill never confronted him about it. He kept the information to himself, noting, "I am *not* a homosexual. I have nothing against homosexuals, but I cannot believe Gary was."

An acquaintance, however, viewed the situation differently and believed from the first day she met Evans that he was gay, regardless of the women he bragged about having sex with. Evans never liked her, she said, and always seemed to avoid her. Perhaps, she later noted, it was his way of not wanting to be figured out.

Another close friend of Evans's talked later in further detail about his paranoia, and how it had spiraled out of control during the same period. Evans would, according to this friend, sneak into the homes of people who spooked him just so he could go through their possessions. Sometimes he would go in at night while they were sleeping and just observe them. Once, while dating a young woman whom he had started to have feelings for, he broke into her home while she was gone so he could hide in the closet and later watch her. By mere habit, perhaps, he decided to bring along a .22-caliber pistol.

While in her bedroom, the woman came home. Evans heard voices, a male and female. So he ducked into the closet in her bedroom.

Standing in the dark, crossing his chest with the pistol as though he were reciting the Pledge of Allegiance, his heart pounding in anxiety, Evans listened as the woman made love to the guy.

"He said he thought about breaking out of the closet and shooting them both," the friend recalled later, "but he decided against it because she had a kid."

Given that he had broken into so many homes throughout the years, many of which were people he knew, some believe he had also been sneaking around Horton's house while Horton, his wife and kids were at home or away.

Faced with this prospect later, Horton said plainly, "If I would have ever caught Gary Evans in my home, I would have killed him . . . and he knew that—because I had warned him about it."

Despite the horror Evans lived as a child of two alcoholics and the blame he later placed on his mother for picking such violent and abusive spouses, Evans loved the women in his life and showered them with gifts of jewelry and expensive vacations. His women throughout the years numbered in the dozens. From underage girls to overweight women, from nice-looking women to women who might have easily passed for men. It was true he didn't discriminate when it came to choosing lovers, and there is no doubt he enjoyed having sex with many different partners.

Some of his women claimed he was a responsive lover who never wanted to do anything out of the ordinary. "Missionary style, that's it!" said one woman. "The only odd thing he liked to do sexually," said another woman, "was perform oral sex on me while I was menstruating. He said it was a natural thing and it didn't bother him."

Like a rock star, Evans took Polaroids of his women while he was having sex with them and kept the photographs in a scrapbook as souvenirs. The photos, scores of them, show Evans and his partners in various positions of sexual pleasure. Evans had even allowed someone close to him, a male, to have sex with some of his women while he participated.

One of his marks had been the daughter (who was underage at the time) of a woman he had dated for some time. The mother of the young girl later swore that Evans had never dated her daughter and that she kept her away from him because she and her daughter were terrified of him. But the

Polaroids show a willing participant—the daughter—giving oral sex to Evans as both smile for the camera. It was all a challenge to him, some later claimed. He loved the idea of being able to show people the women he'd had sex with.

To further bolster the theory that Evans was perhaps confused about his sexuality, other Polaroids depict a man who was, at the least, experimenting. For one, Evans on occasion liked to dress in women's clothes. Wearing a blond wig, makeup and lipstick, he embodied the persona of a female rather affably. Although many might have thought it was nothing more than a Halloween costume, there was also evidence that he had a penchant for transsexuals and dated one while in prison. Not only had he taken Polaroids of a man he had met while in prison who lived life as a female, but later, when she got out of prison and completed her transition to a female, Evans visited her and took more photos. One might ask, why would he visit a transsexual and keep transsexual magazines if, in his prison writings, he ridiculed those same types of people and carried on about how much he hated them?

"If it is true," Horton said later, "he certainly had me and every other cop he had contact with fooled. I had no idea. I would have viewed our relationship entirely different if I would have known then what I know now. He acted like a tough guy and gave me no hint whatsoever that he was bisexual."

Was Evans, when he wrote to Horton how much he envied him, actually showing an attraction for him?

"I felt that it was all business between us," Horton added, "manipulation and a serious game of crime. I've always believed that he killed more than he had admitted to—and if Gary was, in fact, bisexual, well, that opens up an entire new pool of victims. If Gary had it in mind that someone would expose his 'secret life,' he would have killed them in a minute."

Could Evans have been bisexual?

"I can definitely believe it," Horton concluded. "Gary worked so hard to keep it from me that it's most likely true."

CHAPTER 78

Gary Evans and Jeffrey Williams weren't the only major cases Horton was working on by the time spring arrived in 1995. Before meeting Evans at the Monte Mario Motel in Latham, Horton had flown to Alabama to finish a case he had been working on for the past two years. It had been one of the most peculiar cases he had ever investigated. He didn't know it then, but the case would be a precursor to the horrors he was about to discover regarding Evans.

A man in his late thirties—"a real Charles Manson wannabe"—with long hair and a swastika tattooed on his forearm, had beheaded his former boss in front of the man's wife. Bureau investigators found the wife of the victim, who was in the throes of Alzheimer's, sitting up in bed with blood splattered all over her knees, legs and feet. She was rocking back and forth, hugging herself, mumbling words no one could understand.

For years, Horton and other members of the Bureau had tracked the guy from New York to Florida to Alabama. He'd even been profiled on *America's Most Wanted,* the popular television show hosted by John Walsh. Finally, Alabama police picked him up at a vehicle inspection roadblock and, because he was driving a missing woman's car, suspected him of kidnapping her.

The guy, who held two master's degrees, wouldn't talk to anybody. So Horton and Jack Murray, a fellow Bureau investigator, flew down to see if they could get him to confess to the beheading they were investigating in New York.

It had taken them two days to get down south. During that period, the guy still hadn't spoken to anyone. But within a few hours of interviewing him, Horton and Murray got him to confess to the New York murder and the murder of the woman whose car he was driving. He'd even given them a full written statement.

The subsequent confession infuriated the local sheriff and Alabama State Police, who had tried desperately for days to get the guy to talk.

The local DA took Horton and Murray out to dinner that night and further expressed how embarrassed and remorseful they were about not being able to get the guy to talk. "I'm a Civil War buff," the hefty DA said with a noticeable Southern drawl, "and might I commend y'all on what you did today." He raised his glass. Then, "You Yankees kicked our asses in the War and you kicked our asses today."

To Horton, it meant nothing. At the end of the day, the guy had confessed; to whom was insignificant. What mattered was that he was off the street.

It was, however, a matter of respect to those in the South who were involved—and the next few weeks would prove just how personal they took it.

The DA wanted Horton to leave the guy in Alabama for a few days so they could formally charge him. Horton agreed and headed back to New York.

Alabama ultimately couldn't prove its case against the guy because he had cremated the woman. There was no evidence.

In the interim, the NYSP had purchased plane tickets for Horton and Murray so they could fly to Alabama and extradite the guy back to New York to face murder charges in the beheading death of his boss. But a few days before they were set to leave, the local sheriff in Alabama called and explained that there was no need for them to make the trip. The guy was dead. Apparently, while he was talking to his attorney one afternoon in the attorney's fourth-floor office, he jumped up from his chair and dived out the picture window.

But that incident wasn't what caused Horton and Murray to wonder what had gone on between the suspect and county jailers. Because while he was being prepped for surgery that day, the OR nurse discovered something no one could have predicted. As she was looking at his buttocks, she noticed what appeared to be a "tail sticking out of his rectum." After he died later that day and the ME conducted an autopsy, a full-grown rat was found inside his bowels.

Apparently, someone had shoved a rat up his ass.

"He had been chained in a cell by his arms and legs," Horton recalled. "Those Southern cops were jokingly upset that he had given us a confession. Who knows what happened? All I know is that the guy died with a rat up his ass."

Flying back home after a trip he had taken, Horton gazed out the plane window at the land below and became lost in the quilted patterns of circles and squares below him. It had been an unusual year that seemed to gather momentum as each month passed. Evans was in federal prison, stewing over life behind bars, while Horton was trying to figure out a way to get him into a courtroom to testify against Jeffrey Williams—without being viewed as a discredited witness. Evans had done exactly what Horton had told him not to do: he commited a crime while waiting to testify.

There ultimately was no way to present a career criminal as anything but deceitful and dishonest.

"*What* was I thinking?" Horton acknowledged later. "That Gary Evans *wasn't* going to commit a crime while out of jail? It was stupid of me to trust him."

When Horton got back to New York, he went to see Evans. Someone had told him he wasn't doing so well.

"Just hang on, Gar," Horton told Evans. "It's almost over."

"I don't think I can do the rest of the time, Guy."

"Just relax and know that you'll be out of here in a few months."

The Major Crimes Unit of the Bureau had dealt with thirty-four homicides during the past year. With Evans taking up space and the Williams trial looming, Horton began to question how he was going to manage it all.

"Really, I was dealing with the worst society had to offer. It was like routine for me to go to work and find out that there was another beheading or dismemberment. Then I would turn around and have to deal with Gary and his whining about being in jail."

Evans should've counted his lucky stars—because, in truth, he should have gotten twenty-five years to life for the theft of the James Audubon book. A reluctant judge who wanted the book back had worked it out so Evans could be paroled in twenty-seven months. If anything, he should be thanking Horton for sticking his neck out for him. There were several antique dealers in Vermont stirring up problems for the U.S. Attorney's Office, writing letters and making calls, because they had been burgled by Evans. For them, twenty-seven months wasn't enough.

Essentially, Evans had gotten a free pass on, basically, a life sentence—all because he had turned over a book and befriended a cop.

Prosecutor Paul Clyne, who had been looking to nail Jeffrey Williams for years, finally got his day in court in early May. The trial had been going well for Clyne by the time he was ready to call Evans to the stand on May 16, but Clyne and Horton were still a bit leery about how Evans would come across on the stand.

The one thing they didn't want was about to happen: Evans would be showing up in court in an orange jumpsuit, paper slippers, shackled from waist to wrist to ankles. Williams's defense team was going to have a field day.

Evans still hadn't been officially sentenced for the James Audubon book theft and the $75,000 worth of antiques he had stolen from several antiques shops in Vermont. The federal system is a bogged-down conveyor belt of criminals waiting to be sentenced. Evans was in line, in prison for nearly a year waiting to be sentenced. Any time accrued over that period would be time served. But first, he had an obligation to testify in what amounted to be the biggest trial Albany had on its docket in several years. Williams had already escaped a guilty verdict once.

Early in the morning on May 16, Horton sent two troopers to fetch Evans at the federal Pennsylvania prison where he had been serving his time. "Buy him cookies, milk, whatever he wants," Horton told the troopers before they left. "Coddle him if you have to. Just get him here in good spirits."

Later that day, Clyne and Horton were waiting in Clyne's office when they got word Evans had arrived.

Clyne was sitting behind his desk going through some paperwork and taking notes when the door to his office opened and Evans was escorted in, clanking and hopping due to the chains and shackles and handcuffs constraining him.

Horton stood up from the chair he was sitting in while Clyne looked up from his glasses.

"Give us a few minutes," Horton told the troopers.

The plan was to go through exactly what Evans would say when he sat in the witness chair. No surprises. No outbursts of narcissism. Just tell the jury what happened and leave it at that. Clyne and Horton explained to Evans that he would be under a blistering cross-examination from Williams's defense attorney regarding his record.

Evans nodded. He seemed okay with it.

Horton could tell by looking at him that he was embarrassed. The chains and shackles and handcuffs made him feel as if he had let Horton down. He was pale. It was easy to suppose he hadn't slept much.

Looking at Clyne and Horton, Evans said, "I wear the chains I forged in life" as he raised his hands and rattled the chains hanging from his handcuffs.

Clyne stopped what he was doing and just sat there for a moment. "Son of a bitch," he said after a brief pause.

Horton, admittedly less educated than Clyne, didn't recognize at first that the line was from Charles Dickens's *A Christmas Carol.* So he shook his head and wrote it off as another one of Evans's moments of innate clarity. *That's Gary*, Horton told himself, *always making things more dramatic than they actually are.*

"Whatever, Gar . . . ," Horton finally said out loud to break the silence.

Clyne didn't expect anything that dramatic out of Evans. He really didn't know him that well, other than hearing about him from Horton and other cops. But the Dickens line impressed him.

A well-read con . . . what do you know! Clyne thought.

Horton figured it out after Clyne made a reference to Dickens. "Cute, Gar," he said. "Now, we have work to do here."

Evans ultimately stood his ground and gave Clyne the entire summation of the conversation he'd had with Williams. He was on the stand for about a half hour. Williams's defense attorney tried poking holes in his story by bringing up all of his prior convictions, but in the end it was one con's word against another's. From there, the jury could decide.

Four days after Evans testified, Williams was found guilty of kidnapping and murdering Karolyn Lonczak and later sentenced to twenty-five years to life. The conviction, many claimed, was supported by a medallion Williams had supposedly left at the murder scene on the night he purportedly had abducted Lonczak. Only later did Horton dig up a photo of Williams wearing the medallion.

Still, Horton and Clyne agreed, Evans's testimony helped. It was one part of a package of evidence.

After the jury handed down its verdict, Horton telephoned Evans in prison and explained the verdict.

"Guilty," Horton said. "Jeffrey Williams will spend the rest of his life behind bars." Horton was excited. It had been a good day.

Evans didn't say anything at first. Instead, he started crying.

"You all right, Gar?"

"Yeah . . . I'm okay. I'm just happy for you guys. Congratulate Paul and Doug [Wingate] for me, would you?"

"Sure, man, sure. I will. But listen, I need to talk to you about some things now that this Williams thing is behind us."

Evans became quiet. "What's up, Guy?"

"We're through now, Gar. No more. I can't do it any longer." Horton hadn't said it in any type of mean-spirited tone. He was simply relaying how he felt.

"I understand, Guy . . . I do." Evans knew he had let Horton and Wingate down by stealing the book.

"You're way too much of a fucking liability. I need to move on."

"Okay, Guy."

"You should think about leaving New York, Gar. Maybe leaving the Northeast. Consider landscaping or something else."

Evans went silent. Horton told him to remember seriously what it was like in prison—especially the last time they had seen each other when Evans was crying and talking about suicide because he couldn't stand doing any more time.

"I agree with you, Jim. I do," Evans said as he continued to cry.

You'll never do it, Horton said to himself.

"I just need you out of my life, Gar. Take no offense, but you're high maintenance."

Evans was bawling now. "I wish we knew each other under different circumstances, Guy."

"Just try to go straight, Gar. At least give it a chance. I have to go now."

Dial tone.

CHAPTER 79

On June 9, 1995, Evans was formally sentenced to twenty-seven months for the theft of the James Audubon book. A little under a year later, on June 6, 1996, he was released from a federal prison in Vermont and placed on three years' probation because of a time-served credit for spending all those months in prison before his sentencing.

He was nearly forty-two years old. Still as buff as a competition bodybuilder, he had put on a little more weight, but in all the right places. Almost completely bald, he had been robbing people and burglarizing homes, jewelry stores and antique shops for the past twenty-five years. Since 1977, he had been in and out of prison, on average, every third year. Along the way, he had murdered four people, possibly more. He was tired. Beaten down by the system. Resentful of it. A career criminal, he had built his life around prison, killing people and burglary—and what did he have to show for it?

Nothing.

Shortly after he was released from prison, Evans hooked back up with his old friend Tim Rysedorph. Tim was working at BFI Waste Systems in Latham. He hadn't really seen Evans too much over the years. They had exchanged hellos every once in a while and perhaps even turned a few small "jobs" together, but for the most part Evans hadn't seen Tim since they lived together in Troy with Michael Falco back in the early '80s.

Evans later claimed Tim would always call him when he was low on money and "his wife put pressure on him" to come up with some quick cash. But Evans hated Caroline Parker, and was usually reluctant to work with Tim because of her attitude.

Still, Rysedorph kept calling, Evans later said, looking to turn over quick jobs for quick money.

Throughout the winter of 1996 and summer of 1997, Evans went on a burglarizing binge, and when he could, Tim Rysedorph joined him. Scores of jewelry stores, homes and antique shops were hit. Gold. Diamond necklaces. Rare antiques. Baseball cards.

Anything of value.

But it was a pair of gold cuff links worth about $1,500 that would ultimately do Evans in. When he went to sell the cuff links to a local dealer, he signed his own name on the ticket—a mistake he had never made during the past twenty-five years of committing burglaries. Throughout that same period, some later reported, Tim was trying to sell rare coins and jewelry to anyone who could come up with the money. He'd even lugged around a big brass eagle he and Evans had stolen and tried selling it, too.

As they continued to burglarize throughout the fall, Evans grew increasingly more paranoid of Tim and what he would do if they ever got caught. Evans was looking at a life sentence if he ever got pinched again. To him, life in prison meant death.

"I had planned to kill [Tim] for a while," Evans told Horton later, "because the heat was getting closer and he would have rolled on me in a second. He had also ripped me off when we lived in Troy."

Justification—it was all Evans had left. For every person he murdered, he defended his right to do it without remorse. Here it was twelve years after the fact and he hadn't forgotten how Tim Rysedorph had ripped him off and blamed Michael Falco for it. He said he knew the gold cuff links were going to come back to haunt him once the Bureau put Rysedorph in a chair and shone a light in his face. So, from his view of things, there was only one way to avoid such a disaster.

Kill him.

On October 3, 1997, Evans and Rysedorph hooked up at about 12:35 P.M. in the parking lot of T.J. Maxx in Latham, which was directly in front of the apartment complex Lisa Morris had moved into with her daughter, Christina, sometime after Damien Cuomo disappeared.

The plan was, Evans told Tim, to drive over to the Spare Room II storage facility, where Evans and Rysedorph had both rented units, and go through the merchandise they had recently stolen.

"We need to part ways, Timmy," Evans said when he sat down in Tim's car in the parking lot of T.J. Maxx. "It's getting too hot right now."

The idea was to split up the merchandise and not see each other for a while.

"Where are you going?" Tim asked.

"Canada? The West Coast? Not sure," Evans said. "Forget that shit. Follow me to the Spare Room. Okay?"

The Spare Room II was about a two-minute drive from T.J. Maxx. By 12:50 P.M., Evans and Tim were at Spare Room II sifting through what little merchandise they had left.

After they finished, both men drove to Lisa Morris's apartment and had an argument outside in the parking lot as Lisa watched from her balcony.

Lisa later said the argument was over checks Tim had cashed. Evans was upset about it. It was sloppy. They were going to get caught.

"Tim will 'roll over' on me," Evans later told Lisa, "because he has never been arrested before and he has a wife and kid."

Throughout the day, Tim and Evans showed up at various times and took several items from Lisa's apartment. Lisa later said she saw them at about 5:00 P.M. in the parking lot of T.J. Maxx. Evans parked his truck, got into Tim's car and they took off. But a half hour later, they returned to her apartment: Evans driving his truck, Tim his car. By 6:30, they left again in Tim's car after another argument. At 9:00 P.M., Evans called Lisa. "I'm with my partner. . . . Can you pick me up in Troy if I need you to?"

"Sure," Lisa said.

It was the last time Lisa could verify Tim Rysedorph's whereabouts.

As the night of October 3 wore on, Caroline Parker kept calling Tim, asking him when he was coming home. Evans later said it "pissed Tim off" that she wouldn't leave him alone. At 1:03 A.M., on October 4, Tim finally called Caroline and told her he'd be home in forty minutes. He was at the Dunkin' Donuts in Latham, not too far away from the Spare Room II.

"I have to be home soon, Gar," Tim said while getting back into his car. "I've been gone all day."

"One more trip to the storage shed," Evans said. "Help me load up the rest of the shit."

Tim didn't know it, but Evans had his .22-caliber handgun tucked inside the front of his pants.

Back at the storage shed, as Tim was leaning down inside the shed to pick up a box of stolen merchandise, Evans quietly walked up from behind and shot him three times in the back of the head. It was over quickly: *pop, pop, pop.*

With Tim Rysedorph lying dead on the concrete floor of the storage shed, Evans walked over to a box he had placed in the shed a few days earlier. After grabbing a rubber bib, much like what a fish monger might wear, and putting it on, he took out a chain saw and started it. While grabbing one of

Tim's legs, Evans later admitted, he began talking to himself: *You motherfucker . . . you should have never ripped me off.*

Later, while telling the story to Horton, Evans said he "almost got sick at one point" as he proceeded to cut off Tim's legs and arms. He had picked out a burial site in Brunswick days earlier, but it was a steep hill and the only way he could get Tim's body up the hill in one trip was to cut it up and bag it.

CHAPTER 80

After changing clothes and washing the blood off his hands the best he could, Evans drove to the local supermarket and bought a box of plastic black garbage bags and a gallon of bleach. It was light out now. People were beginning to get up, have their morning coffee and head off to work.

Evans, though, had a body—in five pieces—to bury, a weapon to get rid of and a bloody storage shed to clean up.

As he sadistically chopped Tim's body into pieces, blood and bone fragments had sprayed all over the place. Once the cops figured out that Tim had gone missing, Evans believed they would inevitably track down the storage unit Tim had rented and find his name and unit shortly afterward. The unit had to be spotless.

It took about thirty minutes. Evans bagged and taped each part of Tim's body in a separate garbage bag and put the bags into a cardboard box, along with the clothes he had worn while dismembering him. Then he began cleaning the walls and floor of the unit with bleach and paper towels.

As he scrubbed and wiped up the blood, the bleach fumes began to overcome him and, he said later, he nearly passed out. So he walked over to the garage door and opened it about six inches to allow fresh air into the room.

With bloody paper towels and smudged blood all over the floor, as he continued to clean, Evans then heard footsteps.

What the fuck?

Crawling over to the opening of the door, he watched as the manager of Spare Room II, who had been working in his office, began walking toward his unit.

Shit.

Evans then stood up. Ran over to where he had kept one of his shotguns, grabbed hold of it, and hurried back to the garage door.

Standing, pointing the gun directly toward the door at eye level, the end of the barrel touching the inside of the door, he waited.

"As soon as he lifted that door," Evans told Horton later, "I was going to blow his fucking head off."

Oddly enough, however, something beckoned the manager back to his office. As he placed his hands on the bottom of the door to begin lifting it up, he stopped, turned and walked back to the office for some reason.

"That is the luckiest motherfucker in the world," Evans later told Horton. "He has no idea how close he came to being buried next to Tim Rysedorph."

When Evans finished loading Tim's body parts into the cardboard box, he walked up to T.J. Maxx, got in his truck, drove back down to Spare Room II and loaded the box of body parts, the clothes he had worn while he dismembered Tim and the chain saw into the back of his truck. Before leaving, he drove over to the chain-link fence that corralled the grounds of Spare Room II and threw the .22-caliber handgun he had used to kill Tim Rysedorph over the fence and into a small gulch that ran along the interstate.

"Gary drew me a map," Horton said later, "and, unbelievable to us, months later we found the weapon."

After burying Tim's body parts in several shallow graves just over the Troy city line in Brunswick, Evans drove down to a concrete plant on First Street in Troy located on the banks of the Hudson River (merely blocks from where he grew up). He tossed the chain saw and his clothes into the water. Watching the muddy water of the Hudson swallow the bag and chain saw, he decided to take off out west.

Covered with mud from head to toe, he then drove over to Lisa Morris's apartment in Latham, cleaned himself up and had a glass of milk and a box of Freihofer's chocolate-chip cookies. He then went to sleep.

When he awoke hours later, he packed a bag and took off.

When Horton finally convinced Evans to confess to Tim Rysedorph's murder late in the day on June 19, 1998, after the Bureau had captured Evans in Vermont based on a tip Lisa Morris provided, Evans started crying. "It's going to be hard," he said through tears.

Because Horton had been involved in a number of dismemberment cases for a few years leading up to Evans's capture and confession, he said later he "sort of knew what [Evans] meant" when he said "hard." He had a hunch he was talking about the actual killing itself, not his emotional state at the time.

Banking on his instinct, Horton then asked Evans, "What do you mean, 'It's going to be hard' . . . did you cut him up?"

After Evans "regained his composure and stopped crying," he looked up at Horton and smirked, as if to suggest he was proud of what he had done. In his mind, he had graduated: from common murderer—if there ever was such a thing—to a sadistic sociopath who had put another feather in his cap of evil.

Horton, a bit taken aback, then asked, "Did you cut him up or not?"

"Yes," Evans answered plainly, without emotion.

"Did you cut his head off, too?" Horton asked next, realizing at that moment that the man he had been playing cat and mouse with for nearly thirteen years was a vicious serial killer he had not really known at all.

Evans then stared at Horton with a "surprised" look on his face and, with an expression of seriousness only a multiple murderer could conjure, said, "What . . . Do you think I am *sick*—that I would cut someone's head off? Jesus Christ, Guy!"

Horton didn't answer. It was time to find Tim Rysedorph's body and return it to his family. Evans's days of thinking he could control the situation were over.

CHAPTER 81

Jim Horton had spent the better part of eight hours with Gary Evans in the interrogation suite at Bureau headquarters in Loudonville on June 19, 1998, finally getting him to confess to murdering Tim Rysedorph. It had been one of the most labor-intensive and emotionally draining interrogations Horton had ever done in his twenty years of police work. Things were different now. Evans was no longer the criminal he was trying to get to go straight by setting him up with jobs, or helping him get time chipped off a sentence for setting up a dope dealer or returning a book.

"I wasn't one hundred percent sure Gary had actually murdered Michael Falco and Damien Cuomo until that point," Horton recalled later. "I had no idea, of course, that he had taken a chain saw to one of his victims. It was as shocking to me as it would be to the community in the days and weeks to come."

For Evans, there would be no more deals. No more midnight snacks of cookies and milk. No more trading information for prison time. Indeed, no more freedom.

After Evans gave up Tim, he began to descend into a depression that he had never before experienced. He went from "bad to worse" in a matter of minutes while in Horton's company. The circles underneath his eyes had seemingly turned from gray to brown to black in just a few hours. He hadn't shaved for some time, and his face, sunken and seemingly skeletal-looking, took on an entirely new persona.

"He wasn't," Horton recalled, "the Gary Evans I had known all those years. He looked, physically, much different after he admitted murdering Timmy Rysedorph."

Horton didn't want to waste any time. If he had to, he would get the floodlights out and dig up Tim's body parts in the middle of the night. The only thing standing in his way now was the location.

Evans wanted to stay at Troop G and talk about Michael Falco and Damien Cuomo, but Horton kept him focused on Tim Rysedorph. Once he had Tim's body, he could begin talking about the others.

One at a time.

Some of the longest days of the year in the Northeast are in June. Sunset on June 19, 1998, wasn't until 8:36 P.M., which would make it light out until at least 9:00.

With Horton driving and Chuck DeLuca, a Bureau investigator, sitting directly behind him, investigator Jack Murray riding shotgun, a sober-looking, shackled and handcuffed Gary Evans sat quietly behind Murray. A posse of vehicles—the CSI and MCU—followed as they all headed for Brunswick to exhume Tim Rysedorph's body.

This was what Evans enjoyed more than anything. He was in charge, whether Horton wanted to admit it or not. Here they were en route to find Tim's body parts and Evans was calling the shots once again: "Turn here. No, take a right there. Go up that hill. Stop. No, this isn't it. Maybe it's up there somewhere?"

A true indication of a sociopath is his "callousness" and "lack of empathy for his victims." Instead of empathy, he shows "contempt for others' feelings of distress and readily takes advantage of them."

This description would never fit Evans more perfectly than in the coming days and weeks as the Bureau uncovered body after body. While Evans began talking, explaining where he had buried bodies, he started to realize more and more how in control he was of the situation, and thus began using it to work on Horton and those few other people he allowed into his life. Essentially, he had nothing left to bargain with. He knew he was going to prison now for life, and perhaps, since New York had reinstated the death penalty in 1995, he would even get the chair.

What, really, did Evans have to lose?

As they drove, Evans began to say he wasn't exactly sure where the location was.

"Don't fuck with me now, Gar," Horton said as he drove through downtown Troy into Brunswick.

Evans didn't answer.

Jack Murray, sitting in front of Evans, kept turning around and looking at him. Murray was a bit on edge, wondering if Evans was going to reach over the seat and strangle him. DeLuca, sitting beside Evans, had a good bead on the situation. If Evans so much as moved, he would feel the cold steel barrel of DeLuca's 9mm Glock poking at his temple.

"I wasn't screwing around any longer," Horton said. "This was serious."

As they passed a sign welcoming them to Brunswick, Evans began breathing heavily, almost hyperventilating. "Put my window down. . . . Roll my window down," he started yelling. "I need some air . . . motherfucker, I need air."

"What the hell?" Horton said.

"Roll it down, Guy. Come on. . . ."

Horton gave in, but only rolled it down about six inches. Evans, like a dog, stuck his face out the window and took in what little air he could get.

"Gar, *where* are we going?"

"Keep driving . . . keep driving."

Horton looked at Jack Murray, then into his rearview mirror at DeLuca. They didn't say anything to one another. It was more of an eye gesture and a subliminal agreement among them: *You had better not be fucking with us.*

Brunswick is extremely wooded and rural—the perfect spot, in other words, to bury someone.

As Horton came up to a small stream near Shippey Lane, Evans told him to pull over. "Right there. That dirt patch. Hurry up. . . ."

He was about to get sick.

"Don't puke in the car, Gar. Hold on," Horton said.

As the car came to a stop, Evans opened the door and began vomiting.

Horton whispered to Murray and DeLuca, "We must be close."

After Evans finished, he said, "Hey, Guy, I need to talk to you."

"What is it, Gar? Come on. We need to find that body."

Evans made it clear that he wanted to talk to Horton alone. A bit hesitant, Horton asked Murray and DeLuca to excuse themselves for a moment.

"We had come so far up to this point," Horton recalled later. "But without a body, we might as well have been at square one. It was very tense. We were worried that at any second Gary would say, forget it."

The rest of the crime scene entourage had pulled over a few hundred yards behind, waiting for word to continue.

"I need to call [my nephew]," Evans said in a whisper.

"You *what*?"

Evans wanted to talk to his half-sister Robbie's son, Devan.

Without asking why, Horton handed Evans his cell phone. "Take your time, Gar. We can wait."

Robbie answered. "It's me, sis. I need to tell you some things," Evans said immediately.

"It was hard to hear him very well," Robbie recalled later.

"I kept telling him to 'speak up.' His voice was very soft. He was crying."

Evans wanted to explain to the only family he had left what was going to happen over the next few days. He knew once the newspapers got hold of the story, it would turn into a media circus, and he wanted to prepare Robbie and Devan for what was going to happen.

"Sis," Evans continued, "I've done some bad stuff and I don't want you to know all about it. Please don't hate me for what I have done. I had to take care of myself. I never wanted it to end this way. Don't read the papers or get on the Internet. I don't want you to know all the details."

Evans had always been, Robbie said, "protective of her" and Devan. He wanted to shelter them now more than ever. The horror of who he truly was hadn't even been made public, yet he was already beginning to rationalize his behavior.

"I haven't hurt any children or women," Evans added, "only bad people." Again, more justification for the terror he had perpetrated on five victims, two of whom were innocent jewelry shop owners. "Don't hate me for what I've done. I'm not a monster. I just have to get this over."

Horton stood by and tried to give Evans what privacy he needed.

"I'm with Jim," he continued. "I'm okay. He's taking good care of me. . . . I love you." By this point, Robbie recalled later, "he was really sobbing and very pensive."

"Have a good life," Evans then said. "I wish I could have been more, but I am not to be in this world. I chose this life. I'm at peace with myself. I just need to get the pain out of my heart and be done with it all. I'm tired. I want out of this life."

Then, as if he wanted to prove that he could be remorseful, he said, "I wanted to protect the children," meaning the children of his victims. "I go in peace now, whenever that may be. I learned some really hard lessons. I learned a lot I wish I never knew. I did this. Of course, everything has been affected by the things that happened to me as a child—but I still had free choice. I chose my way."

After a brief pause to collect his composure, Evans said, "I hate the world."

"You okay, Gar?" Horton asked.

"Let's go."

CHAPTER 82

About one hundred yards from where Horton and his entourage had pulled off Route 2 to allow Evans a place to vomit and call Robbie, there were large power lines cutting across Route 2, near the corner of Shyne Road.

"Stop the car," Evans said. He looked up into the forest near Shyne Road, where the power lines seemed to run into the woods forever. Across the street was a stream. Evans said he used to swim in it as a kid. He had even taken some of the women he'd dated to the riverbed, he mumbled to Horton, to "get laid and look at the stars."

The incline going up the hill in between Shyne Road and Route 2 was as steep as it could be without it being a wall of rocks. There was a dirt road heading up the hill, but anything other than maybe a dirt bike would have trouble making the trip.

Horton took the shackles off Evans so he could walk up the hill without any trouble. As Evans, Horton, Murray and DeLuca began working their way up the hill, Evans took off his shirt.

"Where?" Horton wanted to know.

"Up there . . . past the crest in the hill," Evans said. He

seemed sure of himself. It had only been about eight months since he'd murdered and buried Tim Rysedorph.

"Shallow grave, right, Gar?" Horton asked.

"Graves," Evans said.

Jesus.

While walking up the hill, Evans launched into a fit of rage. He began breathing heavily and pounding on his chest, screaming and hyperventilating.

At the top of the hill, he led everyone to the right, into the woods. Since it was June, the brush was thick and green, just beginning to come in. "Over here," Evans said, walking deep into the brush, his back and chest getting scraped by prickers and tree branches.

Back down on the street, the team of forensic specialists gathered their shovels and bags, toolboxes and equipment, ready to head up.

"Why here?" Horton asked.

"I like this place."

"Did you mark the grave?"

Evans was scanning the ground, looking for the spot, but couldn't find it.

After about twenty minutes, Chuck DeLuca, who had been roaming around the area by himself, feeling the ground with the bottom of his shoes for a soft spot, said, "Over here, Jim."

Evans and Horton were about fifty yards away. "Is that it, Gar?"

"Yeah, I think so."

The location where DeLuca stood wasn't as grown in as the rest of the area. DeLuca and Murray, along with several other members of the Bureau who had since joined them, began excavating an area about ten by ten.

Evans just stood, staring blankly as they began digging.

"We found something," somebody said within minutes. It looked like a foot wrapped in a plastic garbage bag and taped.

Horton grabbed Evans by the arm and retreated back about

twenty yards. He didn't want Evans to see anything. Horton had done this before. He knew Evans would flip out at the sight of his own work. He needed to know where Falco and Cuomo were buried. If Evans snapped, he might stop talking.

While Evans was putting his T-shirt back on, he whispered, "I'm going to take off, Guy, and . . . run. I want you to shoot me in the back. You'll be the hero."

"Are you crazy? First of all," Horton said softly, putting his arm around Evans's shoulder, "I'll miss you, Gar. No, no, no. You are *not* running away. I am not killing you."

"Come on, Guy. It'll be the perfect end to all of this bullshit."

"No, Gar. We still have more work to do. Let's play this out. You're doing a *good* thing."

As the crew began the horrific task of unearthing Tim Rysedorph's body parts, Horton handcuffed himself to Evans and started walking back down the hill.

"I wasn't taking any chances after he told me he wanted to run away," Horton recalled later. "He was desperate at that point."

Horton then began questioning Evans about how and where he had killed Rysedorph. Evans said he did it across the street by the river. He said they argued. He said he talked Tim into getting out of the car and then shot him in the head and cut his body up in the woods by the river.

"Show me where," Horton said.

"Right there," Evans pointed. There was a narrow patch of road leading down toward the river. Looking at it, Horton became suspicious of the story right away.

"Exactly where?" Horton wanted to know. "Show me the exact spot you shot him and where you cut him up."

Evans first said it was about fifty yards in, and then he changed his story and said it was closer to the river.

"I knew he was lying to me," Horton said later, "but I had no idea why. At that point, there was no reason to."

After Horton got Evans to admit he was lying, and that he had killed Tim at the Spare Room II storage facility, he asked him why he had cut him up.

"You walked up that hill," Evans said.

"So you planned this ahead of time?"

Evans didn't answer.

"What did you do with the chain saw?"

"I threw it in the river [Hudson]."

"Great . . . let's go. You can show us where."

Horton ended up sending out a team of divers to search the area where Evans claimed he had tossed the chain saw into the Hudson, but they turned up nothing after a lengthy search.

CHAPTER 83

By June 23, 1998, the local press had latched onto the story. The *Troy Record,* a newspaper that had followed Evans's career in crime, ran banner headlines: GRUESOME DISCOVERY IN BRUNSWICK: *Saratoga Man's Death Ruled a Homicide; Friend a Suspect.*

This just made things more difficult for Horton, who still had a tremendous amount of work to do with Evans. The media frenzy that ensued became almost unbearable for Horton and the Bureau as they continued to try to get Evans to admit where he had buried Michael Falco and Damien Cuomo. Rumors abounded that he had killed men in Seattle and Florida. Horton was fielding inquiries from law enforcement around the country—everyone, it seemed, had an unsolved murder that Evans could be responsible for.

Evans had said something to Horton that had bothered Horton: "There are others. . . ."

Throughout the past few days, as Horton stopped at Albany County Jail to visit Evans and check on him, he would plant the notion that there would come a time when they would have to discuss what he had meant by "others."

Since news of Tim's murder had broken, Horton and Evans had become local celebrities. All the newspapers and television stations were running nonstop coverage. Wherever Horton went, he was recognized. Evans, who was spending most of his time in Albany County Jail, was also gaining national serial killer celebrity status, like Ted Bundy or John Wayne Gacy.

"I realized quite quickly that all this did was massage Gary's ego," Horton later recalled. "He had been severely depressed since giving up Timmy's body. But now that his face and name were front-page news, he lightened up."

Horton viewed Evans's newfound celebrity as a way to further his agenda. He had been stopping by to see Evans two, three, even four times a day, asking him if he needed anything.

"How are you being treated?"

It was "Mr. Horton" now when he walked into the jail. The guards were "very accommodating." Whatever Horton and Evans needed, they got. No questions asked.

"When you think about the gravity of the situation—we're talking about a serial murderer," Horton said, "it makes you understand how the media turns these guys into celebrities. Gary saw it coming."

Evans was in "protective lockdown." He was considered a high-risk inmate. When Horton stopped by the jail to see him on June 24, Evans indicated that he wanted to go outside and talk.

Horton would arrive at the jail, go see Evans and be asked on the way out by media and guards: "Did you get another body out of him today?" It had become rather surreal, as if people were keeping score.

During one afternoon, Horton brought Evans out to the basketball court in the jail's courtyard. It was a crisp, sunny day. They were alone. "Listen, Gar," Horton said, "you told me 'two others.' What did you mean by that?"

"You mean you didn't find them?"

"There are hundreds of open homicides. I wouldn't even know where to start."

"West! Start looking west."

"Come on . . . don't screw me around."

After Evans had a few moments of psychotic jubilation over the fact that he was still in charge, he gave Horton details that only he could have known about the murders of jewelry shop owners Douglas Berry and Gregory Jouben. Cops run the risk of sometimes accepting that a perpetrator will take responsibility for crimes he did not commit just to bask in the glory. Because of that, cops need details of the crimes only the killer knows.

When Evans finished giving Horton two statements—regarding Berry and Jouben—he realized that there was no way Evans could have been lying; the details, matched up against the police reports from those murders, had striking consistencies.

Later that day, Evans admitted murdering Damien Cuomo and agreed to show Horton where Damien's body was buried.

So again, there they were in Horton's car en route to find another body. As they made their way into Troy, near Damien Cuomo's parents' house and the apartment Damien had shared with Lisa Morris, Horton asked him if he had been back to the scene since burying Cuomo.

"Nope," Evans said stoically. His moods fluctuated. He was up. Then down. Talkative. Then quiet. It was all part of what was going on inside his head. At times, Horton swore, it was as if the entire situation weren't real to Evans. He began talking about a television movie and which actor was best suited to play him. He asked Horton who he wanted to play his role. Horton didn't feed into it, but instead kept directing Evans back to what was important.

Tropical heat had invaded the Albany region over the past few days. By midafternoon, as Horton, Evans and the forensic crew reached the wooded area where Damien was buried, the humidity was brutal.

"I cut a tree down," Evans said, "to mark the area. But it all looks so different now up here."

It had been nearly ten years since Evans had murdered

Damien. The entire area had grown in. What were weeds back then were now small trees.

Horton handcuffed himself to Evans as they made their way through the brush.

"So you cut down a tree. . . . Well, the stump should still be here somewhere," Horton offered. No sooner had he said it, then they located a tree that had been lopped off near the base of its trunk. "This has to be it."

"No, I don't think so."

"Come on, how many trees do you see cut down around here?"

"I'm not sure, Guy."

"You're supposed to be an outdoorsman. . . . This tree is cut off. How many others do you see like it around here?"

Evans again said he wasn't sure.

"Let's just pretend, then, that this is it."

"Sixty paces straight ahead," Evans said in a near whisper.

Horton and Evans counted the sixty paces. "Start digging here," Horton yelled while pointing to the ground below his feet.

"Topsoil," Evans said. "When you find empty white bags of topsoil, you've found Damien."

Within fifteen minutes, Bureau investigators located a piece of rope tied in a knot and two empty bags of topsoil from a local hardware store. A minute later, digging farther, they located an upside-down sneaker.

It was Damien Cuomo's right foot.

Walking back to the car with Evans as the Bureau finished digging up the remains of Damien Cuomo, Horton thought, *That poor bastard . . . he knew he was going to die long before he was murdered.* He looked at Evans, who smirked sarcastically as they walked. *You cold son of a bitch. I never really knew how sick you were.*

Horton, Chuck "Sully" Sullivan and Evans left the scene as the CSI unit began its tedious excavation process. Evans wanted a copy of the local newspapers and something to eat. Horton knew it would be a long day. He still had to get Evans to write an official statement regarding the events of the day. There was a Cumberland Farms convenience store right down the street.

"Let's stop here," Horton said, pulling into the parking lot. He sent Sully into the store. "Get him some orange juice, the newspapers, some chocolate-chip cookies."

"Thanks, Guy," Evans said from the backseat.

With Sully inside the store, Horton leaned over the front seat and, handing Evans his cell phone, said, "Call Lisa Morris."

Evans froze. *What?*

"Call Lisa and tell her what you did to her boyfriend, the father of her child. You've led her on for all these years . . . making her believe Damien was still alive. I want you to tell her what you did. You owe her that much!"

Evans took the phone, sat back, stared at it and started crying.

"Call her!"

Evans slowly dialed the number.

"Lisa? That you?"

Lisa Morris's life, by June 1998, had spiraled out of control. She was drinking heavily, abusing hard drugs and spending much of her time in local bars. She hadn't worked in quite some time. Befriending Horton in 1997 and setting up Evans for his fall in Vermont had indeed taken its toll. She had loved Evans. She believed in her heart Damien had run out on her and Christina. Even with the latest news coverage, she still didn't want to believe Evans had killed Damien.

"I was grief stricken about the whole thing," Lisa said later. "Gary was my best friend. I had lost the love of my life when Damien disappeared. Gary filled that role. Regardless of what people have said, [Gary] was good for Christina. He loved her. When I saw in the newspaper that he was giving up bodies, I couldn't believe what they were saying about him."

Crying, Evans said, "I'm sorry. . . ."

"What do you mean, you're 'sorry'?" Lisa asked.

"I gotta do this favor for these guys. . . . I didn't mean to do this to you," Evans said.

In the end, Evans refused to tell Lisa that he had killed Damien.

"But I knew," she recalled later.

Horton sat there, watching, listening.

Lisa finally said, "Put Jim back on the phone."

Evans handed Horton the phone and stared out the window.

Lisa couldn't speak when Horton got on the phone.

"I'm very sorry, Lisa. I am," Horton said. "I'll call you later."

CHAPTER 84

Dealing with Gary Evans over the past week had been exhausting for Jim Horton, physically and mentally. Evans had given up four bodies. He was manic: up one minute, down the next. He demanded Horton visit him in jail every day. In addition, Lisa Morris was now calling and asking questions that Horton didn't have answers to.

And then there was the media.

"The press was on me like crazy," Horton said later. "About five or six reporters suddenly wanted to be my best friends. Both television and print. Every day they wanted to talk directly to me to see what Gary had said."

Horton couldn't even go to the jails Evans was being shuffled in between, he said, without reporters knowing about it. He believed each jail had a guard feeding the media information about his movements.

"I needed a break from Gary Evans."

Ever since Horton had worked himself into a bout with spinal meningitis back in the late '80s, he had reassessed his life. He couldn't work seventeen-, eighteen-, twenty-four-hour days without paying a price. He was forty-three years old now—same as Evans. The spinal meningitis had knocked him down for months. Doctors said a lot of it was due to the rigorous work schedule he kept.

This time, he wasn't going to let the job—more specifically, Evans—ruin his health. He needed to stay focused and be ready when Evans was willing to talk about other murders. In all likelihood, Tim Rysedorph, Damien Cuomo, Gregory Jouben and Douglas Berry were only the beginning. There was no telling how many more bodies would turn up.

By June 24, a Wednesday, Horton had set two goals: One, he wanted Evans to give up Michael Falco; and two, he needed a long weekend away with his wife and children to regroup.

After a long discussion with Evans later that day, Evans admitted to Horton that he had killed Michael Falco and buried his body in Florida.

"Where?" Horton wanted to know.

"Near my sister's house," Evans said, "in Lake Worth."

Horton immediately contacted the Florida Department of Law Enforcement (FDLE) and informed them that the Bureau needed aerial photographs of an area in Lake Worth near a golf course. Evans told Horton he could pick out the spot where Falco was buried but, "I would rather you take me there so I can show you myself. I'm not positive I can find it on a map."

An hour or so later, Horton went back and told Evans he had spoken to his boss about flying him down to Florida. "Having you travel in any fashion," Horton said, "is out of the question. They just won't okay it. Sorry, Gar. But I can't do anything this time."

Evans was an escape risk. He had been telling the people who were visiting him that he was going to escape. He was asking for razor blades. Nobody knew it, but he had swallowed a handcuff key when he was taken into custody in Vermont and had been recycling it while in jail. Throughout his years of incarceration, Evans had sometimes slept with his index finger lodged in his right nostril for the purpose of forging a tunnel in his sinus where he could hide a handcuff key.

"I didn't even broach the subject with my boss of Gary flying to Florida," Horton recalled later. "But I lied to Gary and told him he had said no. Not that I didn't trust Gary to a point, but something told me not to move him."

A short while later, when Horton stopped in to see Evans, he found out how accurate his instincts were. Evans said, "I would have jumped out of the plane on the way back from Florida."

"We would have been in a jet. I would have been sucked out as well."

Evans shrugged his shoulders.

Horton assigned Sully to go to Florida with the Bureau's ID Unit to oversee the search and excavation of Michael Falco's body. But before Sully could leave, Horton wanted to introduce him to Evans so Evans could show Sully, using aerial photographs, where Falco was buried. Horton had made plans to leave for the weekend. He wasn't breaking them.

"Gary didn't want me to leave, nor did I want to go," Horton recalled. "But I had to delegate some things. Gary felt comfortable with Sully, who has a calming, trusting nature."

So, as Sully and the boys made preparations for a trip to Florida, Horton and his family drove east to spend the weekend at a family-owned cottage in Connecticut. "I had worked many days in a row," Horton said. "Gary just gave up Falco. The guys were headed south. Even if Gary had another body to give me during the time I was away, there was really nobody available (that I wanted) to help me. He was becoming more depressed and just wanted to talk, but he also seemed to change and become clingier toward me. He wanted me to come to the jail just to be there. I was interested in more bodies, while he was turning to me as someone he could talk to, a father figure, a friend, means of support."

As it turned out, while Horton was in Connecticut climbing the walls—calling work four, five times a day with the feeling that something was going to happen in his absence—Evans ended up phoning him several times.

"There wasn't a vacation I ever took where I wasn't like this. I would call work every day, which is probably not too healthy. But being away from Gary, especially, gave me a lot of anxiety. I knew he was planning something—I just didn't know what."

Indeed, there were only three people who later admitted that they knew what Evans was planning, but they either didn't take him seriously enough to go to the authorities with the information, didn't think he could pull it off or abetted him the entire way.

CHAPTER 85

Isn't it a pity, isn't it a shame
Evans plays a vicious game
And seeing how you like to tell people things
I wish you could tell me . . . is it dark in that hole?

Discovered years later, Evans had written a letter in verse from prison to one of his victims before he had killed him. He didn't name the person, but it was clear years later that it was either Michael Falco or Damien Cuomo, both of whom had been buried in holes.

Today is so nice, it's a shame to die on such a day. Now I'm wondering if you feel anything—can you feel your death coming to meet you? Did you ever think that I spent every day + night for years thinking of how you should die? I wonder what you gained when you told on me?

The 1½-page letter was unrelenting in its accusatory manner. Evans wanted his victim to know that because he had "told" on him, he had to die. In what had become his trademark throughout the years, he began the letter with a smiley face and ended it the same way, as if speaking of death and premeditated murder was what made him the happiest.

Letter writing had always been an outlet for Evans while he was incarcerated. He used letters to manipulate people, and each letter was methodically tailored to coddle each specific person's character.

In early July, as prosecutors prepared what was shaping up to be a death penalty case against him, Evans began a letter-writing campaign to those people in his life he trusted the most. In a letter addressed to Horton on July 3, he spoke about their entire life of cat and mouse together, flavoring the letter with anecdotes from his childhood and teenage years of burglary: *I look at the things I've done and say in the mirror, "I did that?" And I know I did and I know it's all over soon.*

"The remorseful Gary Evans."

Then he talked about his "magical princess," Doris Sheehan, a woman he credited with getting him over the love of his life, Stacy.

Near the end of the letter, Evans reminisced about the "red light" he had run in Cohoes back in 1985 on the night he met Horton. As if fate were the driving force, he equated the meeting to some sort of astrological aligning of the stars.

He admitted he "looked up" to Horton, "because I can't look down on you."

Finally at peace, no more pain—that's freedom. It's over finally. Thank you Jim for being Jim. You're a great guy and my friend.

He lastly told Horton he didn't want him to love him: *I'm that much better off.*

On July 10, as the Bureau began looking for Michael Falco's remains in Florida, Evans penned a letter to Bill Murphy, the only "true friend in the world" he claimed he ever had.

He begged Bill to come to the jail: *It's safe now, no filming, etc, no publicity. . . . Boy did I fuck up.* He wrote he needed to say *some serious things—views of life from the Evans observatory.*

"The feel-sorry-for-me Gary Evans."

He then explained how regretful he was for the reporters who had been bothering Bill at work. Then: *I made mistakes and it's almost finishing time.*

Bill, he said, had been his friend longer than anyone: *I hope you come see me soon, it's almost too late already. Please come, I need to . . . say good-bye.*

CHAPTER 86

Jo Rehm had been Evans's baby-sitter, surrogate mother, friend and protector. As kids growing up in Troy during the late '60s, Evans and Jo Rehm were inseparable. Jo took care of little Gary while Flora Mae and Roy Evans drank themselves silly. Years later, when Jo got married and moved away, she took Evans in for a summer after he had run away from home. After he left Jo's home later that year, however, she never really saw him again—that is, until Evans was facing the end of his life and wanted to let her know how much she had meant to him all these years.

The letter Evans wrote to Jo was drenched with "don't blame yourself" rhetoric that only Evans could dish out with his usual saccharine cadence. Jo had written to Evans and explained how she had been hard on herself for not taking better care of him when he was a child.

It was nonsense. Jo was just a kid herself, looking to get the hell out of Troy and begin a life of her own.

And listen, Evans wrote after demanding Jo stop beating herself up, *this is important, I'm OK. I'm at peace with myself. I accomplished a very important thing. And when my time is up, I'll laugh. . . .*

He wrote fervently that he *never hurt a girl or innocent*

person ever. Every one of them was a criminal that did at least as bad as me—and a couple were worse.

"Gary Evans, the justifier."

Apparently, he had forgotten the heartless fact that he had murdered one shop owner while he was asleep and another while he was viewing a piece of jewelry. Both were hard-working family men who never bothered anybody.

No more mail, Evans ended the letter with. *I get too sad, OK?*

Horton received another letter from Evans, on July 11.

Times running, Guy. I feel very sad and a little bit scared, too. . . . Lotta bullshit in the paper. I hope you'll always be OK, I know you will. I'm so sorry about my life.

"The concerned Gary Evans."

The local newspapers had been running daily stories about Evans and Horton now for the past three weeks. People were beginning to call Evans a "monster," a term that infuriated him. He was worried that Robbie and his nephew, Devan, would get caught in the whirlwind of press reports. He didn't want the media bothering them. And Lisa Morris, well: *Can you figure out a way to get [her] in line?* he asked.

Lisa was giving the press photographs of Evans and telling stories about her life with him. He wanted Horton to collect all of his personal items from her.

Major Bart R. Johnson, commander of Troop G, released a formal statement explaining how, on July 14, 1998, Michael Falco's remains had been found in Florida and, with the help of dental records, positively identified.

With the death toll now at five and rising, when Horton asked Evans about the trip he took out west after murdering Tim Rysedorph, Evans said he was "finished giving up bodies."

Horton figured when the time was right, he would start talking again.

Jo Rehm hadn't seen Gary Evans for almost twenty-five years. They had bumped into each other at a local retail store back in 1995, but beyond that two-minute encounter, Jo hadn't spoken to him.

When Jo read about how depressed he was, she picked up the phone, called the jail and made arrangements to go see him.

As soon as they made eye contact a day later, they started crying. It had been a long road. Yet here they were now at what seemed like the end trying to figure out what had happened and where everything had gone so horribly wrong.

"I've done a lot of bad things, Jo," Evans said. "I'm sick."

"Do they know you're sick?" Jo understood him wrong; she thought he was physically ill. "The flu," she later said, "or something."

"No, you don't understand," Evans said, pointing to his head. "I'm sick here."

For the next thirty minutes, they talked about old times. Then Evans launched into an attack against Robbie. He said he didn't want to see her. He was mad at her, but he did want to see Devan.

The next day, Jo went back. Lisa Morris was there when she arrived. It was a short visit.

A few days after that, Horton called Jo after Evans asked him to, because Evans wanted to see Jo again, but said he was having trouble getting word to her.

Jo didn't trust Horton. "I'll pick you up," Horton offered, "if you want me to?"

"No! I've read about you in the papers. I'll take my own car, thank you."

That day, when Jo saw Evans, she asked him about Horton.

"Jim is okay," Evans said. "He's my friend." He paused for a moment, crying, "I . . . I love Jim Horton."

Jo then thought, *If he's good enough for Gary, he's good enough for me.*

"Make sure you keep in touch with Jim," Evans said after collecting himself. "He'll always be there for you."

"Okay, Gary."

From there, Evans started talking in a manner that led Jo to believe the end was near—not, specifically, that Evans was preparing himself emotionally for a death sentence, but that he was planning on doing something to himself. Something big, something people would remember him by.

As the days dragged on and a capital felony murder case was being built against him, Evans started writing to Jo and Horton nearly every day.

On Tuesday, July 28, he wrote to Horton: *It would have been nice to have you as a brother, growing up somewhere nice instead of the trolls that kidnapped me from nice people when I was a baby.* Then he described a scene from Dickens's *A Christmas Carol,* comparing his life to the Ghost of Jacob Marley.

Next he initiated an attack on the justice system, pushing the blame for the murders he committed on a system, he said, that should allow a "thief to do a thief's time" He wrote: *Nothing would have happened to* those *people [Falco, Cuomo, Berry, Jouben and Rysedorph] if I didn't have to worry about getting life for stealing.*

In other words, if the courts would have just allowed him the opportunity to be a serial burglar without serious punishment, he would not have killed anyone.

Don't you see? It's all their fault! he was implying.

Near the end of the letter, he began to question whether what was happening had all been predetermined: *So was it fate [that] we met in a dingy little holding cell in Cohoes and thirteen years later [we] say good-bye here? Were we meant to learn something from our interaction as cops n' robbers and more?*

Reading the letter, Horton could only shake his head in disbelief. "Gary had an excuse for everything; he wanted to believe it wasn't his fault."

Days later, worried about his emotional state, Horton stopped in to see him. As they talked, Evans admitted he was planning an escape.

"You don't want to do that, Gar," Horton encouraged.

"I have to, Guy. I can't die in here."

A few days prior to Horton's visit, Evans had told Lisa Morris nearly the same thing, adding, "If I die in here, they win. . . . If I die out there, I win."

"Well," Horton said, "if you do try something, all I ask is that you don't hurt anyone. . . . And don't do it while in state police custody. Don't make me or the state police look like fools for trusting you."

Evans said he understood.

Leaving the jail, Horton put in a call to the DA's office and the Rensselaer County Sheriff's Office, who were responsible for holding Evans. He told both that Evans was planning an escape attempt. "I don't know how or when, but he told me he is going to try." Like he had said numerous times throughout his career to many different law enforcement agencies, Horton ended the conversation with a familiar caveat: "He will crawl through a straw if he has to. Don't underestimate him. To get away, he will do anything he has to. Remember, he has nothing to lose."

Please believe what I am telling you, Horton silently pleaded.

CHAPTER 87

Evans would write notes for Lisa Morris on the back of chewing-gum wrappers or small pieces of paper, roll them into tiny scrolls, stuff them up in his sinuses and, when no one was looking, slip them to Lisa when she visited him at Albany County Jail. In one, he explained how he wanted Lisa to find him a special handcuff key, and even drew a picture of it after explaining where she could find it. Although Lisa had turned Evans in and he had vowed never to see her again, the game, so to speak, was over. Lisa still loved Evans, she said later. She was one of only a handful of people he had left and she wasn't about to turn her back on him now.

Lisa would never admit that she had fulfilled Evans's request, but it would be clear in the coming days that Evans either had a handcuff key already, or obtained one from someone who visited him. When asked about it later, Horton said he believed Evans had smuggled a key into the jail by swallowing it in Vermont and kept it hidden inside his nose the entire time he was in jail.

Regardless, it was clear he was going to make an escape attempt. The questions were: when and how?

* * *

By August 3, a grand jury had convened to decide Evans's fate. In all likelihood, he would be indicted by week's end and charged with eight counts of first-degree murder. Would the case, in the end, meet the strict guidelines for capital punishment, which had been reinstated in New York on September 1, 1995? District Attorney Kenneth Bruno, who was in charge of prosecuting Evans, was doing his best to prove it did. The one item of importance, Bruno suggested, was the fact that Evans had killed Tim Rysedorph in an attempt to stop him from testifying against him for a string of burglaries they had committed together.

The death penalty issue only instigated a new wave of media coverage. Evans was being billed as a serial killer. To assuage his insecurities over being put into the same monstrous category as Ted Bundy, John Wayne Gacy and several other high-profile serial killers, Horton set up an exclusive interview between Evans and the *Albany Times Union* newspaper. The two-page interview, including photos of Evans behind bars, gave him the opportunity to explain himself. Like he had all along, he said he never wanted for his life to turn out the way it had. "The things I did," he told the *Times Union*, "related to business."

Evans looked tired in the photographs that ran with the article. He had bags under his eyes. His demeanor appeared dark. Cold. Vacant. Horton later said he had taken on an entirely new persona by this time: from remorseful and saddened over everything he had done, to an admitted killer, both terrified and paranoid of the future.

Meanwhile, family members of Evans's many victims assailed him in the press. Caroline Parker, for one, was telling any reporter who would listen that Evans had chosen to kill, and for that reason he should die a horrible death like that of his victims.

With his first court appearance to face charges of murder only a week away, and the information Horton had provided to the DA regarding Evans's desire to escape, Evans was placed in solitary confinement. With nothing left to do, he began to pen what would be his final two letters to Horton—letters that would, later, serve as a crystal ball.

On August 5, it appeared that he wanted to—if only half-heartedly—take responsibility for his actions. He wrote to Horton: *I fucked up my life repeatedly . . . my decisions, my fault. I thought I was too smart and I was, for a long time. But I got stupid and here I am. My fault.*

He wrote he especially felt sorry for Christina Morris, Lisa Morris and Damien Cuomo's daughter. He apologized for misleading Lisa all those years and, in turn, Lisa having to lie to Christina: *I wrecked lives. I was unfeeling toward survivors of victims. . . . It's cold but true. So I deserve what's coming. I got worse and worse and when the trap was coming I killed to avoid it. Cold bloodedly. . . . And I don't want someone like me in society myself.*

Two days later, another letter showed up on Horton's desk, the most bizarre to date.

Evans's handwriting fluctuated from steady and readable, to blurry and scribbled. He used large and small font. Cursive and print. A fan of haiku and poetry his entire life, he wrote in verse:

Many strange dark paths
led me to this place and time.
Sad I am I came.
Oh, buddy, y'know it's hard to do a 'no fear' act
when you're a little, l-i-t-t-l-e bit scared.
I'm so far gone
I ain't never comin' back.
It's getting hard to keep the head right.
Hey, does it snow?
Ha, ha, oh, man . . . I'm fucked up here.

Then he gave Robbie's phone number in Florida to Horton, encouraging him to call her when "it" was "all over."

"He was really breaking down," Horton said later. "At

that time, a lot of what he was saying and writing wasn't making much sense. But, boy, did it all add up a week later."

There was a two-page addendum attached to the letter: a drawing and more verse-like musings. The drawing was of a man breaking through a piece of glass, flying through the air while holding on to what looked like a surfboard. Evans drew shards of broken glass and clouds all around the man: *Turning and bending and all I can hear is the wind—even. That is trying to push me off and my hold keeps crumbling away. If I look up, I get dizzy and lose my balance, so I can't look up or I'll fall. I can't shut my eyes because I have to watch which way it's going to turn. And I'm getting tired.*

CHAPTER 88

On August 9, a Sunday, Evans wrote to Jo Rehm: *My mind is screaming.*

So many negative thoughts. So many strange ideas.

Not much time left.

Jo was a different person from the naive teenager Evans had known back on First Street in Troy when they were kids. After marrying at twenty, she had been through a divorce. She had worked hard all her life. She lived in Troy once again, but on the opposite side of town: a little house up on a hill, nearly overlooking the Troy-Menands Bridge that spanned the magnificent Hudson River leading into town. She had a dog, a garden, and a caring new husband, Ed, who adored her.

Evans was, perhaps, still that little boy she'd tried so desperately to shelter from abusive parents.

Over the next few days, Jo received several letters. In each one, Evans tried to convince her to stop blaming herself for the way things had turned out. Jo was still whipping herself with guilt.

Pick a date, he wrote, and *[you and Doris Sheehan get together and] get rid of things about me: pix, etc, clothes. . . . Start fresh.*

Oooo man my head is going back and forth so fast. . . . Listen, you shit, that guilt nonsense you're hammering yourself with has got to stop here and now.

A few days prior to receiving the letters, Jo had gone to see him. Robbie was there. It turned into a shouting match, Jo explained, between Evans and Robbie. If there wasn't a glass partition in between them, Jo believed Evans would have strangled his half sister.

"You couldn't believe how he was when I would go down there to see him," Jo recalled. "I would come home crying. Because he was in such . . . mental . . . He was just so emotional. Crying and crying. Screaming. He wanted to kill Robbie that day. And would have if he wasn't restrained."

Robbie was supposed to bring Devan, Evans's nephew. But she didn't. Evans went "nuts," yelling and screaming, carrying on about the way she had brought Devan up. He was upset, Jo recalled, because Robbie had given Devan to their mother, Flora Mae, at one time. Evans was scared Flora Mae had sexually abused Devan, Jo heard him yell, because, he said, she had done it to him. Robbie had also, Evans lashed out, went to a local bar the previous night, got drunk and talked about him. A few guards from the jail happened to be present and told Evans about it the next morning.

But there were also lighter moments, Jo explained. When she was with him alone one day, he held up his shackles, smiled and said, "Hey, you want to see me get out of these?"

"What?"

"Close your eyes," Evans said, looking around to see if any of the guards were watching.

A moment later, as if he were Houdini, Evans was out of his shackles, waving his hands in the air. "See . . ."

In what seemed like only seconds later, without Jo even noticing, he was back in the cuffs.

The way Evans saw it during that second week of August, he wrote that Jo *had it all backwards. . . . [Robbie,] the pig bitch, should have come crying to me, begging forgiveness for being rotten all her life to me. . . .*

He ended the letter with a poem, telling Jo not to come see him anymore.

It was all over. There was no reason to come back.

Later that night, however, he changed his mind and got word to Jo to come in on Monday, August 10, and Tuesday, August 11. There were some "last-minute" issues he needed resolved.

On Monday, when Jo showed up, he informed her that she would have power of attorney in all his affairs.

"Why, Gary? What's going on?"

All the paperwork was done, Evans explained, and in the mail. He said he'd had everything notarized. "I am going to do something on Friday . . . ," he added in a stoic tone, as serious as he had ever been, Jo recalled.

"What, Gary?" she asked.

For the next few minutes, Evans laid out his entire plan, explaining every detail: when, where, how.

"I want you to stay home on Friday, Jo," he added near the end of the conversation. "Don't leave your house."

By Wednesday, August 12, Evans was formally charged with eight counts of murder. The DA's office promised it would decide within 120 days if he would be tried as a capital offender and face the possibility of death by lethal injection.

On Thursday, August 13, in Little Falls, New York, Evans was charged with Gregory Jouben's murder. Inside of one week, the DA's office promised that he would be charged with the murder of Douglas Berry in Watertown.

In a photograph taken by the *Troy Record*, Evans was shown walking down the Little Falls Courthouse stairs, smirking. While in court, facing the judge, he "smiled" and, some later said, acted like it was just another routine day in the life of Gary Evans. He had taken on an air of serenity, it seemed.

Security had been more visible during both court appearances. With the Little Falls City Hall completely evacuated, the street near the courthouse had been cordoned off. There was a shotgun-toting trooper walking out in front of the building and several troopers with police dogs roaming around the area. In both instances, Evans wore leg chains and wrist shackles, both of which were connected to a waist chain. Apparently, the local authorities weren't taking any chances; Horton's constant beating of his "he will crawl through a straw" drum had worked.

The authorities were, obviously, listening.

Horton decided to visit Evans at Rensselaer County Jail after his court date on August 13. He sensed time was short, but insisted later that Evans had "never told [him] what he was going to do beyond 'an escape attempt,'" which Horton had reported to all of the appropriate authorities. Because of all the press coverage and the constant bombardment of requests for interviews, and Evans calling his home several times a day, Horton had sent Mary Pat and the kids to Connecticut to get away from it all. Friends and coworkers were badgering Mary Pat for the "inside story," and she found herself having to retell various news accounts of Jim's involvement.

When Horton arrived at the jail, he was given a private room to meet with Evans. The door to the room had a window, and Horton made sure he and Evans were always in full view of the guards. "Not for my protection," Horton recalled, "but so there would be no question as to any collusion between us."

There they were once again in a jail, whispering to each other, just like that first meeting in Cohoes.

"There were a couple of uniform guards right outside the door trying to hear what we were saying so they could go run to the newspapers, I suspect. They were also curious to see this infamous guy and me—the only person, besides Jo Rehm and Lisa Morris, he would really talk to."

Evans was depressed. He began to cry. He said he was

scared. With that, Horton saw a vulnerability. *Maybe he wants to talk?*

"Tell me about those other murders you mentioned," Horton threw out, hoping to get Evans to admit to what he believed were four more murders.

The recent *Times Union* article, at least in Evans's mind, had branded him a "monster." Because of that, he said, "No more. I'm finished giving up bodies."

"He was saying things about our friendship and how much he admired me," Horton said later. "He would laugh and cry in the same breath. It was like he had been sentenced to death already and was saying his good-byes to me."

Evans talked about the first time he and Horton had met, mentioning again his belief that it had been fate that had brought them together.

"I tried being a good listener. Believe it or not, it was sad to me. When I left, we hugged. I told the guards we were done. When Gary walked away, he kept looking back at me, saying things. 'Take care of [Doris]. Be careful. Thanks for trying.'"

"Gary," Horton said at one point, "whatever it is you are going to do, please, please, do not hurt anyone."

"Well, Guy, this is it. But don't worry. I won't hurt anyone."

Horton believed Evans was going to hang himself or slit his wrists. He had warned everyone that he was suicidal and an "extreme" escape risk. Beyond that, he didn't know what else to do.

Finally, before the steel doors closed behind him, Evans looked back at Horton one last time and mouthed, *I love you.*

Outside the jail, Horton sat in his car and began "feeling very strange, not knowing exactly how he should feel." While Evans, he learned later, was in his cell whimpering.

"I knew at that moment our relationship had ended and I was relieved by that," Horton said later. "I also knew that there would never be a trial for Gary. . . . He was going to see to it that it never came to that. That being said, I also had empathy for him. Even though he was a cold-blooded multiple murderer, we spent a significant amount of time together. By that I mean, most of our time was high intensity and high pressure. Our conversations and time together was never a chitchat, walk-in-the-park type of thing. We were feeling each other out constantly. Spending time with someone, no matter what they are, can cause you to do strange things. In this case, Gary and I were brought together not as a normal friendship would begin, but because we were 'natural enemies.' I was, basically, even from 1985, there to take away all of his freedoms. But here we were . . . friends."

Later that same night, Evans sat in his cell and wrote two letters: one to Horton and another addressed to nobody in particular—although it would be perfectly clear within the next twenty-four hours for whom that second letter was meant.

Horton left the jail and drove to Doris Sheehan's trailer in upstate New York. Evans had asked him to give Doris some letters he had written to her over the past few weeks.

While Horton was at Doris's, talking to her over a beer, the phone rang.

"Gary was crying and somewhat incoherent," Horton remembered. "He basically repeated everything he had said to me earlier at the jail. I knew I would never see or hear from him again. When he told me about what he was going to do during the plane ride to Florida if we had taken him along, he said he would have a smile on his face the whole way down . . . screaming at the world with his middle fingers both up, indicating what he thought of everyone: 'Fuck you.'"

CHAPTER 89

The fog coming off the Hudson River on some mornings is so dense one might feel compelled to reach out and touch it. August 14, 1998, was a Friday. The day had dawned crisp and cool in the Capital District. Weathermen predicted temperatures would climb into the high seventies to low eighties by midday, but the morning air still held a churlish hint that fall was right around the corner.

Jim Horton awoke early that morning with one thought on his mind: an appointment he had scheduled with DA Kenneth Bruno's assistant, Nancy Lynn Ferrini, at 10:00 A.M., to discuss the case against Gary Evans. Horton would be a major part of the case, of course. He had spent weeks preparing a large three-ring binder regarding the murder of Tim Rysedorph. Today was the day to hand it off to the DA's office and begin letting go.

Evans had a parole hearing scheduled for midmorning in Albany. Because Albany County Jail, in Colonie, had been under construction and Evans had been caught glaring at certain sections of the jail, perhaps looking for a way out, he had been transferred on June 29 to Rensselaer County Jail in downtown Troy, merely blocks from his old home on First Street. Rensselaer County had been remodeled and updated within the past few years. Everyone agreed it was a far more secure facility for a prisoner who was hell-bent on attempting an escape.

Jo Rehm got up early on August 14. Evans had told her just days before: "Don't leave your house." But Jo had an errand to run. She had no choice but to go out.

Getting dressed, Ed, her husband, asked her why she was up so early.

"I have to go to the bank . . . make my car payment."

"Yeah . . . so?"

"Today is Gary's last day on earth," Jo blurted out, choking up. Then she looked down at the floor and tried to figure out why she had said it.

Not taking her seriously, Ed laughed. "Drive safely."

By 9:30 A.M., Jo had finished her errands and was back at home, where she would spend the remainder of the day.

Two armed U.S. Marshals escorted Evans from the Rensselaer County Jail prisoner staging area to a light brown Chevrolet Astro minivan waiting for him. The van, which the United States Marshal Service (USMS) routinely used as a prisoner transport vehicle, was no different from the millions Chevrolet had sold to families throughout the world.

Dressed in a fluorescent orange jumpsuit, Evans was handcuffed at his wrists and shackled at the ankles, but the USMS didn't see the need for an additional waist chain around his hips that would have connected his handcuffs to his shackles. Even more surprising, no one had scanned Evans with a metal detector (or "wand," as it is called) to see if he was hiding contraband.

A second vehicle, carrying two additional armed marshals, followed behind the van as it left Rensselaer County en route to Albany.

Inside the van, a "security cage" made of Plexiglas directly behind the front seat separated Evans, who was alone in the backseat, from the marshals. Moreover, the security cage did not cover the five 3-by-2-feet glass windows, which were locked down with simple plastic clips, on both sides of the vehicle and in back of Evans. Thus, the only material separating Evans from the outside world was a piece of half-inch-thick glass, no different from the glass Chevrolet put in all of its vans.

According to the USMS, for the past 215 years it has been "protectors and defenders of our freedoms." Primarily, marshals serve as watchdogs, transporting federal prisoners, protecting federal witnesses and making sure federal jurors and judges are sheltered from the obvious dangers they might face. Marshals work for the U.S. government; there is no association between the USMS and state police.

"Don't hurt anyone. . . . And don't do it while in state police custody."

As of now, Evans was a federal prisoner. The state police had nothing to do with him.

He was calm as the van began its trek into the U.S. District Court in Albany. It was his third court appearance in as many days.

The previous day, Thursday, August 13, Randolph Treece, Evans's court-appointed capital defender, met with him to discuss what was going to happen over the course of the next few weeks. Treece, an astute, tall, good-looking black man with a deep voice, instilled in Evans that he was prepared to do everything in his power to fight the death penalty.

Treece later said that at some point during the conversation, Evans said, "Thanks. You guys have been really wonderful. But this is all over."

At the time, Treece thought Evans meant "something was going to take place in the jail . . . that he wasn't going through with the trial. . . ." So the phrase—"this is all over"—seemed to be nothing more than an inane set of frustrating words any prisoner in Evans's position might dredge up.

At about 10:16 A.M., Evans was signed into the U.S. Marshal's Office at the U.S. District Court in Albany. By 10:30, U.S. District Court judge Thomas McAvoy had sentenced Evans to two years in federal prison for violating the terms of his parole. Evans was particularly passive while in court, behaving "strangely," the judge commented later.

Nonresponsive. Anxious. Unfocused.

Evans just wasn't himself.

Michael Desautels, Evans's public defender, had a meeting to attend down the road with Treece and his boss at 11:00 A.M. While Desautels was packing up his briefcase, Evans handed him a package of "legal papers."

"There's a letter in there for Treece," Evans said. "Make sure he gets it."

By 10:38 A.M., Evans was loaded back into the U.S. Marshals' van for his trip back to Rensselaer County Jail in Troy. It was about a ten-minute ride: a straight shot up Interstate 787, a quick jaunt over the Troy-Menands Bridge into downtown Troy, and onto River Street.

Again, the same two armed marshals sat in the front seat of the minivan while Evans sat in back alone, and an escort of two armed marshals followed closely behind.

For the second time that day, Evans wasn't "wanded" to see if he was carrying any type of contraband. Essentially, he had been in and out of court for the past three days without any problems. What could possibly go wrong now?

As Evans headed back to jail, Mike Desautels ran up the road to make his meeting on time. On his way up the stairs inside the building, Desautels ran into Treece as he was rushing to the same meeting.

"Listen, Randy," Desautels said, "Gary gave me a ton of papers. He wants you to have them. He said there's a letter in there for you. I left them in the car or in my office, but . . ."

"No problem, Mike," Treece said. "It doesn't seem that important. Let's get together after the meeting."

By 10:45 A.M., Jo Rehm was on the phone talking to her daughter, discussing mundane, domestic issues that often plague life. Midway through the conversation, after her daughter asked, Jo said she was planning on spending the rest of the day at home, doing nothing.

"I'm just going to mope around and stay in."

"Is there anything wrong, Ma?"

"No. Everything's okay."

CHAPTER 90

Kevin Kot was a thirty-seven-year-old electrical contractor who lived a rather simple, ordinary suburban life. Married with two kids, Kot loved his job. On Fridays, it was Kot who delivered payroll to the company's dozens of employees at various job sites throughout the Capital District. Generally speaking, Fridays were Kot's favorite day of the week.

By 11:00 A.M., on August 14, Kot was traveling east over the Troy-Menands Bridge—which connects the village of Menands to Troy—on his way to the Emma Willard School, where his company had been working on a job for the past few weeks. The bridge spans some sixty-two feet above the Hudson River waterline. Traffic travels fast over the four-lane bridge, normally fifty-five to sixty miles per hour.

Driving in the far right lane—two lanes head east, two west—Kot saw a "very nondescript Astro van" coming up from behind him on the left side, in the left lane. He took notice of the van only because he had one just like it sitting in his driveway at home.

As the van crept up alongside his Pontiac Firebird, a fine mist of what Kot initially thought were "sand pebbles" began bouncing off his front windshield. Originally, it sounded to Kot as if he had been in back of a state plow truck dropping sand and salt on the roads during winter. But as the van passed, Kot's vision was quickly shrouded as he realized that what at first he thought to be sand pebbles was actually shards of glass pelting his windshield.

"I was thinking," Kot said later, "it was stuff falling from the top of the bridge." The bridge was old. It needed work.

Yet, as quickly as Kot thought that the bridge was falling apart, he looked to his left and saw the Astro van lock up its brakes and begin to skid sideways into his lane. At that point, he saw what appeared to be an "orange jumpsuit coming out of the side window of the van."

What the hell?

It was Evans. He had kicked out the side window of the van and was climbing out from it.

Kot then slammed on his brakes and began to skid.

In back of the van was the second USMS vehicle, a Ford Expedition; it, too, locked up its brakes and went into a tailspin.

They were about three-quarters of the way over the bridge.

As Evans kicked out the passenger-side window and jumped out, he got hung up for a moment on the broken glass and dangled there, his feet hitting the ground as the van continued skidding to a stop.

Unnerved by what he was witnessing, Kot watched as Evans, with the finesse of a stuntman, then took a headfirst dive onto the pavement after shimmying himself free from the window and rolled on the tar with the momentum of the van.

"For a noticeable amount of time," Kot said, "he was struggling to get loose. He hit the pavement and just started tumbling."

With the tires squealing and Kot's Pontiac beginning to come to a stop, he almost hit Evans as he bounced off the tar, rolled a few times and popped up off the ground and onto his feet as if the scene had been scripted for him.

As Evans got up off the ground, he hopped over the guardrail and made it onto the sidewalk that ran along the bridge on both sides. Once there, he made a mad dash, Kot insisted, for the *center* of the bridge.

After racing out of the vehicle, the two marshals in the Expedition in back of Kot's Pontiac headed Evans off from one side of the bridge, while the two marshals in the van, after jumping out and running, trailed him from behind.

When Evans saw that he was cornered and had nowhere left to run, he glanced quickly back at the marshals coming up from behind, then turned and looked at the marshals in front of him.

There's no way out.

Faced with being bottled in on both sides and traffic completely stopped, Evans looked up toward the sky, bowed his head and then tucked his body underneath the second guardrail—a solid piece of metal running along the outer side of the sidewalk.

With sixty-two feet between him and the water below, Evans jumped.

CHAPTER 91

Kevin Kot, after watching Evans run by his car and head for the middle of the bridge, immediately dialed 911 from his cell phone. The four marshals, realizing what Evans had done, stood by the side of Kot's car staring over the side of the bridge.

Holy shit.

"I'm on the Troy-Menands Bridge . . . ," Kot said hurriedly, "lawmen have an escaped prisoner who went over the side of the bridge."

"You're where?" the startled dispatcher asked. "Can you repeat that?"

Looking at the marshals, Kot couldn't understand why they were so calm. There was a boat heading upriver toward the exact spot where Evans had jumped. The marshals weren't dashing for the lower part of the bridge or drawing their weapons.

"I thought it was some master plan," Kot said later. "Your mind does crazy things. I saw the boat, [Evans] had jumped, and I was thinking . . . 'They're just going to let him get away?' "

* * *

At 11:07 A.M., Jo Rehm was still on the phone with her daughter. During the conversation, Jo heard a commotion going on outside her home and told her daughter to hang on for a moment. "I'll be right back."

Jo walked out her front door, which basically overlooked the Troy-Menands Bridge, and heard what sounded to her like "thousands" of sirens blaring and wailing and heading for the bridge.

"I'll call you back later," she told her daughter in a whisper. "I have to go."

A minute later, as Jo stood near her garden, a helicopter came sweeping over her house so close, she remembered later, she felt as if she could have reached up and grabbed hold of it.

Standing, looking toward the bridge, she placed her hands over her mouth and started crying.

Chaos reigned supreme back at the bridge as cops, fire trucks, U.S. Marshals, local and state police, countless other law enforcement, rescue personnel and media rushed to the scene: Gary Evans had escaped. He's on the loose.

Down below the bridge, near the Troy side of the banks of the Hudson, Evans lay in about twelve inches of water, approximately ten feet from shore.

While Horton was meeting with Nancy Lynn Ferrini, discussing the Tim Rysedorph murder, his pager went off. *911,* it said on the screen—which meant big trouble.

"Excuse me one minute, Nancy," Horton said. At that moment, the phones in the DA's office began screaming. People started shuffling about, huddling in corners, talking, scrambling around as if the governor had called an air raid.

Horton found an empty room and called Troop G. Within moments, he had administrative Bureau senior investigator John Caulfield on the phone.

"What's up?"

"As far as I know," John said, "Gary is . . ."

I fucking knew it! Horton thought.

"What the hell happened?"

"Well, apparently, he escaped and jumped off the Troy-Menands Bridge."

Horton dropped the phone and ran toward the door. Nancy Lynn asked if she could go with him.

"Yeah, but let's go right now!"

Gary Evans, his face bloodied from an incredible sixty-two-foot fall, lay faceup and still as any one of the thousands of stones in the water around him.

He was dead.

Oddly, he had two sets of handcuffs attached to his hands: one connecting both hands around his back; and a second pair connected to one wrist, the other end dangling. His legs were still shackled together.

The first person on the scene was one of the marshals. He had walked over, dragged Evans out of the water and flipped him over. Just then, a local Troy officer appeared from the wooded area near the bank of the river.

"Give me your handcuffs," the marshal yelled up to the cop.

The cop then tossed his set of cuffs down to the marshal and ran back up to an area directly underneath the bridge to direct the onslaught of vehicles arriving on the scene.

After cuffing Evans, the marshal stood and looked at him. There was blood streaking down the side of his mouth and nose. Several of his teeth had been knocked out from the fall. His eyes were open. There was a large gash on the right side of his head that had been made by a piece of rebar sticking out of the water where he had landed. Quite bizarrely, Evans's right hand was frozen in a position of "fuck you"; his middle finger sticking straight up with his other fingers curled down. In a way, he had done exactly what he had told Horton he would do: go down saying "fuck you" to the world.

* * *

By the time Horton arrived on the scene, there must have been, he later said, "fifty to sixty law enforcement vehicles parked near the immediate area."

"There were Troy, Albany County, Colonie, state police, along with cops I had never seen before, when I got there. It was a circus-type atmosphere. Even sergeants with desk jobs who hadn't been on the road in years were wandering around. Everyone wanted to touch Gary Evans. I saw troopers assigned to the Police Academy roaming around and I thought, 'What the hell is this?'"

The area where Evans had landed was near an old oil-refining plant. There were rusted and empty oil tanks and train tracks separating the river from the road. A chain-link fence kept the media far enough back so they couldn't see anything, or take any photos. A photo of a dead Gary Evans would be priceless.

As Horton walked around the scene, sizing up Evans, he yelled out, "What's this? Why does he have *two* sets of handcuffs on him?"

"I know Gary Evans," one of the local Troy cops said, "I was worried he would escape."

"He fell sixty feet and landed on a piece of rebar. . . . You think he was going anywhere?"

Barney fucking Fife, Horton thought, walking away. *Jesus Christ.*

Horton then reached down and checked the serial numbers on both sets of handcuffs. The cuffs that were attached to both of Evans's wrists, holding his arms behind his back, were from the Troy Police Department; the cuffs dangling from his right wrist, attached to only one arm, were from the USMS.

What the hell? Horton said to himself. *How did he get out of his cuffs?*

"Hey, Horton, what's going on?" somebody yelled from behind the fence as Horton stood up. "Tell us what's happening. . . . Come talk to us."

Media were everywhere, scurrying around on the opposite side of the fence. Word had spread in record time that the infamous Gary Evans had made an escape attempt and failed. News organizations, of course, wanted that exclusive story from the one man who knew Evans best.

CHAPTER 92

Not long after Evans had been pronounced dead at the scene by Dr. Barbara Wolf, a renowned forensic pathologist who freelanced for the Albany County Coroner's Office, Horton made a decision to leave the scene.

"Dozens of cops were trying to be a part of it," he said later, "who absolutely had no legitimate purpose for being there. The press were really hounding me. Civilians were rubbernecking and gawking. I couldn't take it anymore. My beeper was going off nonstop."

Horton's mother had been home watching television when she heard the news and immediately paged him to see how he was holding up.

"Hello, Ma."

She said she only wanted to know one thing: "How do you feel about what's happened?"

"Not sure," Horton said. "I don't feel anything, actually."

"Ambivalent," she said with an influence only a mother could evoke. "You feel ambivalent. That's good. That's how you *should* feel."

After speaking to his mother, Horton turned off his pager, found Jack Murray and Bud York, and said, "Get me outta here."

When it came down to it, there was no reason for Horton to stay at the scene. What was done, was done. From there, it was paperwork, questions and, hopefully, answers.

The autopsy was another matter. Horton insisted he be present for it. It would be a while, Barbara Wolf said, but she would see that it was done that night.

By nature, an autopsy is designed to clear up any unanswered questions. But Horton and Barbara Wolf were about to learn that Evans's autopsy would only unearth new questions about Gary Evans and how he had managed to escape under the radar of four armed U.S. Marshals.

From the death scene at the bridge, Horton, York and Murray drove into downtown Troy and stopped at a local pub to get something to eat and, deservedly, a stiff drink.

Nobody in the bar knew who they were, but the crowd was glued to the television, hanging on every detail about the Evans escape that was slowly trickling out. Incredibly, not three hours after Evans had been pronounced dead, the bar was pushing a drink it called "Gary on the Rocks." Vodka, cranberry juice and ice. The dark red cranberry juice, Horton learned by reading the chalkboard announcing the new special as you walked into the bar, represented the blood of Troy's most famous serial killer.

When he read it, Horton's appetite diminished. Additionally, he felt the need to be doing other things back at work, including talking to his bosses and preparing to attend Evans's autopsy. A neighborhood bar seemed like the last place in the world he should be.

CHAPTER 93

Once word of what Evans had done made its way to Randolph Treece, he realized he was probably in possession of a suicide letter Evans had written. Sitting in his office, watching the story unfold on television, Treece's mind shifted away from the television as he recollected what Michael Desautels had said to him earlier as they made their way up the stairs: *"[Gary] said there's a letter in there for you."*

Treece immediately called Desautels. "Mike, you said Gary's got papers for me?"

"Yeah, and one of them is a letter addressed to you."

"Get those things over to me. . . . No, I'll send my investigator over there right now."

Rummaging through the stack of papers about an hour later, Treece picked up the letter and opened it.

I'd like it known why I can't allow myself to be imprisoned, the two-page letter began. *Because of all the things taken from me. . . .*

If there was any doubt Evans had designed his escape for any other purpose besides suicide—which was certainly the feeling by some early on—Evans's own words made it clear that his sole intention was to kill himself.

He went on to write that he couldn't live in a world knowing he would never get to experience certain "things" again. Most important, he wrote, was *all the magic moments with the girl I love [Doris Sheehan]. . . .*

Then he talked about living "in a cage forever."

In the middle of the clearly printed letter, he wrote about the things in life that had made him the happiest: Jet Skiing in Florida, viewing the stars in Alaska, swimming with sharks, touching a sleeping pelican, watching a moose, saving an octopus and feeling the "deepest love imaginable" for a person. The future, he wrote, would be nothing but *torment, torture and misery forever. And to allow my life to be taken from me by the enemy is not something I will do. Slow death or fast, makes no difference. They can't have it.*

Beginning on the top of the second page, Evans had circled an entire section and explained to Treece in a side note that he wanted it released to the media.

Paper and TV, he wrote. *TV's better, the papers lie a lot.*

My lessons here are learned = on to a better place now. My friends are happy, and I'm already there. With Canis Minor and a beautiful blue moon. With a smile stars surround me and peace and love are mine. They can't be taken or touched.

Lastly, he wrote, *I win.*

He made a note on the bottom of the page: *Mail it to Jo Rehm . . . and tell her to give it to my girl I love.* Underneath that: *And my words to her [Doris] are: Be happy for me, don't be sad. For you, us, I'm OK now.* He drew a smiley face. Then, *No drinking. I love you always. Live long, you'll be an awesome mom. Hey Boogie! See ya next place.*

Words he had spoken to Lisa Morris and Jim Horton merely days earlier were scattered, if only by impression, all over the letter: "If I die in here, they win. If I die out there, I win."

CHAPTER 94

Kenneth Bruno released a statement only hours after Evans had made his fatal leap. After explaining what had happened in figurative detail, Bruno said that "although the criminal prosecution against Gary Evans is over, my office will continue to make ourselves available to" the families of his victims. He talked about "mixed emotions" during what was going to be a time of uncertainty. Finally, "No one celebrates the death of any individual, even if death would have been the appropriate consequence for his actions. That's a decision that I won't have to make in this case."

What was, essentially, mere politically correct sentiment didn't bode well with public opinion, however. One man told reporters that Evans had "saved the taxpayers a lot of money." Another said, "I'm glad he's dead." Yet another commented, "I'm not an advocate of anyone dying, but you have to make an exception in this case."

One of Michael Falco's brothers told the *Times Union*, "I think there was a higher court looking to judge this one. His death, the way it all happened, it's called 'poetic justice.'"

* * *

Regardless of how people felt, Evans was dead. He wasn't going to hurt anyone again. For Horton and his colleagues, though, they needed answers to several questions—one of which being, how in the hell did a prisoner who was considered an escape risk, to begin with, get out of his handcuffs and hurl himself over a bridge in broad daylight in the presence of four armed marshals?

None of it made sense.

Horton, Dr. Barbara Wolf and several Bureau investigators met at Dr. Wolf's Albany office later that night to go through Evans's body with a magnifying glass. Hopefully, they would find some answers. Dr. Wolf had done thousands of autopsies in a career that had spanned decades. She was appointed to collect forensic evidence after the ill-fated TWA Flight 800 crash off Long Island Sound. Well-respected, Wolf was known throughout the forensic community as someone who took her work seriously. If Evans's body held secrets, Dr. Wolf would find them.

Almost immediately, Evans's corpse yielded clues as to how far he was prepared to go in order to carry out his plan. After undressing him, Dr. Wolf made note of all his tattoos as Horton and the others looked on. Down near Evans's Achilles' heel, they found a paper clip and a blade from a razor taped to his leg underneath his sock. A quick search by anyone at the jail or courthouse would have found it easily.

Horton picked it up and looked at it. "What the hell? How did he get this? How come nobody found it?"

There were some who later insisted that it had to have been a guard at Rensselaer County Jail, but it would never be proven. While others swore it had been Horton, Lisa Morris or Jo Rehm.

The next order of business was to do a full-body X ray.

"That's when things really got bizarre," Horton said later.

Bizarre wouldn't even begin to describe what they found next.

Taking the X ray took some time. But as the X rays came

back from the lab and Dr. Wolf and Horton started going through them, they couldn't believe their eyes.

Buried inside Evans's left nostril, up inside his sinus, was a handcuff key. About 1½ inches long, the loop end of the key was facing up, while the serrated end pointed down.

Dr. Wolf, with a pair of tweezers, reached up, extracted the key and held it under the light.

Obviously puzzled, Horton and Dr. Wolf looked at each other.

"It was like everyone in the room, at that moment, said, 'Why, that son of a bitch!'" Horton said later.

Things began to make sense to Horton. The two sets of handcuffs, one of which was unattached from one of Evans's wrist and the long pinkie fingernail.

He hid that key and retrieved it while they were making their way across the bridge.

Looking closer at the X ray, Dr. Wolf discovered something else. Underneath Evans's palate, deep in his sinus, what appeared to be a piece of metal with some sort of string attached to it emerged. To get it, however, Dr. Wolf would have to do some internal probing.

With a scalpel in hand, Dr. Wolf cut an incision along the top of Evans's forehead and along both sides of his face, around the inside of his ears, leaving the area below his chin intact. She carefully peeled back his face and rolled it down off his skull as if it were a children's rubber Halloween mask.

Immediately, when the inner cavity of Evans's sinuses was exposed, everyone took a step back because of the rancid stench.

"It was the most profound and grotesque aroma I have ever smelled," Horton said, "and I have been around a lot."

The smell was caused by the decaying and rusting metal buried underneath Evans's palate. Dr. Wolf again took a pair of tweezers, sifted through the bloody tissue and extracted it.

Sure enough, it was a small blade from a razor, about the

size of a dime. Most interesting, though, was what Evans had done to the blade. He had drilled a tiny hole in one end and, after taking about fifteen of his hairs and braiding them into a piece of man-made rope, tied it to the blade. Apparently, he had shoved it so far up into his sinus that it forever became part of his body after tissue had entombed it.

Up underneath the left side of his jaw, Dr. Wolf extracted another small blade that Evans had worked in between his jaw and gum, as if it were a piece of chewing tobacco.

From there, Dr. Wolf cut the cap of Evans's skull off and removed his brain. There were contusions and bruises on the right side, which had turned the white tissue red; the left side was still white, uninjured.

"That's what killed him," someone said. "That piece of rebar that hit his head."

Over the next few hours, Dr. Wolf examined Evans's entire body, taking it apart, piece by piece, and putting it back together again.

Nothing else abnormal was uncovered. In the end, Dr. Wolf decided the cause of death was "blunt-force injuries of head and torso with basilar skull fracture," the result of a "jump from [a] bridge."

CHAPTER 95

The weekend of August 15 and 16 produced a torrent of newspaper and television reports of the Gary Evans saga. Horton and Jo Rehm refused to speak to anyone. They just wanted to let it all go, decide what to do with Evans's body and try to move on.

Well-wishers and old "girlfriends" of Evans's seemingly came from everywhere to talk about their brush with him. Lisa Morris—confused, upset, angry—spoke to the press, and she used the interviews as a way to sort through her feelings. She was shell-shocked by the totality of what had taken place. Like Jo Rehm, she may have been told by Evans what was going to occur, but it didn't mean she believed it, or had prepared a way to deal with it after it happened.

By Saturday, August 15, Horton had received a letter in the mail from Evans. Quite matter-of-fact, the letter was devoid of any conscience or guilt. In large part, it was a detailed list of instructions for Horton to give to Doris Sheehan. Most compelling was what Evans, who referred to himself in the third person throughout much of the letter, wanted Horton to relay to Doris about his desire to commit suicide: *It's what he wanted, instead of suffering and dying every day. You know you wouldn't want him to live in misery,* you *[Doris] know what [hell is] like.*

For Evans, ending his life was the only way to quash the obvious suffering he felt in his soul. It was, like his life, all about him—egotism and selfishness to the umpteenth power. Evans was wielding his self-absorbed sword once more in death, as he had in life so many times before.

He wanted Doris to know, he wrote, that he was *counting on her to have a great life.*

As he had written to the world, Evans couldn't resist the temptation to tell Horton the same thing: *I win.*

The letter, one could argue, was Evans's final move in a game of psychological chess he and Horton had played for almost thirteen years.

Doris Sheehan had called Jo Rehm late in the day on Friday after Evans had committed suicide to "talk," Jo later said. The conversation didn't yield any breakthroughs in the sense of new information, but instead allowed the two women Evans loved the most to begin what would be a long process of mourning.

"Every time I hear a helicopter, sirens or a train," Jo said later, "I think of that day."

Evans told Jo just days before his death that he wanted to be cremated. "You *don't* have to pay for any of it, either," he added. "The state will pay for it."

At the time, Jo thought it surreal to be talking about cremation, but she listened.

"I want you to give my ashes to Jim Horton," Evans added. "You and [Doris] take some, too."

On Saturday, August 15, Jo went down to a local funeral parlor and explained the situation. "I don't want anything in the newspapers," she said. "I don't want to be hounded."

"Don't worry, ma'am, we'll take care of everything."

Horton, Doris Sheehan, and Jo and Ed Rehm went down to the funeral parlor on Sunday to sit with Evans before his body was sent off to the crematorium. It wasn't a formal wake or funeral service, but more of a way to say good-bye one last time.

Doris and Jo ended up having "words," Jo recalled. Doris wanted to "take photographs of Evans lying in his casket," but Jo refused to allow it. Then Doris started asking about Evans's possessions: jewelry, a mountain bike, gold, rings.

She wanted it all.

"It was odd, actually," Horton said. "She was worried about material things while Jo and I were there to say good-bye. Her boyfriend was waiting for her in the car outside the funeral home. He had no business being inside, and he knew that. I was a bit wary about being there to begin with. Her odd behavior only made it all that more strange for me."

Back at home the following week, Horton sat down on his couch and poured himself a glass of scotch and began thinking about the past few weeks. How surreal it had all been. How much of a blur it seemed like now—almost as if it were some sort of dream.

Sitting, sipping from his scotch, going through some of the paperwork connected to the case, Horton came across Evans's death certificate. For a moment, he just stared at it, not reading it. Seeing it again brought back memories of the autopsy.

"During the autopsy, I really felt a sense of relief," Horton recalled. "It was truly over. Again, I had some ambivalence, but it was only because, with all the work I had done, I realized I would never get the opportunity to prosecute Gary—which was my main focus once I found out he was a serial murderer."

After placing the death certificate down, Horton picked up a book of autopsy photographs and began flipping through the pages.

Not only were Evans's eyes open during the autopsy, but—Horton noticed—he had a smirk on his face throughout the entire procedure, undoubtedly frozen in that position by the mere nature and process of death as the body goes through it.

"It almost looked like," Horton said, "he was alive and was going to say something. Not unlike all the other times when he didn't want to tell me something, but he couldn't resist. I actually think he wanted to brag to me over the years about killing Michael Falco and Damien Cuomo, but couldn't for obvious reasons."

That smirk, Horton concluded, was, at least at the core of all the sensationalism attached to the life of Gary Evans, perhaps Evans, one last time, saying, "I win."

As if the past thirteen years had been some sort of elaborate game of psychological chess, Horton raised his scotch in a mock salute to his twisted friend and opponent. . . .

Checkmate!

EPILOGUE

Avid chess players say that the most "obscure and least-used move" in the game is the *En passant*, which I used as a title for the third and final section of this book. Indeed, in keeping with the metaphorical nature of *En passant*, Gary Evans certainly used an obscure, if not bizarre, final move to avoid not only facing Jim Horton again, but one of his worst fears: spending his life behind bars. For me, writing about Gary Evans has been one of the most interesting and exciting experiences I've had as a writer. I could not have written a novel that—even remotely—compares to the life of Gary Evans.

Since September 9, 1999, Jim Horton has been deputy chief investigator for the New York State Attorney General's Office, Department of Law. Leaving the state police wasn't something Horton *wanted* to do; he lived for the thrill of the chase and loves the idea, I'm convinced, of hands-on work out in the field. Today he is confined to an office, supervising investigations of a different kind, an environment that contains his obvious talents as an investigator. I believe the public is suffering a great loss because of that.

"I didn't even have a résumé when I got the call asking if I was interested in taking the job at the AG's office," Horton recalled later. "Hardest decision I ever had to make—leaving the troopers. It was a job that I loved and still do."

As one might guess, Gary Evans had a major impact on Horton's life. There's not a week that goes by where Horton doesn't field some sort of question about Evans. Today he looks at it all as an anomaly; he couldn't control Evans, he says, "only react to his behavior."

When I discovered that Evans was perhaps involved in a second life that may have included transsexuals, I posed a question we shall leave to the imagination to Horton, who was quite shocked—to say the least—by my findings.

"He fooled me all those years," Horton said, shaking his head. "I should have known!" Horton seemed disappointed in himself that he had allowed Evans—in death—to one-up him one last time. "I believe I made the most out of every bad situation in every instance where it pertained to Gary. It was *always* a bad situation with him: burglaries, arson, guns, stolen property, murder. People have (and will) criticize me for the relationship Gary and I had. I will only say that those people are small-minded; they don't understand the facts. Police have to deal with the worst society has to offer—and dealing with Gary was part of that."

Throughout the many interviews, hundreds of e-mails and scores of phone calls with Horton, I got a sense that he would, occasionally, go out of his way to prove to me how compassionate he was to victims and their families. You see, there are some people who truly misunderstand Horton and the extent of his job, the people he deals with and the horrors he has seen human beings perpetrate against one another. Anyone who is not in his shoes cannot possibly comprehend the atrocities and violence and abuse he and his former Bureau colleagues dealt with every day. So it is easy for people to sit back, read newspaper accounts of Horton's relationship with Evans, hear sound bites on radio, see clips on television and then judge him.

At best, the disparaging comments regarding Horton's integrity I heard from a few people as I conducted interviews were immature and slanderous; at worst, they undermine the character and integrity of a cop who, at least in my opinion, went above and beyond the call of duty whenever the circumstances warranted it. If you re-read the first section of the book with this dynamic in mind, you will see how Horton taught himself to think outside the box in order to make sure he put those he believed to be an immediate danger to society in jail, where they belonged. He empathized with the criminals he tracked in order to understand them better. If we go back and look at history, we will find that some of our greatest generals did the same thing during the bloodiest of wars.

The USMS would not comment on whether or not procedures were changed as a result of Gary Evans's escape. Yet, it doesn't take a genius to figure out that since Evans's escape, policies have been changed regarding the way the USMS transports its prisoners—mainly, the vehicles they now use.

Off the record, I was told by a source close to the USMS that because of Gary Evans the USMS now chooses to use those white trucks we see on our roads; trucks that, in fact, entomb prisoners in cages during transport.

Regarding the USMS, Horton would only say this: "Gary Evans was going to do whatever he was going to do no matter who was transporting him. The individuals involved did everything and more as far as 'official procedure' was concerned, knowing full well about Gary and how dangerous he was. They [the marshals] were as white as ghosts when I saw them on the riverbank that day. I'm sure they changed their procedure, i.e., windowless vehicles or having a marshal in the seat with the prisoner. But I just don't know for sure if it was because of Gary Evans."

* * *

As I was finishing this book, I came across a few letters written by the Son of Sam to Gary Evans that I had not seen before. Mostly, the writing was that same dark, sarcastic nature I outlined in the book. Yet, in a few of the letters that the Son of Sam had written to Evans, he talked about the novel *Red Dragon* by Thomas Harris. Apparently, Evans loved the book, had ranted and raved about it, and was trying to get the Son of Sam to read it. The Son of Sam ultimately wrote off Evans's persistence and told him he had no interest in "those types of books."

I had always viewed the obvious parallels between *Red Dragon* and *The Silence of the Lambs*, Harris's follow-up to *Dragon*, and Gary Evans's story as, at best, coincidental. Murder is murder. I've learned that killers will do the same things without even trying. Crime fiction is often based on real events. We all know that. Sure, there are certain elements of Evans's story that one could easily argue he had pulled directly from the pages of Harris's books. But is there a definitive connection?

Evans, it seemed to me, wasn't necessarily using the books as a script for life, but instead had perhaps subconsciously incorporated some of the same situations from the books into his life without trying to.

After re-reading those letters between the Son of Sam and Evans, I decided to go back and re-read both books before I handed the manuscript of *Every Move You Make* into my editor. I wanted to be certain I wasn't missing something obvious. It had been years since I had read both books; the images and characters I had in my mind were from film—hardly a way to make any comparison.

I found several comparisons. Not exact, mind you. But strangely similar. I encourage readers to e-mail me or write to me and tell me what you think regarding the comparisons between Gary Evans and Hannibal Lecter. I can be reached by e-mail at *mwilliamphelps@mwilliamphelps.com,* or by snail-mail at P.O. Box 3215, Vernon, CT 06066.

* * *

Amazing to me was that what started out as a journey to find a story that had certain elements I look for when choosing a true-crime story for a book then turned into a saga the best fiction writers of today couldn't have dreamed up. Gary Charles Evans is probably the most interesting criminal I have ever had the opportunity to research and write about; he is the epitome of the criminal mastermind. There is a layer of his character no one will ever uncover; but I believe, in my fourteen months of full-time research and writing, interviewing dozens of people and spending, literally, hundreds of hours talking to Jim Horton, along with scouring thousands of pages of public records associated with the case, I've gotten to the core of who Gary Evans was as both a person and criminal.

ACKNOWLEDGMENTS

This book would not have been possible if Jim Horton hadn't trusted me with all the information he had been harboring in his soul for years, waiting for the right writer to come along. I want to extend my gratitude and appreciation to Jim and all he has done to make this book what it is. The few people who truly know Jim Horton—of whom I can be added to that short list—understand that the humility he exudes is one of the most distinguishing and profound characteristics that sets him apart. He is extremely protective over his memories of Evans and the thirteen years he spent involved in his life. I want to thank Horton for allowing me into his world, and also Mary Pat, Alison and Jim for always being courteous and answering my questions. Horton's career—of which only a small fraction was covered in this book—spans more than two decades and is heaving with bravery, honor, respect, dignity and, most important, integrity. Jim has made hundreds of arrests, all of them important.

The psychotherapy checklists of Dr. H. Cleckley and Dr. R. Hare were very helpful to me as I studied Gary Evans. I quoted from those checklists in a few places throughout the book.

I acquired a new literary agent shortly before beginning this book. Peter Miller (PMA Literary & Film Management, Inc.) has been a blessing to me at this point in my career. Like Peter, his entire staff has been kind, gracious and always available to take my calls. I thank all of you for that.

There is no book I can write without thanking . . . William Acosta, J.G., A.R., R.K.

Gregg Olsen, a brilliant author who has become an inspiration and mentor, thank you for your friendship.

Johnny Crime and editor-in-chief Michaela Hamilton at Kensington have been superb people to work with. I am lucky to have such talented people in my corner. I also owe a considerable amount of gratitude and thanks to copyeditor Stephanie Finnegan, who was really helpful, not to mention instrumental, in shaping the book and making the final product what it is. Copyeditors are hard-working people; their work is often overlooked.

To those of you whose names I changed in the book at your request: thank you for sharing your stories, letters, documents and other helpful memories and materials.

The late great author Jack Olsen once said that a crime book without a few name changes is a crime story not worth telling, simply because the entire story is not being told. In my opinion, this book proves Jack's theory.

Bill Murphy and Jan Murphy: Thank you for allowing me into your home and sharing with me your anecdotes and memories. That visit changed this book. Also, Tina Spata, Tom Wessels, Kate Murphy.

I need to acknowledge all the law enforcement officers involved in the life and crimes of Gary Evans. Although a lot of you weren't mentioned by name in the book, it is important to note that your work was instrumental in the entire scope of the Gary Evans saga. In no particular order: Ron Campano, Kevin Chevrier, Jim O'Connor, John Camp, John Couch, Mary DeSantis, Steve Ercole, John Mays, Dennis Moessner, John Carey, John Egan, Jeff Ullman, Drew McDonald, Eric Cullum, George McNally, Leo Blanchard, Walt Goodell, Donte Annicelli, John-Paul Sinclair, Marty Hatch, Patrick Devenger, Darren Annis—and, of course, Thor, the K-9 who ultimately caught Gary Evans.

Doug Wingate: thank you, sir.

Robbie Evans was a treasure trove of information. The

letters, photographs, cards and e-mails partly made this book what it is. Thank you, Robbie, for helping me.

Jo Rehm: You are the true hero in this story. Let go and allow yourself the space to accept the fact that you were never responsible for anything Gary Evans did throughout his life. Your help in this project was commendable. Without it, the book would have suffered greatly.

My children and my wife of many years: How can I write a book without thanking you for listening to my stories, allowing me the space to fill the house with horrific tales of Gary Evans's life, and supporting me 100 percent. I love you all. You know that.

I know I forgot someone, perhaps several. If that is the case, I apologize.